PSYCHOEDUCATIONAL ASSESSMENT
OF MINORITY GROUP CHILDREN:
A Casebook

PSYCHOEDUCATIONAL ASSESSMENT OF MINORITY GROUP CHILDREN:
A Casebook

Reginald L. Jones, Editor

Cobb & Henry • Publishers
Berkeley, California

PSYCHOEDUCATIONAL ASSESSMENT OF
MINORITY GROUP CHILDREN: A Casebook

Copyright © 1988 Reginald L. Jones

Cobb & Henry • Publishers
P.O. Box 4900
Berkeley, California 94704–4900

Book design and typesetting by Cragmont Publications, Oakland, California

Manufactured in the United States of America

Library of Congress Cataloging–in–Publication Data:

Psychoeducational assessment of minority group children.

  Includes bibliographies and indexes.
  1. Psychological tests for children—Case studies.
2. Educational tests and measurements—Case studies.
3. Psychological tests for minorities—Case studies.
I. Jones, Reginald Lanier, 1931–
BF722.P77   1988   155.4'5   87–20861
ISBN 0–943539–00–5

Contributors

William H. Anderson, Jr.
David W. Barnett
Herbert G.W. Bischoff
Hermes T. Cervantes
Margaret G. Dabney
Alan T. Fisher
Ralph M. Hausman
H. Carl Haywood
Henriette W. Langdon

Marcia L. McEvoy
Deborah L. McIntosh
James A. Morrison
Leigh S. Scott
Mark R. Shinn
John M. Taylor
Lorraine Taylor
Gerald A. Tindal

Consultants

Harold Dent
Daniel Reschly
Jose Rodriguez

John M. Taylor
Josephine Young

CONTENTS

Part 6
Other Methods/Procedures

PREFACE

The present volume is devoted to psychoeducational procedures for assessing minority group children. It grows out of the mandate of Public Law 94-142 which states that testing and evaluation procedures are to be nondiscriminatory. Concern for the development of such procedures is the result of litigation which had as its core the view that minority group children, especially those labeled mentally retarded, were disproportionately represented in special education classes, and that biased assessment instruments were in large measure responsible for such overrepresentation. I believe the complex problem of psychoeducational assessment must be addressed on at least two levels. First, we must continue research on models of test bias, new instrument development, and the analysis of procedures and practices that work against fair assessment. Second, we must take advantage of the knowledge, experiences and insights of practitioners. School psychologists and other specialists are drawing upon their experiences to develop procedures they believe are nondiscriminatory and to revise procedures thought to be nondiscriminatory. The objective of the present volume is to make these procedures available through case studies. Cases which highlight examples of practices designed to provide nondiscriminatory assessment can be instructive to practitioners—who must make judgments using existing instruments and procedures—and also to researchers who will evaluate the practices and procedures that have been designed. While the present volume describes potentially useful clinical procedures for assessing minority group children, it is not the last word on these procedures. Some of them are relatively new and are in the forefront of assessment practices. Others have been around for some time and are in need of systematic study in order to determine their effectiveness. One purpose of this volume is to bring a variety of assessment procedures into the spotlight so that researchers and practitioners can begin to think about ways of validating the approaches. The volume will have served its purpose if readers are encouraged to utilize and to modify procedures described herein, to subject them to rigorous scientific scrutiny, and to report the results of these activities to their colleagues.

I am grateful to many persons who made the completion of this work possible. First are the authors of case studies who shared their ideas and were willing to subject their work to the scrutiny of their peers. Without their willingness to share their experiences and expertise, this volume would not have been possible. I am also indebted to a number of individuals at the University of California, Berkeley, who helped bring the work to conclusion: Ms. Antonia Costa was helpful in administrative matters at a critical juncture in the project, as were Ms. Frances Carter, Ms. Elmirie Robinson and Dr. Carolyn Mitchell (now at Santa Clara University) who provided valuable assistance in manuscript preparation. Ms. Katherine Stauffer was with the project from its inception and performed many valuable services in editing and manuscript preparation. All of us—editor and authors alike—owe her a special debt of gratitude. And finally, Mrs. Linda Polsby did an excellent job of preparing the manuscript for publication.

The project was supported by a grant from the Office of Special Education, U.S. Department of Education. Obviously, views expressed herein are those of the editor and individual authors and do not represent those of the Office of Special Education.

Reginald L. Jones
University of California, Berkeley

PSYCHOEDUCATIONAL ASSESSMENT OF MINORITY GROUP CHILDREN: ISSUES AND PERSPECTIVES

Reginald L. Jones

Introduction

Crisis: a turning point in the course of anything; decisive or crucial time, stage, or event. A time of great danger or trouble, whose outcome decides whether possible bad consequences will follow. (*Webster's New World Dictionary of the American Language.* William Collins. World Publishing Co., Inc., 1978. p. 336).

A crisis exists in the psychoeducational assessment of minority group children. There are several reasons for this state of affairs. First, immigrant and refugee children, some of whom will be candidates for special education programs, are coming to U.S. public school systems in increasing numbers. Unfortunately, language–appropriate instruments for the psychoeducational assessment of these newcomers have not been developed. Second, Public Law 94–142, The Education For All Handicapped Children Act, requires that children be evaluated using instruments that are not racially or culturally biased. Again, procedures to accomplish this end are wanting. Third, in the State of California IQ tests cannot be used to assess black children for placement in special education programs. In response to this judicial mandate, alternatives to the use of IQ tests are in very early and halting stages of development. And finally, scholars and researchers, the courts, and lay people are increasingly placing pressure on school districts to develop procedures that ensure equitable placement of minority group children in school programs. In spite of these diverse sources of pressure, little progress has been made to develop and implement unbiased procedures for assessing minority group children.

The present volume has been developed to help fill this real void by presenting procedures, for the psychoeducational assessment of minority group children, that are thought to be unbiased.

Fair/non–discriminatory assessment is at the heart of Public Law 94–142. The law states that tests and procedures for evaluating and placing handicapped children must be selected and administered so as not to be racially or culturally discriminatory. Specifically, the tests and evaluation materials must meet four criteria: (1) they must be provided and administered in the child's native language; (2) they must have been validated for the purpose for which they are used; (3) they must be administered by trained personnel; and (4) they must be tailored to areas of specific educational need. The thread running through the procedures is that they be valid for the purposes for which they are used. While the concept is simple, implementation is difficult (Jones, 1979).

The concern with non–discriminatory assessment stems from the fact that minority group students are overrepresented in special education classes—especially classes for mentally retarded children. Critics allege that a major reason for such overrepresentation is that IQ tests, which are a major tool in the special education assessment process, are biased against minority group children and thus lead to their placement in classes for the mentally retarded when the students are, in fact, not mentally retarded. Moreover, critics allege that educable mentally retarded (EMR) classes offer few valid educational services, and they channel students into tracks that impede their return to regular school programs. Because these programs are said to be stigmatizing, the claim is made that the social adjustment of students enrolled in the classes is impaired as well.

Evidence which supports assessment bias, or a lack thereof, is presented later on. However, disproportionate representation of minority children in certain special education categories has been conclusively documented. An analysis of data on EMR placement conducted by the National Academy of Sciences Panel on Selection and Placement of Students in Programs for the Mentally Retarded revealed that the average proportion of minorities exceeds the average for whites in every state except New Hampshire, West Virginia, Vermont, and Iowa, each with a very small number of minority students. Of states with more than 10 percent minority enrollment, the median EMR assignment rate for minorities is 3.35 percent while it is 1.17 percent for whites (Heller, Holtzman, & Messick, 1982). These findings indicate that the greater representation of minorities in classes for the mentally retarded is a nationwide phenomenon, and as such reflects values and practices that extend beyond any given locale or region.

Several authors have presented analyses, suggestions, and guidelines for assessing minority populations (Alley & Foster, 1978; Barnes, N.D.; Bay Area Association of Black Psychologists, 1972; Carroll, Gurski, Hinsdale, & McIntyre, 1977; Cervantes, 1974; Coordinating Office of the Regional Resource Center, N.D.; Cudnick, 1970; DeAvila, 1976; Dent, 1976; Deutsch, Fishman, Logan, North, & Whiteman, 1964; Franklin, 1977; McDiarmind, 1979; Mercer & Lewis, 1978; Mukherjee, 1976; Nava, 1970; Quinto & McKenna, 1977; Ramirez & Gonzalez, 1971; Ramirez, Taylor, & Peterson, 1971; Samuda, 1976; Sattler, 1973, 1974; Savage & Adair, 1978; Scales & Smith, 1974; Talerico & Brown, 1963; Ysseldyke, 1978; and Zintz, 1962). A shortcoming of the above methods and procedures is that most deal with only a single aspect of the bias problem. They fail to recognize that the problem of bias is multifaceted (Jones, 1979; Reschly, 1980). Jones (1979) noted, for example, that bias can exist at the content level, where decisions are first made about what items to include in a test (the perspectives and experiences of minority group children are often thought to be excluded), at the level of standardization, where decisions are made about the population for whom the test is appropriate, at the level of administration, in which tests are administered by persons unfamiliar with the patterns of language, behavior, and customs of the person being examined, and at the level of validation, where efforts are undertaken to determine whether or not the tests accomplish what they were designed to accomplish.

Testing practices have been specifically singled out for scrutiny. For example, Laosa (1977) identified major criticisms of testing practices as follows:

1. Standardized tests are biased and unfair to persons from cultural and socioeconomic minorities since most tests reflect largely white, middle class values and attitudes, and they do not reflect the experience and the linguistic, cognitive, and other cultural styles and values of minority group persons.
2. Standardized measurement procedures have fostered undemocratic attitudes by their use in forming homogeneous classroom groups which severely limit educational, vocational, economic, and other societal opportunities.
3. Sometimes assessments are conducted incompetently by persons who do not understand the culture and language of minority group children and who thus are unable to elicit a level of performance which accurately reflects the child's underlying competence.
4. Testing practices foster expectations that may be damaging by contributing to the self–fulfilling prophecy which ensures low–level achievement for persons who score low on tests.

5. Standardized measurements rigidly shape school curricula and restrict educational change.
6. Norm–referenced measures are not useful for instructional purposes.
7. The limited scope of many standardized tests appraises only a part of the changes in children that schools should be interested in producing.
8. Standardized testing practices foster a view of human beings as having only innate and fixed abilities and characteristics.
9. Certain use of tests represents an invasion of privacy. (pp. 10–11)

Controversy surrounds most of the criticisms and possible sources of bias cited above. Cleary, Humphreys, Kendrick, and Wesman (1975), for example, argue that research does not support evidence of a differential predictive bias. The subjects of studies cited by Cleary et al., however, were college students. How or whether such findings generalize to elementary age minority students who are enrolled in or candidates for special education placement is unknown. Moreover, studies of predictive bias have rarely acknowledged that bias can exist in the criterion as well as in the predictor(s). Questions surrounding examiner bias have similarly been the subject of a mixed literature (Barnes, N.D.; Jensen, 1980; Sattler, 1974).

Jensen (1980) concluded that "by and large, current standardized tests of general mental ability and scholastic achievement as well as many vocational aptitude tests, are not biased with respect to any native born, English speaking minority groups in the United States, and, moreover, this generalization can be extended in the case of non–verbal tests to native–born non–English minority groups as well" (p. 715). A number of scholars and the courts, however, have reached conclusions which are at variance with those of Jensen. Judge Peckham, in Larry P. vs. Riles, concluded that IQ tests were biased. He banned their use in assessing black children for placement in special education programs in California schools. However, Judge John F. Grady in PASE vs. The Board of Education concluded on the basis of personal inspection that virtually all items in the Stanford–Binet and WISC–R were free of bias and hence were appropriate for use with minority group children in the Chicago Public Schools (Heller, Holtzman, & Messick, 1982).

Comprehensive review of issues associated with bias in mental tests is beyond the scope of this volume. For diverse perspectives on the subject, the reader should consult, among others, Berk, 1982; Bureau of Education for the Handicapped, 1979; Heller, Holtzman, & Messick, 1982; Hunter & Schmidt, 1976; Jackson, 1975; Jensen, 1980; Oakland,

1977; Reynolds, 1982; Reynolds & Brown, 1982; Sattler, 1984; Wigdor & Garner, 1982; and Williams, 1971.

Not all assessments lead to labeling and special education placement. Ashurst and Meyers (1973) analyzed 269 cases of children referred by teachers or principals as probably mentally retarded during three consecutive years in the school district of a medium–sized western city (the ethnic distribution in the schools was 80% Caucasian, 11% Mexican–American, and 8% black). Five varieties of case processing through the steps of teacher referral, psychologist determination, and placement were identified:

1. Teacher suspected, psychologist labeled, placed: Children referred as mentally retarded by teachers and/or principals, tested by a school psychologist and labeled mentally retarded by the psychologist and placed in a special education class (86 children).
2. Teacher suspected, psychologist labeled, not placed: Children referred as mentally retarded by teachers and/or principals, tested by a school psychologist and labeled as mentally retarded but not placed in a special education class (63 children).
3. Teacher suspected, not labeled by psychologist, not placed: Children referred by teachers and/or principals as mentally retarded, tested by a school psychologist and not labeled as mentally retarded by a school psychologist, and not placed in a special education class (116 children).
4. Otherwise teacher referred, labeled by psychologist, placed: Children referred to not as mentally retarded by teachers and/or principals, tested by a school psychologist, labeled mentally retarded and placed in a special education class (one child).
5. Otherwise teacher referred, labeled by psychologist, not placed: Children referred but not as mentally retarded, tested by a school psychologist and labeled mentally retarded, but not placed in a special education class.

Ashurst and Meyers hypothesized that teachers and psychologists will agree more in labeling Caucasian than ethnic minority children. In formulating this hypothesis, the authors reasoned that sociocultural factors can confound teachers of minority children causing the child to be labeled mentally retarded upon referral to the psychologist. Ashurst and Meyers reasoned that psychologists, using standardized and clinical techniques, should be able to distinguish between environmental and intellectual deficits as the causative agents for the learning problem presented by the child in the classroom situation. The hypothesis was supported. The study by Ashurst and Meyers does not address the issue of alleged bias in the assessment process. It does, however, alert us to the real possibility that referral and testing do not necessarily lead to placement in classes for mentally retarded children.

Given the focus of the present work, which is to present innovative assessment practices with minority group children, it will not be possible to present all of the literature on the highly charged controversy around race and intelligence, test bias, and related topics. It will suffice to note that psychologists, test instruments, and testing practices have been heavily implicated in allegations of bias and that exploration of promising assessment directions and practices may represent one step in reducing inappropriate placement.

The importance of psychologists and psychological evaluation in evaluating children for special education placement following 94–142 guidelines has been documented in several investigations. Bickel (1982) surveyed trends in assessment revealed by a number of studies (Marver & David, 1978; Poland, Ysseldyke, Thurlow, & Mirkin, 1979; Stearns, Greene & David, 1979; Thouvenelle & Hebbeler, 1978) and concluded that "in general, the [assessment] process has shifted away from one of a single psychologist administering one or more tests toward the creation of assessment teams reviewing multiple data sources..." (p. 194). Nevertheless, Poland et al. reported that despite the above trend, there is still to be found a heavy reliance on psychological assessment data as the basis for a decision (Bickel, 1982). A study by the National State Directors of Special Education (1980) similarly found that placement teams tended to be dominated by administrative personnel or psychologists. There is good reason, then, to give attention to psychological assessments in the special education process. At the same time, as I will note in the section on limitations and caveats, problems exist at other levels of the identification–assessment–placement process and these problems also need attention if minority group children are to be accurately assessed. Nevertheless, since psychoeducational testing is an integral part of the assessment process, there is good reason to devote attention to innovative psychoeducational procedures that have special relevance to minority group children.

Limitations and Caveats

The present volume is devoted to test instruments and procedures which seem especially promising and useful in assessing minority group children. In a few instances, assessment systems are presented. The reader should be aware, then, that the *Casebook* cannot be relied upon as the sole source of information on the assessment of minority group children; testing is only one aspect of assessment, and comprehensive treatment of assessment—of minority group or other children—must include not only psychoeducational testing but other dimensions as well (see Jones, 1979).

The following section addresses considerations that must be part of a comprehensive assessment of minority group children. It includes discussion of (1) dimensions of the assessment process and possible sources of bias at all points therein, (2) possible bias in parental involvement in the assessment process, (3) the educational relevance of assessments, and (4) the need for a theory of teaching–learning as a conduit for assessment information (and other data useful in educational programming).

The Assessment Process

A variety of models of the identification–assessment–placement process in special education have been proposed (Abeson, Bolick, & Hass, 1975; Brinegar, 1976; Carroll, Gurski, Hinsdale, & McIntyre, 1977; Harrison, 1976; National Association of State Directors of Special Education, 1976, a, 1976, b; Sabatino, 1976; and Tucker, 1976). A synthesis of the models suggests a process somewhat as follows: First, a school related problem is identified. The problem may be one of behavior, of achievement, of appropriateness of class placement, or some combination of the above. Second, if formal assessments are deemed necessary, permission to engage in such activities is sought from parents or parent surrogates. Third, formal observations and assessments by various specialists (e.g., school psychologists, school social workers, resource consultants, speech therapists, physicians, and others) are conducted. Fourth, a planning team is constituted to integrate information received about a child and to make recommendations for further case disposition. Fifth, an instructional plan may be formulated. Sixth, followup is required. Obviously, not all identification–assessment–placement activities follow the above model in the order presented, but most include the components indicated, or similar ones.

Material in the present volume is directed only to step three of the identification–assessment–placement process, i.e., actual observations and testing of minority group children, and interpretation and conclusions derived from these activities. Of course, bias can, and does, occur at steps that precede and follow those just outlined. For example, at the level of initial referral, Tomlinson, Acker, Conter, and Lindborg

(1977) found that the rate of referral of minority students was 14% higher than their enrollment in school. A study conducted in Florida, in which a sample of 359 elementary school teachers was asked to review 16 hypothetical students in which race and sex were independent variables, revealed that "black students, although with the very same mental capacity and achievement test scores, were referred to EMR classes...more frequently than were their white contemporaries (regardless of race of referring teachers)." (p. 169)

Craig, Kaskowitz, and Maloire (1978), who studied 7,000 students recommended for special education, found that despite inconsistency among indicators, more students from lower socioeconomic groups tended to be identified as handicapped, and teachers recommended disproportionate numbers of blacks for EMR and ED placements. Zucker, Prieto, and Rutherford (1979) studied the influence of race and sex on teacher recommendations of the placement of Hispanic students in classes for the educable mentally retarded and concluded that "regardless of sex of students...teachers scored special class placement more appropriate for Mexican American children than they did for white children." (p. 4)

In interpreting the above findings, we must be sensitive to a number of factors that influence referral recommendations, including system identification factors. MacMillan, Meyers, and Morrison (1980) called attention to the variety of factors that impinge upon the identification of mildly mentally retarded children, including teacher referral tendencies—for example, "some teachers seem to feel that a regular class teacher's responsibility is to help all children in the regular program, while others believe that the best course of action is to refer such children and thereby have more time for the majority of children in their classes." (p. 109) MacMillan et al. also note variability in teachers' referral behavior as related to differences in students' social class and differences in average competence levels between schools and classes. In upper class schools, a student with an IQ score slightly below 100 might be judged as requiring special help, whereas a child in a school where the average ability was lower would not be referred.

Variations in the screening of referrals must also be considered. Robbins, Mercer, and Meyers (1967) noted two sources of variability in rate of referrals by school units: the service available (availability of programs and staff was also found to influence rate of referrals by Stearns et al. [1979]), and the school principal. Some principals request help only under the most dire circumstances since they believe that problems should be handled locally; other principals seek all help available.

Differences in interdistrict referral policies represent additional factors to be considered. Despite guidelines and policies for identification set forth by state and national bodies, many variations exist among school districts in their referrals of children—minority group and others—for possible special education placement. Districts also vary in their use of tests, in cutoff scores, and in procedures used to evaluate and classify children.

Lastly, there are sociopolitical considerations. A major impetus for P.L. 94–142 was the overrepresentation of minority group children in special education classes. The subject of considerable litigation, in some instances the net effect of this law has been to make school personnel sensitive to referring minority group children for special education placements, except in clear cut cases. MacMillan et al. (1980) list several developments that add variability to the system– identification process: (1) the Diana decision which mandated that school districts must avoid a disproportionate number of ethnic minority children in EMR placements; (2) the Larry P. decision which prohibited the use of mental tests in EMR placement of black children; (3) the Meyen and Moran (1979) report of the reluctance of regular class teachers to refer students with mild learning handicaps, since referral would require the teacher to prepare a time–consuming assessment, attend a placement conference, and if the child were certified as handicapped, participate in the development of an Individualized Education Program (IEP). Further, the child would remain in the classroom where the teacher would then be held accountable for progress; (4) parental involvement in the special education referral–assessment–placement process, with parental right of appeal, has made school districts cautious in referrals of minority group children.

Parental Involvement in Assessment

The participation of minority parents in the assessment process is required under P.L. 94–142 guidelines. Carol, Gurski, Hinsdale, and McIntyre (1977) observe that:

> Parental involvement in the assessment process has been shown to have immediate benefit to educators. For instance, it has become apparent that the parents of children in need of intensive assessment may be enlisted in becoming valuable sources of diagnostic information, especially with regard to the child's peer and family interactions, health and play habits, developmental history and medical history. Moreover, parents who become actively involved in the as-

sessment process often are willing to assist in actual program implementation, thereby providing a sense of continuity between home and school. Finally, parental involvement in ssessment and programming adds a new dimension to the concept of accountability in educators—the direct accountability of educators to the parents whose children they shape. In the context of culturally appropriate assessment, this accountability to parents is particularly meaningful since it implies accountability to the child's cultural and linguistic heritage as well. (p. 323)

The existence of bias against the participation of parents in the assessment process must also be considered. Even though P.L. 94–142 mandates parents being involved in assessment and placement decisions, existing evidence indicates that this is not the case. The problem has several dimensions: (1) school personnel attitudes toward parental involvement, (2) parental attitudes, and (3) the attitudes generated by interaction of parents and school personnel.

Many middle class parents have always been more active in decisions about their children than minority group parents. P.L. 94–142 was designed, in part, to eliminate such problems. Unfortunately, there are factors which conspire against active participation of minority parents in developing educational programs for their children. A first factor concerns beliefs of school personnel about parent involvement. For example, in one 1980 National Association of State Directors of Special Education Report on school personnel views about parent participation, it was noted that school personnel believed that educational program development should be left to the professional educator and that parents do not have the skills necessary for this activity. The personnel also stated that for some cases, the cost of notification and consent procedures outweighed the potential benefits of participation. These attitudes, combined with pressures resulting from the large number of cases to be processed, probably explain why in a survey of 100 special education directors in 49 states, 79% of the responding directors indicated that there were occasions when parents were not present at meetings which were held prior to the placement team meeting, to resolve differences among team members concerning placement options.

Consider these facts alongside findings from a large study involving three states, California, Massachusetts, and Montana on 94–142 related practices: (1) in these states, the IEP had often been informally drafted prior to the meeting with the parents (with the researchers reporting, "This was apparently not resented by the parents"); (2) placement was selected in the context of available services; (3) the use of overly technical language hindered communication with parents; (4)

the special education teacher was fearful about being held accountable for the achievement of objectives and preferred to keep IEPs as general as possible; and (5) some districts used the same goals for all students— there was no individualization of programs.

The impact of the above pattern can be especially devastating for low socioeconomic (SES) minority parents who are confronted with a group of united professionals using language which the parents do not understand. The parents probably are less likely to disagree with the professionals, even if they are inclined to believe the recommendations and proposals are not in the best interests of their children. We should not be surprised to find, for the above and other reasons, that in the study of appeals in one state, parents in these appeals were overwhelmingly middle and upper income whites. Less than 5% of the appeals involved minority or low income parents.

Educational Relevance of Assessments

Even though we may develop tests and measures which are not racially or culturally discriminatory, they may not predict educationally meaningful performance or provide information that facilitates the development of instructional activities. Thus, even when appropriate bias–free tests are developed, we may still be faced with more serious problems involving (a) the absence of established relationships between the attributes measured and school performance, and (b) the absence of a theory (theories) of teaching–learning in special education. The two voids are, of course, closely interrelated (Jones, 1979).

In commenting on the first void, Orasanu, McDermott and Boykin (1977) remind us that

> ...in order for a test to be useful in the description of what a child knows relative to what is to be learned, the test must offer well defined tasks which are essential components of what must be done in the performance of some complex skilled behavior, such as reading. That is, we cannot give a child a reading test until we can show that the items on the test are well defined in the test taker's eyes and that they relate to the skill we are trying to teach. This requirement presumes that a complete and adequate analysis of the target skill is available. Adequate task analysis describes what a person must do in order to perform successfully on the final task, e.g., read and comprehend a page of text; furthermore, it must identify subskills so that tests can be constructed which will monitor a child's progress on these components. (p. 62)

Heller, Holtzman, and Messick (1982) in summarizing the work of the National Academy of Sciences Panel on Selection and Placement of Students in Programs for the Mentally Retarded reached these conclusions about desirable relationships between assessment and educational practice:

> The primary justification for the use of any assessment technique is... its contribution to educational practice. from this perspective a valid assessment must display two characteristics. First, measurement instruments should assess a child's functional needs and should thereby be evaluated on the basis of their relevance to educational decisions. Functional needs may be categories of academically relevant skills (e.g., reading, mathematics), cognitive–process skills (e.g., generalization, self–monitoring), adaptive and motivational skills (e.g., impulse control, social skills), or physical problems that hamper learning (e.g., defective vision or hearing). Second, functional needs should be identified only if there exist potentially effective interventions. Thus, assessments can be judged in terms of their utility in moving the child toward appropriate educational goals. (pp. 98–99)

Heller et al. acknowledge that assessment techniques need not always identify functional characteristics of the individual that can be corrected through intervention since such an emphasis might discourage research on new instructional practices that may, in the future, ameliorate children's educational performance. They urge, however, that assessment procedures employed by school systems focus on individual characteristics that are relevant to classroom performance and susceptible to remediation. Such a focus, Heller et al. note, would concentrate attention on the responsibilities of the school rather than on the shortcomings of the child. Reschly (1980) advocated a similar link between assessment and instruction:

> ...Illumination of improved practices in psychology and education, especially procedures that would expand opportunities and improve competencies of children, have been conspicuously absent.... (p. 1)

Reschly speculates that the difficulty in discussions of non–biased assessment stems from a focus on the wrong problems and questions. He notes that the major concern in non–biased assessment has been with the assessment of minorities, and he agrees that issues related to tests used with minority populations are legitimate and important to raise, but he suggests that "a more significant issue to address is whether we can ensure educational experiences that maximize competencies and opportunities for minority students." Bias in tests or bias in assessment generally, Reschly writes, should be evaluated according to outcomes for individuals:

> The concern for outcomes for individuals directs our efforts toward ensuring that assessment activities yield information useful for educational and psychological interventions, and toward the effectiveness of these interventions. (p. 1)

Assessment which leads to improvement in instructional practices should be undertaken whenever possible, but such a view should not be used to denigrate activities such as Mercer's System of Multicultural Pluralistic Assessment (SOMPA) procedures which have as their goal determining appropriate classification or educational placement. No single test or assessment system will satisfactorily address all of the educational problems of any given child. We can (and should) expect that a number of complementary assessment procedures will often be required to determine what is appropriate for any given child. Thus, for example, when results of the SOMPA procedures suggest that a child is not eligible for labeling as mentally retarded, other methods and procedures may be needed to determine what educational programming is appropriate.

Theory and the Teaching–Learning Process

The use of tests and test results in IEP development also requires our attention. In using tests for such purposes, it is assumed that we possess valid information about the growth and development of academic and social abilities of children who comprise special populations, that we know something about the conditions under which such growth and development of the children take place, that we can predict the upper level of growth for various kinds of achievement for different populations of handicapped (or indeed non–handicapped) children, and that existing tests and measures are developed well enough to be sensitive to changes that might in fact occur (Jones, Guskin, Yoshida, 1978).

Regrettably, we cannot say with certainty how much growth can be expected to occur in students with various learning and/or behavioral profiles taught by method A or by method B. Nor can we be certain that existing measurement instruments are developed well enough to enable us to measure pupil gains in achievement confidently, a critical requirement for evaluating IEP effectiveness (Jones, 1979).

Moreover, Morrisey and Safer (1977) note that

...to measure program/IEP's effectiveness in terms of pupil change indicators (e.g., achievement), it would be necessary to confirm that what was prescribed was implemented, and that the variance that was observed/measured could be accounted for in terms of implementation. This would be a particularly difficult charge since IEP related activities will have varying correspondence to elements of the prescribed educational plan and take up varying amounts of the instructional day. These problems, coupled with the inherent difficulties in pre–test/post–test methods of measuring/recording pupil performances, suggest that it may be methodologically difficult to assess IEP effectiveness in this way. Moreover, the precision and frequency of documentation that would be required to collect reliable data, make use of such methods prohibitive. Therefore, it may be most desirable to consider multiple and varied methods of effectiveness—cost, resources, satisfaction and pupil measures. At any rate, determining appropriate measures of effectiveness will be an initial difficult task.... (pp. 35–36)

Theory is critical to the development of instructional activities, and regrettably, little theory of the teaching–learning process in special education exists. While many tests have been used to predict special education outcomes, only rarely has the selection of measures been guided by theoretical models or considerations which generate the basis for their selection, which predict various special education outcomes, or which explain how they function singly, or in interaction, to lead to some specified educational accomplishment (Jones, 1978). It is difficult to see how tests and other evaluation procedures can be used effectively in developing IEPs in the absence of such knowledge.

In the context of their discussion of competency–based teacher education in special education, Semmel, Semmel and Morrisey (1976) stated the need for theory quite well. They noted that

...Theoretical conceptions must seek to identify those instructional and pupil characteristics which most probably relate to pupil growth. This implies more than the construction of hypotheses related to the effects of one type of administrative arrangement over another. What is needed are efforts to construct models which suggest that teachers with special characteristics, who demonstrate specified observable teacher behaviors, with pupils having specified learning characteristics will produce desired pupil outcomes within the limits of specified educational contexts. The complexity of searching for functional relationships between presage, process, and product variables in the study of teacher behavior demands a sizable effort... Theory is a powerful tool for organizing such an endeavor. It is, to be sure, not the only promising strategy for uncovering meaningful relationships between teacher behavior and pupil growth. But it is, in our opinion, a necessary component of a total effort.... (Semmel et al., 1976, pp. 200–201)

The sum and substance of considerations introduced in this section are as follows: concern with bias in assessment cannot be limited to test instruments and procedures or to examiner characteristics alone; we must give attention to possible bias in all facets of the identification–assessment–placement system including bias in the referral and screening process, the influence of bias on parental involvement, the educational validity of procedures adopted, as well as to theories of teaching–learning which explain the accomplishments of defined subgroups of learners. Only when these factors are considered in tandem can we expect to have a system of special education that will be truly effective for all learners.

Selection of Cases

Cases for the volume were solicited through several means: (1) brief letters describing the project were sent to chief school psychologists and heads of special education in state Departments of Education in the fifty states. These individuals were asked to identify school districts or individual school psychologists known to be engaged in innovative and/or nondiscriminatory assessment practices with minority group children; (2) selected individuals in special education known to be interested in assessment were queried; and (3) individuals associated with established systems or specific practices related to nondiscriminatory assessment were asked to identify persons known to be noteworthy practitioners of nondiscriminatory procedures.

Individuals or school districts identified through the above means were sent a brief statement describing the project. They were asked to send an abstract which included information on their procedures as applied to a specific case. They were also asked to provide information on the case study client's age, sex, race, nationality, socioeconomic status, suspected category of exceptionality, the kind of data that entered into the assessment process/placement decision, specific techniques or considerations which made the case noteworthy, and the unique practices and procedures which would justify inclusion of the case in a volume devoted to innovative assessment practices with minority group children.

Approximately 55 abstracts were received. All were read by the editor and a five–person consultant panel consisting of a practicing school psychologist (Chicano) in a Western state, a professor of school psychology (Caucasian) in the Midwest noted for his research and writings on nonbiased assessment, a psychologist and former director of pupil personnel (Black) in a medium–sized school district in the Western United States, and chairman (Black) of the Committee on Assessment of the Association of Black Psychologists, a supervising school psychologist (Black) in a large urban school district, and a state director (Caucasian) of school psychological services in a Southern state.

The editor and panelists read and evaluated each case for innovativeness, clarity, and potential usefulness. For cases recommended for possible inclusion in the casebook, evaluators provided suggestions to authors for preparing cases. Consultants were asked to appraise each case for potential usefulness to assessment practitioners and, when appropriate, to raise questions that would help authors highlight unique elements and practices represented by their cases.

The review process led to the selection of 24 cases, fourteen of which are included in the present volume. Cases were selected that reflected innovative practices thought to have a high probability of utility for practitioners. Exotic case studies, those judged to reflect idealized and presently unattainable goals, and those thought to be inordinately time consuming, while yielding only modestly useful information, were excluded.

Each author selected was asked to describe the rationale for the procedure utilized—to indicate whether the basis for the practice was to be found in personal experiences or in the literature—and to present a case, drawn from actual practice, which illustrated the principles they had previously described. No specific guidelines for the preparation of cases were given; authors had wide latitude in format and length.

The first draft of each case was reviewed by the editor, at least three consultants, and two or three contributors (a requirement of participation in the project was that each participant evaluate two or three cases). The six or seven evaluations were synthesized by the editor and sent to the author for response. Contributors were asked to modify their cases in order to accommodate the evaluations, all of which had been screened for relevance and appropriateness by the editor. Revised cases were returned to the editor who made certain that the requested modifications had been made. Cases included in this volume, then, are those which were judged to be generally responsive to the reviewers' and the editor's major suggestions for revision.

Obviously, case critiques were limited to the perspectives of the reviewers, and none of us claims that further improvements could not be made. We invite you, the reader, to use and explore the procedures described and discussed herein, to further refine and validate their usefulness through practice and research and, finally, to communicate the results of these activities for use, modification, and research. It is only through such an iterative process that improvement in assessment practices with minority group children is likely to occur.

Overview of Case Studies

The cases describe a number of methods and techniques that are potentially useful in testing and assessing minority group children. Because rationales for the procedures are discussed comprehensively in the introduction to each case, they will not be presented in this section. It will suffice to note that several individual methods and procedures are included (Sections 1–4): dynamic and learning potential assessment, adaptive behavior assessment, behavioral assessment, and bilingual assessment. A fifth section presents methods useful with groups, while Section 6, Potpourri, includes methods and procedures for assessing preschool children, a Piagetian approach, the introduction of cultural factors into assessment, and a procedure based on the direct measurement of achievement.

The subjects of cases are in the elementary grades since most assessments for special education placement take place at this level. The race and nationalities of the case study subjects are black, Chinese, Native American, Laotian, Vietnamese, and Mexican–American. Reasons for referral include actual or suspected mental retardation, emotional disturbance, hearing impairment, giftedness, learning disability, hyperactivity, and aggressive behavior.

The cases and their rationale have not been presented uncritically. Haywood, for example, in his discussion of the Learning Potential Assessment Device (LPAD), calls attention to the fact that validity studies which link LPAD performance to school achievement have yet to be undertaken; he also presents a number of caveats that users of the LPAD need to consider. Anderson reminds us that behavioral techniques— noted for their objectivity—also are subject to bias; he critically analyzes the behavioral assessment process. Lorraine Taylor analyzes Piagetian assessment procedures, and Morrison presents a comprehensive overview of criticisms of the SOMPA. Many authors presented critical analyses of existing procedures since perceived limitation of these procedures often were the reasons for exploring alternative assessment approaches.

As previously noted, procedures presented in this volume relate most directly to testing—as opposed to assessment. Assessment includes the integration of test results with information from other sources such as interviews, observations, teacher and parent reports, etc., to classify or to provide a basis for educational programming or intervention. While some of the cases described show how tests are used in the assessment process—often leading to conclusions which are at variance with outcomes that would have resulted if the specially adapted procedures and methods had not been used—many cases describe only the methods and procedures themselves, and leave it to the readers to apply the techniques to their own situations.

References

Abeson, A., Bolick, N., & Hass, J. (1975). *A primer on due process*. Reston, VA: The Council for Exceptional Children.

Alley, G., & Foster, C. (1978). Nondiscriminatory testing of minority and exceptional children. *Focus on Exceptional Chldren, 9*, 1–14.

Amira, S., Abramowitz, S.I., & Gomes–Schwartz, B. (1977). Socially–charged pupil and psychologist effects on psychoeducational decisions. *Journal of Special Education, 11*, 433–440.

Ashurst, D.I., & Meyers, C.E. (1973). Social system and clinical model in school identification of the educable mentally retarded. In R.K. Eyman, C.E. Meyers, & G. Tarjan (Eds.), *Socio–behavioral studies in mental retardation* (pp. 150–163). Washington: American Association on Mental Deficiency.

Barnes, E. (N.D.). *IQ testing and minority school children: Imperatives for change* (p. 8). Storrs, CT: National Leadership Institute Teacher Education/Early Childhood, The University of Connecticut.

Bay Area Association of Black Psychologists (1972). Position statement on use of IQ and ability tests. In R.L. Jones (Ed.), *Black psychology* (1982) (pp. 92–94). New York: Harper & Row.

Berk, R.A. (1982). *Handbook of methods for detecting test bias*. Baltimore: The Johns Hopkins University Press.

Bersoff, D.N. (1979). Regarding psychologists testily: Regulation of psychological assessment in the public schools. *Maryland Law Review, 39*, 27–120.

Bickel, W.E. (1982). Classifying mentally retarded students: A review of placement practices in special education. In K.A. Heller, W.H. Holtzman, & S. Messick (Eds.), *Placing children in special education: A strategy for equity*. Washington, D.C.: National Academy Press.

Budoff, M. (1968). Learning potential assessment procedure: Rationale and supporting data. In B.W. Richards (Ed.), *Proceedings of the First Congress of the International Association for the Scientific Study of Mental Deficiency*. Reigate (Surrey): M. Jackson.

Bureau of Education for the Handicapped (1979). *Developing criteria for the evaluation of protection in evaluation procedures provisions*. Philadelphia: Research for Better Schools.

Carroll, A., Gurski, G., Hinsdale, K., McIntyre, K. (1977). *Culturally appropriate assessment. A source book for practitioners.* Los Angeles: Regional Resource Center.

Cervantes, R.A. (1974, April). *Problems and alternatives in testing Mexican American students.* Unpublished paper presented at the Annual Meeting of the American Educational Research Association, Chicago.

Cleary, T.A., Humphreys, L.G., Kendrick, S.A., & Wesman, A. (1975). Educational uses of tests with disadvantaged students. *American Psychologist, 30,* 15–41.

Committee on Child Development Research, National Academy of Sciences (1980). *Trends in special education placement as revealed by the OCR school surveys.* Unpublished study. 53 pp.

Coordinating Office of the Regional Resource Centers (N.D.). *With bias toward none.* Lexington, KY: Coordinating Office of the Regional Resource Centers.

Craig, P.A., Kaskowitz, D.H., & Malgoire, M.A. (1978). *Teacher identification of handicapped pupils (ages 6–11) compared with identification using other indicators* (Vol. II). Menlo Park, CA: Educational Policy Research Center, Stanford Research Institute.

Cudnick, B.P. (1970). Measures of intelligence of Southwest Indian students. *Journal of Social Psychology, 81,* 151–156.

DeAvila, E. (1976). Mainstreaming ethnically and linguistically different children: An exercise in paradox or a new approach? In R.L. Jones (Ed.), *Mainstreaming and the minority child* (pp. 93–108). Reston, VA: The Council for Exceptional Children.

Dent, H.E. (1976). Assessing black children for mainstream placement. In R.L. Jones (Ed.), *Mainstreaming and the minority child* (pp. 77–92). Reston, VA: The Council for Exceptional Children.

Deutsch, M., Fishman, J.A., Kogan, L., North, R., & Whiteman, M. (1964). Guidelines for testing minority group children. *Journal of Social Issues, 20.*

Diana v. State Board of Education (1970). C–70–37 (RFP Dist N. California).

Feuerstein, R. (1979). *The dynamic assessment of retarded performers.* Baltimore: University Park Press.

Fisher, A.T. (1977). *Four approaches to classification of mentally retarded.* Paper presented at the meeting of the American Psychological Association, Toronto. ERIC Document Reproduction Service No. ED 172–495.

Franklin, A.J. What clinicians need to know about testing black students. *Negro Educational Review.* (prepublication copy)

Heller, K.A., Holtzman, W.H., & Messick, S. (1982). *Placing children in special education: A strategy for equity.* Washington, D.C.: National Academy Press.

Hobbs, N. (Ed.) (1975). *Issues in the classification of children* (2 vols.). San Francisco, CA: Jossey–Bass.

Hobsen v. Hansen (1967). 269 F–Suppl. 401 (D.D.C.)

Hunter, J.E., & Schmidt, F.L. (1976). A critical analysis of the statistical and ethical implications of various definitions of "test bias." *Psychological Bulletin, 83,* 1053–1071.

Irvine, S.H., & Carroll, W.K. (1980). Testing and assessment across cultures: Issues and methodology and theory. In H.C. Triandis & J.W. Berry (Eds.), *Handbook of crosscultural psychology –Methodology, Volume 2*. Boston: Allyn & Bacon.

Jackson, C.D. (1975). On the report of the ad hoc committee on educational uses of tests with disadvantaged students: Another psychological view from the Association of Black Psychologists. *American Psychologist, 30*, 86–90.

Jensen, A.R. (1980). *Bias in mental testing*. New York: Free Press.

Johnson, V.M. (1977). *Salient features and sorting factors in the diagnosis and classification of exceptional children*. Doctoral dissertation, Pennsylvania State University. *Dissertation Abstracts International* 37:4282–A. University microfilm No. 76–29,649.

Jones, R.L. (1973). Accountability in special education: Some problems. *Exceptional Children, 39*, 631–643.

Jones, R.L. (1979). Protection in evaluation procedures: Criteria and recommendations. In PEP: *Developing criteria for the evaluation of protection in evaluation procedures provisions* (pp. 15–84). Philadelphia: Research for Better Schools.

Jones, R.L., Gottlieb, J., Guskin, S., & Yoshida, R. (1978). Evaluating mainstreaming programs: Models, caveats, considerations, and guidelines. *Exceptional Children, 44*, 588–601.

Jones, R.L., & Wilderson, F. (1976). Mainstreaming and the minority child: An overview of issues and a perspective. In R.L. Jones (Ed.), *Mainstreaming and the minority child* (pp. 1–14). Reston, VA: The Council for Exceptional Children.

Kaskowitz, D.H. (1977). *Validation of state counts of handicapped children* (Vol. II). Menlo Park, CA: Stanford Research Institute.

Lanier, J., & Wittmer, J. (1977). Teacher prejudice in referral of students to EMR programs. *The School Counselor, 24*, 165–170.

Laosa, L.M. (1977). Nonbiased assessment of children's abilities: Historical antecedents and current issues. In T. Oakland (Ed.), *Psychological and educational assessment of minority children* (pp. 1–20). New York: Brunner/Mazel.

Larry P. et al. v. Wilson Riles, Superintendent of Public Instruction for the State of California et al.(1979, October 11). No. C–71–2270 (N.D. Cal.).

Linn, R.L. (1978). Single–group validity, differential validity, and differential prediction. *Journal of Applied Psychology, 63*, 507–512.

MacMillan, D., Meyers, C.E., & Morrison, G.M. (1980). System identification of mildly mentally retarded children: Implications for interpreting and conducting research. *American Journal of Mental Deficiency, 85*, 108–115.

Marver, J.D., & David, J.L. (1978). *Three states' experiences with IEP requirements similar to P.L. 94–142*. Menlo Park, CA: SRI International, Educational Policy Research center.

Matuszek, P., & Oakland, T. (1979). Factors influencing teachers' and psychologists' recommendations regarding special class placement. *Journal of School Psychology, 17*, 116–125.

McDiarmind, G.L. (1971, Sept.). *The hazards of testing Indian children.* In F.L. Denmark (chm.), *Implications of minority group testing for more effective learning.* Unpublished symposium paper presented at the Annual Convention of the American Psychological Association, Washington, D.C.

Mercer, J., & Lewis, J. (1978). *System of Multicultural Pluralistic Assessment.* New York: Psychological Corporation.

Meyen, E.L., & Moran, M.R. (1979). A perspective on the unserved mildly handicapped. *Exceptional Children, 45,* 526–530.

Meyers, C.E., MacMillan, D.L., & Yoshida, R.K. (1978). Validity of psychologists' identification of educable mentally retarded students in the perspective of the California decertification experience. *Journal of School Psychology, 16,* 4–15.

Moran, R.E. (1974). *Observations and recommendations on the Puerto Rican version of the Wechsler Intelligence Scale for Children.* Rio Piedras, Puerto Rico: University of Puerto Rico. ERIC Document Reproduction Service No. ED 088 932.

Morrisey, P.A., & Safer, N. (1977). Implications for special education: The individualized education program. *Viewpoints, 53,* 31–38.

Mukherjee, A.K. (1976). *Measurement of the intellectual potential of Mexican–American school–age children.* Austin, TX: Texas Education Agency. ERIC Document Reproduction Service No. ED 138 034.

NAACP (1976). *NAACP report on minority testing.* New York: NAACP.

National Association of State Directors of Special Education (1976,a). *Functions of the placement committee in special education.* Washington: National Association of State Directors of Special Education.

National Association of State Directors of Special Education (1976,b). *The Prince William Model: A planning guide for the development and implementation of full services for all handicapped children.* Washington: National Association of State Directors of Special Education.

National Association of State Directors of Special Education (1978). *The implementation of due process in Massachusetts.* Washington, D.C.: National Association of State Directors of Special Education.

National Association of State Directors of Special Education (1980). *Summary of research findings on IEPs.* Washington: National Association of State Directors of Special Education.

Nava, J. (1970). Cultural backgrounds and barriers that affect learning by Spanish–speaking children. In J.H. Burma (Ed.), *Mexican Americans in the United States: A reader* (pp. 125–133). Cambridge, MASS: Schenkman.

Oakland, T. (Ed.)(1977). *Psychological and educational assessment of minority children.* New York: Brunner/Mazel.

Orasanu, J., McDermott, R., & Boykin, W.A. (1977). A critique of test standardization. *Social Policy, 8,* 61–67.

Petersen, C.R., & Hart, D.H. (1978). Use of multiple discriminant function analysis in evaluation of a state–wide system for identification of educationally handicapped children. *Psychological Reports, 43,* 742–755.

Peterson, N.S., & Navick, M.R. (1976). An evaluation of some models for culture fair selection. *Journal of Educational Measurement, 13,* 3–29.

Poland, S., Ysseldyke, J., Thurlow, M., & Mirkin, P. (1979). *Current assessment and decision making practices in school settings as reported by directors of special education*. Research Report No. 14. Minneapolis, MN: Institute of Learning Disabilities.

Quinto, F., & McKenna, B. (1977). *Alternatives to standardized testing*. Washington: National Education Association.

Ramirez, M. III, & Gonzalez, A. (1971). *Mexican–Americans and intelligence testing: Racism in the schools*. Unpublished manuscript, University of California, Riverside.

Reschly, D.J. (1980). *Nonbiased assessment*. Des Moines, IA: State of Iowa Department of Public Instruction.

Reynolds, C.R. (1982). The problem of bias in psychological assessment. In C.R. Reynolds & T.B. Gutkin (Eds.), *The handbook of school psychology*. New York: Wiley.

Reynolds, C.R., & Brown, R.T. (1982). *Perspectives on bias in mental testing*. New York: Plenum

Robbins, R.C., Mercer, J.R., & Meyers, C.E. (1967). The school as a selecting–labeling system. *Journal of School Psychology, 5,* 270–279.

Sabatino, D. (Ed.) (1976). *Learning disabilities handbook: A technical guide to program development*. DeKalb, Illinois: Northern Illinois University Press.

Sattler, J.M. (1973). Intelligence testing of ethnic minority group and culturally disadvantaged children. In L. Mann & D. Sabatino (Eds.), *The first review of special education* (Vol. 2) (pp. 161–201). Philadelphia: The JST Press.

Sattler, J.M. (1974). *Assessment of children's intelligence*. Philadelphia: W.B. Saunders.

Savage, J.E., & Adair, A. (1980). Testing minorities: Developing more culturally relevant assessment systems. In R.L. Jones (Ed.), *Black psychology* (2nd ed.) (pp. 196–200). New York: Harper & Row.

Scales, A.M., & Smith, G.S. (1974). Strategies for humanizing the testing of minorities. *Negro Educational Review, 25,* 174–180.

Semmel, M.I., Semmel, D.S., & Morrisey, P.A. (1976). *Competency–based teacher education in special education: A review of research and training programs*. Bloomington, IN: Center for Innovation in Teaching the Handicapped, Indiana University.

Stearns, M.S., Greene, D., & David, J.L. (1979). *Local implementation of P.L. 94–142*. Menlo Park, CA: SRI International.

Stevens, F.I. (1980). *The impact of the Larry P. case on urban school districts*. Paper presented at the meeting of the National Council on Measurement in Education, Boston, MA.

Swanson, E.N., & Deblassie, R.R. (1979). Interpreter and Spanish administration effects on the WISC performance of Mexican–American children. *Journal of School Psychology, 19,* 231–236.

Talerico, M., & Brown, F. (1963). Intelligence test patterns of Puerto Rican children seen in child psychiatry. *Journal of Social Psychology, 61,* 57–66.

Thouvenelle, S., & Hebbeler, K. (1978). *Placement procedures for determining the least restrictive environment placement for handicapped children*. Silver Springs, MD: Applied Management Sciences.

Thurlow, M.L., & Ysseldyke, J.E. (1979). *Current assessment and decision–making practice in model programs for the learning disabled.* Research Report No. 11. Minneapolis, MN: Institute for Research on Learning Disabilities, University of Minnesota.

Thurlow, M.L., & Ysseldyke, J.E. (1980). *Factors influential on the psychoeducational decisions reached by teams of educators.* Research Report No. 25. Minneapolis, MN: Institute for Research on Learning Disabilities, University of Minnesota.

Tomlinson, J.R., Acker, N., Conter, A., & Lindborg, S. (1977). Minority status and school psychological services. *Psychology in the Schools, 14,* 456–460.

U.S. Department of Health, Education and Welfare (1979). *Service delivery assessment: Education for the handicapped.* Unpublished report. Inspector General's Office, U.S. Department of HEW.

Wigdon, A.K., & Garner, W. (1982). *Ability testing: Uses, consequences, and controversies* (Parts I and 2). Washington, D.C.: National Academy of Sciences.

Williams, R.L. (1971). Abuses and misuses in testing black children. *Counseling Psychologist, 2,* 62–77.

Ysseldyke, J.E. (1978). Implementing the protection in evaluation procedures provisions of P.L. 94–142. In Bureau of Education for the Handicapped (Ed.), *Developing criteria for the evaluation of protection in evaluation procedures provisions* (pp. 143–194). Washington, D.C.: Bureau of Education for the Handicapped.

Zucker, S.H., Prieto, A.G., & Rutherford, R.B. (1979). *Racial determinants of teachers' perceptions of placement of the educable mentally retarded.* Paper presented at the meeting of the Council for Exceptional Children, Dallas, TX. ERIC Document Reproduction Service No. ED 191 015.

Part 1
Dynamic Assessment

DYNAMIC ASSESSMENT: THE LEARNING POTENTIAL ASSESSMENT DEVICE

H. Carl Haywood

Description of the Technique

"Dynamic assessment" (Feuerstein, Rand, & Hoffman, 1979; Haywood, 1977) refers to a general method of psychological assessment that can be employed with many different testing instruments. It is both parent and child to a systematic view of the nature, development, and educability of intelligent behavior known as structural cognitive modifiability; i.e., while it was experience with clinical dynamic assessment that stimulated Feuerstein's conceptual thought about structural cognitive modifiability, development of the structural cognitive modifiability concepts provides an intellectual basis for continuous refinement of the assessment methods (see Feuerstein, 1968, 1977; Feuerstein & Rand, 1974; Feuerstein, Rand, & Hoffman, 1979). Dynamic assessment differs from "normative" assessment in the following fundamental ways: (a) its *principal goal* is to assess subjects' potential for modifying their basic cognitive structures—and, thereby, for improving the effectiveness and efficiency of their learning, thinking, and problem solving; (b) its *primary method* is to examine the processes of perception, thought, learning, and problem solving by attempting to change them, i.e., by actually teaching cognitive principles and problem-solving attitudes and strategies during the examination and measuring the subjects' generalization of those principles to the solution of new problems; (c) its *products* are identification of both effective and deficient cognitive functions, estimation of the kind and amount of investment required to overcome identified deficits, and prescriptions—usually but not always educational—for modifying deficient cognitive functions (Haywood, 1977). Dynamic assessment requires tests that can be used in a teaching process and as indices of generalization of newly acquired cognitive principles and strategies. Examiners must abandon their psychometric neutrality to become teacher-observers, while subjects become learner-performers (Feuerstein, Rand, & Hoffman, 1979). Other important characteristics of dynamic assessment as opposed to static or normative assessment are: search for maximal rather than typical performance; emphasis on processes (during new learning) rather than on the products of presumed prior opportunities to learn; the assumption that subjects will not have had the same opportunities to learn rather than the contrary assumption of normative tests (Haywood, 1977).

There are other systematic approaches that are called "dynamic assessment" but do not share all of these characteristics of the approach of Feuerstein and collaborators. These include principally procedures that owe a great debt to Vygotsky (e.g., 1962, 1978) and/or Piaget (e.g., 1947, 1973, 1974; Piaget & Inhelder, 1955, 1959). Ann Brown and her colleagues (Brown & Ferrara, 1980; Brown & French, 1979; Hall & Day, 1982) have used a prompting method in which subjects are encouraged to find answers and solutions by being given a carefully ordered succession of increasingly explicit prompts or clues. Similarly, Budoff and associates (e.g., 1969; Budoff & Friedman, 1964; Budoff, Meskin, & Harrison, 1971) have used a test-teach-test procedure to classify subjects into categories of "high scorers," "gainers," and "non-gainers." Both the Brown and the Budoff procedures are "dynamic" in the sense that they involve some teaching between tests, but they differ from the Feuerstein methods in that the latter place much greater emphasis on the teaching of generalizable principles of thought, learning and problem solving rather than on correct answers. (These and similar assessment procedures have been reviewed by Vye, in press.) The approach most similar to the Feuerstein one is a laboratory method being used in France for cognitive developmental research (see Orsini-Bouichou, 1977; Orsini-Bouichou & Malacria-Rocco, 1978; Paour, 1975, 1978 a, 1978 b, 1979, 1980; Robeants, 1982). Called "l'apprentissage opératoire" (the learning of concrete operations), and applied primarily to children just at or clearly below the developmental stage of concrete operations, this method requires assessment of cognitive developmental stage by Piagetian tests (e.g., of conservation), followed by teaching of the specific behavior required to advance developmentally to the level of concrete operations. Post-tests are then given to determine whether the changes produced by teaching were structural changes, i.e., whether the newly acquired understanding is durable and generalizable. These investigators characteristically produce structural cognitive change across developmental stages even in mildly and moderately mentally retarded children.

The principles of structural cognitive modifiability and the requirements of dynamic assessment have been incorporated by

Feuerstein into an assessment procedure and set of "instruments" called the Learning Potential Assessment Device (LPAD) (Feuerstein, Rand, & Hoffman, 1979; Feuerstein, Haywood, Rand, & Hoffman, 1981, 1982; Haywood, Filler, Shifman, & Chatelanat, 1975). LPAD has both individual and group forms, with 15 tests or "instruments" currently available for individual clinical use and 9 for group administration, of which no more than 5 -7 are given ordinarily in any individual case. Feuerstein et al. (1982) state in the *Examiner Manuals* for the LPAD that:

> Selection of instruments is an important part of the clinical process, and derives from the nature of the presenting problem, the clinician's initial judgment of the probable areas of cognitive deficiency, the particular questions one wishes to answer, and subjects' response to the initial task. (p. 10)

The authors state further that:

> Some of the instruments are especially rich in their demand for multiple and complex cognitive functions (e.g., the matrix problems, including Set Variations I and Set Variations II, as well as the Representational Stencil Design Test) and are almost always used, while others have a more specific character (e.g., Plateaux, Positional Learning Test, Test of Functional Associative Recall, Test of Verbal Abstracting) and are used when examiners pose specific questions (e.g., regarding organization of memory for spatial relationships, stability of perceptual schemata, use of mnemonic strategies, identification of obstacles to verbal/abstract categorization). (p. 10)

The tests that are currently part of LPAD are listed in Table 1, along with an indication of individual or group administration. All are available in English and Hebrew, and most in French.

LPAD is not a normative procedure; i.e., its purposes do not include classification or ranking within groups, so there are no norms. There are reliability data and data on the effectiveness of the "examiner-as-teacher" procedures, reported in the *Examiner Manuals* (and to a limited extent in the book by Feuerstein et al., 1979), but there are so far few "validity" data of the predictive sort linking LPAD performance to subsequent school learning. The manual gives detailed instructions for administration, intervention, recording, and interpretation. While at the moment of writing many of the instruments are not commercially available and have been distributed in the past only through training workshops, arrangements are in progress leading to standard commercial publication and distribution. In the meantime, the authors of the manual and several colleagues continue to offer periodic workshops for the training of examiners. Responsible clinical use of the LPAD by examiners who are already qualified as clinical psychologists or

41

Table 1

Instruments Used in Learning Potential Assessment Device

Name of Instrument	Author	Administration
*Organization of Dots	Adapted from Rey	Individual and Group
*Coloured Progressive Matrices (A, Ab, B)	Raven	Individual and Group
Standard Progressive Matrices (A, B, C, D, E)	Raven	Individual and Group
*LPAD Set Variations I (Matrices)	Feuerstein	Individual and Group
Representational Stencil Design Test	Adapted from Arthur	Individual and Group
Numerical Progressions	Feuerstein	Individual and Group
*Complex Figure Drawing	Ray	Individual only
Positional Learning Test	Adapted from Rey	Individual and Group
*Functional Associative Recall	Adapted from Rey	Individual only
*Test of Verbal Abstracting	Haywood	Individual and Group
*Plateaux	Rey	Individual only
Word Memory Test	Adapted from Rey	Individual only
The Organizer	Feuerstein	Individual only
Propositional Reasoning	Feuerstein	Individual only

psychometrists requires an initial investment of approximately 40 hours of training in theory and methods, followed by a period of trial use of the instruments and a supervised practicum of perhaps another 40 hours. (Information on research and training in LPAD may be obtained from Haywood [Box 9, Peabody Station, Vanderbilt University, Nashville, Tennessee 37203], Reuven Feuerstein [Hadassah-WIZO-Canada Research Institute, 6 Karmon Street, Beit HaKerem, Jerusalem 96308 Israel], or from Mogens Jensen, [Yale University, Department of Psychology, 2 Hillhouse Avenue, New Haven, CT 06520].)

Special Applicability to Minority Group Children

The dynamic assessment of learning potential, as it is represented in the Learning Potential Assessment Device, meets a special set of needs in minority children and is especially appropriate for their psychoeducational assessment. Children who come from minority ethnic groups, economically disadvantaged families, and high-density inner-city residences, often present psychoeducational patterns of low school achievement and low scholastic aptitude as measured by standard normative tests (see Haywood, 1982, for a discussion in the context of "compensatory" education), and they are usually overrepresented in special education classes (see, e.g., Mercer, 1970, 1973, 1975). A point of view well worth considering is that many such children are underachievers in the sense that their scholastic achievement scores and even their scholastic aptitude scores (IQ) do not represent their potential to learn as faithfully as such scores function for children from majority cultures or from more advantaged circumstances. These children experience a syndrome of cultural deprivation, not in the misguided sense in which that notion was used so popularly in the 1960s (i.e., the idea that some subcultures were incapable of providing the necessary conditions for optimal cognitive and social development) but in the more direct sense that environmental circumstances (such as poverty, poor parental education, social discrimination) make it difficult for the full benefits of their own culture and subculture to be transmitted to the children (see, e.g., Feuerstein, 1970; Feuerstein et al., 1979, 1982). Thus, the problem is not in the culture, nor in the children, but primarily in the unavailability of processes of intergenerational cultural transfer— i.e., it is an ecological problem. Those aspects of any human culture that must be transmitted from one generation to the next in order to promote effective cognitive development (and subsequent "good" learning and school achievement) include patterns of systematic thought, rules, rule-making techniques, attitudes toward learning, strategies of problem solving, achievement motivation, and many other cognitively fundamental aspects. Cultural deprivation so defined can and does occur in all cultures and is not intrinsic to minority subcultures. It is, however, thought to be more likely to occur when families are poor, victims of social discrimination, and have limited access to social institutions.

Since many minority children cannot be assumed to have had the same opportunities to learn the content domains of static intelligence tests as have other children (i.e., the majority of children in the tests' normative samples), it is inappropriate to use such static achievement-oriented tests to estimate the children's future learning potential. A more appropriate approach is to give them new learning tasks that have not been encountered before, observe their learning processes, teach them some principles of learning and problem solving, observe how readily they learn *given teaching*, and then require them to apply the principles to the solution of new problems. In other words, the best predictor of learning is learning, not knowledge that one presumes to have accumulated in situations that examiners do not know and could not control. That is precisely the method of LPAD. With LPAD, one searches for maximal rather than typical performance, for cognitive processes rathr than products of presumed prior opportunities to learn, for the amount of teaching needed to achieve certain levels and types of learning rather than for success/failure ratios, and for specific process deficiencies (and the means for their correction) that underlie previous learning failure, rather than merely for evidence that certain content areas have not been mastered.

As the authors of the *Examiner Manuals* point out (Feuerstein et al., 1982):

> The dynamic assessment of learning potential through LPAD is not for everybody. It is not indicated for persons who are successful with conventional tests... It is for use with children and adolescents who are having difficulty in performance of academic work and in cognitive growth generally... Any attempt to use these procedures as a standard test of intelligence in order to derive a global estimate of ability... will be misguided and will result in a waste of time and effort. The special purpose of the LPAD is to assess the *modifiability* of specific processes of thought, observe the processes of change under the very special condition of direct teaching of principles of reasoning, perception, and problem solving, and thereby prescribe remedial measures. (pp. 10-11)

LPAD is indicated when there are:

(a) low psychometric scores (e.g., IQ) on normative tests, plus low achievement scores; (b) high psychometric scores plus low achievement; (c) low psychometric scores plus high achievement [for explaining the discrepancy]; (e) a diagnosis or other suggestion of mental retardation or emotional disturbance with accompanying learning deficits. (Feuerstein et al., 1982, p. 11)

The Case of Carlos

I present here, briefly, the Case of Carlos in order to illustrate the use of the LPAD for identification of specific cognitive deficiencies and to suggest methods for their remediation. The case is ideal in some respects, but far from it in others. To be sure, Carlos represents a minority subculture—children of Hispanic origin in the American southwest—for whom static, normative tests often fail to estimate academic aptitude accurately (leading sometimes to self-fulfilling prophecies), as well as a category of special education, learning disability, that is not well understood wth respect to its origins, its specific clinical components, its distribution in the population, its effective treatment, or its prognosis (see, e.g., Haywood, 1980; Lambert & Sandoval, 1980; Quay, 1980). On the other hand, we do not have available much anamnestic information, not all the LPAD instruments were used, and there are not yet any follow up-data. In addition, Carlos was examined in the unusual setting of a demonstration workshop on LPAD. In spite of these limitations, it is possible to see in this case some illustrative ways in which LPAD may be used, especially with minority children, to diagnose the cognitive roots of specific learning difficulty and to recommend specific remediation.

The Subject

Carlos, an attractive and apparently healthy 11 year old son of Hispanic parents in the American southwest, was given a learning potential assessment on three successive days as part of a training workshop for psychologists. Carlos is a student in a special class for children with learning disabilities. One reason for the assessment was to try to determine whether there are specific deficits in cognitive functioning that could be identified and assessed with respect to the possibility of focused remediation. Another reason was simply to search for and explain the sources of some problems in academic achievement that his teacher refused to attribute to low intelligence.

Carlos's mother is very involved in his education. She accompanied him to the examination and accepted readily the examiner's invitation to participate as an observer in the assessment. She talked about wanting school-related activities to do at home for the purpose of encouraging learning progress, and asked for a report of the assessment.

The assessment setting was unusual in that student examiners were often present in the room, and the examiner sometimes interrupted the examination in order to call the students' attention to some aspects of the examination. Interpretation of the results must be done taking these circumstances into account. These factors seemed to have little if any negative effect; and the presence of the students even seemed occasionally to enhance an already satisfactory level of motivation.

This situation is unusual also in that the examiner did not have the usual access to social, educational, developmental, and health histories, and had not had opportunity to do extensive pre-assessment interviewing and data gathering. An optimal learning potential assessment takes advantage of all sources of valid and relevant information. Of these, the social history is the most important prior to the examination itself, even though often some assumptions based on generalizations from the social history are found to be untenable as a result of performance in the assessment itself.

In general, Carlos was pleasant, cooperative, interested in the tasks, willing to work hard, and willing to persist in the tasks. At the same time, one must note that he was not obviously forthcoming; i.e., he gave only minimal verbal responses, he spoke—when he spoke at all—in a very quiet voice, and while he responded to the examiner's requests, he certainly could not be said to have attacked the tasks eagerly or confidently. He appeared to have a negative self-evaluation, particularly with respect to his ability to engage in intellectual activity, and his behavior was typically characterized by failure-avoiding motives rather than by success-striving motives. His negative self-evaluation, his motivation to avoid failure (which reduced greatly his willingness to take risks and to commit himself to an answer even when he "knew" that it was the correct one), and his reluctance to engage in verbal interaction all combined to produce a general mood and appearance that would make others get an impression of dullness, which would be incorrect and unfortunate!

The Instruments and Their Results

The following material is a description of each of the seven LPAD instruments (tests) used in the assessment of Carlos's learning potential, followed in each case by a discussion of Carlos's performance and the most obvious inferences that were derived from his work on that instrument. (More detailed descriptions are given in the *Examiner Manuals for the LPAD* by Feuerstein et al., 1982). Discussions of his work on individual instruments are followed by an integrated interpretation. As with most really useful psychological assessment procedures, some interpretation is made from the sum of the instruments as well as from each instrument. In the LPAD, examiners want to see evidence of a deficient cognitive function and of its remediation on more than one instrument, or if that is not possible, then certainly across problems within an instrument. That is to say, reliability of observation is important and is a major responsibility of an LPAD examiner. Although they are not presented here, there are scoring and recording procedures whose primary function is to aid in intra-observer reliability. Another safeguard against strong examiner bias is the use of independent observer/recorders, i.e., having the performance recording done by a person other than the examiner. This is usual procedure with LPAD, not least because an LPAD examiner has an enormous job to do in presenting tasks, observing responses, teaching (mediating), and testing.

Plateaux

Description. The Plateaux Test of André Rey consists of four square "plates" (actually flat boards) measuring approximately 15 cm x 15 cm. On each plate are nine buttons arranged in a 3 x 3 matrix. Eight of the buttons on each plate are easily removable, while one is fixed. The position of the fixed button differs from plate to plate, but of course it is constant within each plate. The plates are presented to the subject in a standard order and orientation. The subject's task is to locate the fixed button on each plate in turn and to remember these locations across successive plates. The first efforts, of course, are trial-and-error. The plates are presented in constant order until the subject has identified the fixed button on all four plates on three successive errorless trials. The plates are then removed and the subject is asked to produce a schema, on paper, representing with the numbers one through four the positions in the 3 x 3 matrix of the fixed buttons on the four successive plates. When the subject has given evidence of a well-established schema, the plates are represented, and in view of the subject, they are rotated through 90 degrees, the subject being then required to reach the same criterion. This is followed by a rotation of 180 degrees.

The examiner uses this test to observe, first, evidence of systematic exploratory behavior and control of impulsive responding, then indications of availability and use of mnemonic strategies and a concept of sequentiality, response to teaching of these functions, ease (or difficulty) in establishing spatial-sequential schemata, and sturdiness and transpositionality of established schemata (i.e., through rotations in space). The examiner records the number of errors (wrong buttons touched), number of trials to criterion, and accuracy of production of the positional schema. This test is often used early in an LPAD with subjects who appear to need, at least initially, to be able to manipulate concrete objects in space rather than to rely entirely on symbolic and representational thought. It "breaks the ice."

Performance. Carlos did well on this test, especially so considering that many children who have been diagnosed as learned disabled are thought to have visual-perceptual and perceptual-motor deficits. He learned to criterion in fewer than the average number of trials required by children of his age in several studies (Feuerstein et al., 1979, pp. 147, 178-189). Even so, performance on Plateaux helped to reveal some deficiencies in his cognitive functions. At first he tested buttons in a seemingly random fashion, even returning to buttons that he had already tested and had found to be incorrect. Second, he revealed some impulsive responding by trying buttons before he had given himself time to recall the position-sequence relationship, as if each presentation was necessarily a new experience. Third, the positional schema was only tenuously established after reaching the initial criterion of learning, as shown by the fact that it did not survive rotation of the boards without relearning. This supported also an inference of deficiency in summative behavior, i.e., in the disposition to view events in relation to prior and/or future related events (each event being seen as isolated in time and space). There were also some very positive indications: (a) Relearning after rotation required successively fewer trials, indicating that even with a fragile and insecure schema, he could benefit from cumulative experience. (b) Even though he showed no evidence at the outset of systematic search behavior or mnemonic strategies, he developed and employed such strategies when required to do so. (c) His impulsive responding was overcome with absolutely minimal effort, and he was able quickly to redirect his efforts in a more planful and systematic way once he had been given some mediation in this modality, albeit with occasional lapses into impulsivity.

Organization of Dots

Description. This is a deceptively simple-looking instrument that is actually a very rich source of insight into subjects' cognitive functioning. Introduced originally by André Rey (Rey and Dupont, 1953), it consists of apparently amorphous groups of dots within which one has to find and duplicate model geometric figures by connecting the right dots. The problem is complicated by the figures' changing orientation, by their lines "crashing through" each other, and by misleading close (but incorrect) approximations. In order to do this task completely, one must at least (a) project orderly relationships into unconnected dots; (b) develop and maintain stable definitions of the figures; (c) exercise precision and accuracy both in information intake and in production; (d) develop and use systematic sequential strategies; (e) inhibit impulsive responding and substitute planful behavior in its place; (f) compare proposed solutions to standard models, and be critical of one's own productions; (g) segregate parts from wholes, analyze a perceptual field, and reorganize the elements into a new whole. In a training task subjects are helped to learn rules whose application will make it possible to do the tasks properly and efficiently. Test problems are then given to examine the extent to which subjects have learned and generalized the rules and concepts. Speed is not emphasized.

Performance. Carlos understood the task immediately and set to work, a bit impulsively. His response to regulation of his impulsive behavior was to become too tentative, suggesting that he was unusually afraid of failure, an attitude that restrained his behavior even when he was fairly certain that he was correct. At first he was satisfied to produce figures that were almost, but not quite, correct. This fact, combined with his clear ability to detect incorrect aspects when he was required to compare his figures to the model figures, suggested an insufficiently developed need for precision and accuracy that lay more at the expressive level than at the receptive level. With teaching, he learned quickly the "rules" of the tasks, the mathematical requirements of the figures, some useful strategies (e.g., find the square before the triangle, start with an outside dot, "see" the figure before you start to connect dots, compare your proposed figure to the model for exact size and shape), and some "cognitive constants" (e.g., a square is a square regardless of its orientation in space if it meets the mathematical requirements, figures may be superimposed without losing their identity). These concepts were applied, with only minimal reminding, to subsequent problems. Verbalizing the rules, which he began to do spontaneously, seemed to help him to apply them. Carlos completed this task with fewer-than-average errors and had little relearning to do on the test problems (on which mediation of cognitive principles and strategies by the examiner is confined to what is required to sustain work on the task). Some of his remarks during this task, as well as the tentative nature of some of his responses, suggested that he sees himself as generally not very capable.

The Matrix Tasks

Description. Carlos was given Raven's Coloured Progressive Matrices (RCPM; A, Ab, B) as a training procedure, followed by LPAD Set Variations I as a generalization task and test of "near transfer." (For LPAD Set Variations I problems, see Feuerstein et al., 1979, p. 96). These tasks were chosen (a) because they require logical operations that are assumed to be beyond the capacity of mildly mentally retarded persons and even of many nonretarded persons in minority subcultures (see e.g., Jensen, 1969, 1970; Raven, 1965), (b) because they are arranged in a "power" series with relatively simple problems leading to quite complex ones, (c) because the materials themselves appear to be attractive to children, and (d) because they call upon some quite fundamental cognitive functions.

With Carlos, RCPM was used to explore how easy or difficult it would be for him to acquire such basic cognitive functions as spontaneous comparative behavior, summative behavior, need for and use of logical evidence, use of multiple sources of information simultaneously, transformations, and sequentiality. LPAD Set Variations I consists of a set of matrix problems similar to the B-8 through B-12 problems of Raven. Following usual LPAD procedure, for each type of problem there is first a training task, and that is followed by 6 "near transfer" tasks that require the same principles for solution but have varied elements. It is an excellent way to measure the extent to which a subject has mastered and is able to generalize the cognitive principles and strategies required in all the variations. The problems in this series cannot be solved by simple identity or "match-to-sample" techniques, but require instead more complex functions.

Performance. Carlos solved the early problems easily, although even on those he was a bit tentative and was always reluctant to engage in verbal interaction. When the problems required more complex processes, he slowed down and made errors. He revealed difficulty in planning, anticipation, and sequencing. At first the idea of transformation (A *becomes* B) was resisted, but with mediation, it was learned and applied readily. Even after learning new cognitive strategies, Carlos would sometimes revert to older, more comfortable (but unfortunately ineffective) strategies when the problems became difficult. After more mediation and several correct applications, his newly acquired principles and strategies became more stable and he generalized them more confidently. Specific cognitive deficits revealed on RCPM—and, to some extent, on LPAD I—included: (a) initial difficulty in using multiple sources of information (e.g., when form, color, and orientation would vary simultaneously); (b) reluctance to express solutions even after it was clear that he had them available; (c) poor independent memory, i.e., unless supplied with referents, combined with lack of adequate summative behavior; (d) an initial lack of need for logical evidence. All of these deficient areas responded to mediation, as shown by his remarkable good performance on LPAD I following training. Even so, there remained some inadequacy in planning, anticipation, and sequencing, and in using multiple sources of information.

Functional Associative Recall

Description. This test is an elaboration and extension of a much simpler test of André Rey (1966). The original Associative Recall instrument is described by Feuerstein et al. (1979) as one that "studies the capacity of the individual to use increasingly reduced stimuli as a support for his memory of 20 figures presented to him in the first phase of the test" (p. 350). Feuerstein has made a new instrument by requiring functional associations in order to remember the items. For example, confronted with a picture of a hole in the ground, the functionally associated item is the instrument used to produce the hole, a shovel. Upon seeing a schematically reduced hole in the ground, the subject must respond not with identity but with the functional association (shovel). Not only are cues reduced in successive presentations, but ordinal position is changed, eliminating this potential cue.

A primary function of this test is to examine availability and use of mnemonic strategies and stability of associations once established.

Performance. Carlos performed very well indeed on this task, especially after the functional associative strategy was mediated to him. He made very few errors, and those few were mainly intralist intrusions and results of impulsive responding. Results suggested that he has great potential for modifiability, especially in the use of effective cognitive (in this case, mnemonic) strategies to aid learning and memory.

Test of Verbal Abstracting (TVA)

Description. Using the "Similarities" mode, this instrument is designed to assess verbal abstracting (categorizing) abilities, to locate deficiencies at the input, elaboration, or output levels, and to determine readiness of response to the teaching of principles and strategies of categorization. Based upon the research of Haywood and his students (e.g., Call, 1973; Gordon & Haywood, 1979; Haywood & Switzky, 1974; Tymchuk, 1973), the TVA consists of 20 verbal concepts (e.g., fruit, domestic animals, writing implements), each with either two (apple, banana) or five (apple, banana, peach, plum, pear) exemplars. A subject's task is to indicate in what way the exemplars are alike. The two-exemplar version is given first, followed by the five-exemplar version after interpolated activity (other testing). There are mediational teaching procedures that are used in a prescribed sequence depending on the level of success at each stage (see Feuerstein et al., 1982).

Performance. Carlos demonstrated some apparent deficiency in abstracting. On the two-exemplar test, he obtained a score of 15 out of a possible 40 (scoring criteria similar to those of the Similarities subtest of the Wechsler scales), achieving only four two-point (i.e., abstract) responses in 20 items. This is low for his age and general level of functioning. Many children from minority subcultures do poorly on the two-exemplar test but much better when given five exemplars of each item. Carlos did not. His score on the five-exemplar version was only 16, including five two-point responses. Reasons for his low score and for his failure to improve with added exemplars seemed clear. First, he has some plain information deficit; i.e., his vocabulary is inadequate and he has failed to learn in a categorical fashion. Second, he did not improve with five exemplars because his difficulty is not at the input level (which the "enriched" presentation has been shown to overcome) but rather at the output level as shown on other parts of the LPAD. Because of limited time and the unusual circumstances of this administration, training in strategies for categorizing was not done, but there is evidence from other parts of the LPAD to suggest that he would respond well to such training. One can only speculate on the origins of verbal abstracting deficits. In bilingual children, such apparent deficits may be related to learning in two different languages, but Carlos functioned in English quite comfortably at school, at home, and at play, and his parents, both well educated, have excellent facility in English. Nevertheless, this could be a factor.

Complex Figure Test

Description. This is another test of André Rey (1959). Subjects are shown a line drawing that constitutes a rather complex figure (with a single exception, composed entirely of straight lines). The structure of the figure is organized sequentially in such a way that if one follows a logical, preplanned sequence (basic structure first followed by certain kinds of elaboration, with external "decorative" or nonstructural features last), the figure is reproduced and remembered easily; otherwise, subjects may be stymied by its complexity. Subjects are asked to draw the figure, as much like the model as possible, first by copying from sight and subsequently from memory. Occasionally children who do not typically employ organizational and sequential strategies spontaneously will produce a much better drawing from memory than from sight, since in the memory performance, they are almost forced to employ some sequential strategies in order to complete the task at all. As with the other LPAD tasks, this one is done in a test-teach-test sequence, with identification of ineffective approaches, obstacles to good performance, and specific cognitive deficits based partly upon initial performance. Teaching is then focused upon removal of such obstacles and acquisition, elaboration, or strengthening of relevant cognitive functions, followed by a "test" production of the figure.

Performance. Copying from sight, Carlos produced a figure that had all the elements of the model figure in it, but the elements were out of proportion because he had not followed a sequential strategy in organizing his efforts. He was obviously bothered by the poor proportionality of his figure. In this case, since we had evidence from other tasks that he could learn and use cognitive strategies and since time was quite limited, extensive teaching was not done. (In the usual procedure, principles would be mediated to the subject both on the basis of deficiencies detected with initial performance on this task and in an effort to assess the generality of deficiencies noted with preceding tasks.) He was, however, required to produce the figure from memory. This latter production contained fewer than one-half of the elements that had been incorporated into his first drawing of the figure. In addition, some major elements were incorrectly oriented in space and were grossly disproportionate. When asked how he tried to remember what to put into the figure, he did not reveal any systematic strategies.

This task yielded evidence of inadequate development of anticipatory planning and squencing behavior and of (possible related) deficiencies in spontaneous memory functions. Whether the memory deficits would have yielded easily to mediation of principles of sequentiality and mnemonic strategies is not known. What is clear is that he did not use such strategies spontaneously. The two performances revealed the need to develop habits of systematic approach to problem solving, an analytical approach to problem definition, and mnemonic strategies.

Interpretation of Learning Potential

(The following is a slightly edited version of the Interpretation and Recommendation sections of the actual clinical report written by the author following this assessment.)

With respect to his cognitive functioning specifically, the first thing to note is that he performed very well—at least at an average level and often above an average level for his age—on several tasks requiring associational memory or associational learning: he learned easily to remember objects by virtue of their functional association with other objects, and retained that association under conditions of reduced cues. Second, in several of the tasks in this series, his initial performance (i.e., prior to training) was at least at the average level.

(Astute readers may observe here a seeming contradiction in this appeal to normative concepts. In fact, dynamic assessment does not require that normative procedures be rejected. What is rejected is the interpretation that statistically subnormal performance, compared to peers, is evidence of inability. Many LPAD examiners find normative data useful, especially as baseline data against whih to compare performance after mediation. Logically, good performance is good evidence of ability, but poor performance is not evidence of inability.)

There are some areas of specific cognitive deficiency, and all are areas that can be expected to develop if he is given focused cognitive remediation.

Carlos appears to need help in developing "summative behavior;" i.e., perception of contemporary events in light of their history and their future, summation of objects in space, and summation of events in time. If what happens at point C or D depends upon an outcome at point A, he is likely to make errors. Efforts to bring about change in this function were relatively successful, indicating that progress could be made with modest investment of focused cognitive education. Second, he seemed to have some deficiency in independent memory, i.e., he did well in tasks requiring associative memory but less well when no associative stimuli or strategies were available. This function is easily remediable by giving successively longer lists for memorization and by teaching mnemonic strategies (and requiring him to produce mnemonic strategies). Third, he has some difficulty in planning, anticipating, and sequencing—a set of difficulties that showed up consistently on the various tasks that require such activity. The principal difficulty here appears to be dispositional and experiential rather than in ability itself; i.e., it is not a question of inability to plan, anticipate, or sequence so much as lack of habits of doing so (as shown by his marked increase in such behavior when taught and required to do it). Fourth, he appears to have some deficiency in verbal abstracting (i.e., grouping objects and events into categories and assigning abstract labels to the categories), but on closer examination it is clear that the deficiency again is not one in ability to perform this function. Further, the difficulty is not at the input level, i.e., it is not a deficiency in ability to take in information in chunks of varying size and transfer that information to a central processing (elaboration) system. The difficulty here appears to be of two kinds: informational and expressive. The information component is simply that he cannot assign verbal labels that he does not possess, and his vocabulary, especially with respect to abstractions is somewhat limited. When correct labels are supplied, he learns them and uses them correctly, both immediately and later. Fifth, he appears to have limited facility in using multiple sources of information simultaneously. This was demonstrated especially in problems that required him to keep in mind several dimensions (e.g., shape, size, color, and number) at the same time and in which those dimensions could vary independent of each other. As with the other deficient functions, this one appeared to be readily remediable. Finally, most of Carlos's cognitive deficits appear to be at the expressive level; i.e., he appears to need help particularly in expressing solutions, answers, plans, and strategies that are already available to him. Help with a variety of modes of expression should be pursued with respect to each of the deficient areas of cognitive functioning.

Recommendations

Overall, Carlos appears to be capable of doing acceptable school work at a level at least on a par with his age peers, and in addition, he specifically shows the ability to engage in abstract thought at a complex level of the kind that will be required in the upper grades. His performance in several areas of basic cognitive functioning (supra) needs remediation if he is to reach his learning potential. His self-evaluation is depressed, particularly with respect to school work and general ability to learn. He has come to see himself as a slow learner and is reluctant to try when he is not certain; he is not a risk taker, but is capable of developing task-intrinsic motivation under conditions in which his task performance is rewarded with opportunities to do increasingly interesting and complex tasks, as was often the case during this assessment.

Carlos should be held to a high academic standard and not excused for poor or inadequate performance. He can be given a good amount of academic work to do without great fear of overload. His teachers might work on his independent memory functioning. They could (a) give him increasingly long lists of materials to learn, both by rote and by association, and test those lists by the three methods of anticipation (i.e., serial position constant), free recall, and associative recall; (b) teach him mnemonic strategies; and (c) require him to produce original mnemonic strategies. Teachers could also require sequenced performance in a variety of tasks, in longer and longer sequences, in both linear and branching modes (i.e., do first a, then b, and c, then d...; do a, then if a+, do b but if a-, do b'. Teachers should encourage and actually require elaborated verbal expression of solutions to problems that he has devised, and in fact should not accept minimal responses. He should be expected to explain his answers fully including correct answers, in order to develop a need for logical evidence and some facility in marshaling such evidence toward problem solutions. He should be given practice in using multiple sources of information simultaneously. If that does not produce an immediate improvement in this function, he should be taught some strategies for retaining and manipulating 2, 3, 4, and even more dimensions of problems simultaneously, then given practice doing it in the solution of problems.

At home, his mother might encourage two general kinds of activities: planning and reporting. In the planning realm, she might offer him opportunities to participate in favored activities (such as movies, picnics, family outings) on the condition that he present careful and sequenced plans, taking into account the variety of considerations that must be part of such activities. In the reporting realm, she should get him to relate events such as movies or television programs that he has seen but she has not, encouraging him to give rich but elevant detail; in fact, she might also encourage the use of fantasy by asking for original stories about events in which he is interested already, such as sports.

Carlos should not be made to feel different. His difficulties are not so severe that he has to feel apart from his age peers. All of his cognitive deficits appear to be remediable with relatively modest investment, but the investment must be sharply focused upon those very areas of cognitive deficits rather than constituting simply more of an academic program with which he may continue to have difficulty if his cognitive deficits are not dealt with directly. If it were possible to have him in an Instrumental Enrichment (Feuerstein et al., 1980) class, that would be a good partial solution. If that is not possible, his present teachers and his family can take the responsibility and provide structured remediation focused upon these areas of cognitive deficiency.

Summary: Unique Applicability of LPAD in this Case

Carlos's identification as a learning-disabled child had put a name on his difficulty with school learning, but had not explained it. Minority group children are especially likely to be merely labeled, or labeled and placed in special classes that do not completely meet their needs or address the roots of their manifest learning difficulty. We did not need to assess school achievement because we knew already that in certain areas it was low. We did not need a static, normative estimate of intelligence because that had been done. From the combination of the two, it would have been possible to conclude that Carlos could not succeed in academic subjects. Some teachers had already questioned that interpretation, conceding that Carlos needed some kind of special help, but feeling that such special help should be somehow different from—perhaps supplemental to—what he was getting in a special education class. His referral for learning potential assessment was insightful and quite correct.

With LPAD, it was possible to ask very different questions: to search for the sources of his learning difficulties among cognitive functions that are so basic and general that they must underlie a wide range of learning and thinking tasks. Instead of asking how much he could not do, it became possible to ask what were his specific cognitive deficiencies and how much investment would be required to bring about more effective use of basic cognitive functions. The answers to the latter part of the question was: surprisingly little!

Use of LPAD made it clear that Carlos is capable of perceiving and manipulating abstract relationships, but that he does not typically do so in his school work for two major reasons: (a) he has not acquired (but is clearly capable of learning) certain basic cognitive functions (see below), including attitudes, habits, and dispositions toward intellectual work; (b) he has developed a self-defeating image of himself as one who is not capable of doing or learning complex intellectual tasks. Neither set of deficiencies is fixed, as shown by the ease with which he learned in the LPAD, and some evidence of slight positive changes in self-concept as a learner when he had success at some of the tasks. Thus, the basis of his school problems was seen to be experiential and remediable rather than constitutional and irremediable.

Carlos's specific pattern of cognitive (including affective/motivational) deficits included:
- Unsystematic exploratory behavior
- Impulsive responding
- Inadequate summative behavior
- Lack of need for precision and accuracy both in data gathering and in constructing responses/solutions
- Negative self-concept as a learner/performer
- Motivational system based on failure avoiding rather than success striving
- Difficulty in planning, anticipation, sequencing
- Difficulty developing a transformation schema
- Difficulty using multiple sources of information
- Lack of need for logical evidence
- Deficiency in vocabulary and general information
- Deficient use of mnemonic strategies
- "Total" rather than "analytic" approach to problem definition

With such a list in hand (and the clinical evidence to support it), plus evidence of at-least-average general ability and evidence that deficient cognitive structures could be modified with relatively little focused investment, it was possible to recommend specific remediational activities.

Some Caveats

Cost. LPAD is unquestionably expensive in terms of a subject's time and an examiner's time. It is too costly in the individual form to be used for "screening" or classification, but such uses would in any event be inconsistent with its conceptual basis. These procedures should be used to answer specific questions regarding the possible cognitive sources of learning or behavior problems, including: identification of both effective and deficient cognitive functions; response to mediation of principles of thought; quality and quantity of investment required to produce generalizable change. When used for such specific purposes, the cost should be much less than the cost of not finding such answers! Of course, the cost is greatly reduced by using group administration, but one sacrifices thereby much of the dynamic character of the procedures and misses potentially rich individual data. Group administration can be used to identify students who do well initially or with a minimum of intervention, those who make large gains, and those for whom the group teaching is not sufficient to produce significant performance gains. From such groups, one can then select specific students for further assessment with individual administration. Economy by limited use (i.e., with few subjects) is at present far preferable to economy by abbreviation of the procedures.

Outcomes. Those who have observed LPAD in use comment often that virtually all children are found to have greater potential for learning than is manifest either in their school performance or on normative tests. That is certainly the case, and would be unacceptable if one's goal were simply to determine whether or not each subject has learning potential or whether or not a subject's cognitive structures are modifiable. Use of LPAD to answer such questions will yield zero variance! Instead, one assumes that every person has learning potential and seeks to identify the specific areas in which help both is needed and will produce generalizable change.

Measurement Characteristics. It is neither possible nor reasonable to establish reliability or validity of LPAD instruments in the same sense that one does for normative tests. To begin with, the object of the "dynamic" aspect, i.e., the intervention, is to defeat the prediction of future performance based on baseline performance—a situation in which test-retest reliability is an inappropriate criterion. Data are reported in the *Examiner Manuals* that indicate satisfactory internal consistency. In test-retest administrations with and without intervening teaching, the test-retest correlation is typically substantially lower with intervening teaching than without, indicating that the teaching has at least reordered the subjects' performances.

One approach to validity is to determine whether or not the intervening teaching works, i.e., whether scores after the teaching of cognitive principles are higher than before (a greater increase than is observed in subjects who have not been taught between tests). Data from the *Examiner Manuals* indicate that there typically is significant improvement in performance attributable to teaching, and that these changes are both generalizable and surprisingly durable for such a brief intervention.

There is some construct validity inherent in the dynamic approach. That is to say, when one infers the existence of a specific cognitive deficiency, then gives the subject mediated learning designed to overcome that particular deficiency, and subsequently is able to record improved performance in the operations served by the cognitive function that was thought to be deficient, that situation constitutes some evidence both that the deficiency did exist and that such deficiencies are remediable.

It should be possible to establish validity of the clinical inferences derived from the LPAD procedure (as opposed to the validity of specific instruments) by determining to what extent prognostic statements, given the prescribed intervention, are borne out in the form of subsequent improved school learning. Such data are not yet available.

A final word of caution: It is easy to make optimistic forecasts, and difficult to deliver significantly improved performance under normal circumstances. All the positive indications of cognitive modifiability—and of consequent improved academic learning—that have come from this assessment are predicated on the availability of cognitive remedial procedures. If teaching of certain cognitive functions by way of a mediational teaching style is not done, the forecast benefits will almost certainly not accrue. Thus, it is very important that LPAD be followed by vigorous efforts to see that the children who have been so assessed actually get programs of cognitive education (such as Instrumental Enrichment, based on the same theoretical structure as LPAD). Maintaining that children have heretofore unsuspected learning ability and then not giving them appropriate teaching leaves them in an even worse position than they occupied prior to the assessment. Predictions of improved learning must be qualified with the phrase "given cognitive remediation and adequate content teaching." If systematic assessment of learning potential by the methods of dynamic assessment is followed by specific and focused cognitive remediation, the benefits, especially for minority group children and adolescents, can be rewarding indeed!

References

Brown, A., & Ferrara, R. (1980). *Diagnosing zones of proximal development: An alternative to standardized testing? Paper presented at Conference on Culture, Communication, and Cognition: Vygotskian Perspectives. Chicago: Center for Psychosocial Studies.*

Brown, A., & French, L. (1979). The zone of potential development: Implications for intelligence testing in the year 2000. *Intelligence, 3,* 255-273.

Budoff, M. (1969). Learning Potential: A supplementary procedure for assessing the ability fo reason. *Seminars in Psychiatry, 1,* pp. 293-309.

Budoff, M., & Friedman, M. (1964). "Learning potential" as an assessment approach to the adolescent mentally retarded. *Journal of Consulting Psychology, 28,* 434-439.

Budoff, M., Meskin, J., & Harrison, R. (1971). Educational test of the learning potential hypothesis. *American Journal of Mental Deficiency, 76,* 159-169.

Call, R. (1973). *Verbal abstracting performance of low SES children: An exploration of Jensen's theory of mental retardation.* Unpublished doctoral dissertation, George Peabody College.

Feuerstein, R. (1968). The Learning Potential Assessment Device. In B. W. Richards (Ed.), *Proceedings of the First Congress of the International Association for the Scientific Study of Mental Deficiency* (pp. 562-565). Reigate, Surrey (England): Michael Jackson.

Feuerstein, R. (1970). A dynamic approach to the causation, prevention, and alleviation of retarded performance. In H.C. Haywood (Ed.), *Social-cultural aspects of mental retardation* (pp. 341-377). New York: Appleton-Century-Crofts.

Feuerstein, R. (1977). Mediated learning experience: A theoretical basis for cognitive human modifiability during adolescence. In P. Mittler (Ed.), *Research to practice in mental retardation: Proceedings of the 4th Congress of IASSMD: Vol. 2. Education and training* (pp. 105-116). Baltimore: University Park Press.

Feuerstein, R., Haywood, H.C., Rand, Y., & Hoffman, M.B. (1981). *Examiner's manuals for the Learning Potential Assessment Device.* Jerusalem: Hadassah-WIZO-Canada Research Institute.

Feuerstein, R., Haywood, H.C., Rand, Y., & Hoffman, M.B. (1982). *Examiner's manuals for the Learning Potential Assessment Device* (rev. ed.). Jerusalem: Hadassah-Wizo-Canada Research Institute.

Feuerstein, R., & Rand, Y. (1974). Mediated learning experiences: An outline of the proximal etiology for differential development of cognitive functions. In L.G. Fein (Ed.), *International understandings* (pp. 7-37).

Feuerstein, R., Rand, Y., & Hoffman, M.B. (1979). *The dynamic assessment of retarded performers: The Learning Potential Assessment Device, theory, instruments, and techniques.* Baltimore: University Park Press.

Gordon, J.E., & Haywood, H.C. (1969). Input deficit in cultural-familial retardates: Effects of stimulus enrichment. *American Journal of Mental Deficiency, 73,* 604-610.

Hall, L.K., & Day, J.D. (1982, March). *A comparison of the zone of proximal development in learning disabled, mentally retarded, and normal children.* Paper presented at the Annual Meeting of the American Educational Research Association, New York.

Haywood, H.C. (1977). Alternatives to normative assessment. In P. Mittler (Ed.), *Research to practice in mental retardation: Proceedings of the 4th Congress of IASSMD: Vol 2. Education and training.* Baltimore: University Park Press.

Haywood, H.C. (1980). Introduction to special issue on learning disabilities. *Journal of Abnormal Child Psychology, 8,* 3-4.

Haywood, H.C. (1982). Compensatory education. *Peabody Journal of Education, 59,* 272-300.

Haywood, H.C., Filler, J.W., Jr., Shifman, M.A., & Chatelanat, G. (1975). Behavioral assessment in mental retardation. In P. McReynolds (Ed.), *Advances in psychological assessment* (Vol. 3) (pp. 96-136). San Francisco: Jossey-Bass.

Haywood, H.C., & Switzky, H.N. (1974). Children's verbal abstracting: Effects of enriched input, age, and IQ. *American Journal of Mental Deficiency, 78*, 556-565.

Jensen, A.R. (1979). How much can we boost IQ and scholastic achievement? *Harvard Educational Review, 39*, 1-123.

Jensen, A.R. (1970). A theory of primary and secondary familial mental retardation. In N.R. Ellis (Ed.), *International review of research in mental retardation* (Vol. 4)(pp. 33-105). New York: Academic Press.

Lambert, N., & Sandoval, J. (1980). The prevalence of learning disabilities in a sample of children considered hyperactive. *Journal of Abnormal Child Psychology, 8*, 33-50.

Mercer, J.R. (1970). Sociological perspectives on mild mental retardation. In H.C. Haywood (Ed.), *Social-cultural aspects of mental retardation* (pp. 378-391). New York: Appleton-Century-Crofts.

Mercer, J.R. (1973). *Labeling the mentally retarded.* Berkeley: University of California Press.

Mercer, J.R. (1975). Psychological assessment and the rights of children. In N. Hobbs (Ed.), *Issues in the classification of children* (Vol. 1) (pp. 130-158). San Francisco: Jossey-Bass.

Orsini-Bouichou, F. (1977). A propos du concept piagétien de schème et d'apprentissage [Concerning the Piagetian concept of schema and learning]. *Bulletin de Psychologie, 327*, 323-330.

Orsini-Bouichou, F., & Malacria-Rocco, J. (1978). Des regularités à l'induction opératoire [Some regularities in operatory induction]. *Cahiers de Psychologie, 21*, 139-162.

Paour, J.L. (1975). Effet d'un entrainement cognitif sur la compréhension et la production d'enoncés passifs chez des enfants déficients mentaux [Effect of cognitive training on the understanding and production of passive statements in mentally retarded children]. *Etudes de Linguistique Appliquée, 20*, 88-110.

Paour, J.L. (1978, a). Une expérience d'induction des structures logiques chez des enfants déficients mentaux [An experiment on the induction of logical structures in mentally retarded children]. *Cahiers de Psychologie, 21*, 79-98.

Paour, J.L. (1978, b). Dynamique de la construction opératoire chez les déficients mentaux: Etude exploratoire des facteurs déterminant l'induction expérimentale et la genese spontanée des opérations concrètes [Dynamics of operatory construction in the mentally retarded: Exploratory study of factors determining experimental induction and the spontaneous development of concrete operations]. *Cahiers de Psychologie, 21*, 183-195.

Paour, J.L. (1979). Apprentissage de notions de conservation et induction de la pensée opératoire concrète chez les débiles mentaux [Learning of ideas of conservation and induction of concrete operatory thought in the mentally retarded]. In R. Zazzo (Ed.), *Les débilitiés mentales*, (pp. 421-465).

Paour, J.L. (1980). *Construction et fonctionnement des structures opératoires concrètes chez l'enfant débile mental: Rapport des expériences d'apprentissage et d'induction opératoires* [Construction and functioning of concrete operatory structures in the mentally retarded child]. Unpublished doctoral thesis, University of Provence.

Piaget, J. (1947). *La psychologie de l'intelligence* [The psychology of intelligence]. Paris: Armand Colin.

Piaget, J. (1973). *Introduction a l'épistémologie génétique. Vol I: La pensée mathématique* [Introduction to genetic epistemology. Vol I: Mathematical thought] (2nd ed.). Paris: Presses Universitaires de France.

Piaget, J. (1974). Introduction to B. Inhelder, H. Sinclair, & M. Bovet, *Apprentissages et structures de la connaissances* [Learning and cognition structures]. Paris: Presses Universitaires de France.

Piaget, J., & Inhelder, B. (1955). *De la logique de l'enfant à la logique de l'adolescent. Essai sur la construction des structures opératoires formelles* [From the logic of the child to the logic of the adolescent. On the construction of formal operatory structures.] Paris: Presses Universitaires de France.

Piaget, J., & Inhelder, B. (1959). *La genèse des structures logiques élémentaires. Classifications et sériations* [The development of elementary logical structures. Classifications and seriations]. Geneva: Delachaux et Niestle.

Quay, L., & Weld, G.L. (1980). Visual and auditory selective attention and reflection-impulsivity in normal and learning disabled boys at two age levels. *Journal of Abnormal Child Psychology, 8,* 117-125.

Raven, J.C. (1965). *Guide to using the coloured progressive matrices, sets A, Ab, B.* London: H.K. Lewis.

Rey, A. (1959). *Testes de copie d'une figure complexe. Manual* [Tests of copying of a complex figure]. Manual. Paris: Centre de Psychologie Appliquee.

Rey, A. (1966). *Les troubles de la memoire et leur éxamen psychométrique* [Memory problems and their psychometric examination]. Brussels: Charles Dessart.

Rey, A., & Dupont, J.B. (1953). Organization des groups des points en figures géométriques simples [Organization of groups of dots in simple geometric figures]. *Monographs de Psychologie Appliquée, 3,* 39-65.

Robeants, M.J. (1982). *Une première approche du fonctionnement cognitif de jeunes enfants haitiens* [An initial approach to the cognitive functioning of young Haitian children]. Unpublished master's thesis, University of Provence.

Tymchuk, A.J. (1973). Effects of concept familiarization vs. stimulus enhancement on verbal abstracting in institutionalized retarded delinquent boys. *American Journal of Mental Deficiency, 77,* 551-555.

Vye, N.J. (in press). Procedures for the dynamic assessment of learning potential: A review. *Journal of Human Learning.*

Vygotsky L. (1972). *Thought and language.* Cambridge, Mass: MIT Press.

Vygotsky, L. (1978). *Mind in society: The development of higher psychological processes.* Cambridge, Mass: Harvard University Press.

THE USE OF BUDOFF'S LEARNING POTENTIAL ASSESSMENT TECHNIQUES WITH A MEXICAN-AMERICAN, MODERATELY HANDICAPPED STUDENT

Ralph M. Hausman

As dissatisfaction with IQ tests increases (Hamilton & Budoff, 1973), assessment specialists have developed procedures which are designed to be non-discriminatory for "culturally and/or experientially atypical" children. The procedures have encompassed a variety of strategies and include nonsense syllables, direct translations into other languages, and use of novel stimuli as culture-fair tests. A test-teach-retest strategy, which is the focus of this paper, is also being used.

In general, the test-teach-retest procedure consists of the presentation of a novel or familiar task to a student in a manner similar to a pretest in an experiment. The examiner then teaches the youngster the basic principles underlying the general task (in the case of a reasoning task) or structures a miniature learning session (in the case of a reading task). Finally, the examiner re-presents the task in the form of a hierarchy of subtasks that become progressively more difficult. In this manner, the examiner is able to determine whether the student was able to profit from instruction, and if so, how much he/she was able to profit. In addition, the examiner would have an idea of the amount of instructional investment required to produce a gain in the student's performance and, by altering the task dimensions, would also be able to determine the student's preferred learning modality, i.e., visual, auditory, and/or kinesthetic. The tasks developed for this type of assessment approach could be described as either molecular, i.e., consisting of a single task or task classes, or molar, i.e., consisting of a battery of task or task classes.

As early as 1950, work was begun in Israel on a relatively molar approach to the assessment of children's potential for learning in general by Reuven Feuerstein (1967, 1968, 1970) after he had come to the realization that the conventional psychometric tools available were highly inappropriate for culturally deprived Moroccan youngsters.

Having tried various approaches, including non-verbal performance tests, he developed the Learning Potential Assessment Device (LPAD) by modifying existing tests such as Raven's Coloured Progressive Matrices (1956) and developing new tasks such as the Arrangement of Points Tests and the Pyramid Test. The specific information relating to the LPAD and the research ata supporting such an approach are detailed in Feuerstein's (1979) text. (Also see Haywood's chapter in the present volume.)

Budoff (1965), on the other hand, took a rather molecular tack in his research with educable mentally retarded children. Cognizant that the educable mentally retarded child was more capable of learning and reasoning than the verbally based intelligence scores indicated, Budoff hypothesized that "…when given the opportunity to learn how to solve a non-verbal reasoning task through the medium of a systematic learning experience, the educable retardate (sic) would markedly improve his performance beyond the expectations based on his IQ ratings" (Budoff, 1965, p. 2).

To provide evidence for this hypothesis, the Kohs Block Designs Test (1923) was chosen as it was not markedly related to verbal ability, background experience, or school work, yet required reasoning ability for its successful solution. To counteract the traditionally reported history of repeated failures in school learning, an instructional procedure was designed which involved teaching the principles involved in block design construction while allowing the subject to enjoy maximum success. In general, the procedure involved pretesting on 15 test designs and 5 coaching designs, followed six days later by an individual coaching session. On the following day and one month later, the subjects were retested on the test series.

Results of a series of studies (Budoff & Friedman, 1964; Budoff, 1967, 1968; Babad & Budoff, 1971) indicated that within the traditional educable mentally retarded classification (IQ 50—80), children evidenced three distinct levels of learning potential (LP) status: GAINERS (subjects demonstrating markedly increased proficiency on the posttraining test designs); HIGH SCORERS (subjects demonstrating pretest proficiency on at least one of the complex 9-block test designs); and NONGAINERS (subjects failing to demonstrate increased proficiency on test designs following training). Although the functional definitions employed for these levels now use regression equation-based norms, the three distinct levels remain intact.

During his early research, Budoff noted that approximately 60 percent of his EMR samples attained GAINER (G) and HIGH SCORER (HS) status, while approximately 40 percent attained NONGAINER (NG) status. On this basis, Budoff concluded that individuals had a maximal probability of attaining G and HS status if they were members of lower socioeconomic groups who lived in situations associated with poor school performance, e.g., recent immigrants, children whose parents do not speak English, or children from exceptionally large families (Budoff, 1969).

Budoff and his associates also adapted the Raven's Coloured Progressive Matrices (1956) for use with the LP version of the Kohs Block Design Test and they developed an elaborate coaching series and structured its administration in a manner similar to that of the LP-Kohs Test (Frank, 1969). Their purpose was to expand the "test-teach-retest" assessment strategy to other tasks that would not only prove useful with younger children (as Kohs Block Designs appear unable to distinguish LP status accurately with children below 12 years of age) but would also tap a variety of cognitive abilities. According to Corman and Budoff (1973), each of the subtests of Raven's Test equally contained the following four structures: (a) continuity and reconstruction of simple and complex structures, (b) discrete pattern completion, (c) reasoning by analogy, and (d) simple continuous pattern completion.

Budoff (1972) noted that depending on the sample age level, the learning potential version of Raven's Test could be used just as effectively as the learning potential version of the Kohs Test; hence, the two versions could be used separately or in conjunction as the situation warranted. In various studies, Budoff and/or his colleagues found that learning potential assessment data predicted performance on problem solving or learning tasks (Budoff, 1967; Pines & Budoff, 1970; Budoff, Meskin, & Harrison, 1971), tasks purporting to assess rigidity (Budoff & Pagell, 1968), self-report, self concept or vocational status scales (Harrison, 1970), students' reactions to frustration (Pines and Budoff, 1970), and learning disabilities students' abilities to profit from resource room placement (Milleret, 1974).

The first major application of Budoff's learning potential procedures with elementary age Mexican-American students was completed by Hausman (1972). In an exploratory analysis, the predictive validity of and relationship among a variety of tests (including traditional tests administered in English or Spanish, and several learning potential assessment instruments) were examined. The results were interpreted as suggesting the use of a multifaceted assessment model consisting of, at least, measures of intellectual functioning (standardized on local populations and administered in both languages), learning potential, and motivational orientation when important decisions regarding young, bilingual, Mexican-American children of low socioeconomic status must be made. In terms of Budoff's learning potential instruments, while the gain scores obtained on the Kohs version failed to contribute significantly in predicting the academic criterion measure, the Raven mental age gain score was found to be highly predictive. At the time, the failure of the Kohs as a predictor of later performance with children under 12 years of age was not unexpected in view of previous research.

Since 1972, Budoff's learning potential assessment procedures have been extensively utilized with a variety of sample populations with similar results(Budoff, 1974; Budoff, 1975; Budoff & Hamilton, 1976; Folman & Budoff, 1971). (The latest versions of the instruments are available directly from Dr. Milton Budoff at the Research Institute for Educational Problems, 29 Ware Street, Cambridge, Massachusetts 02138). Since my initial experience with learning potential procedures, I have used them with a variety of students. One case which makes use of Budoff's original learning potential versions of the Kohs and Raven tests is presented below.

Case Study: Miguel

Miguel, a ten year old boy of Mexican-American parentage, was referred for evaluation because his teacher felt he was capable of functioning on a higher level than standardized test scores indicated. At the time of referral, he was located in a small town, public school based program for TMR students.

Background Data

Miguel lived at home with his natural parents and five siblings (two of whom were in special education classes for EMR students). His parents had been migrant workers until approximately two years prior to the assessment session. At the time of assessment, Miguel's father was a bricklayer and his mother a housewife. Miguel was born at home with a midwife in attendance. At age 4, Miguel is reported to have suffered a "head injury" due to the collapse of a bricklayer's scaffold. It appears that the medical treatment was restricted to emergency room treatment of the visible damage. According to Miguel's mother, hospitalization and follow-up were declined due to the family's limited resources. When he was five years of age, Miguel had reportedly experienced a high fever and was in the hospital for a week. When observed at the age of ten, several scars were still easily visible throughout the scalp area. According to several special education teachers, Miguel was considered to be "brain damaged" due to the previous accident. Yet there appeared to be no medical records on file to substantiate such a condition.

Previous test data were obtained by the administration of the Peabody Picture Vocabulary Test (PPVT; Dunn, 1959) and the Wechsler Intelligence Scale for Children (WISC; Wechsler, 1949). Both tests had been administered three years previously by a bilingual school counselor using a direct translation format. On the PPVT, Miguel had obtained an IQ of 48; on the WISC he produced a verbal IQ of 56, a Performance IQ of 89, and a Full Scale IQ of 69. Following an initial placement in a predominantly English-speaking EMR classroom, Miguel was placed in the TMR classroom, reportedly because of his inability to respond appropriately. Further, the reference in his file to a "head injury" and, later, hospitalization for a high fever combined with the visually obvious scalp scars apparently led the school personnel to believe he had suffered some degree of permanent neurological insult.

Evaluation Procedure

Shortly before the original referral was initiated, Miguel was individually administered an English version of the Metropolitan Reading Test. According to his teacher, he obtained a 1.7 grade equivalency on Word Knowledge, a 1.6 grade equivalency on Word Discrimination, and a 1.0 grade equivalency on overall reading ability. As a result of the referral, Miguel was informally interviewed to assess his English language proficiency. During the three-year interval since his previous testing, Miguel seemed to have developed a minimal proficiency which allowed for relative ease in communication and the ready establishment of rapport. Throughout the evaluation process, the combination of English and Spanish prevalent in the geographical region was employed by both student and examiner. When the WISC was replicated in the standard English format (replacing the Block Design Test with the Mazes to prevent a practice effect on the Kohs designs and accepting either an English or Spanish response, Miguel obtained a Verbal IQ of 61, a Performance IQ of 79, and a Full Scale IQ of 69.

Kohs Block Test—Budoff's Learning Potential Version

On the day after the WISC was administered, the learning potential procedures were implemented. As the procedures involved manipulation of blocks, the learning potential version of the Kohs was administered first. In Budoff's original version, five coaching designs were inserted within the 16 test designs (all following one introductory design) originally included in the Kohs test. The introductory design was labeled A, the test designs were A1 through A16, and the coaching designs were numbered 1 through 5. Designs A and A1 through A7 as well as the coaching designs numbered 1, 2 and 3 involved four-block designs, while test designs A8 through A10 and the remaining coaching designs involved nine-block designs. Two sets of multi-colored blocks from the WISC (Wechsler, 1949) were required as the student was presented with four, nine, and sixteen blocks (depending on the stimulus design requirements).

Following the instructions specified, the blocks are introduced to the student and, following completion of the introductory design by the examiner, the student is asked to complete the same, introductory design. Afterwards, the student is asked to complete each design as he or she sees it. The test is stopped after the student has incorrectly completed three consecutive designs. Regardless of the actual ceiling level, each student is always administered all five coaching designs. The total number of designs completed correctly then form the pretest value. On designs A9 through A17, "marginally correct" designs (i.e., those completed with 125% of the allowed time with two or less incorrectly aligned blocks or those completed correctly within 150% of the time) were also tabulated. On the pretest, Miguel correctly completed test designs A1 and A2 and the coaching designs 1 and 2, all of which involved four block designs. He was, however, unable to successfully complete any other designs presented.

On the following day, the coaching session was implemented. (Although Budoff originally required a six day delay between initial testing and the coaching session for experimental purposes, the writer has found such an extensive delay inappropriate in most field-based assessment situations. Thus in recent years, the writer has consistently reduced the pretest-coaching interval to a single day, with little or no apparent change in the results of the assessment data obtained.)

Following a relatively structured set of coaching instructions, the student is carefully and systematically led through all five coaching designs. On each design he is initially asked to align his blocks according to the design presented. Each row of blocks in the design is then carefully separated from the others and, on sequential cards, each block is distinguished from the adjacent block by a black line. The student is then asked to consider each row of his blocks in isolation and, later, as part of the whole design. On the fifth coaching design, the student is carefully taught how to align the half-white and half-red sides of the blocks to form a continuous white or red line. (Although Budoff uses the word "coaching" when referring to this session and to the specific target designs, he is actually teaching the students the basic skills required to solve similar block design problems rather than simply attempting to improve their scores on specific designs.)

On the coaching designs, Miguel demonstrated a high level of interest and an amazingly quick grasp of the essential skills involved in correctly aligning the blocks on the first design. Although he reported not knowing the name of the color yellow, Miguel was easily able to align the blocks correctly according to the stimulus card without additional instruction. He proved similarly proficient on a four-block design rotated to form a diamond shape and on the first of the nine-block designs. Although unable to align correctly the second nine-block design (involving the "stripe") on the first trial, as soon as he was shown the effects of grouping the blocks into a square, he was able to copy the design successfully on the second trial. The total time lapse during the coaching session was 21 minutes.

Approximately 24 hours after pretesting, Miguel was again presented with the original stimulus cards and the correct number of blocks with the same instructions employed on the pretest. In spite of his age, Miguel displayed a dramatic increase in performance. While he had been able to solve only the first four designs on the pretest, following a relatively brief coaching session he was able to complete all but one of the four block designs and three of the five nine-block designs successfully.

While two of the three nine-block designs were coaching designs, the third was a design he had not previously seen. The four-block design which he completed incorrectly involved the use of the half-red and half-white block sides to form a red "hour" glass design. He was apparently able to work the red and white colored nine-block designs successfully, but seemed unable to transfer to the blue and yellow design or to recover successfully on the following red and white design.

When presented with the sixteen-block designs, Miguel correctly aligned only four blocks on the first design and then quickly ceased trying on the two subsequent designs. (Throughout the three sessions, he appeared to be highly dependent on the examiner for emotional support.) On the posttest, Miguel correctly aligned a total of 7 test designs and all 5 of the coaching designs, for a gain score of 5 designs. Thus, in spite of his youthful chronological age, Miguel demonstrated an ability to profit from instruction and hence was considered a "gainer."

Raven Coloured Progressive Matrices— Budoff's Learning Potential Version

Immediately following the administration of the Kohs-LP version pretest, Miguel was presented the Raven Coloured Progressive Matrices (Forms A, AB, and B). Miguel obtained a total raw score of 15 (out of a total of 36 possible points), which translated into a mental age of 6 years, 6 months. The resultant IQ was 65.

As with the Kohs (and for the same reasons), the Raven coaching plates were presented approximately twenty-four hours later. Unlike the Kohs, the Raven coaching plates are both extensive in number and relatively time-consuming. During the coaching session, each student is systematically exposed to and required to respond in various ways to 65 separate stimulus figures. The first few figures simply require the student to complete a partially drawn figure at the end of a series of approximations of the figure. Later the student is required to point to the "missing portion" of the stimulus figure. Still later, he is asked to select from a field of six possible designs the design that would complete the stimulus figure at the top of the page.

Throughout the coaching plates, the student is systematically and progressively presented with samples of each way a pictorial analogy could be solved. A response is required for each plate, followed by immediate feedback relative to the correctness of his response. Miguel required 66 minutes to progress through the complete coaching sessions (a relatively long period compared to others of similar age). Although he appeared to have difficulty whenever a new stimulus dimension was introduced, only rarely did he require a third trial to complete the focal task successfully.

Approximately 24 hours later, the Raven posttest was presented to Miguel immediately following the administration of the Kohs posttest. On the Raven posttest, he obtained a total raw score of 20, which translated into a mental age of 8 years, 6 months. The resultant IQ was 85. Thus, with but 66 minutes of individual instruction, Miguel obtained a short term gain of two years in mental age and a gain of 20 IQ points on the Raven Coloured Progressive Matrices.

Discussion

Although Miguel was apparently accepted as a neurologically involved TMR student for over two years and in spite of the similarity of his WISC Full Scale IQ scores (i.e., 69 on the Spanish version followed three years later by 67 on an English version), his performance on the learning potential assessment devices suggests that he was capable of functioning on an appreciably higher level (at least on nonverbal reasoning tasks). Based on the writer's experience with these learning potential assessment devices when administered to other Mexican-American students of similar chronological age and with similar traditional test results, Miguel's performance on the Kohs could be considered highly unusual.

Typically, children as young as Miguel have difficulty achieving past the four-block design level even when extensive coaching effort is expended. While Miguel's overall performance did not support the teacher-posited contention of a neurological deficit, Miguel did appear stimulus bound and rigidly unable to transfer the effects of his learning when the color stimulus was changed on the more complex, nine-block designs. This apparent rigidity may have been influenced by a cognitive difficulty in that Miguel had previously indicated a lack of knowledge of the name of the color "yellow." (The lack of the appropriate verbal mediator, i.e., the color name, may consequently have hindered either color recall or perception.) Further, the full effect of his apparent dependence on adults for guidance and support on his assessment performance remains in the realm of conjecture.

His performance on the learning potential version of the Raven, however, is disconcertedly unremarkable in that similar gains have been noted by the writer among other minority-member students, particularly if they are members of migrant workers' families. Still, the relatively large differences between his pretest and posttest performances would seem to indicate that Miguel was previously "misdiagnosed" by the professionals involved in the interpretation of all of the traditional tests purporting to measure his intellect. Indeed, it would seem he was capable of profiting from instruction when instruction was presented on an individual basis and in a systematic, highly structured and relatively concrete manner.

As a direct result of the use of Budoff's learning potential assessment instruments, Miguel was quickly transferred to a bilingual EMR unit. Having been apprised of the implications of Miguel's performance on the various assessment instruments, his new teacher was, reportedly, quite interested in providing a high degree of intellectual and academic stimulation during the rest of the school year. When the special education administrator was queried later, he indicated that Miguel appeared to be gaining steadily for the short period prior to the end of the school year.

References

Babad, E., & Budoff, M.(1971). Sensitivity of learning potential measurement in three levels of ability. *Studies in Learning Potential, 2,* No. 22.

Budoff, M.(1965). *Learning potential among the educable retarded.* Progress report. Unpublished manuscript. Cambridge, Mass.: Mental Health Clinic.

Budoff, M.(1967). Learning potential among institutionalized young adult retardates. *American Journal of Mental Deficiency, 72,* 404-411.

Budoff, M.(1968). *Description of the findings on the social and test data for the community EMR school age sample.* Unpublished manuscript. Cambridge, Mass.: Research Unit, Cambridge Mental Health Association, Inc.

Budoff, M.(1969). *R.I.E.P. Annual Report.* Unpublished manuscript. Cambridge, Mass.: Mental Health Clinic.

Budoff, M.(1972). Measuring learning potential: An alternative to the traditional intelligence test. *Studies in Learning Potential, 3,* No. 39.

Budoff, M.(1974). *Final report: Learning potential and educability among the educable mentally retarded* (N.I.M.H. Grant No. OEG-0-8-8-506-4597). Cambridge, Mass. Research Institute for Educational Problems.

Budoff, M.(1975). *Final report: Learning potential among educable retarded pupils* (N.I.M.H. Grant No. RO1 MH 18553-03). Cambridge, Mass. Research Institute for Educational Problems.

Budoff, M., & Friedman, M.(1964). Learning potential as an assessment approach to the adolescent mentally retarded. *Journal of Consulting Psychology, 28,* 434-439.

Budoff, M., & Hamilton, J.L.(1976) Optimizing test performance of moderately and severely mentally retarded adolescents and adults. *American Journal of Mental Deficiency, 81,* 49-57.

Budoff, M., Meskin, J., & Harrison, R.H.(1971). Educational test of the learning potential hypothesis. *American Journal of Mental Deficiency, 76,* 159-169.

Budoff, M., & Pagell, W.(1968). Learning potential and rigidity in the adolescent mentally retarded. *Journal of Abnormal Psychology, 73,* 479-486.

Corman, L., & Budoff, M.(1973). Factor structures of retarded and nonretarded children on Raven's Progressive Matrices. *Studies in Learning Potential, 3,* No. 54.

Dunn, L.M.(1959). *Peabody Picture Vocabulary Test.* Minneapolis, MN: American Guidance Services, Inc.

Feuerstein, R.(1967). *Problems of assessment and evaluation of the mentally retarded and culturally deprived child and adolescent: The Learning Potential Assessment Device.* Unpublished manuscript. Presented at the First Congress of the International Association for the Scientific Study of Mental Deficiency, Montpelier, Vermont.

Feuerstein, R.(1968). *The Learning Potential Assessment Device: A new method for assessing modifiability of the cognitive functioning of socioculturally disadvantaged adolescents.* Unpublished manuscript. Presented to Israel Foundations Trustees, Tel Aviv, Israel.

Feuerstein, R.(1970). A dynamic approach to the causation, prevention and alleviation of retarded performance. In H.C. Haywood (Ed.), *Social-cultural aspects of mental retardation* (pp. 341-377). New York: Appleton-Century-Crofts.

Feuerstein, R.(1979). *The dynamic assessment of retarded performers: The Learning Potential Assessment Device, theory, instruments, and techniques.* Baltimore: University Park Press.

Folman, R., & Budoff, M.(1971). Learning potential and vocational aspiration of retarded adolescents. *Exceptional Children, 38,* 121-130.

Frank, L.(1969). *Development of Raven's Coaching Procedures and preliminary data analysis by sets.* Unpublished manuscript. Cambridge, Mass.: Research Institute for Educational Problems.

Hamilton, J.C., & Budoff, M.(1973). Learning potential among the moderately and severely mentally retarded. *Studies in Learning Potential, 3,* No. 52.

Harrison, R.H.(1970). Summary: A factor analysis of the Laurelton Self Concept and Bialer Locus of Control scales in an educable mental retardate sample. *Studies in Learning Potential, 3,* No. 7.

Hausman, R.M.(1972). *Efficacy of three Learning Potential Assessment Procedures with Mexican-American educable mentally retarded children.* Unpublished doctoral dissertation. Nashville, TN: Peabody College for Teachers.

Kohs, S.C.(1923). *Intelligence Measurement.* New York: Macmillan.

Milleret, M.E.(1974). *Learning potential as a predictor of L.D. junior high students' behavior in the classroom and in the resource room.* Unpublished master's thesis. University of Kansas.

Pines, A., & Budoff, M.(1970). Performance on the Stroop Color-Word Test as related to learning potential status of educable mentally retarded adolescents. *Studies in Learning Potential, 3,* No. 11.

Raven, J.C.(1965). *Guide to using the Coloured Progressive Matrices.* London, England: H.K. Lewis & Co.

Wechsler, D.(1949). *Wechsler Intelligence Scale for Children* (rev.). New York: The Psychological Corporation.

Part 2
Adaptive Behavior Assessment

RUDY GARCIA: A SOMPA CASE STUDY

James A. Morrison

Litigation (Covarrubias v. San Diego Unified School District, 1971; Diana v. State Board of Education, 1970 & 1973; Larry P. v. Riles, 1972) and legislation (PL 94-142) have necessitated the development of innovative nondiscriminatory assessment instruments. The System of Multicultural Pluralistic Assessment or SOMPA (Mercer and Lewis, 1978) is a unique series of evaluation instruments designed to assess children from culturally diverse backgrounds. SOMPA differs from traditional assessment approaches in its explicit pluralistic view of American society. From this perspective, American society consists of a dominant Anglo core culture and many other unique cultural groups that vary in their degree of identification with the dominant culture. As Figueroa (1979) states, "The more distinct and homogeneous the ethnic group, the greater the difference in the life experience of the children and the greater the need to look at the child within the context of his or her experience" (p. 30). SOMPA assumes that all cultures have equal worth and value which should be reflected in both the assessment and educational process. Accordingly, SOMPA is designed to assess the current functioning and "potential" of Anglo, Hispanic and Black children, ages 5 through 11. The measures are standardized on approximately 2100 children, 700 from each ethnic group and are representative of the population of students attending public schools in California.

In addition to SOMPA's pluralistic view of American society, SOMPA also differs from traditional assessment approaches in its use of three conceptual assessment models: The Medical Model, the Social System Model, and the Pluralistic Model. Each model is based on a different definition of abnormality and a distinct set of assumptions, characteristics, measurement properties, and ethical code. Thus, in contrast to current assessment procedures which tend to view the child only from the dominant core culture perspective, or fail to specify the underlying assumptions of the evaluation process, SOMPA evaluates the child's performance from three separate and explicitly described perspectives.

The Medical Model assumes that pathological symptoms are caused by biological conditions and that sociocultural factors are not relevant to diagnosis or treatment. Accordingly, Medical Model measures focus upon deficits or pathology within the person being assessed. SOMPA includes six instruments with its Medical Model: Physical Dexterity Tasks, Bender-Gestalt Test, Health History Inventories, Weight by Height, and Vision and Hearing Screenings. The purpose of these measures is to screen for possible neurological or central nervous system anomalies, perceptual-motor difficulties, possible biological insult, nutritional or developmental problems, and deficits in visual and auditory acuity which may interfere with school performance.

The Social System Model defines normality/abnormality in terms of conformity and social deviance. Behavior is "abnormal" if it violates social system norms, and "normal" if it meets the social system's expectations. Thus, this model assumes that there are multiple definitions of normal with different standards for each role in each system, that norms are not determined by biology but are defined in the political process, and that tests enforce the norms of the dominant social system group. Accordingly, the Social System Model is both an asset and a deficit model where deviance is a judgment about behavior and not an attribute of the person. Social System instruments reflect and measure the norms of the dominant group and correlate with group ratings of performance. SOMPA has two measures meeting the assumptions of the Social System Model: the widely used Wechsler Intelligence Scale for Children—Revised (WISC-R) and the Adaptive Behavior Inventory for Children (ABIC). From Mercer and Lewis' perspective, the WISC-R is considered a Social System measure because it correlates with successful performance in the student role within the social system of the school and is termed a measure of School Level Functioning (SLF). The ABIC measures the child's role behavior in the family, community, peer group, nonacademic school roles, self-maintenance, and earner-consumer roles from the family's (generally the mother's) perspective. Thus, the Social System Model's instruments attempt to measure the child's functioning in the role of student and a variety of roles from the parent's perspective.

The Pluralistic Model defines normality/abnormality in reference to the individual's own sociocultural group. Subnormal is defined as a low score for one's sociocultural group. The Pluralistic Model assumes that all "achievement" and "intelligence" tests measure learning; that sociocultural backgrounds affect opportunity and motivation to learn; that all sociocultural groups have the same biological potential for learning; and that to estimate potential, the child must be compared with others who have the same opportunity and motivation. Thus there are multiple normal distributions, one for each sociocultural group. Performance is completely culture bound relative to the ranking within the individual's sociocultural group. It is an asset model, uncovering "potential" (an attribute of the person) masked by cultural differences, and maintains that learning potential is revealed in current functioning when sociocultural factors are held constant.

The WISC-R using SOMPA pluralistic norms is the only measure in the Pluralistic Model. Through use of the WISC-R and pluralistic norms, an Estimated Learning Potential (ELP) can be obtained. To derive the ELP, SOMPA includes four Sociocultural Scales: Urban Acculturation, Socioeconomic Status, Family Structure, and Family Size. These scales are used to place the child in his "sociocultural space in American society" and to determine how much the individual's world differs from the Anglo Core Culture. Through the use of multiple regression procedures, sociocultural variables (as measured by the Sociocultural Scales) in the WISC-R score are held constant yielding the Estimated Learning Potential. Thus Estimated Learning Potential is a WISC-R score adjusted for differences in the child's sociocultural environment. Additional description and a brief technical critique of the instruments unique to SOMPA will be provided in the *Appendix*.

In summary, SOMPA differs from traditional assessment procedures because it views the child from three explicitly stated frames of reference, Medical, Social System and Pluralistic Models, and uses pluralistic norms and controls for sociocultural factors to estimate learning potential. The following case study is presented to illustrate both the potential strengths and limitations of SOMPA, and the necessity for supplemental assessment and careful examiner observation and judgment.

Rudy Garcia, Age 11-3

Background Information

Rudy (all names have been changed to ensure confidentiality) is an 11-3 year old Mexican-American boy. According to the State Home Language Survey, the family is Spanish-speaking. However, Rudy's mother reports that although she speaks Spanish to Rudy and his younger brother, they tend to answer her in English and to speak English to each other. Rudy's health records and previous psychological reports indicate an involved and significant medical and developmental history of laryngoscopy, breech delivery with possible brain damage secondary to birth trauma, drooling, convulsions and limited use of his right hand. Currently administered SOMPA Health History Inventories indicate that Rudy is "at risk" (below the 16th percentile) in the areas of Prenatal/Postnatal Trauma, Disease and Illness, and Vision. These findings generally validate earlier collected data. However, Rudy's visual and auditory acuity are within normal limits as well as his weight by height ratio (as screened by the school nurse). Rudy's familial and sociocultural background is also highly significant. Rudy's natural mother and father were both born and partially raised in small rural towns in Mexico. When Rudy's natural mother and father were approximately 10 years old, their respective parents migrated to Southern California in search of employment. According to Mrs. Benson (Rudy's mother), she and Rudy's natural father attended school in Southern California to the tenth grade where they met and were subsequently married at age 17 due to Mrs. Benson's pregnancy with Rudy. Mrs. Benson states that the marriage was characterized by constant conflict centered primarily upon financial difficulties, and "immaturity," causing the young family to move several times and to live with relatives. The marriage lasted five years and ended when Rudy's father left the family and moved to another state, leaving Mrs. Benson unsupported with Rudy (then age five and entering kindergarten) and his one year old brother. Rudy has had no contact with his natural father since that time. Mrs. Benson reports that Rudy was not close to his natural father and had spent very little time with him, but seemed to be "upset" by the couple's quarreling. Mrs. Benson further indicated that Rudy's father had never been able to accept Rudy's "disabilities" and she felt that he had rejected Rudy.

Approximately eight months later, Mrs. Benson married an "Anglo" (monolingual English-speaking) auto mechanic. This marriage was also fraught with conflict due to Mr. Benson's apparent alcoholism which interfered with his ability to keep a job, again causing the family to have to move and live with relatives. When sober, Mr. Benson related positively to the children, taking them on weekend excursions. However, when drinking he would sometimes be gone for several days and would verbally abuse the children and his wife. The marriage recently ended with Mr. Benson abandoning the family. When this case study was conducted, Rudy, his mother and younger brother were living with an aunt. Mrs. Benson was in the process of applying for welfare. However, during two of Rudy's testing sessions, Mrs. Benson was actually in the hospital for surgery (hysterectomy). Thus, the case study took place at a time of great emotional stress and change in Rudy's life. This will be discussed further in a later section of the paper.

Educational History and Previous Testing

Rudy has been evaluated several times, with a number of discrepancies in the resulting test scores. He was initially diagnosed while in kindergarten to be of average intelligence (Leiter IQ of 90) with severe learning disabilities attributed to possible neurological involvement. Subsequent testing on the WISC-R in English seven months later revealed a Full Scale IQ of 57 (Verbal and Performance IQs and subtest data were not cited in the Psychological Report). Emotional problems and behavior difficulties were also noted, and Rudy was placed in the EMR (educable mentally retarded) program at the end of his kindergarten year. However, no measure of adaptive behavior was administered.

After four years of EMR placement, Rudy was reevaluated by the school psychologist in July, 1977. He obtained a mental age score of 6-9 and an IQ of 69 (CA 10-6) on the Leiter International Performance Scale (Leiter, 1948) and WISC-R (Wechsler, 1974) scores of Verbal Scale, 72; Performance Scale, 70; and Full Scale, 69. Performance on the Peabody Picture Vocabulary Test (PPVT) (Dunn, 1959), yielded a mental age of 7-10 and an IQ of 74. No measure of adaptive behavior was administered. Severe delays in fine-motor coordination and in all academic areas were also reported. Continued placement in the EMR program was recommended.

At the time of this study, April, 1977, Rudy was enrolled in a special day class for Learning Handicapped students (educationally retarded), with adaptive physical education as a designated instructional service. There was no integration in the regular classroom indicated in his Individual Education Plan (IEP). Rudy stated that he "hates the special class" and "wants out!" As a result of Rudy's unhappiness in the special class, Mrs. Benson asked the school district to conduct an assessment by an independent Spanish-speaking examiner and reportedly threatened to take the district through state level due process hearings. At this point, the author was hired as a consultant to conduct an independent reevaluation and assessment. The author recommended to Mrs. Benson that the assessment be postponed due to her recent marital separation, (then) pending surgery and tentative living arrangements. The author suggested that the present emotionally stressful situation might adversely affect Rudy's test performance. However, Mrs. Benson insisted that the evaluation continue as scheduled.

Questions to be Answered by the Assessment

Mrs. Benson and the director of the district's Special Education Department, in consultation with the author, agreed that the assessment should be conducted to answer the following questions:

(1) What are Rudy's current linguistic, cognitive, sensorimotor, academic and social/emotional functioning levels?
(2) Is Rudy presently eligible for special education services?
(3) If qualified for services, what is the appropriate special education eligibility classification?
(4) What is the "least restrictive" educational placement that will best meet Rudy's educational needs?
(5) What recommendations can be made to the family to help them cope with their present crisis?

Rationale for the Use of SOMPA in this Case Study

Rudy's sociocultural and educational history revealed a complex interaction between medical, social and cultural variables. The examiner hypothesized that SOMPA's three assessment models might clarify the nature and influence of medical, social and cultural variables on school performance. For example, data from SOMPA's Health History Inventories and Physical Dexterity Tasks would yield an objective, standardized cross validation of material reported in previously collected medical data and provide a sound empirical basis on which to make a referral for further medical evaluation. Moreover, because there were inconsistent results in previous evaluations and a failure to consider adaptive behavioral functioning, English language proficiency and sociocultural variables, the examiner felt that the ABIC combined with the WISC-R School Functioning Level (SFL) would give a more complete picture of Rudy in a variety of social roles. Finally, the examiner thought that SOMPA's pluralistic norms and controls for sociocultural factors in the derivation of Estimated Learning Potential (ELP) would contribute to the nondiscriminatory determination of a special education eligibility classification and lead to an appropriate educational placement.

Test Data and Interpretation

Linguistically, Rudy stated that he prefers speaking English. Performance on the Dos Amigos Verbal Language Scales (Critchlow, 1973), a verbal opposite test, shows a slight superiority in Spanish percentile ranking (English 25%ile, Spanish, 40%ile). Rudy scored at Level 5 in English and Level 4 in Spanish on the Bilingual Syntax Measure (Burt, Dulay, & Hernandez, 1976), indicating that his syntactic and morphological development appears to be better in English than in Spanish. In addition, all of Rudy's formal education had been conducted in English. Thus the data indicated that Rudy was English-dominant and would be able to take the WISC-R in English.

However, because Rudy's native language is Spanish, he might obtain a higher and more accurate intellectual assessment if also tested in Spanish. At the time of this case study, there were no Spanish language intelligence tests normed on U.S. populations. There was a Puerto Rican version of the WISC, but much of its vocabulary was unfamiliar to Mexican-American children and its norms were not applicable. Spanish translations of existing English tests were also available but had inherent difficulties summarized by Sattler (1982).

(1) Many concepts either have no equivalent in another language or are difficult to render without engendering ambiguity. Thus, the meaning of important phrases may be lost in translations.

(2) Translations are usually made into standard Spanish, with no provision for dialectical or regional variations. The word "kite," for example, may be translated as *cometa, huila, volatin, papalote,* or *chiringa,* depending on the country of origin.

(3) The language familiar to Spanish-speaking children may be a combination of two languages ("Pocho", "pidgin," or "Tex-Mex") so that a monolingual translation may be inappropriate.

(4) Some words may have different meanings for Mexican-Americans, Puerto Ricans, Cubans, and other Hispanics. For example, *toston* refers to a half dollar for a Chicano child, but to a Puerto Rican child, it means a squashed section of a fried banana.

(5) The difficulty level of words may change as a result of translation. For example, the word "pet", a common English word, becomes in its Spanish equivalent *animal domestico,* an uncommon phrase.

(6) Translation can alter the meanings of words. For example, seemingly harmless English words may translate into Spanish

profanity. "Egg" translated as *huevon* may be literally correct, but the Spanish term has more earthy connotations. (p. 371)

Sattler further indicates that the use of Spanish translations of intelligence tests has yielded inconsistent results and does not necessarily provide more valid test scores. Consequently, because of the lack of valid and reliable Spanish assessment instruments, and the difficulties inherent in translations, and, more significantly, because parent report, language dominance testing, student preference, and educational history (all formal education received in English) suggested that Rudy was a dominant English speaker, the author decided that the most appropriate intelligence instrument would be the WISC-R as employed within SOMPA's Social System and Pluralistic Models.

Accordingly, in cognitive areas, using standard WISC-R norms (School Function Level or SFL), Rudy was functioning within the mentally deficient range of cognitive skills with a Verbal score of 69, Performance 70, and Full Scale 68. There was no significant subtest variation on either the Verbal or Performance Scales. His Leiter IQ was 64. It is possible that Rudy's test scores were lowered by emotional/environmental factors (family crisis). However, when the SOMPA Pluralistic Model norms and regression equations controlling for family size, family structure, socioeconomic status, and urban acculturation were applied (to the WISC-R scores), Rudy obtained an Estimated Learning Potential (ELP) of Verbal 89, Performance 83, and Full Scale 79. Thus when sociocultural factors were taken into consideration, Rudy's potential intellectual functioning fell within the low average range. Mercer and Lewis (1977) state that a difference of 15 points or more between SFL and ELP scores should be interpreted as probably indicating that there is greater potential than expressed in the traditional WISC-R score. The difference between Rudy's Verbal SFL and ELP was 20 points. Mercer and Lewis (1977) further suggest that ELP interpretation should focus on the Verbal ELP because these scores are more correlated with academic and interpersonal relationships as rated by teachers and have more cultural loading, especially for Spanish surnamed children. Thus the use of the SOMPA ELP, especially the Verbal ELP, from the Mercer and Lewis perspective would seem to indicate that Rudy had higher intellectual potential than the traditional WISC-R score revealed.

Academically, Rudy was functioning at the 1.5 level in reading recognition, 1.9 in reading comprehension, 2.6 in spelling, and 2.4 in general information (with standard scores of below 65, below 65, 69 and 74 respectively) as measured by the Peabody Individual Achievement Test (PIAT) (Dunn, 1970). Rudy had a sight vocabulary of approximately 40 words on the graded Dolch Word List and was functioning at the preprimer level. He also had severe difficulties in phonetic analysis skills as measured by the USC Phonics Test (Ransom, 1978). He had mastered the consonant sounds w, v, h, j, x, z, s, n, g, b, c, f, m, l, and d. However, he still had difficulties with consonant digraphs and blends, and confused long and short vowel sounds. Rudy appeared frustrated throughout the phonics test. However, in mathematics, Rudy was functioning at the 4.4 level (PIAT—standard score 87), consistent with the SOMPA Pluralistic Model Estimated Learning Potential. Further testing in mathematics on the Key Math Diagnostic Arithmetic Test (Connolly, Nachtman, and Pritchett, 1971) revealed notable strengths in word problems and the use of money and time arithmetic problems where Rudy was functioning at the 4.3, 6.2, and 5.3 grade levels respectively, again consistent with his ELP. In computational skills, Rudy was able to add and subtract with regrouping and was beginning multiplication and division.

In sensorimotor integration (as measured by the SOMPA Physical Dexterity Tasks, a standardized series of tests of the intactness and capability of the motor and sensory pathways involved in physical exercise) Rudy was "at risk" (below the 16th percentile) in the areas of ambulation, fine-motor sequencing, finger-tongue dexterity, and involuntary movement. Equilibrium and placement were found to be within normal limits; however, the total score was "at risk". Rudy's teacher reported that when compared to his classmates assigned to the EMR class, he was able to run adequately, roller skate, was "good in kickball," and enjoyed participating in classroom physical education activities. Perceptually, Rudy had severe difficulties in fine-motor coordination where he was functioning at approximately the six-year-old level as measured by the Bender-Gestalt (Bender, 1946) and Developmental Test of Visual-Motor Integration (Beery, 1967). Rudy also had marked problems in visual memory and discrimination on the Ransom Visual Memory and Discrimination Tests (Ransom, 1978) of letters, words and phrases. For example, Rudy still confused b, d, p, and q. Although his auditory discrimination skills were age appropriate on the Wepman Auditory Discrimination Test (Wepman, 1973), he had extreme difficulty analyzing, sequencing, and remembering sounds on the Test of Auditory Analysis Skills (Rosner, 1975). These weaknesses in visual and auditory perceptual skills appeared to be contributing to Rudy's difficulty in reading and spelling.

Emotionally, Rudy appeared to have strong feelings of insecurity probably related to the recent loss of his father, home (through divorce) and temporary separation from his mother (through hospitalization). At the time of the case study, Rudy was truly without the support of parent figures. He also exhibited poor self-concept, perhaps due to his history of learning and behavioral difficulties. Rudy tended to see school as a place of frustration whre the work was too hard for him, where his peers thought he was "crazy and dumb," and where his efforts seemed to lead to incorrect answers and disappointment (Sentence Completion Test; Educational Apperception Test). Rudy seemed to react to academic frustration through aggressive misbehavior evidenced in the fighting and provoking behaviors described by previous teachers. However, his present teacher stated that although Rudy could "be a behavior problem," he responded positively to rewards and teacher praise and functioned "independently and adequately" in classroom tasks. In the area of adaptive behavior, as measured by the SOMPA Adaptive Behavior Inventory for Children (ABIC) (administered in Spanish with Mrs. Benson as informant), Rudy was "at risk" (below the 2nd percentile) in the areas of family, community, peer relations, nonacademic school roles, and self maintenance skills. Rudy was in the 5th percentile in the earner consumer role. However, it was this examiner's impression that Rudy had a higher level of maturity, adaptability, and awareness than was indicated by the ABIC ratings. For example, during the testing session, Rudy and the examiner took a break. Rudy was able to fix himself a cup of hot chocolate and the examiner a cup of coffee with a minimum of instruction using the office coffee maker. The examiner and Rudy also had lunch together at Jack in the Box. Rudy paid for his meal with a $5 bill and received change. When the examiner asked Rudy how he know that he had received the correct change, Rudy responded that since his food had cost $1.53 and he had given "the lady" $5, he should receive $3.47. Although he did the computation with his fingers, he then proceeded to count the change to see if he was correct, which he was. This also confirmed, in a practical situation, the measured strengths in the use of money on the diagnostic math test. It is also significant that Rudy in no way differed from any other customer eating and ordering at Jack in the Box on this particular day. Rudy also evidenced considerable concern about his mother (who was hospitalized at the time of the testing sessions) and stated that he was going to call her at the hospital to see how she was feeling. He did so during the break, dialing the number appropriately, and securing the correct extension.

In addition, Rudy was extremely aware of the E.A.S. (Educational Assessment Service) procedure and processes and was aware of the Resource Specialist Program as a possible alternative for him. According to Mrs. Benson, it was Rudy who reminded her of the examiner's appointment with her for the SOMPA parent interview. Thus, Rudy in his own way was trying to take responsibility for his educational future, reflecting the potential for highly developed social behavior. Finally, Mrs. Benson, the ABIC informant, appeared to be extremely depressed at the time of the parent interview. She was recovering physically from a hysterectomy, psychologically from abandonment by her husband, and for the immediate future, she did not have a home of her own. Her physical and psychological circumstances may have lowered her perceptions of Rudy's abilities.

Summary and Recommendations

The evaluation data and recommendations generated by the case study will be discussed in relation to the "Questions to be Answered by the Assessment" previously formulated.

(1) What are Rudy's current linguistic, cognitive, sensorimotor, academic and social/emotional functioning levels?
The psychoeducational assessment indicated that Rudy appeared to be English-dominant. In addition, because all of Rudy's formal education had been received in English, cognitive assessment was conducted in English using the WISC-R as employed within the SOMPA Social System and Pluralistic Models. All other tests were also administered in English. Cognitively, Rudy's School Functioning Level (SFL) fell within the mentally deficient range. (The examiner noted that the scores may have been lowered due to emotional factors.) However, his Estimated Learning Potential (ELP) generally fell within the low average range. In sensorimotor areas, Rudy was "at risk" in ambulation, fine-motor sequencing, finger-tongue dexterity, and involuntary movement while equilibrium and placement were within normal limits. Severe delays were noted in fine-motor coordination, visual, and auditory perception. Academically, Rudy's scores ranged from the 1.5 to the 2.6 level in reading and spelling. However, math performance ranged from the 4.3 to the 6.2 level and appeared to be commensurate with the ELP. In social/emotional areas, feelings of insecurity due to the family's present precarious situation and poor self-concept resulting from a history of learning and behavioral problems were noted. Ratings on the ABIC fell within the 2nd to 5th percentile but may have been underestimated due to the informant's (Rudy's mother) depressed emotional state. In addition, higher level adaptive behavior functioning was observed by the author.

(2) and (3) Is Rudy eligible for special education, and if so, what is the appropriate special education eligibility classification?

Because the SOMPA Estimated Learning Potentials (especially the Verbal ELP) performance in mathematics and examiner observed adaptive behavior together suggest low average learning potential, continued placement in the Learning Handicapped class with the eligibility classification of "mental retardation" was inappropriate. However, the assessment suggested a severe discrepancy between Estimated Learning Potential and academic achievement in the areas of reading and written language skills, qualifying Rudy for special education services with the eligibility classification of "specific learning disability."

(4) What is the least restrictive educational placement that will best meet Rudy's educational needs?

The assessment results indicated that Rudy had severe delays in reading and written language skills. Moreover, Rudy had not participated in a regular classroom for five years. It was recommended, therefore, that he continue in the Learning Handicapped Special Day Class on the basis of a "specific learning disability." Integration into the regular classroom for mathematics instruction with appropriate modifications in the length of written assignments due to his difficulties in fine-motor coordination was also recommended. Finally, the examiner suggested that the school counselor, in conjunction with the resource specialist, develop a hierarchy of academic and behavioral tasks and a reinforcement program to enable Rudy to increase the amount of time spent in the regular classroom.

(5) What recommendations can be made to the family to help them cope with their present crisis?

The author suggested that the Bilingual School Community Liaison help Mrs. Benson (e.g., with transportation, translating, filling out forms, etc.) in securing welfare benefits and that the Liaison also facilitate contacts with the medical social worker. The author suggested that Mrs. Benson seek professional counseling from a local mental health agency (which accepted Medi-Cal) to help cope with her present life crisis. Finally, the author recommended that Rudy receive a neurological evaluation to update his medical status.

Unique Contribution of SOMPA in Responding to Assessment Questions

After studying the assessment results, one may question if the recommendations made for Rudy could have been derived through a thorough interpretation of the data obtained in a traditional evaluation process. While it certainly would have been possible to formulate the recommendations through a thorough interpretation of the data obtained by current methods, it is evident from the case study that the use of SOMPA made a unique contribution. From the Medical Model perspective, data from the Health History Inventories, Physical Dexterity Tasks and Bender-Gestalt supported in an *objective and standardized manner* evidence of possible neurological dysfunction that had been suggested in previous health and developmental histories and provided a sound basis on which to make a referral for further medical evaluation. From the Social Systems Model viewpoint, the SFL seemed to reflect what had been reported in two previous psychoeducational evaluations. In this particular case, the ABIC (as would any other measure of adaptive behavior where the mother was the informant) seemed to underestimate Rudy's adaptive behavioral functioning due to his mother's depressed emotional state. From the Pluralistic Model perspective, the ELP supported evidence of higher mental ability suggested by low average to average performance in computational and numerical reasoning skills, which was not apparent from the SFL score alone. Thus, the use of SOMPA in this case provided cross validation of significant medical variables and learning potential not evident in the SFL. This additional data combined with linguistic and edumetric assessment and careful examiner observation provided the basis to determine a nondiscriminatory special education eligibility classification, in this instance "specific learning disability" (perhaps attributed to neurological dysfunction).

Follow-up Data

The presented recommendations were accepted by school level personnel, Mrs. Benson, and the District Educational Assessment Service and written into Rudy's Individual Educational Plan (IEP). Rudy's Special Day Class teacher was surprised that he was able to perform so well in numerical reasoning problems. However, the teacher did have concerns that Rudy needed to improve his attending and task completion behaviors prior to integration into the regular classroom.

Accordingly, the examiner and Rudy's Special Day Class teacher developed a behavior modification program to provide the structure for Rudy to make a successful integration into the regular classroom. Four target behaviors were identified, as follows: (1) establishing eye contact with teacher when hearing directions, (2) raising hand quietly if the instructions are not understood, (3) working quietly, and (4) completing assignment within required time periods. Numbers(1) through (3) were given a point value of 1 and (4) given a value of 2. Rudy was positively reinforced if he performed at the 80% level (4/5 points). Thus, in order to meet the criteria, his work had to be completed due to the 2 point weight assigned to this behavior. Positive reinforcement consisted primarily of time spent in the regular classroom which was very motivating for Rudy. Additional reinforcers consisted of awards and certificates, going out to lunch or for an ice cream cone with the teacher, and class time to play a game with a friend. The author and the Special Day Class teacher explained to Rudy that his participation in regular classroom activities would be contingent upon his performance on the four target behaviors. Rudy indicated that he understood and seemed enthusiastic about beginning the process. The program was to be implemented in the Special Day Class and, if successful, extended into the regular classroom. The regular sixth grade classroom teacher had previously worked with the Special Day Class teacher in the integration of other students and consequently, his students were accustomed to having children from the Special Day Class come into their room for part of the day. This teacher agreed to work with Rudy when appropriate.

Because Rudy was extremely motivated to participate in the regular classroom, he quickly met the task completion objective (to complete a minimum of 80% of his written math assignments within required time periods). This behavior modification program was then extended into the regular classroom where Rudy was integrated into the low math group. Task completion was charted by the regular classroom teacher with rewards dispensed by the Special Day Class teacher. However, the length of his written assignments had to be modified due to Rudy's fine-motor coordination difficulties. Limited follow-up data indicated that Rudy performed in an acceptable level, meeting the 80% task completion objective and earning a grade of "C" in the regular math class at the end of the year. Rudy was also able to participate successfully in selected music, art, and social science activities. However, his minimal progress in reading and written language skills did not permit further integration in other academic areas. Both the Special Day Class and regular classroom teachers reported that at the end of the year, Rudy appeared to be content with the intervention and noted an improvement in self confidence, self-concept and peer relationships. The regular classroom teacher observed that Rudy was accepted by the class because he was able to complete his work. However, he also indicated that Rudy did not develop any close friendships during the five months spent in his classroom. In contrast, Rudy seemed to feel that he was accepted by the class (as per examiner interview). In addition, Mrs. Benson secured her welfare payments and agreed to see a counselor at a local mental health agency. The family moved at the end of the year, and further follow-up information was not available.

Discussion of Recommendations and Follow-up Data

The purpose of this section is to amplify the rationale for the case study recommendations to reclassify Rudy as "specific learning disabled," to integrate him into a regular classroom for mathematics instruction, and to discuss the follow-up data further. Where applicable, relevant research will be cited.

The recommendation to reclassify Rudy's special education eligibility classification from "mental retardation" to "specific learning disability" was based on data from the Verbal ELP, mathematics performance, and examiner observed adaptive behavior, which, taken together, suggested low average learning potential. It is noteworthy that Rudy was originally diagnosed as having a severe learning disability attributed to possible neurological dysfunction and that he had a Leiter IQ of 90 in kindergarten. Yet, approximately six months later, on the basis of a Full Scale WISC-R score of 57 and reported behavioral difficulties, he was placed in a class for the educable mentally retarded. According to Mrs. Benson, this was a time of extreme tension and stress for the family, caused primarily by marital conflict with her first husband, culminating in their separation and eventual divorce. In addition, school psychological records are unfortunately incomplete and do not give the breakdown between verbal and performance skills, or subtest data; nor was there an attempt to assess Rudy's degree of language proficiency in either English or Spanish. It appears probable that the original diagnosis was correct and that extreme family tension combined with severe learning difficulties made it impossible for Rudy to function in a regular classroom. When retested on a WISC-R after four years of EMR placement, his performance was commensurate with the program in which he was placed, as was the parent-requested testing (conducted by this author) using the traditional norms eight months later. As stated previously, it is also possible that Rudy's performance was lowered by emotional factors.

However, when sociocultural variables were controlled, the Verbal and Performance ELPs went up 20 and 13 points respectively, consistent with the ability demonstrated by early Leiter results. In addition, the hypothesis that the Verbal ELP may represent a better estimate of Rudy's learning potential was supported by his math performance on the PIAT, a test which appears to rely more on numerical reasoning skills than computation, and his scores on the word problem, time, and money subtests of the Key Math. Moreover, studies on the math performance of the mentally retarded indicate that in arithmetic computation, they achieve at a level near that of "normal," comparable mental age students. However, in arithmetical reasoning, mentally retarded students lag significantly behind their mental age peers (MacMillan, 1977). Rudy had the opposite pattern of abilities and exhibited wide discrepancies in academic skill functioning (severe deficits in reading and written language and strengths in mathematics), a characteristic of children with specific learning disabilities. More significantly, Rudy's positive response to the behavior modification program and acceptable performance in the regular classroom in math also suggest higher "learning potential." Thus, for Rudy the ELP appeared to be a better estimate of his learning potential than the traditional WISC-R norms, for the ELP corresponded with low average performance in arithmetical reasoning and computational skills and actual classroom functioning in math. If the ELP is accepted, then the interpretation can be made that Rudy evidenced a severe discrepancy between mental ability and academic achievement in reading and written language skills and met the eligibility criteria for "specific learning disability."

In using the ELP, because of the lack of validity data (refer to Appendix), the author sought supporting evidence for higher potential. In other words, the author viewed the ELP as a hypothesis in need of confirmation. The use of the ELP in Rudy's case also points to the difficulty in attempting to validate the ELP (on a broad scale) through correlations with academic achievement. Such correlational studies may be confounded by the presence of specific learning disabilities in populations classified as mentally retarded. In Rudy's case, the SFL was a better predictor of reading and written language skills, while the ELP correlated with performance in math. For other students, the correlational pattern may vary according to the area(s) of specific disability.

The recommendation for reclassification as specific learning disabled, continued placement in the Special Day Class, and integration into the regular sixth grade class for math instruction indicates that use of the ELP does not necessarily lead to a loss of special education services as suggested by Clarizo (1979a, 1979b). For example, in California where this case study was conducted, there are Special Day Classes for the "learning handicapped." A student may be found eligible on the basis of a "specific learning disability" or "mental retardation." Both classifications may be found within one Special Day Class. In Rudy's case, the label was changed from mental retardation to specific learning disability, but the classroom and special education service remained essentially the same. Because Rudy was functioning within the low average range in mathematics, integration in the regular classroom was suggested in this area. Both recommendations for reclassification and integration for mathematics are consistent with the P.L. 94-142 dictum "the least restrictive environment" and did not result in a reduction in special education service.

Before discussing the follow-up data, a few comments about Rudy's ABIC scores are necessary. As stated previously, the examiner's professional judgment was that the ABIC may have underestimated Rudy's level of adaptive, behavioral functioning due to the possible depressed condition of his mother, the ABIC informant. Examiner observation of Rudy in the classroom and community setting seemed to suggest a higher level of adaptive behavioral functioning. However, Rudy did have emotional difficulties associated with the loss of his father, anxiety about possible loss of his mother, tenuous living arrangements, and severe learning handicaps, as was clearly indicated by his responses to sentence completion and thematic apperception materials.

In summary, the use of the SOMPA battery with prerequisite linguistic assessment, further edumetric, observational, and projective measures revealed that Rudy was an ll-3 year old Mexican-American, English-dominant boy of low average learning potential (ELP). There appeared to be a severe discrepancy between his estimated learning potential and academic performance in reading and written language skills, suggesting severe learning disabilities in these areas. Performance in mathematics seemed to be commensurate with his ELP. At risk scores on the Medical Model measures, Health History Inventories, Physical Dexterity Tasks, and Bender-Gestalt suggested that these learning disabilities might be neurologically based. Although Rudy's Total Score on the ABIC was "at risk," his mother's possible depression and examiner classroom and community observation suggested a higher level of adaptive behavioral functioning than indicated by the ABIC ratings. However, generalized feelings of insecurity due to a tenuous home situation and difficulties in self-concept development associated with Rudy's severe learning difficulties were noted.

Although the family moved out of the area toward the end of the school year, the limited available follow-up data indicated that Rudy responded well to the behavior modification program and corresponding integration into the regular classroom program for math instruction and eventually for selected art, music, and social science activities. There is empirical evidence to support the integration recommendation and its apparent success. For example, Budoff and Gottlieb (1976) found that high learning potential, formerly classified as EMR students (as assessed by the Budoff learning potential paradigm), after a year in an integrated placement with resource center support, felt that other students perceived them more positively when they were mainstreamed than when they were placed in segregated classes, and tended to "feel oppressed" by the Special Day Class placement. Although Rudy was not integrated to the degree of the high learning potential subjects of the Budoff and Gottlieb study, as a high ELP student in a segregated special education class, he did appear to feel "oppressed" and he "wanted out." After the limited integration, his mother and teacher reported that Rudy appeared to be more confident. In response to interview questions by the examiner, Rudy indicated that he "got along o.k." in the regular class and that he was "happy" with the intervention.

In addition, a study by Gottlieb, Semmel, and Veldman (1978) found that EMR social acceptance and social rejection by nonretarded peers were separate dimensions. Perceptions of misbehavior were associated with social rejection while academic competence was associated with social acceptance. It is possible that in Rudy's case, the effective use of behavior modification to increase task completion reduced social rejection while his competence in arithmetic and numerical reasoning facilitated social acceptance in the classroom.

It is also possible that Rudy's reported increase in positive self-concept is attributable to the availability of multiple comparative social reference groups. Strang, Smith and Rogers (1978), applying Festinger's social comparison theory, found that learning handicapped children who were mainstreamed for part of the school day, significantly increased their self esteem while mainstreamed academically handicapped students, restricted to regular classroom peers in making social comparisons, showed a decrease in self-concept. Thus, Rudy's reported increase in self-concept may have been a function of his selective use of two available, comparative social reference groups. For math, Rudy may have used regular classroom peers as a comparative group, while using his Special Day Class companions for reading, written language, and perhaps social relationships, and as a result "enjoyed the best of both worlds."

APPENDIX
SOMPA: A BRIEF TECHNICAL CRITIQUE

The purpose of this appendix is to consider some of the technical aspects of SOMPA's development and to review and critique the instruments unique to SOMPA. Test administration and materials, standardization sample, Medical, Social System, and Pluralistic Model measures will be discussed. The WISC-R will not be presented because it has been the subject of extensive study elsewhere. (Kaufman, 1979).

Test Administration and Materials

Brown (1979a) states it is unlikely that one individual would have either the time or the skill to administer all the SOMPA instruments. Oakland (1979a, 1979b) states that the complete administration of the SOMPA battery may take up to five hours. Mercer (1979) maintains that it will add 90 minutes of additional time to a conventional psychoeducational assessment. It is this author's (a trained SOMPA administrator) experience that the administration and scoring of just the Physical Dexterity Tasks, Parent Interview (Health History Inventory, Sociocultural Scales, and ABIC), and scoring and derivation of the ELP, extends the traditional psychoeducational evaluation approximately two hours. However, with P.L. 94-142 requirements that children be evaluated by an assessment team, there is no need for one person to administer all the measures. For example, a school nurse can conduct the hearing and vision screening and height by weight measurement; an adaptive/remedial physical education specialist can administer the Physical Dexterity Tasks, leaving the WISC-R, the Parent Interview, and the Bender to the psychologist. If necessary, a social worker or a paraprofessional can conduct the Parent Interview. A resource specialist can conduct an academic assessment with edumetric measures. In regard to the skill necessary to administer the SOMPA battery, Mercer has developed a comprehensive training program to provide potential users with the conceptual basis and practical experience to administer, score, and interpret the SOMPA instruments.

In addition, there are excellent Spanish translations of the Physical Dexterity Tasks, Health History Inventories, Sociocultural Scales, and ABIC. However, the complete SOMPA system can only be used with children who speak English well enough to take the WISC-R *in English*. Consequently, when working with Hispanic children, the examiner must determine the child's language proficiency in English and in Spanish before choosing an assessment approach. Thus, SOMPA does not provide a verbal measure of intelligence for the Spanish-speaking child, a tool urgently needed for a complete assessment.

The Standardization Sample

As stated earlier, SOMPA was standardized on approximately 2100 children, 700 each, black, Hispanic, and white students attending public school in California. However, Sattler (1982) expresses concern about the adequacy of the California based norms, indicating that the SOMPA manual presents no information regarding the sample's socioeconomic distribution. This makes an evaluation of sample representativeness problematic. Moreover, Sattler further states that the use of total sample norms will give a distorted picture because equal distribution of the three racial/ethnic groups does not exist in the state. Brown (1979, a) further questions if generalizations can be made to other samples such as Puerto Ricans in New York or Mexican-Americans in New Mexico and Texas. Oakland (1979, a) reports data suggesting that the California norms should be used with caution in other geographical locations. For example, Buckley and Oakland (1977) found that Mexican-American children in Austin and Corpus Christi, Texas, had significantly lower ABIC scores than the Mexican-American children in Mercer's California sample on four of the six subtests with the most significant differences in the lower class Mexican-American children. Scott, Mastenbrook, Fisher, and Gridley (1982) also found that low SES Mexican-Americans had significantly lower ABIC scores than Anglos or blacks in a Corpus Christi sample. Thus, Oakland (1979, a) states that more Mexican-American children would qualify for special education, using the California norms. Oakland (1979, a) also compared data from the Sociocultural Scales using the Austin and California samples. He found that the Austin Anglo children tended to score lower on family structure and urban acculturation than the California children. Black and Mexican-American children tended to come from higher SES homes than the children in the California sample. Finally, Tebeleff and Oakland (1977) found that the correlations between the WISC-R and achievement were significantly different in the Austin and California samples. The WISC-R accounted for approximately 38% of the variance in achievement in Austin, but only 9 to 20% in the California sample. This difference was especially notable for minority students where in the Austin sample, IQ accounted for 38% of the variance in achievement and only 8% in California. Thus, the California norms should be used with caution in other states.

In addition, as indicated by Brown (1979, a), differences in norming samples might also affect the weighting constants used to transform the WISC-R scores to ELPs. This point will be discussed further in the section on Pluralistic Model measures.

Medical Model Measures

Three of the six Medical Model measures will be discussed because two, the Physical Dexterity Tasks and Health History Inventories, are unique to SOMPA, and the inclusion of a third (Bender-Gestalt) within the Medical Model is controversial. The Physical Dexterity Tasks include a series of behaviors often used by physicians in neurological evaluations to assess sensorimotor coordination and to screen for "soft" signs of neurological impairment. These tests were specifically developed for SOMPA and represent a unique contribution to medical and psychological assessment which has gone largely unrecognized by the critics. The Physical Dexterity Tasks are important because they have been standardized on a *normal* sample of children from three ethnic and racial groups. Moreover, sociocultural variables account for less than 4% of the variance, indicating that the Physical Dexterity Tasks meet the transcultural assumptions of the Medical Model (Mercer & Lewis, 1977). Split half reliabilities range from .61 to .94 for differing age levels and .71 to .90 for the total sample.

Also uniquely developed in SOMPA are the Health History Inventories. These inventories include a series of questions for parents about children's pre- and postnatal events, traumas, diseases, and problems related to vision and hearing. The purpose of these measures is to identify children having biological insults which may lead to difficulty in school learning. The SOMPA Health History Inventories represent a significant advance over traditional developmental screenings because item validity is determined by significant correlations with the Bender-Gestalt and Physical Dexterity Tasks (tasks associated with "soft" signs of neurological impairment). Scores below the 16th percentile are categorized as "at risk" and warrant further evaluation by a medical specialist. Thus, the examiner has an empirically based health history. Sociocultural variables account for less than one percent of the variance, indicating that the inventories meet the transcultural assumptions of the Medical Model (Mercer & Lewis, 1977). Although Brown (1979, a) and Sattler (1982) state that empirical relationships between Medical Model measures and school variables need to be demonstrated, results of testing with the Physical Dexterity Tasks and Health History Inventories combined with the other Medical Model measures provide the assessment team with relevant data for the decision to refer or not to refer the student for further medical evaluation.

In addition, reviewers such as Goodman (1979, a; 1979b) have severely criticized the inclusion of the Bender-Gestalt as a Medical Model measure. Citing a variety of studies on Bender-Gestalt performance, Goodman argues that lower class children perform significantly worse than middle class subjects, disadvantaged black students more poorly than similarly situated white children, and that Navahos and Mexican-Americans do more poorly than whites, contradicting the transcultural assumption of the Medical Model. Goodman (1979, a) also indicates that Mercer and Lewis' (1977) data show a significantly high (.46) correlation with the WISC-R, and argues that the Bender reflects disturbed adjustment and other personality variables. Moreover, Sattler and Gwynne (1982) in an analysis of Table 16 of the SOMPA manual state that there are significant differences among blacks, whites, and Hispanics at several age levels, suggesting the need for separate norms. However, Mercer (1979) and Mercer and Lewis (1977) maintain that the Bender-Gestalt was included in the Medical Model because sociocultural variables accounted for less than 2% of the variance. Mercer (1979) argues that the Bender is only one of 18 scores in the medical profile, and as part of this larger picture, it is less likely to be overinterpreted.

In summary, SOMPA's Medical Model measures seem to provide a comprehensive screening for possible medical variables traditionally thought to affect the child's school performance. In addition, these measures provide ample data for the examiner or assessment team to make the decision to refer or not to refer, to a medical specialist for further evaluation. Moreover, the Physical Dexterity Tasks, standardized on normal children, and the empirically based Health History Inventories represent a significant contribution to the field. However, empirical relationships between Medical Model measures and school learning need to be demonstrated. There are also data to suggest that the Bender-Gestalt may not meet the Medical Model's assumptions.

Social System Model Measures

The measures in the Social System Model include the ABIC and the WISC-R. It is beyond the scope of this paper to review the WISC-R. Accordingly, the discussion will focus primarily on the ABIC. Mercer and Lewis (1977) conceptualize adaptive behavior as the "achieving of an adaptive fit or situational functioning through the development of interpersonal ties in social systems and the acquisition of specific skills required to fulfill the task functions associated with particular roles" (p.

123). Thus, the ABIC attempts to estimate (through a parent interview) a child's role performance in six areas: family, community, peer relations, nonacademic school roles, earner/consumer, and self maintenance.

The ABIC was developed from extensive interviews with mothers from Hispanic, black and Anglo cultures. The mothers were questioned about the types of behaviors allowed and observed in their children. The items in each of the six roles inquire about the children's competence in progressively more complex social tasks. The items were assigned to one of the six roles on the basis of ratings by 10 independent judges. Mercer and Lewis (1977) report that overall there were no significant differences between males and females or ethnic groups, and sociocultural variables accounted for less than 4% of the variance. As a result, separate norms were not developed. Split half reliabilities for each age level in the standardization sample and for each ethnic group were calculated with Total Score reliability coefficients for the composite and each ethnic group at .95 or above, and subscale reliabilities ranging from .78 to .92 with a median r of .86. Thus, the ABIC appears to be a reliable instrument.

ABIC validity is supported by its apparent conceptual and statistical independence from both intelligence as measured by the WISC-R (Mercer & Lewis, 1977; Oakland, 1980; Tebeleff & Oakland, 1977) and academic achievement (Tebeleff & Oakland, 1977). Moreover, Oakland and Feigenbaum (in Oakland, 1979, a) conducted an assessment of bias using item analysis, multiple regression, analysis of variance and factor analysis to determine whether there were biases due to children's racial-ethnicity, sex, age, birth order, health history, family size, urban acculturation or SES as reflected in the ABIC's internal consistency, item difficulty, item-total correlations, concurrent validity, and construct validity. The only evidence of ABIC bias was that item difficulty was influenced by birth order, age, and SES, tending to substantiate Mercer and Lewis' (1977) original data. However, Scott, Mastenbrook, Fisher, and Gridley (1982) in a Corpus Christi sample, found significantly lower ABIC scores for low SES Mexican-Americans and recommended separate norms for this group.

In addition, factorial validity of the ABIC is questionable. Mercer and Lewis (1977) state that the intercorrelations between the ABIC subscales are generally .65, which they cite as justification for a Total Score. However, the median subscale intercorrelation is .77 (Sattler, 1982), and as Brown (1979, a) indicates, these data can also be used to argue against the use of subscale scores. Given these high subscale intercorrelations, extreme caution should be used in interpreting individual subscale scores.

Moreover, ABIC validity may be limited by its "no opportunity" score. Reviewers such as Sattler (1982) maintain that the ABIC does not consider the child's opportunity to learn adaptive behaviors. The fact that low SES Mexican-Americans obtain significantly lower ABIC scores than other groups might be a function of lack of opportunity and differential parental expectations for the acquisition of adaptive behavioral skills (Mastenbrook, Scott, & Marriott, 1978). As stated by Sattler (1982), the "no opportunity" score on the ABIC "results in a lowering of the adaptive behavior score, not in an explanation of why there is no opportunity" (p. 314).

ABIC validity is also limited by its use of the mother as the primary informant. Goodman (1979, a; 1979b) states that although the ABIC is intended to reflect the child's role performance in a variety of social settings, the sole informant is the mother. She argues that the ABIC may be "more a test of parental perception than of child role behavior." Indeed, Wall and Paradise (1981) found little agreement between mother and teacher on abbreviated ABIC ratings; mothers also tended to rate their children significantly higher than teachers. Goodman (1979, a) also states that although the central purpose of SOMPA is to assess learning abilities, "at no point is the teacher's analysis and judgment requested" (p. 54). Mercer (1979) also expresses regret for not providing a direct measure of role performance in the school. This represents a major weakness in the SOMPA Social System Model.

In summary, the ABIC is a reliable standardized measure of adaptive behavioral functioning (from the parent perspective) which appears to be both conceptually and statistically independent of intelligence and academic achievement. Preliminary data, however, suggest that some lower SES Mexican-Americans (e.g., Corpus Christi sample) have significantly lower ABIC scores than other groups. Factorial validity is questionable because of the high interscale correlations. Accordingly, extreme caution should be used in interpreting individual subscale sores. Moreover, ABIC validity is also limited by the "no opportunity" scores. Lack of opportunity to acquire an adaptive behavior may lower a child's score while not actually reflecting the child's lack of ability. Finally, a fundamental weakness of the ABIC and SOMPA Social System Model in general is the failure to provide a set of teacher ratings to directly assess directly role performance in school.

Pluralistic Model Measures

The WISC-R is the only measure in the Pluralistic Model and uses pluralistic norms and the sociocultural scales to derive the Estimated

Learning Potential (ELP). As stated earlier, the Sociocultural Scales determine how much an individual's world differs from the Anglo core culture in four areas: family size, family structure, socioeconomic status, and urban acculturation. These scales are used as a basis for converting the WISC-R scores into ELPs. Accordingly, the ELP is the WISC-R score with the sociocultural variables held constant through the use of multiple regression procedures. However, Brown (1979, a) questions the generalizability of the weighting constants used to transform the WISC-R scores to ELPs. To the extent that the California sample differs from the local population, the greater the scores will be in error. Preliminary studies by Oakland (1979, a) in Texas, Dewey (1978) in Iowa, and Reschley (1978) in Arizona, reveal significant difference in ELPs derived from geographically distinct regression equations.

This leads to the question of ELP validity. With the exception of the fact the ELP is a WISC-R score controlled for sociocultural variables, there is no clear operational definition of estimated learning potential. Perhaps the situation is best summarized by Brown (1979b) who states, "The algebra works, but what does it mean?" This apparent lack of a clear operational definition of the ELP results in disagreement as to what approach or criteria for ELP validation should be employed. For example, investigators (Dewey, 1978; Oakland, 1977, 1980; Reschly, 1978) have attempted to validate the ELP as a predictor of academic achievement by comparing its predictive power to that of the WISC-R score(SFL). The results of these studies suggest that although the ELP is significantly correlated with academic performance, the SFL is a significantly better predictor of academic achievement and accounts for as much as twice the variance.

However, Mercer (1979) objects to this method of validating the ELP. She asserts that it is an error to validate measures across assessment models. According to Mercer, validity should be defined by the instrument's intended use. When a test is used to infer "intelligence" within the Pluralistic Model, validity is determined by the extent to which opportunity to learn the materials in the test, motivation to learn, and other intervening variables have been controlled. Thus, Mercer maintains that the appropriate test of ELP validity is the amount of variance in the WISC-R score accounted for by the sociocultural variables in the regression equation. The more the sociocultural component of the test score is controlled, the more valid its inferences.

Moreover, Mercer (1979) states that the proposal to validate the ELP using the achievement tests as criteria has inherent statistical problems. She argues that cultural exposure acts as an intervening variable enhancing the relationship between the SFL and academic achievement tests because there is a systematic cultural effect favoring Anglo core-culture children in both measures. Removing the cultural effect in one of the scores reduces the correlation between the scores. But as Brown (1979, a) states, even if Mercer's definition of ELP validity is accepted, the SOMPA Sociocultural Scales only account for between 6 and 28% of the variance. Brown (1979, a) also raises the issue of whether all four sociocultural scales are necessary inasmuch as the data indicate that most of the variance is accounted for by the Urban Acculturation Scale

But more basic, the ELP as presently defined provides no information regarding the relation of scores to educationally relevant variables. Nor is there evidence that the ELP will result in a more accurate assessment that will facilitate more appropriate educational planning. Because Mercer rejects school achievement as a criterion measure, the establishment of ELP external validity is problematic. Perhaps as Brown (1979, a) suggests, SFL or ELP scores could be used to predict performance on a new learning task as in the Budoff (1975) or Feuerstein (1979) paradigms. Another approach suggested by Brown (1979, a) and Mercer and Lewis (1977) is to compare the learning task performance of students equated for SFLs but differing significantly in ELPs. Thus, problems in construct validation stem from lack of a clear operational definition of the Pluralistic Model's Estimated Learning Potential.

However, if the intent of SOMPA is nondiscriminatory assessment in the labeling and placement process, one aspect of its validity might be established by showing that its use significantly decreases the number of minority students identified as mentally retarded. Fisher (1977) found that the use of the ABIC had this effect in the reevaluation of students classified as TMR and EMR. Reschly (1978) found that the use of the ELP helped decrease the percentage of minority students identified as EMR. However, Clarizo (1979a, 1979b) asserts that the use of SOMPA may deprive children of special education services they truly need. Mercer (1979) does not deny there would be a loss of special education services to some students. However, she questions the appropriateness of maintaining such placement because special education programs may not be markedly better than regular class or compensatory education programs, and the negative consequences of the mentally retarded label and isolation from normal peers may not be compensated by the quality of the special education class. This opens the issue of the efficacy of Special Day Classes and mainstreaming which is beyond the scope of this paper. However, the situation is cogently summarized by Figueroa (1979), who states, high Estimated Learning Potential "will do nothing without educational placements that reflect linguistic and cultural diversity." (p. 34)

References

Beery, K.E. (1967). *Developmental test of visual-motor integration*. Chicago: Follett Educational Corporation.

Bender, L. (1946). *Manual for instruction and test cards for Visual Motor Gestalt Test*. New Yrk: American Orthopsychiatric Association.

Brown, F.G. (1979a). The SOMPA: A system of measuring potential abilities? *School Psychology Digest, 8*, 37-46. (a).

Brown, F.G. (1979b). The algebra works—but what does it mean? *School Psychology Digest, 8*, 213-218. (b).

Buckley, K., & Oakland, T. (1977). Contrasting localized norms for Mexican-America children and the ABIC. Paper presented at the annual meeting of the American Psychological Association, San Francisco, CA.

Budoff, M., & Gottlieb, J. (1976). Special class EMR children mainstreamed: A study of aptitude (learning potential) x treatment interaction. *American Journal of Mental Deficiency, 81*, 1-11.

Burt, M.K., Dulay, H.C., & Hernandez, C.E. (1976) *Bilingual Syntax Measure*. New York: Harcourt, Brace Jovanovich.

Clarizo, H.F. (1979a). In defense of the IQ test. *School Psychology Digest, 8*, 79-88. (a).

Clarizo, H.F. (1979b). SOMPA: A symposium continued: Commentaries. *School Psychology Digest, 8*, 207-209. (b).

Connolly, A.J., Nachtman, W., & Pritchett, E.M. (1971). *The Key Math Diagnostic Arithmetic Test*. Circle Pines, Minn.: American Guidance Service.

Covarrubias v. San Diego Unified School District (Southern California) No. 70-394-T (S.D. Cal. February, 1971).

Critchlow, D.E. (1973). *Dos Amigos Verbal Language Scales*. San Rafael, CA: Academic Therapy Publications.

Dewey, S.J. (1978). *An investigation of the validity of the Estimated Learning Potential from the System of Multicultural Pluralistic Assessment*. Unpublished master's thesis, Iowa State University, Ames.

Diana v. State Board of Education. (1973, June 18). Civil Action No. C-70 37 RFP. (N.D. Cal. Jan. 7, 1970).

Dunn, L.M. (1959). *Peabody Picture Vocabulary Test*. Minneapolis: American Guidance Service.

Dunn, L.M., & Markwardt, F.C., Jr. (1970) *Peabody Individual Achievement Test*. Circle Pines, Minn.: American Guidance Service.

Figueroa, R.A. (1979). The System of Multicultural Pluralistic Assessment. *School Psychology Digest, 8*, 28-36.

Feuerstein, R. (1979). *The dynamic assessment of retarded performers: The Learning Potential Device, theory, instruments, and techniques*. Baltimore: University Park Press.

Goodman, J.F. (1979a). Is tissue the issue? A critique of SOMPA's models and tests. *School Psychology Digest, 8*, 47-61. (a).

Goodman, J.F. (1979b). Ignorance versus stupidity—the basic disagreement. *School Psychology Digest, 8*, 218-223. (b).

Gottlieb, J., Semmel, M.I., & Veldman, D.J. (1978). Correlates of social status among mainstreamed mentally retarded children. *Journal of Educational Psychology, 70*, 396-405.

Kaufman, A.S. (1979). *Intelligent testing with the WISC-R*. New York: Wiley Interscience.

Larry P. v. Riles. (1972) Civil Actions No. C-71-2270 343 F. Supp. 1306. (N.D. Cal.).

Leiter, R.G. (1948). *Leiter International Performance Scale*. Chicago: Stoelting.

MacMillan, D.J. (1977). *Mental retardation in school and society*. Boston: Little, Brown.

Mastenbrook, J., Scott, L, & Marriott, S. (1978, Sept.). Use of the ABIC in special education. Paper presented at the meeting of the American Psychological Association, Toronto.

Mercer, J.R. (1979). In defense of racially and culturally nondiscriminatory assessment. *School Psychology Digest, 8*, 89-115.

Mercer, J.R., & Lewis, J.F. (1977). *SOMPA conceptual and technical manual*. Riverside: Institute for Pluralistic Assessment Research and Training. (At the time of the case study, this was the only edition of the technical manual available.)

Mercer, J.R., & Lewis, J.F. (1978). *System of Multicultural Pluralistic Assessment*. New York: Psychological Corporation.

Oakland, T. (1979a). Research on the Adaptive Behavior Inventory for Children and the Estimated Learning Potential. *School Psychology Digest, 8*, 63-70. (a).

Oakland, T. (1979b). Research on the ABIC and ELP: a revisit to an old topic. School Psychology Digest, *8*, 209-218. (b).

Oakland, T. (1980). An evaluation of the ABIC, pluralistic norms, and estimated learning potential. *Journal of School Psychology, 18*, 3-11.

Ransom, G.A. (1978). USC Phonics Test. In G.A. Ransom, *Preparing to teach reading* (pp. 180-184). Boston: Little, Brown.

Ransom, G.A. (1978) Visual memory and discrimination tests. In G.A. Ransom, *Preparing to teach reading* (pp. 178-180). Boston: Little, Brown.

Reschly, D. (1978). Comparisons of bias in assessment with conventional and pluralistic measures. Paper presented at the annual meeting of the Council for Exceptional Children, Kansas City, Mo.

Rosner, J. (1975). *Test of Auditory Analysis Skills*. Novato, CA: Academic Therapy Publications.

Sattler, J.M. (1982). *Assessment of children's intelligence and special abilities* (2nd ed.). Boston: Allyn and Bacon.

Sattler, J.M., & Gwynne, J. (1982). Ethnicity and Bender Visual Motor Gestalt Test performance. *Journal of School Psychology, 20), (1)*.

Scott, L.S., Mastenbrook, J.L., Fisher, A.T., & Gridley, G.C. (1982). Adaptive Behavior Inventory for Children: The need for local norms. *Journal of School Psychology, 20), 39-44*.

Strang, L., Smith, M.D., & Rogers, C.M. (1978). Social comparison, multiple reference groups, and the self-concepts of academically handicapped children before and after mainstreaming. *Journal of Educational Psychology, 70*, 487-497.

Tebeleff, M., & Oakland, T. (1977). Relationships between the ABIC, WISC-R, and achievement. Paper presented at the annual meeting of the American Psychological Association, San Francisco, CA.

Wall, S.M., & Paradise, L.V. (1981). A comparison of parent and teacher reports of selected adaptive behaviors of children. *Journal of School Psychology, 19,* 73-77.

Wechsler, D. (1974). *Wechsler Intelligence Scale for Children—Revised.* New York: Psychological Corporation.

Wepman, J.M. (1973). *The Auditory Discrimination Test.* Chicago: Language Research.

THE TEXAS ENVIRONMENTAL ADAPTATION MEASURE: TEST DEVELOPMENT AND STANDARDIZATION, AND A CASE STUDY

Leigh S. Scott and Alan T. Fisher

The Texas Environmental Adaptation Measure (TEAM) was developed to determine a student's adaptive behavior from the perspective of his/her particular social-emotional environment. It was a natural outgrowth of the study, in both an applied and a research setting, of the concept of adaptive behavior and the instruments which purport to measure it (Scott, 1978, a). TEAM was standardized on a sample of students from the Corpus Christi (Texas) Independent School District (CCISD) during the 1977-78 school year. Since that time, it has been used almost exclusively in the adaptive behavior assessment of CCISD students (aged 5-18) and has also been used in several other Texas school districts (see Author's Note 1, p. 131).

The purpose of this chapter is to demonstrate the usefulness of the TEAM in preventing the misclassification as mentally retarded of minority group children. Discussion will focus upon the historical antecedents of adaptive behavior assessment and its impact on misclassification, research which served as impetus for the development of the TEAM, the instrument and its standardization, and the presentation of a case which illustrates the use of the TEAM in assessment for special education eligibility.

Historical Antecedents

Adaptive behavior in non-school environments has not traditionally been one of the criteria for assessing mental retardation, although the concept of adaptive behavior has many historical antecedents. In the 19th century, definitions of retardation usually dealt with factors relating to what is presently called adaptive behavior. "Since the early 1800s, pioneers in the field of mental retardation, Itard and Haslam, Seguin, Vaisin, Howe, and Goddard spoke in terms of social competency, skills training, moral training, social norms, the power of fending for one's self in life and efficiency of social value rather than in terms of heredity, educational achievement, or an I.Q. sort of criterion in defining retardation." (Horton, 1966)

In 1959, the American Association on Mental Deficiency (AAMD) rediscovered adaptive behavior and used it in the definition and determination of mental retardation. During the early sixties, adaptive behavior was defined by Heber (1961, p. 61) as including two major factors: (a) the degree to which the individual is able to function and maintain himself independently, and (2) the degree to which he meets satisfactorily the culturally imposed demands of personal and social responsibility. In 1973, the AAMD defined adaptive behavior as the effectiveness with which the individual copes with the natural and social demands of his environment (Grossman, 1973).

Misclassification

In the 1950s, many children from poor and ethnic environments appeared to be classified mentally retarded solely on the basis of standardized intelligence and school achievement tests. Observers felt that many of these children might be exceptionally adaptive to the situations and community in which they lived even though they performed poorly on intelligence tests and in school. Observers noticed that a significantly greater percentage of non-Anglo school-age persons were classified mentally retarded than were persons too young or too old to be in school. This seemed to indicate that schools might be classifying as mentally retarded people who later were able to live normal lives in their environments (Garza, Marriott, Mastenbrook, & Scott, 1977).

Because of these factors, psychology and education professionals began to place emphasis on adaptive behavior in the assessment of mental retardation; this concern was reflected in the AAMD's and the National Institute of Mental Health's (NIMH) project for the development of an adaptive behavior scale. (The scale was standardized on an institutionalized population and was later revised and standardized [Lambert, Windmiller, Cole, Figueroa, 1975] for use with public school children as the Adaptive Behavior Scale—Public School Version.) As awareness of discrimination against the poor and minority groups in the U.S. increased in the 1960s, studies began to document the disproportionate labeling of low SES and minority group children as mentally retarded by the schools. Most of these children were still being labeled on the basis of performance on standardized IQ tests without reference to their level of adaptive behavior in other environments (Mercer, 1973). Professionals in psychology and education also began to document the middle class, Anglo perspective of IQ and achievement tests. They felt that the values and learning opportunities in some subcultures differed markedly from those of the middle class Anglo culture. Therefore, IQ and achievement tests were not accurately assessing the abilities of children in different subcultures (Mercer, 1971).

In 1969, the President's Committee on Mental Retardation reviewed the problem concerning school district placement of disproportionately large numbers of minority children into special classes for the mentally retarded. The Committee concluded that many of the minority group children who were labeled educable mentally retarded were capable of functioning normally outside the school setting. They believed that if a child could function well in his or her home, neighborhood, or playground without being labeled by others, there was no reason to label the child in school. The Committee recommended that the child's behavior in the home and in the neighborhood be assessed and found to be mentally retarded before the child could be labeled as mentally retarded (President's Commission on Mental Retardation, 1969). These recommendations were ultimately included in the Education for All Handicapped Children Act of 1975 (PL 94-142).

During the 1970s, much of the documentation of the disproportionate referral and labeling of minority group children as mentally retarded was done by Jane Mercer at the University of California, Riverside. Mercer studied the percentage of blacks, Mexican-Americans, and Anglos at each stage in the classification process for programs for the mentally retarded. Mexican-Americans and blacks were overrepresented as compared to population percentages, and the degree of overrepresentation increased as the process went from referral to placement (Mercer, 1974).

Mercer's research efforts resulted in the creation of an instrument to assess the behavior of children in non-school environments: the Adaptive Behavior Inventory for Children (ABIC), a part of the System of Multicultural Pluralistic Assessment (SOMPA) (Mercer & Lewis, 1977).

In the ABIC, "adaptive behavior is conceptualized as achieving an adaptive fit through the development of interpersonal ties in social systems and the acquisition of specific skills required to fulfill the task functions associated with particular roles" (Mercer & Lewis, 1979, p. 123).

Mercer and Lewis' SOMPA also incorporated a second approach in the modification of traditional psychometric techniques to achieve

111

nondiscriminatory assessment—the use of pluralistic norms. The term "pluralistic" refers to the development of separate norms for each sociocultural group; in assessment, an individual is then compared only to the sociocultural group of which he/she is a member. This concept has been operationalized by Mercer and Lewis in Estimated Learning Potential (ELP). Data from the SOMPA Sociocultural Scales (family size, family structure, SES, degree of acculturation) are used in a multiple regression equation to estimate mean WISC-R scores for the child's particular sociocultural group. The child's attained WISC-R scores are then compared to the means for his/her sociocultural group to determine estimated learning potential. The ELP differs from a traditional IQ score in that the child is compared only with children from a similar sociocultural environment rather than with children from a general population sample (Fisher, 1978).

Impact of Adaptive Behavior Assessment

The overrepresentation of minority and low SES students in classes for the mentally retarded has been well documented (Mercer, 1971, 1973). The impact of adaptive behavior assessment and the ELP on this apparent misclassification of students has been investigated by Mercer (1973) and Fisher (1978).

Mercer (1973) reported that the use of the ABIC and a traditional IQ test, utilizing scores below the third percentile as indicators of mental retardation on both, resulted in the declassification of 60-90% of Mexican-American and black students as mentally retarded. The use of pluralistic norms (ELP) also declassified sizable percentages of minority and low SES students.

Further investigation of the effects of adaptive behavior assessment on classification was reported by Fisher (1978). Four approaches to classification were compared. The approaches included the use of IQ tests utilizing the traditional 3rd percentile cut-off, a psychometric approach using multiple traditional tests and cut-off scores, adaptive behavior (i.e., ABIC), and the Estimated Learning Potential. The results revealed that sizable differences in the percentage of students being classified as mentally retarded occurred when the four approaches were compared, with the ABIC and ELP declassifying a sizable number of students (ABIC, 60-85%; ELP, 35-70%).

With the passage of Public Law 94-142, formal assessment of the adaptive behavior of school age children was mandated in order to determine eligibility for classes for mentally retarded children, yet few instruments were available for its measurement and there remained a need for further research on adaptive behavior as it related to school-age children and on the appropriateness of the instruments themselves.

Impetus for the Texas Environmental Adaptation Measure

In 1976, the Pluralistic Diagnostic Team research project was initiated in the Corpus Christi (Texas) Independent School District with a Title IV C grant from the Texas Education Agency. The purpose of the project was to study problems inherent in the implementation of adaptive behavior assessment in the appraisal process of a large urban school district. Research initially focused on study of the construct of adaptive behavior and the instruments available for its measurement.

During the 1976-77 school year, local CCISD norms (Scott, Mastenbrook, Fisher, & Gridley, 1982) were established on Mercer and Lewis' (1977) Adaptive Behavior Inventory for Children (ABIC). Research results on the ABIC revealed the need for separate norms for only one subgroup of the sample (N = 420) used in the study. This subgroup, the Mexican-Americans with low socioeconomic status (SES), scored significantly lower than the other five Corpus Christi subgroups (low, high SES Anglos; low, high SES blacks; and high SES Mexican-Americans) and lower than the California sample used by Mercer in the standardization of the ABIC.

Critique of Available Scales

While the local norming of the ABIC was in progress, research also focused on study and analysis of the AAMD Adaptive Behavior Scale—Public School Version (ABS-PSV) (Lambert, et al., 1975) and the Vineland Social Maturity Scale (Doll, 1965). During this same period, the research team was involved in using these measures of adaptive behavior in determining the eligibility of students for special education classes in the Corpus Christi Independent School District. Following critical analysis and use of each of the available adaptive behavior scales—ABIC, ABS-PSV, and the Vineland—the team concluded that the instruments overlapped in content to a degree and that none was without drawbacks (Scott, 1981).

ABIC. The ABIC, a parent interview questionnaire, available in both English and Spanish, contains 242 questions and provides an ABIC total score and scaled scores in each of six subscales.

The ABIC standardization was made on a sample of 2,085 California public school children, ages 5-11, representing (in almost equal numbers) three racial-ethnic groups: blacks, Spanish surnamed Americans, and Anglos. Results of the standardization procedures revealed a mean ABIC total score of 50 and a standard deviation of 15 for each subscale (Scott, et al., 1982).

The Family subscale of the ABIC attempts to measure the ability of the child to relate to and communicate with family members and to obey and respond to parents. The Community subscale attempts to measure a child's interest and participation in community affairs, altruistic involvement with neighbors and relationship with adults, and degree of independent functioning as it relates to locomotion. The Peer Relations subscale attempts to discover the ways in which the child interacts with other children and the kinds of activities they engage in together. The Non-Academic School Roles subscale attempts to determine the child's relationship with teachers and classmates and the amount of responsibility the child feels toward school. The Earner-Consumer subscale attempts to measure a child's knowledge and use of money. The Self-Maintenance subscale attempts to measure a child's ability to care for his/her own needs, the child's general independence of activity, and general personality characteristics. The Veracity subscale consists of questions placed at inappropriate age levels to check the truthfulness of the respondent's answer and to interrupt the respondent's response set.

Corpus Christi researchers reported several identifiable problems and limitations of the ABIC in the assessment of mental retardation for special education eligibility. These problems and limitations were reported in two major areas: (1) failure to take into account environmental factors which may affect the acquisition of adaptive behaviors and (2) structural characteristics which inhibit the usefulness of ABIC scores (Mastenbrook, Scott, & Marriott, 1978).

The ABIC fails to identify effectively lack of opportunity due to socioeconomic or cultural background and fails to single out factors in a particular child's home environment, apart from SES or culture, which may inhibit the acquisition of school and adaptive behavior skills (e.g., low parental expectations). Neither does the ABIC address motivational factors which contribute to a failure to learn certain adaptive behaviors (Mastenbrook, et al., 1978). Structural characteristics of the ABIC which have also been a source of problems in the use of the instrument in special education assessment include the method of administration (e.g., giving credit for items below the baseline, yielding sometimes spurious results) and question content (e.g., questions related to personality variables rather than ability). The excessive amount of time required to ad-

114

minister the parent interview has also been seen as a problem with the ABIC (Oakland, 1979).

ABS-PSV. Behaviors assessed in Part I of the AAMD Adaptive Behavior Scale—Public School Version range from general to specific developmental and maturational aspects of life (Garza, et al., 1977). Areas of questioning include Independent Functioning, Physical Development, Economic Activity, Language Development, Numbers and Time, Vocational Activity, Self-Direction, Responsibility, and Socialization.

According to the authors, Independent Functioning, Economic Activity, and Vocational Activity "represent functional skills required to maintain personal independence in daily living and to meet a basic level of social responsibility" (Lambert, et al., 1975, p. 8). Questions on Physical Development are used to assess visual and auditory acuity and fine and gross motor coordination. Questions on Language Development and Numbers and Time are used to assess cognitive development. Self-direction and Responsibility questions tend to focus on peer relationships, emphasizing social interaction and consideration for others.

Corpus Christi researchers found several problems with the ABS-PSV in determining the eligibility of students for placement in classes for the mentally retarded. According to Mastenbrook (1977, b), because the ABS-PSV measures primarily low level behaviors, ABS-PSV assessment of the mildly mentally retarded must be done cautiously in order to prevent a truly mentally retarded child from being denied access to a lass for the mentally retarded. Mastenbrook (1977, b) has also determined that the ABS-PSV norms do not represent a normal distribution and that only four of the eight subscales in Part I successfully differentiate between students in regular classes and those in classes for the mentally retarded. The ABS-PSV has recently been revised as the AAMD Adaptive Behavior Scale—School Edition (Lambert, Windmiller, Tharinger, & Cole, 1981).

Vineland. The Vineland Social Maturity Scale has questions in eight categories: Self-help (General), Self-help (Eating), Self-help (Dressing), Self-direction, Occupation, Communication, Locomotion, and Socialization.

Problems with use of the Vineland center about its primarily developmental scope and the scarcity of items on several subscales, a condition which limits the measurement of a full range of adaptive behaviors across age levels. Despite these problems, the Vineland can be useful in the adaptive behavior assessment of young children, due to its developmental nature and the fact that norms on children under age 5 are not available for other instruments.

Concept of Adaptive Behavior

The study of available adaptive behavior scales produced not only questions about the adequacy of these scales but also questions concerning the concept of adaptive behavior on which each was based.

According to Mastenbrook (1977, a), problems with the popular conceptualization of adaptive behavior focus upon the failure to take into account personality and motivational factors and the uniqueness of the particular environments to which children must adapt. The concept of "adaptive fit" developed by Jane Mercer (1977) envisions the adaptation of a child as the ability to gain entry into an increasing number of social systems—family, school, peers, community, etc. However, as Mastenbrook has pointed out, this results in a quantitative rather than qualitative construct in which little or no weight is given to psychological factors. The definition of adaptive behavior accepted by the American Association on Mental Deficiency, the degree to which the individual is able to maintain himself independently and satisfactorily meet the culturally-imposed demands of personal and social responsibility (Grossman, 1973), refers to "culturally-imposed" demands, but does not emphasize how diverse these cultures may be.

In an attempt to increase the viability of adaptive behavior as a usable concept, the Corpus Christi researchers developed a construct of adaptive behavior which incorporates both personality and motivational factors as well as the uniqueness of individual environments (Scott, 1978, b). This construct of adaptive behavior takes into account "(1) the physical and social environmental demands, expectations, and values of the particular person's environment, (2) the personality characteristics and motivations of the person which influence how his/her skills are manifested in particular adaptive behaviors, and (3) how the person has adapted to his/her environmental demands and expectations" (Mastenbrook, 1977, a). These aspects of adaptive behavior were operationalized in a new instrument for use in adaptive behavior assessment—The Texas Environmental Adaptation Measure (TEAM).

Description of the Instrument

TEAM is based upon the assumption that analysis of the individual child's environment and personality is prerequisite to the assessment of his/her adaptive behavior (Scott, 1978, b).

The Texas Environmental Adaptation Measure is a parent interview consisting of three sections: Family Environment Assessment (sociocultural and family dynamics information), Personality Assessment (developmental and personality adjustment information), and Adaptive Behavior Assessment (Scott, 1979, a). TEAM has been designed in such a way that information from each section complements that of the others; information from the first two sections provides the background necessary for accurate interpretation of adaptive behavior results.

Although TEAM is designed to be administered in its entirety, it is so constructed that the adaptive behavior section, the only part which provides a numerical score, can be given separately or in conjunction with either of the other measures. TEAM has been developed as a home interview, using the parent, guardian, or other person familiar with the child and the home as respondent. Administration time is approximately one hour.

Family Environment Assessment

The Family Environment Assessment section addresses two broad areas: background information and home environment.

Background Information. The Background Information section of TEAM covers necessary demographic information as well as information related to the child's sociocultural environment. Information in six areas is included: (1) family background (age, marital status, race of parents, age and sex of siblings, number of people living in the home, etc.); (2) educational background (educational level of parents and siblings, problems in school); (3) medical background (chronic or recurrent health problems that interfere with family activities); (4) economic information (occupations of parents, principal source of income, etc.); (5) housing (type of residence, description of home); (6) description of neighborhood (income level, type of neighborhood, etc.). This section of TEAM differs from the Sociocultural Scales of Mercer's SOMPA in that it provides much more information and is designed to aid in understanding a particular child rather than to provide numbers to insert into a multiple regression equation.

Home Environment. The Home Environment section of TEAM provides a picture of factors in a child's day-to-day existence which may affect his or her adaptive behavior. Among these factors are the actual physical proximity of the home t recreation areas, food stores, schools, and the availability of sleeping quarters, telephone, and automobile. A second group of factors involves family dynamics issues including such things as relationship of the family to neighbors, child care, family structure (rules, discipline), expressiveness (decisionmaking, attitudes toward emotional expression), and parental expectations (family goals, desired educational achievement). The Home Environment section also includes factors relating to the child's environmental opportunity including where the child is allowed to play, what household chores are required, what access to money the child has, and what social, community or recreational activities the child engages in. A fourth group of factors addresses the family's school orientation. Included are the availability of reading material, parental involvement with the school and homework, the child's style of problem-solving, and language models in the home.

Personality Assessment

The Personality Assessment section of TEAM was designed to reveal emotional and motivational aspects of a child's functioning. Questions concern developmental aspects—pre/postnatal problems, unusual, rapid, or delayed speech and/or locomotion, changes in rate of development, problems with toilet training, temper tantrums, etc. Information is gathered concerning the child's typical response to discipline and frustration—sulking, crying, anger, anxiety, acting-out, etc. The child's usual mode of interaction with peers, siblings, teachers, parents, etc., is also investigated. Information is requested about recent trauma (accident, illness, death in the family, divorce, separation, etc.) and school adjustment (frequent absences, early morning illness, fear and/or dislike of school or classmates, etc.)

Adaptive Behavior Assessment

The Adaptive Behavior Assessment of TEAM shows both similarities and differences when compared to other available adaptive behavior instruments. The authors are indebted to the ABIC, the AAMD ABS-PSV, and the Vineland for many suggestions for possible questions. Questions are written in a format similar to that of the ABIC—

multiple choice with three possible responses: null or minimal performance, intermediate or performed with assistance, and maximal or independent performance. The adaptive behavior section of TEAM has a total of 102 questions, as opposed to the 66 of the ABS-PSV and the 242 of the ABIC. The Adaptive Behavior section of TEAM was designed so that an examiner may ask all the questions within about 20 minutes, a short period of time compared to the 45-60 minute administration time of the ABIC. Scoring is simpler than that of any of the aforementioned scales and can be completed in about five minutes.

The Adaptive Behavior Assessment of TEAM also differs from current instruments in that it focuses on a wider range of behaviors than the ABS-PSV and, unlike the ABIC, provides a look at what a child can actually do, rather than a look at what his school, economic condition, and community offer. The Adaptive Behavior Assessment has also been designed for use in a conversational manner, without adherence to the dictum of verbatim questioning used by Mercer. Another major difference between the new instrument and others is that it includes questions appropriate for the 12-16 year age group.

The Adaptive Behavior Assessment contained in the TEAM investigats activities in six areas: Autonomous Activities, Mechanical Skills, Play and Recreation, Communication and Social Skills, Responsibility, and Economic Activity.

The Autonomous Activites subscale consists of 26 questions concerning independent self-help activities. Among these are personal hygiene activities such as bathing, hair washing, dressing, caring for fingernails, and independent toilet activities. Questions also concern feeding activities: using utensils, pouring, using a bottle opener, preparing sandwiches, cooking, baking, and washing dishes. Household cleaning activities such as clothes washing, housecleaning, and yard work also provide areas of inquiry in the Autonomous Activities subscale.

The Mechanical Skills subscale focuses upon simple to complex items in 16 questions. Among these are simple activiies such as operating the television, turning light switches on and off, unplugging electrical appliances, and changing light bulbs and batteries. More complex activities include using power tools, repairing appliances, using a sewing machine, and driving and maintaining an automobile or motorcycle.

Age-appropriate games and play activities and independent recreational activities are the major areas of inquiry in the Play and Recreation subscale. Typical children's play activities include "pretend" games such as "house" or "school," creating imaginary characters and emulating TV heroes. Also included are outside activities such as tag,

119

chase, hide-and-seek, bike riding, sports activities, and camping. Table games, crafts, and puzzles are also mentioned in the Play and Recreation subscale. The 16 questions in this subscale were designed to determine not only the types of activities in which the child engages, but also the degree of complexity and the independence required in these activities.

The 21 questions of the Communication and Social Skills subscale range from assessment of minimal abilities to communicate with others to social awareness and interaction skills. Complexity of the language used by the child, knowledge of parents' occupations, telephone numbers, etc., are areas of inquiry. Questions also concern perception of the social environment, interaction with friends and members of the opposite sex, participation in organizations, and arrangement of social affairs.

The Responsibility subscale concerns the child's ability to care for himself/herself and others and to fulfill his/her obligations. The 14 questions focus on independent locomotion, ranging from simple negotiation of the unsupervised trip from house to yard, to independent trips to school or bus stop, to the grocery store, or to the movies. Information is also obtained on how long the child is left alone at home, and the child's use of public transportation, care of pets and elderly people, and ability to handle emergency situations. The child's responsibility for his/her own activities is also assessed: owning mistakes, doing homework and household chores without prodding, arriving on time, keeping promises, and fulfilling obligations.

The Economic Activity subscale consists of nine questions about the child's use of money. Questions concern how the child gets money (from a job, allowance, etc.) and what he/she does with it (buys candy, toys, records, pays for entertainment). Inquiry is also made into the child's ability to make change, run errands, and use banking facilities.

A copy of TEAM may be found in the Appendix.

Use of TEAM in Educational Planning

The Texas Environmental Adaptation Measure provides a wealth of information about the child's family background, personality, and adaptive behaviors, some of which may give only an idea of the barriers to a child's progress and some of which may provide actual tools for remediation which can be incorporated into the child's individualized educational plan (IEP).

General Information

Scott (1979, b) has pointed out that general information necessary for an understanding of a child's problems and determining the need for further testing can be gleaned from each section of TEAM. For example, information from The Family Environment Assessment may reveal that a child shares a bedroom with five others in a small home in a low socioeconomic area with little access to shopping or recreation areas—factors which may influence study habits, motivation, and opportunity to learn social skills. Poor academic achievement may be better understood with knowledge that the child receives no help with homework, or that the parents have relatively low educational expectations for their child.

The Personality Assessment section also provides information which can be useful in understanding poor school achievement and may reveal maladaptive behaviors which may be interfering with a child's functioning. A parent's portrait of a child as typically withdrawn in the face of discipline or frustration and emotionally passive and shy with peers and teachers may provide an explanation for the child's failure to achieve or to adjust to school. Frequent moves, a divorce or death in the family, or other environmental changes may also help explain a child's failure to adjust to school. Responses to the Personality Assessment section may help explain why a child does or does not engage in certain adaptive behaviors.

Information from the Adaptive Behavior Assessment may reveal a lack of opportunity to engage in the adaptive behaviors expected of a child of the same age and ethnic group.

Information indicating a need for further testing can also be found in TEAM. For instance, both medical and developmental information are available as a result of TEAM; this information may suggest the presence of seizures, convulsions, or hearing/vision problems and may point up the need for a complete physical examination, an electroencephalogram, a diagnosis of speech problems, or other screening. The indication that only Spanish is spoken in the home, despite a parent's indication of English on a permission-to-test form, will reveal the need for bilingual evaluation. A parent's indication in the Personality Assessment section that the child shows inappropriate affect and difficulty in interpersonal relationships may reveal a need for an evaluation to determine the extent, if any, of emotional disturbance.

Specific Information for IEPs

Specific information which can be incorporated into a child's IEP may be found as a result of TEAM evaluation. For example, if a parent reports that a child prefers to work alone, individual rather than group activities may be stressed in the child's IEP; if the parent reports a particularly successful method he or she uses to draw out a shy or withdrawn child or to calm an overactive child, these methods may be incorporated into an IEP. (In Texas, the IEP is developed by a committee which includes the child's parent, teacher, school administrator, and appraisal personnel.)

The Adaptive Behavior Assessment section of TEAM is of particular importance in the development of educational plans for a child. Each of the six subscales is a possible source of recommendations for IEPs.

The Autonomous Activities subscale reveals where the child is lacking in self-help skills. The Mechanical Skills subscale may indicate the presence or absence of mechanical abilities which may affect the feasibility of a vocational-technical program for an individual child. The games which the child prefers to play, as indicated by the parent in the Play and Recreation subscale, may be incorporated for specific learning tasks on the IEP. The Communication and Social Skills subscale may provide evidence of problems in these areas which should be addressed. The Responsibility subscale may be especially useful in incorporating parent tasks into an IEP; for instance, specific home activities in which the child should be given more responsibility may be delineated. The Economic Activity subscale may indicate a need for money-handling skills to be addressed in the IEP.

Case Study

Use of the Texas Environmental Adaptation Measure (TEAM) to determine possible special education eligibility is described in the following case study. This case study exemplifies an approach to assessment which combines the traditional psychometric approach with the assessment of sociocultural status, personality factors, and adaptive behavior.

Maria, a six year old Mexican-American girl, was referred for evaluation by her kindergarten teacher. According to the teacher, Maria appeared to have a limited vocabulary in Spanish as well as in English, immature speech patterns, and an inability to express ideas adequately.

She appeared distractible, restless, and overly dependent on the teacher. She seldom completed classwork. Vision and hearing screening by the school nurse and a health history taken by the school counselor revealed no physical problems which might be affecting Maria's success in the classroom. Prior to the psychoeducational evaluation, Maria had been evaluated by a bilingual speech therapist using the Spanish version of the Test of Auditory Comprehension of Language (Carrow, 1973); Maria reportedly either echoed the examiner's response or made no response at all.

Psychoeducational Evaluation

Maria was referred to the school's diagnostic team (an associate school psychologist and an educational diagnostician) for a psychoeducational evaluation to determine her eligibility and possible need for special education services.

The evaluation was conducted in a small room at Maria's elementary school. Tests were administered bilingually and included the Stanford-Binet Intelligence Scale (Terman & Merrill, 1960 [see Authors' Note 2]), the Beery Developmental Test of Visual Motor Integration (Beery, 1967), the Wide Range Achievement Test (Jastak, Bijou, & Jastak, 1965), and the Peabody Picture Vocabulary Test (Dunn & Markwardt, 1965).

In their observations, the diagnostic team noted that initially, Maria would not respond to the examiner; however, as the evaluation progressed, she became talkative and restless, often smiling and laughing and swinging on the table. Her speech was often unintelligible; she spoke both English and Spanish and tended to omit the beginning sounds of words.

Results of the Stanford-Binet revealed a mental age of four years, two months and an IQ of 61, placing Maria's estimated level of general intelligence within the educable mentally retarded range. Compared to her agemates, she demonstrated no apparent strengths; however, relative to her own performance, Maria demonstrated a strength in visual motor skills requiring the manipulation of materials in problem-solving situations. For example, she was able to complete a picture of a man, sort buttons, and copy a circle. A relative strength was also found in Maria's memory and concentration. Primary weaknesses were found in her inability to integrate components into a meaningful relationship, numerical associations, word association skills, verbal expression, abstract problem-solving, discrimination, and comparison.

According to the PPVT, Maria's receptive vocabulary skills fell within the trainable mentally retarded range (mental age 3.4; IQ = 51).

Maria's visual motor skills, as measured by the Beery VMI, were severely below average, comparable to those of a 3.2 year old child.

Results of the evaluation of Maria's preacademic achievement, using the WRAT, revealed prekindergarten skills in spelling and arithmetic, both with standard scores of 56. Maria was unable to print her first name, and she accurately reproduced only four of eighteen geometric figures. She was able to count from one to six, but was unable to recognize one or two digit numerals or to count objects; neither was she able to indicate which numbers were "more" or "less." Maria exhibited kindergarten level skills in reading recognition with a standard score of 78. She was able to match capital letters in isolation but made no verbal responses when asked to name letters or words.

TEAM Evaluation

In general, results of the psychoeducational evaluation appeared to indicate that Maria might be appropriately classified as educable mentally retarded. However, according to the policies and administrative procedures established by the Texas Education Agency, in accordance with Public Law 94-142, intellectual functioning incorporates not only verbal and performance abilities (generally measured by individually administered intelligence tests) but adaptive behavior as well. To qualify for services as mentally retarded, a student must score at least two standard deviations below the mean in verbal and performance skills and adaptive behavior (Texas Education Agency, 1979).

Maria was, therefore, referred to the school district's adaptive behavior team for an evaluation of her adaptive behavior skills. At that time, the team consisted of an associate school psychologist, two social psychologists, and a bachelor's level adaptive behavior interviewer who had formerly been employed as a social worker.

Upon receipt of the referral which included a summary of Maria's test scores and diagnostic team comments, the evaluation was assigned to the bilingual adaptive behavior interviewer who scheduled an appointment with Maria's mother for the administration of the Texas Environmental Adaptation Measure (TEAM).

The interviewer met with Maria and her mother in their home in a primarily low income residential section of the city. Although the mother was to serve as respondent for the adaptive behavior interview, the interviewer interacted briefly with Maria during the interview. According to the interviewer, Maria appeared to have speech problems. Although cooperative and friendly, she appeared to have a sad demeanor and looked first at her mother before answering any question.

The interviewer initially administered the Family Environment Assessment and Personality Assessment to the mother in Spanish in a structured interview format.

Family Environment Assessment

Results of the Family Environment Assessment revealed that Maria resides with her natural mother and stepfather. She is the oldest of five children, having three half-brothers and one half-sister. A brother-in-law resides in the home. The mother is a housewife, and the stepfather is a deliveryman. The mother's formal education ended in elementary school and the stepfather's educational level is unknown. The family receives no public financial assistance.

According to her mother, Maria is allowed to play only in her own yard. Household chores required of Maria include picking up toys, clothes, and trash. Spanish is the language most often used in the home. The family does not subscribe to or read any magazines or newspapers and does not have books in the home.

Personality Assessment

Results of the Personality Assessment interview indicated that Maria is generally a friendly child who can be assertive with her sister, but who gets along well with her brothers. According to her mother, Maria gets along better with her stepfather than with her mother to whom Maria "talks back." Maria's mother stated that Maria sometimes has temper tantrums, kicking and crying when she cannot have her own way. She appears to have little interaction with neighborhood children and usually plays with one close friend. In response to questions about Maria's development, her mother reported that Maria was born anemic and was kept in the hospital until she was about one month old. Maria began walking at age 1 1/2 and talked at 2 years of age. In terms of school adjustment, Maria's mother reported that she likes school, is rarely absent, and sometimes plays "school" at home.

Adaptive Behavior Assessment

Following administration of the Family Environment and Personality sections of TEAM, Adaptive Behavior Assessment was administered to Maria's mother in Spanish, with the interviewer translating the questions in such a way as to be as understandable as possible to her.

On the Adaptive Behavior Assessment section of TEAM, Maria achieved a total raw score of 110. She showed strength in the areas of autonomous activities and responsibility. On the autonomous activities subscale, which measures self-help skills and household activities, Maria received 37 of a maximum of 52 points (71%). She functions independently when it comes to bathing, washing her hair, dressing, feeding and toileting; she cleans her room, folds clothes and does other minor household chores. She also assists her mother with dishwashing, clothes washing, and other household activities. On the responsibility subscale, Maria received 20 of a possible 28 points (71%). She apparently does homework and household chores without prodding, cares for her four younger siblings, voluntarily assists others, and keeps promises.

Maria achieved a score of 50% or greater in the areas of play and recreation and communication and social skills. In play and recreation, she achieved a score of 17 of a possible 32 points. According to the informant, Maria plays age appropriate games and participates in group or family activities involving sports, movies, and other activities. She does not, however, ride a bicycle or rollerskate. In communication and social skills, Maria received 21 of 42 possible points. Maria voluntarily relates events, joins in children's conversations, has a best friend, and shares her belongings. She does not use complex sentences or use the telephone and does not know her address or her stepfather's occupation.

Maria's weaknesses in adaptive behavior were evidenced in the subscales of mechanical skills (11 of 32 points or 34%) and economic activity (4 of 18 points or 22%). Maria's mechanical skills appear to be limited to operating the television, light switches, water faucets, and door locks. She plugs and unplugs electrical cords and changes flashlight batteries only with assistance; she does not change light bulbs, use electrical appliances, sew, iron, or use tools. In terms of economic activity, Maria runs errands and uses money for purchases only with assistance; she knows some money equivalents (e.g., five pennies = one nickel) but she cannot make change.

Interpretation

Using information from the Family Environment Assessment concerning family size, income, type of neighborhood, language dominance and parental attitudes, the interviewer determined that Maria's adaptive behavior skills could be appropriately compared to those of children in Group 2 of the TEAM norming sample (see Table 2 in *Appendix*).

Information from the Family Environment Assessment revealed a sociocultural environment which did not appear significantly different from that of the norm group. An analysis of environmental opportunities for Maria did not reveal a significant lack of opportunity, and no "N.O.'s" indicating no opportunity to engage in specific adaptive behaviors were found in TEAM scoring. Therefore, Maria's Adaptive Behavior Assessment score appeared to be a valid indicator of her adaptive behavior skills. (See Authors' Note 3.) The mean total score expected on TEAM Adaptive Behavior Assessment for children of Maria's age, ethnicity, and socioeconomic status was 111; Maria's score of 110 placed her adaptive behavior skills within the average range.

For some children, information from the Personality Assessment may indicate a number of emotional factors and personality characteristics which prompt the adaptive behavior evaluator to regard the adaptive scores as extremely depressed due to the interference of emotional problems. Fortunately, this was not the case for Maria. The Personality Assessment did indicate, however, a possible problem with peer interaction which may have had a slight effect on Maria's adaptive behavior scores. Maria's temper tantrums, although disturbing to those around her, do not appear to be a significant factor in the interpretation of adaptive behavior results. As reported earlier, such behavior appeared to be reported more often in Maria's norm group.

Although Maria did not score within the mentally retarded range on TEAM, the adaptive behavior interviewer did note evidence of language development problems and reported a perceived need for special education services for Maria.

Disposition

Teacher reports and the results of a psychoeducational evaluation appeared to indicate that Maria was unable to function academically in a regular classroom setting. However, results of the adaptive behavior evaluation appeared to indicate that Maria was functioning adequately in the home and neighborhood. Because of these disparate results,

Maria was not eligible for special education services as mentally retarded. When this information was presented to the Admission, Review and Dismissal/Individualized Educational Plan (ARD/IEP) committee, the committee determined that Maria was eligible for services as learning disabled; using Maria's adaptive behavior as the estimate of her highest intellectual potential, a discrepancy of more than one standard deviation existed between her intellectual functioning and academic achievement, meeting criteria established by the Texas Education Agency for learning disabled students. Results of a speech evaluation indicated that Maria was eligible for speech therapy as a related service. Maria was placed in a self-contained Early Childhood Education Classroom which utilized a low student-teacher ratio to provide individualized instruction. When Maria was reevaluated three years later, results of the reevaluation revealed a performance IQ on the Wechsler Intelligence Scale for Children (Wechsler, 1949) which fell within the borderline range, thus verifying the inappropriateness of the mentally retarded label which Maria would have received had her adaptive behavior *not* been evaluated. She continued to qualify for special education services as learning disabled. Maria was served in a self-contained classroom for academically low functioning students with learning or behavioral problems.

Educational Planning

Maria's adaptive behavior assessment provided the teacher information which could help in providing the most appropriate educational program for Maria.

TEAM revealed that Maria lives in an impoverished environment with few educational resources such as books or magazines. As the eldest child of parents with little education, she has no role model from whom to learn successful academic behavior. She apparently also has little peer interaction. In addition, results of Adaptive Behavior Assessment revealed weaknesses in mechanical skills and economic activity although Maria showed strengths in the areas of autonomous activities and responsibility.

Using this information, the Early Childhood Education teacher could structure an environment for Maria which would capitalize on her areas of strength and improve her weaknesses. For instance, using Maria's good self-help skills as a model for other children in the class could enhance her self-concept as well as improve peer relationships; rewarding Maria by asking her to perform duties and run errands in the classroom would take advantage of her strong sense of responsibility.

Maria's weaknesses in mechanical skills and economic activity could be addressed in the classroom using visual motor tasks, playing games with money, etc. An awareness of Maria's background could assist the teacher in selecting materials and teaching strategies; for instance, educational materials could be provided for use at home, and an older child could be used as a tutor and role model for Maria.

Uniqueness of TEAM Approach

Maria's case is noteworthy for several reasons: (1) it exemplifies the use of a measure of adaptive functioning to rule out mental retardation; (2) it illustrates the use of a method of assessment which places more reliance on interpretation of the scores than the scores themselves; and (3) it involves an assessment instrument in which racial-ethnic and socioeconomic factors were taken into account in its standardization and on which local norms were established. In addition, Maria's case illustrates the use of an adaptive behavior instrument which was designed to provide data for both special education classification and educational planning. (See Coulter and Morrow, 1978)

Inquiry

This chapter has presented a brief look at the historical antecedents and research which led to the development of the Texas Environmental Adaptation Measure (TEAM), its description and standardization, and an illustration of TEAM's use in assessing a child's eligibility for special education services. This information may have left a number of questions unanswered; the following discussion may answer some of them.

Raw Scores vs. Standard Scores

A question about TEAM standardization involves the lack of standard scores. At TEAM's inception, the development of standard scores was intended. Following completion of the research, however, it was determined that the sample size should be substantially increased prior to establishing standard scores. Unfortunately, because of funding problems, this was not possible. In addition, as use of TEAM in special education assessment progressed, the researchers believed that although TEAM was easier to use and provided more information than other available measures, it needed refinement and could be substantially improved. Using the results of TEAM item analysis, a new adaptive behavior section was developed; this version has not yet been standardized, however. Despite these factors, TEAM appears to be an appropriate measure of adaptive behavior for children in Corpus Christi and is preferred over other available measures due to the ease of administration and the wealth of information provided.

In the case presented, TEAM was administered in Spanish in an extemporaneous translation. Readers may ask why no written Spanish translation is available. Previous research with the ABIC (Scott, et al., 1982) had shown limited usefulness of Mercer's Spanish version of the ABIC, leading to the preparation of a new South Texas version. Even using the new translation, examiners sometimes noted that respondents' receptive vocabulary for specific Spanish words varied a great deal; language used by respondents often involved a combination of English and Spanish in varying degrees. For these reasons, and because TEAM was designed to be administered conversationally, adjusting to the needs of the respondent, and not verbatim, no Spanish translation was developed. For further discussion of the problems inherent in the use of translations, see Sattler (1982, p. 371).

Sequencing of Evaluation

In CCISD, the evaluation of adaptive behavior generally follows the completion of a more traditional psychoeducational battery for two reasons: (1) CCISD adaptive behavior assessment is performed by professionals funded solely for that purpose and children are initially referred through the school to the diagnostic team assigned to that school, and (2) formal adaptive behavior evaluations are required only for students who may be classified as mentally retarded and, therefore, an IQ measure is administered first in order to limit the number of adaptive behavior evaluations necessary. (Although evaluating adaptive behavior first might rule out mental retardation, Texas guidelines still require a multistage psychoeducational assessment for each child referred.)

Benefits of Non-MR Classification

Maria's case illustrates the fact that adaptive behavior assessment does serve to prevent the misclassification of minority group children.

In all probability, however, it did not change the type of educational classroom, i.e., self-contained classroom, into which Maria was placed (although this may not generally be the case). If this is the case, of what real benefit to the child is a LD diagnosis as opposed to classification as mentally retarded? This issue was addressed by Mastenbrook (1978) when he indicated that the educational and vocational expectations for persons classified as mentally retarded are usually lower than for persons who fall under other special education handicapping conditions. "Children labeled as mentally retarded are often seen as having less potential, regardless of the reasons for the children's low functioning. Because of their low functioning and these low expectations, the educational instruction provided these children is restricted, particularly in terms of the content of the curriculum, the repetitiveness of the instruction, and the expectations for the children's rate and complexity of learning. The classification of mental retardation is the most restrictive classification in terms of educational services for a child and, therefore, should be the most conservative classification." (p. 2)

In other cases, because of nonretarded adaptive behavior scores, a student may not qualify for any type of special education services; the student is still failing academically despite a high level of adaptive functioning. It would appear that in an attempt not to discriminate against a student on the basis of ethnicity culture or SES, the very help that he or she may need to succeed in school may no longer be available. Besides eliminating the stigma of being labeled mentally retarded, the use of adaptive behavior assessment in these cases may ultimately benefit these students by forcing educators to adapt the regular education curriculum to meet the needs of such students.

Authors' Notes

Requests for more information regarding the TEAM should be sent to:
Leigh S. Scott, 820 Buffalo, Corpus Christi, Texas 78401

1. In Texas, at the time data gathering began, only instruments approved by the Texas Education Agency were allowed to be used by public schools to measure adaptive behavior as well as IQ.
2. Due to the large number of performance-type items on the Stanford-Binet at the lower age levels (2-6), it was not considered inappropriate for Maria's assessment. From the practitioner's

standpoint, the Stanford-Binet often appears to be more "fun" for younger children and, therefore, seems to elicit better responses, providing a good understanding of the child's present level of functioning.

3. For some children, an analysis of environmental opportunity may reveal an environment severely restrictive in terms of the types of activities available to the child. This information is used to interpret scores on the Adaptive Behavior Assessment and may result in the examiner's reporting "a minimal estimate of adaptive behavior skills based on lack of opportunity." Such a child would not be classified mentally retarded.

References

Beery, K.E. (1967). *Developmental test of visual motor integration.* Chicago: Follett.

Carrow, E. (1973). *Test for auditory comprehension of language.* Hingham, MASS: Teaching Resources.

Coulter, W.A., & Morrow, H.W. (1978). *Adaptive behavior: Concepts and measurements.* New York: Grune & Stratton.

Doll, E.A. (1953, 1965). *Vineland Social Maturity Scale.* Circle Pines, MN: American Guidance Service.

Dunn, L.M., & Markwardt, F.C. (1965). *Peabody Picture Vocabulary Test.* Circle Pines, MN: American Guidance Service.

Fisher, A.T. (1978, Aug). *Four approaches to classification of mental retardation.* Paper presented at annual meeting of the American Psychological Association, Toronto.

Garza, M., Marriott, S., Mastenbrook, J., & Scott, L. (1977). *1976-77 Final report, pluralistic diagnostic team report.* Unpublished manuscript.

Gourevitch, V. (1965). *Statistical methods: A problem-solving approach.* Boston: Allyn & Bacon.

Grossman, H.J. (1973). *Manual on terminology and classification in mental retardation.* Washington, D.C.: American Association on Mental Deficiency.

Heber, R.A. (1961). Manual on terminology and classification in mental retardation. *American Journal of Mental Deficiency Monograph.*

Horton, L. (1966, May). *The historical development of the concept of adaptive behavior.* Paper presented at the annual meeting of the Kansas Psychiatric Association, Wichita, Kansas.

Jastak, J.F., Bijou, S.W., & Jastak, S.R. (1965). *The Wide Range Achievement Test.* Wilmington, Delaware: Guidance Associates of Delaware.

Lambert, N., Windmiller, M., Cole, L., & Figueroa, R. (1975). *AAMD Adaptive Behavior Scale—Public School Version.* Washington, D.C.: American Association on Mental Deficiency.

Lambert, N., Windmiller, M., Tharinger, D., & Cole, L. (1981). *AAMD Adaptive Behavior Scale—School Edition.* Monterey, CA: Publishers Test Service.

Mastenbrook, J. (1977, a, Aug). *Analysis of the concept of adaptive behavior and two assessment instruments.* Paper presented at the annual meeting of the American Psychological Association, San Francisco.

Mastenbrook, J. (1977, b). *Suggestions for the use of the AAMD Adaptive Behavior Scale—Public School Version in the classification of the mentally retarded.* Unpublished paper.

Mastenbrook, J. (1978, Sept). *Future directions in adaptive behavior assessment: The Texas Environmental Adaptation Measure.* Paper presented at the annual meeting of the American Psychological Association, Toronto.

Mastenbrook, J. (1979). *TEAM-ABIC correlations.* Unpublished paper.

Mastenbrook, J., Scott, L., & Marriott, S. (1978, Sept). *Use of the ABIC in special education: Problems and solutions.* Paper presented at the annual meeting of the American Psychological Association, Toronto.

Mercer, J.R. (1971). Sociocultural factors in labeling mental retardates. *Peabody Journal of Education, 48,* 188-203.

Mercer, J.R. (1973). *Labeling the mentally retarded.* Berkeley: University of California Press.

Mercer, J.R. (1974). A policy statement on assessment procedures and the rights of children. *Harvard Educational Review, 44,* 125-141.

Mercer, J.R., & Lewis, J.F. (1977). *System of multicultural pluralistic assessment.* New York: The Psychological Corporation.

Mercer, J.R., & Lewis, J.F. (1979). *SOMPA system of multicultural pluralistic assessment: Conceptual and technical manual.* New York: The Psychological Corporation.

Oakland, T. (1979). Research on the adaptive behavior inventory for children and the estimated learning potential. *School Psychology Digest, 8,* 63-70.

President's Committee on Mental Retardation. (1969). *MR. 69.* Washington, D.C.: U.S. Government Printing Office.

Sattler, J. (1982). *Assessment of children's intelligence and special abilities.* Boston: Allyn & Bacon.

Scott, L. (1978, a, Sept). *Texas Environmental Adaptation Measure: Adaptive behavior in sociocultural, emotional environments.* Paper presented at the annual meeting of the American Psychological Association, Toronto.

Scott, L. (1978, b, Nov). *Research results: The norming of the Texas Environmental Adaptation Measure.* Paper presented at the annual meeting of the Texas Psychological Association, Dallas.

Scott, L. (1979, a, March). *Texas Environmental Adaptation Measure: Its use in classification and planning.* Paper presented at the annual meeting of the National Association of School Psychologists, San Diego.

Scott, L. (1979, b, Nov). *The role of adaptive behavior assessment in the identification of declassified students.* Paper presented at the annual meeting of the Texas Psychological Association, San Antonio.

Scott, L. (1981, Nov). *Use of the Texas Environmental Adaptation Measure in special education assessment.* Paper presented at the annual meeting of the Texas Psychological Association, Houston.

Scott, L., Mastenbrook, J., Fisher, A., & Gridley, G. (1982). Adaptive behavior inventory for children: The need for local norms. *Journal of School Psychology, 20,* 39-44.

Tebeleff, M., & Oakland, T. (1977, Aug). *Relationships between the ABIC, WISC-R, and achievement*. Paper presented at the annual meeting of the American Psychological Association, San Francisco.

Terman, L., & Merrill, M. (1960). *Stanford-Binet Intelligence Scale*. Boston: Houghton Mifflin.

Texas Education Agency (1979). *Policies and administrative procedures for the education of handicapped students*.

Wechsler, D. (1949). *Wechsler Intelligence Scale for Children*. New York: Psychological Corporation.

Appendix
The Texas Environmental Adaptation Measure: Standardization Procedures and Data TEAM Test Booklet and Score Sheet

LEIGH S. SCOTT and ALAN T. FISHER

STANDARDIZATION

TEAM was standardized during the 1977-78 school year on a random stratified sample (3 ethnic, 2 SES groups) of 545 students (ages 5-16) in the Corpus Christi Independent School District (Scott, 1978, b).

Description of Sampling Area

Corpus Christi is a city of approximately 235,000 persons (1980 census), located on Corpus Christi Bay on the South Texas coastline, 210 miles southwest of Houston. "Blue collar" industries (petrochemical plants and oil refineries), agriculture, fishing, and a large military installation provide most of the employment in the Corpus Christi area. Corpus Christi is basically a low-income area whose population according to census figures available at the time of TEAM research was 40.6% Mexican-American, 5.1% black, and 54.3% Anglo. The ethnic make-up of the students in the Corpus Christi Independent School District (CCISD) in 1977-78 was 62% Mexican-American, 6% black, and 32% Anglo.

Method

Research Design

In order to determine the need for separate norms in the standardization of TEAM, the sample was stratified according to age (by year), ethnicity (black, Mexican-American, Anglo), and low or high socioeconomic status (SES) based on qualification or nonqualification for the CCISD free lunch program (using a measure of income by family size).

Subjects

Using a table of random numbers, 545 students, ages 5-16, were chosen from the total population of students enrolled in the CCISD during the 1977-78 school year. For age groups 5-11 (inclusive), 420 children were selected in equal numbers from the three ethnic groups. Equal numbers of females and males and low and high SES students were randomly selected for each age level in each ethnic group (5 per cell). For age groups 12-16 (inclusive), 120 children were selected in equal numbers from the three ethnic groups. Again, equal numbers of females and males and low and high SES students were randomly selected for each age level in each ethnic group. (Due to fluctuations in the availability of students in some age groups, certain cells contain an additional subject.)

Procedure

Eight interviewers were employed either part- or full-time in the administration of the Texas Environmental Adaptation Measure to the parents of the children selected in the sample; however, all eight were not employed during the same period of the norming procedure. Educational level of the interviewers ranged from bachelor's degree to postgraduate level, with the mode being master's level education. Average interviewing experience was approximately two years. Six females (one Mexican-American, one black, four Anglos) and two males (one Mexican-American and one Anglo) were employed. All were trained in the administration and scoring of the TEAM by its authors.

135

Subjects were randomly assigned to interviewers, with the low SES Mexican-American group assigned at random to one of the Mexican-American examiners, who used Spanish when appropriate.

Parents were contacted first by letter and then by telephone or in person, if necessary, to arrange an appointment for the interview. Interviews were held in the parent's home, except in a few instances in which the parent chose another location. The interviewer administered all sections of TEAM to the parent in a conversational manner, eliciting information and probing when appropriate. Information from the Family Environment Assessment and Personality Assessment sections of TEAM was written on the interview form; responses from the Adaptive Behavior Assessment were recorded (0, 1, 2, or No opportunity) on a separate score sheet. Parent permission for the interview was obtained in writing, and confidentiality was maintained.

Results and Discussion

Total raw scores on the 102 items of the Adaptive Behavior Assessment, along with frequency information on the sociocultural, family, and personality characteristics of the sample (107 variables), were analyzed.

Adaptive Behavior

Mean total raw scores for the Adaptive Behavior Assessment for each of six ethnic-SES groups are shown in Table 1. Highest possible

Table 1
Mean Total Scores for TEAM Norm Groups

SES	Ethnicity		
	Anglo	Black	Mexican-American
High	133.6	130.7	127.0
Low	131.0	123.7	116.5

score was 204. Analysis of variance results were significant, F (5) = 4.855, p < .001.

Group by group comparisons of means using Fisher t-tests revealed that the low SES Mexican-American group scored significantly lower than all other groups in the sample, paralleling the results of Corpus Christi's ABIC research (Scott, et al., 1982). Further analysis revealed that scores of low SES blacks, ages 5-8, were also significantly lower than the scores for other children in the sample.

Thus, results of the Adaptive Behavior Assessment analysis indicated the need for separate norms for the low SES Mexican-Americans and for the low SES blacks at the lower age levels (5-8). Table 2 shows

Table 2
Mean Total Adaptive Behavior Scores

Age (in years)	Total Score Means	
	GROUP 1[a]	GROUP 2[b]
5	104	98
6	109	102
7	125	111
8	134	120
9	142	128
10	147	133
11	155	141
12	161	157
13	163	149
14	168	154
15	173	159
16	179	164

Note: Standard Deviation for all groups = 14

[a]High, Low Anglos; High Blacks; High Mexican-Americans; Low Blacks, Ages 9-16.

[b]Low Mexican-Americans; Low Blacks, Ages 5-8.

the raw score means and the standard deviation determined from these data and currently in use in the assessment of special education candidates in the CCISD (Scott, 1979, b).

Research results further revealed no significant differences between male and female total raw scores for the total sample. Significant differences were found between the sexes on the Mechanical Skills subscale for each ethnic group, with males scoring higher. Significant differences between the sexes were also found for the Mexican-American subgroup on the Autonomous Activities subscale, with females scoring higher.

Sociocultural and Family Characteristics

Frequency counts and corresponding percentages revealed interesting subgroup differences in sociocultural and family characteristics.

Results revealed low SES Mexican-Americans to have larger, more intact families than the other subgroups and to have lower parent education levels. The low SES Mexican-Americans also appeared to have fewer mothers employed outside the home. Low SES blacks appeared to have a greater number of female heads of households than the other subgroups.

More low than high SES Mexican-Americans listed Spanish as their primary home language. Low SES Mexican-Americans also reported fewer reading materials available in the home than the other subgroups. With the exception of the home language and family size questions, most of the above-mentioned comparisons appeared to follow a pattern in which the high SES subgroup scored "higher" than the low SES subgroups, with the low SES Mexican-American subgroups scoring "lowest." Another interesting exception to this pattern is found in the occurrence of temper tantrums; it appears that low SES Mexican-American parents reported that their children engaged in tantrum behavior considerably more often than was reported by the parents of children in any of the other subgroups.

Two important indices of parental restrictiveness or overprotection are the number and types of household chores required of a child and the restriction placed on where the child may play. In terms of household chores, results revealed ethnic group differences in the percentage of children who were required to do no household chores or limited household chores (cleaning own room, etc.). These differences are as follows: Anglos, 27% none/limited household chores; blacks, 28.4%; Mexican-Americans, 45% (for ages 5-11).

This trend was again seen in the play area restrictions imposed upon children in the different ethnic groups. The percentages of children (ages 5-11) required to play in their own yards or where they could be watched were as follows: Anglos, 24.2%; blacks, 30.4%; and Mexican-Americans, 45.6%.

These results established the basis for the use of the TEAM in the determination of the eligibility of students for special education programs in the CCISD and revealed the possibility of using information from TEAM in the educational planning for individual students.

Ongoing Data Collection

At the present time, approximately twenty Texas school districts and special education cooperatives have received permission from the Texas Education Agency to use the TEAM to assess the adaptive behavior of students being considered for special education classes for the mentally retarded. (See Reference Note 1) A stipulation of that permission was the provision to the Corpus Christi district of data on each student assessed with the TEAM in order to broaden the TEAM's special education data base. Data were to include the following information about each student assessed: age, sex, socioeconomic status, ethnicity, TEAM adaptive behavior raw scores (subscale and total), IQ scores (verbal, performance, and full scale) and the handicapping condition determined by the ARD/IEP committee.

Scott (1981) has reported results of the comparison of a small group of cases from three Texas school districts with data from 309 Corpus Christi cases. Table 3 shows the number of children in the sample who scored within the mentally retarded range on the TEAM and the number of those who did not.

Of the 25 students from the three districts, 72% scored within the mentally retarded range. Mean IQ scores for the group having mentally retarded TEAM scores was 50.82; for the "not mentally retarded" group, x = 61. Of the total CCISD sample, 65% scored within the mentally retarded range on the TEAM; 35% scored above the mentally retarded range. Results from a similar study utilizing the ABIC, Vineland, ABS-PSV and the TEAM (Scott, 1979, b) revealed that 55% of the 525 students assessed scored within the mentally retarded range on one of the four instruments.

Utilizing data from selected subgroups within the 1981 CCISD sample, Scott compared the IQ scores of those with mentally retarded

Table 3
Comparison of TEAM Results from
Three School Districts[a] and CCISD[b]

| | TEAM Raw Score Range | | | |
| | Mentally Retarded[c] | | Not Mentally Retarded | |
	Three Districts	CCIS	Three Districts	CCISD
Hispanic				
Low SES	7	117	6	78
Middle SES	2	17	0	4
Black				
Low SES	2	17	0	12
Middle SES	0	2	0	1
Anglo				
Low SES	3	29	0	9
Middle SES	4	18	1	5

[a] n = 25

[b] n = 309

[c] raw score more than 2 SD's below the x

TEAM scores (MR subgroup) with IQ scores of students with TEAM scores above the mentally retarded range (NMR subgroup).

Results of this comparison revealed no significant difference between the IQs of those students whose TEAM scores fell within the mentally retarded range and those who scored above the mentally retarded range on the TEAM. Because the data compared were derived from the records of students assessed for possible special education placement over a three year period (1978-1981), it was not possible to control for many intervening variables (use of different IQ measures, variety of examiners, etc.); however, the results would appear to indicate that in terms of IQ scores, the MR and NMR TEAM subgroups tend to be drawn from the same population, thus indicating that it is the level of adaptive functioning rather than IQ which differentiates these groups of students from one another.

According to Scott (1981), results of these comparisons appear to indicate that the TEAM classifies a similar percentage of students mentally retarded in the CCISD as in a small sample of students from other school districts and a somewhat higher percentage of students than did a combination of instruments. Similarity between the CCISD students and students assessed with the TEAM from other districts is noted in terms of mean IQ scores, indicating an apparent similarity in students classified MR and NMR.

Preliminary Validation

Scott (1981) used the CCISD sample to determine the relationship between TEAM scores and IQ. Results revealed a correlation coefficient of .38 (using the Raw Score Formula: Gourevitch, 1965), indicating a low positive correlation between TEAM and IQ scores for this group of students. These results are similar to those of Tebeleff and Oakland (1977), in their comparison of ABIC and WISC-R scores for a group of Austin, Texas, students (r = .28 for Full Scale IQ). Although the CCISD data are rough, they, taken with those of Tebeleff and Oakland, tend to support the conclusion that the abilities measured by an adaptive behavior scale and those measured by a traditional IQ test are different abilities.

TEAM vs. ABIC scores

Using a sample of 18 CCISD students who had been given both the TEAM and the ABIC, Mastenbrook (1979) correlated (Pearson Product Moment) standard deviation levels for the ABIC and the TEAM to give an indication of the similarity in performance levels of children on the TEAM and on the ABIC. The correlation coefficient of .538 (which accounts for approximately 30% of the variance) indicates a significant similarity in performance levels for the TEAM and the ABIC. It also indicates that over 70% of the variance in standard deviation levels is not common to the two tests. Therefore, students score at similar but far from the same levels on the two tests.

The moderate correlation between TEAM and ABIC scores and the similar low correlation between both instruments and IQ provide a small measure of validity for TEAM; however, much more data need to be collected in order to establish TEAM's validity and reliability.

As more data are received from the approximately twenty Texas school districts which are using TEAM, the appropriateness of the

TEAM norms for children in Texas may be established. It must be remembered that these data are from a population of students being assessed for eligibility for special education services. In order for the TEAM to be considered an acceptable measure of the adaptive behavior of students throughout the United States, two alternatives should be considered: (1) it should be standardized on a much larger cross-sectional "normal" population, or (2) each local education agency planning to use the TEAM should determine the need to establish local norms.

TEXAS ENVIRONMENTAL ADAPTATION MEASURE

(TEAM)

EXPERIMENTAL EDITION (Limited Distribution)

FAMILY ENVIRONMENT ASSESSMENT

PERSONALITY ASSESSMENT

ADAPTIVE BEHAVIOR ASSESSMENT

Student's Name: _____School: _____

Address: _____Grade: _____

Date of Birth: _____/_____/_____Teacher: _____

Developed in the Corpus Christi Independent School District under Title IV-C funding from Texas Education Agency

Authors:

Leigh S. Scott, John Mastenbrook, Sara Marriott, Alan T. Fisher

TEXAS ENVIRONMENTAL ADAPTATION MEASURE

Student's Name: School:

Address: Grade:

Telephone No.:   Teacher:

Date of Birth: Date of Interview:

Age: ____yrs. _____mos.   Interviewer:

Background Information

Parent/Guardian

	Relationship		
Name:	to Child	In Home	Not in Home

_____(respondent __yes __no)_____

_____(respondent __yes __no)_____

_____(respondent __yes __no)_____

_____(respondent __yes __no_____

Respondent
Address: _____ Telephone (Home)_____
         _____   (Business)_____

Marital Status: (circle one) single married divorced separated widowed
                    other _____
Ethnicity: (circle one) Caucasian Black Mexican-American
Native-American Oriental Other _____
Place of Birth: (Mother) _____ (Father) _____
Age: (circle one) Mother: below 25 25-55 over 55
 Father: below 25 25-55 over 55

Family Size

Birth order of student _____

Relationship to Child

Names of Siblings	Age	Sex	Full	Half	Step	In home	Not in Home
1.							
2.							
3.							
4.							
5.							
6.							

Other Persons Living in Home   **Relationship to Family**

_____

_____

Total number of people living in home: _____

Educational Background of Family

Name	Number of years Formal Education	Type of Diploma or Degree Received
parent/guardian		
parent/guardian		
other		
other		

School Problems Experienced by Family Members

Name	Relationship to Child	Type of problem Example: academic, behavioral, drop-out, etc.)

Medical Problems Experienced by Family Members

(List only medical problems that interfere with activities or activities of family)

Name	Relationship to Child	Type of Problem

Economic Information

	Mother	Father	Other Person in Home
Occupation: (Title or Description of Job Role)			
Place of Employment:			
Unemployed:			
Seeking Employment:			

Sources of Income

Employment ____   Unemployment Comp. ____   SSI____

Retirement ____   Veterans Benefits ____   Other ____

Social Security ____   AFDC ____   Food Stamps ____

Housing

Place of residence:

house ____   duplex ____   farm or rural area ____
apartment ____   housing project ____
mobile home/trailer ____   other ____

Description of Home and Neighborhood (to be completed by interviewer)

Condition of home: (circle one)

dirty	1	3	5	clean
disheveled	1	3	5	neat
over–crowded	1	3	5	spacious
in disrepair	1	3	5	in good condition

Description of Neighborhood:

Income level: low ____   middle ____   high____

Area is: ____ Primarily residential
                                  ____ Primarily industrial
                                  ____ Primarily business
                                  ____ Primarily !light manufacturing

Briefly describe area in which child lives:

_____

_____

_____

Home Environment

How far away from your home is the nearest park, playground, or other recreation area?

_____

_____

    Do you allow your child to go there? ___Yes ___No   If so,

    How does he/she usually get there?_____

    Who usually accompanies him/her? _____

How far away from your home is the nearest grocery or convenience store?

_____

    Do you allow your child to go there? ___Yes ___No If so,

    How does he/she usually get there?

    Who usually accompanies him/her? _____

How far away from your home is your child's school? _____

How does he/she get to school? _____

Who usually accompanies him/her? _____

Does your child share a bedroom with someone? ___Yes ___No

If Yes, with whom? _____

Do you have a telephone? ___Yes ___No

Does your family have the use of a car? ___Yes ___No

    Who drives it?_____

Relationship with Neighbors

How well do you know your neighbors?

___very well   ___as casual acquaintances

___just to say hello   ___not at all?

How well do the children know the neighbors?

___very well   ___as casual acquaintances

___just to say hello   ___not at all?

Do you consider some of your neighbors to be your good friends?

___Yes   ___No

Do your children?   ___Yes   ___No

Do you visit, exchange favors, and/or borrow from one another?

___Yes   ___No

Do your children?   ___Yes   ___No

Do you have problems with any of your neighbors?

___Yes   ___No

Do your children have problems with the neighbors?

___Yes   ___No

Are there children in the neighborhood your child's age?

___Yes   ___No

If Yes, about how many?_____

Who does your child usually play with? _____

Child Care

After the children get out of school each day, who generally cares for them?

___parent   ___private agency   ___themselves

___older sibling   ___relative   ___housekeeper/maid

___neighbor   ___school   ___other

When you are out at night for several hours, who generally cares for the children?

___older sibling   ___school   ___parents seldom go out

___neighbor   ___themselves   ___children usually
                                              accompany parents

___private agency ___other

___hired babysitter ___relative

Family structure

Do you tell your children what to do and what not to do?

___Yes ___No

Do you have rules about what they are allowed or not allowed to do? For instance, about where they can play, what time they have to be home, etc.?   ___Yes ___No   If yes, give an example:

_____

Does your child obey the rules

___most of the time   ___sometimes   ___very seldom

When _____ does something he/she is not supposed to do, what sort of discipline or punishment do you use? _____

_____

Who generally disciplines him/her? _____

When _____ wants to do something or go somewhere, does he/she

    ___ask either parent for permission

    ___ask mother for permission

    ___ask father for permission

    ___tell you what he/she is about to do

    ___do it, but check in with you from time to time

    ___just do it

Expressiveness

Most of the time, who makes major family decisions?

_____

Most of the time, who makes the minor, day-to-day decisions in your family? _____

If _____ has an accident, a problem, or some other trouble, what does he/she do?

___keeps it to himself/herself

___talks to his mother

___talks to his father

___talks to both parents

___talks to a sibling

___talks to a friend

___other, explain _____

What do you do when _____has a problem?

_____

When _____has been injured physically, what does he/she do?

___cry

___show it hurts, but try to be brave

___become frightened

___over-react to get attention

___show no emotion

Attitudes toward expressiveness

When you are upset about something, do you think it's a sign of strength and maturity to keep it to yourself? ___Yes   ___No

Should children cry or display anger in front of others? ___Yes ___No

Should family members show their affection for one another openly?   ___Yes ___No

Parental Expectations

In comparison with other children his/her own same age, how would you rate your child's ability to take care of himself/herself and to get along at home and in the neighborhood?

    ___excellent

    ___good

    ___fair

    ___poor

Do you have any plans or goals about what you would like your family to be doing several Years from now?   ___Yes   ___No

If yes, can You give an example? _____

How much education would you like your child to get?

    ___high school

    ___high school and vocational or technical school

    ___some college

    ___a college degree

    ___graduate school

    ___less than high school

    ___no preference

How much education do you expect your child to get?

    ___high school

    ___high school and vocational or technical school

    ___some college

    ___a college degree

___graduate school

___less than high school

Environmental Opportunity

Where do you allow your children to play or meet their friends?

___only in their own yard

___where you can watch them

___at the homes of nearby neighbors

___throughout the neighborhood, as long as they are back by a certain time

___wherever they want to, as :long as they tell you where they will be and check in from time to time

___within "yelling" distance

___anywhere

___other (Explain): _____

Where do they play or meet friends most often?_____

What household chores is _____required to do?

Does he/she volunteer to do other chores?   ___No   ___Yes

If Yes, what are they? _____

What chores are other children in the family responsible for?

_____

Who is responsible for the day-to-day cleaning? _____

_____

Do your children have their own money to spend? ___Yes ___No

How do your children get the money that they spend? (Example: job, allowance, from grandparents, etc.) _____

When _____has money to spend, what does he/she usually spend it on? _____

How many of the children that _____ plays or associates with after school do you know?

___most of them

___about half of them

___a few of them

___none of them

What social or community activities does _____ participate in?

___Special events at school or in the community such as dances, concerts, fairs, plays, etc.

___church-related or religious activities

___athletic clubs/teams

___clubs/organizations such as Campfire Girls, Girl Scouts, Boy Scouts, etc.

___extracurricular school activities such as choir, band, drill team, other clubs/organizations

___Other. Explain: _____

Recreational Activities:

What sort of toys, games, sports equipment, or other recreational items do you have in the home? _____

_____

_____

How does _____spend most of his/her spare time?

_____

If he/she could, what would _____ spend most of his/her time doing? _____

School Orientation

Availability of reading material:

What magazine or newspapers does your family read or subscribe to? _____

_____

_____

What type of books do you have available in your home?

____encyclopedia

____dictionary

____other (Give Examples): _____

_____

_____

Parent Involvement:

How often do you visit your child's school? _____

    ___Just when there is a problem

    ___regularly to talk about the child's progress

    ___whenever there is a special program or event of some kind

    ___very seldom

    ___never

Mediated Learning Experience:

How often does your child bring work from school to do at home?

_____

How often does someone in the family or neighborhood help
_____ with school work or school-related word (reading, math,
writing, etc.)? _____

Problem Solving:

Who usually helps him/her? _____

Problem Solving:

When working on school work, does your child prefer

    ___to work alone

    ___to work with one other person

    ___to work with a group of people

    ___or doesn't he/she have a preference

At home when he/she is having trouble finding an answer or solving a problem, does your child

___give up

___ask someone for help

___ask someone to solve the problem for him/her

___keep on trying until he/she succeeds

How would you rate your child's performance at school?

___excellent

___good

___fair

___just getting by

___poor

Language models in the home:

What language(s) is spoken between parents and children most often?

___English　　___Both

___Spanish　　___Other

What language(s) do the children speak most often?

___English　　___Both

___Spanish　　___Other

What language(s) do the parents speak most often?

___English　　___Both

___Spanish　　___Other

What language(s) does the mother read? _____ write? ____

What language(s) does the father read? _____ write? ____

Personality Assessment

Developmental Aspects

Pre/Post Natal Development

Did you have any problems with your pregnancy?

___No   ___Yes   If Yes, explain:

Did you have any problems during childbirth?

___No   ___Yes   If Yes, explain:

Did your child have any problems at birth?

___No   ___Yes   If Yes, explain:

During infancy and early childhood, was your child different from other children in any of the following areas:

	No	Yes	If Yes, in what way?
Amount of crying	_____	_____	_____
Speech/Hearing	_____	_____	_____
Learning to sit-up/walk	_____	_____	_____
Coordination	_____	_____	_____
Becoming toilet trained	_____	_____	_____
Special fears	_____	_____	_____
Tamper tantrums/fighting	_____	_____	_____
Dressing himself/herself	_____	_____	_____
Eating habits	_____	_____	_____

Speech Development

At what age did _____say his/her first words? _____
Were these words ___English ___Spanish ___Other?

After he/she began to talk was _____'s speech hard to understand?
___Yes ___No If Yes, explain: _____
_____

Did speech begin to develop, then stop?
___Yes ___No If Yes, at what age?_____

Miscellaneous Developmental Aspects

Have there been any other sudden changes in development?
___Yes ___No If Yes, explain: _____

Did anything unusual happen immediately preceding this change?
___Yes ___No If Yes, explain: _____

Did your child engage in exploratory behavior as a toddler?
___Yes ___No
Give an example of his/her behavior _____

Was he more or less active than your other children (or other children you have known)? ___Yes ___No
Example: _____
_____

1. Has your child ever had any of the following illness?

___measles   ___mumps   ___chicken pox   ___scarlet fever.

___rheumatic fever   ___whooping cough

2. Has your child ever had seizures or convulsions?

___Yes   ___No   If Yes, explain: _____

_____

3. Has your child ever had a fever over 103°

___Yes   ___No   If Yes, explain: _____

_____

4. Has _____ever had a serious accident or illness?

___Yes   ___No   If Yes, explain: _____

_____

5. Has your child ever been hospitalized for any reason?

___Yes   ___No   If Yes, explain: _____

_____

6. Is your child taking any medication prescribed by the doctor for a long term condition or illness?

___Yes   ___No   If Yes, explain: _____

_____

Has he/she taken such medication in the past?

___Yes   ___No   If Yes, explain: _____

_____

Does _____have any current eating problems? (For example: eating too much, too little, extreme "pickiness", etc.)? ___No ___Yes. If Yes, explain: _____

_____

Affective Behavior

What does your child usually do when he/she has been disciplined or punished for something? Can you describe his/her behavior?

_____

_____

What does Your child usually do when he/she is frustrated by something—when he/she fails to accomplish something no matter how hard he/she tries? Can you describe his/her behavior?

_____

_____

What does your child do when you or others tell him/her that he/she has done something wrong or when you criticize him/her in some other way? Can you describe his/her behavior? _____

_____

_____

What makes your child angry? _____

_____

_____

How do you know when he/she is angry? What does he/she do?

_____

_____

What makes your child happy? _____

_____

_____

How do you know when he/she is happy? What does he/she do?

_____

_____

_____

What makes your child sad or unhappy? _____

_____

How do you know when he/she is sad or unhappy? What does he/she do? _____

_____

Interpersonal Behavior

How does your child usually behave toward people his/her own age?

___passive (ignores them)

___friendly

___assertive (directs activity, tells others what to do, stands up for own rights, etc.)

___aggressive (pushes others around, curses, yells, fights)

___compliant (does what he/she is told, takes directions from others without comment)

___fearful

___reserved, but friendly

___somewhat bashful

___extremely shy

How does your child usually behave toward you?

___passive (ignores you)

___friendly

___assertive (directs activity, tells others what to do, stands up for own rights)

___aggressive (pushes others around, curses, yells, fights)

___compliant (does what he/she is told, takes direction from others without comment)

___fearful

___reserved but friendly

___somewhat bashful

___extremely shy

How does your child usually behave toward his/her other parent?

___passive (ignores him/her)

___friendly

___assertive (directs activity, tells others what to do, stands up for own rights, etc.)

___aggressive (pushes others around, curses, yells, fights)

___compliant (does what he/she is told, takes direction from others without comment)

___fearful

___reserved, but friendly

___somewhat bashful

___extremely shY

How does your child usually behave toward his/her brother(s)?

___passive (ignores him)

___friendly

___assertive (directs activity, tells others what to do, stands up
for own rights)

___aggressive (pushes others around, curses, yells, fights)

___compliant (does what he/she is told, takes direction from
others without comment)

___fearful

___reserved, but friendly

___somewhat bashful

___extremely shy

How does your child usually behave toward his/her sister(s)?

___passive (ignores her)

___friendly

___assertive (directs activity, tells others what to do, stands up
for own rights)

___aggressive (pushes others around, curses, yells, fights)

___compliant (does what he/she is told, takes direction
from others without comment)

___fearful

___reserved, but friendly

___somewhat bashful

___extremely shy

How does your child usually behave toward his/her teachers?

___passive (ignores hisher)

___friendly

___assertive (directs activity, tells others what to do, stands up for own rights)

___aggressive (pushes others around, curses, yells, fights)

___compliant (does what he/she is told, takes direction from others without comment)

___fearful

___reserved, but friendly

___somewhat bashful

___extremely shy

How does your child usually behave toward adults who are strangers to him/her?

___passive (ignores them)

___friendly

___assertive (directs activity, tells others what to do, stands up for own rights)

___aggressive (pushes others around, curses, yells, fights)

___compliant (does what he/she is told, takes direction from others without comment)

___fearful

___reserved, but friendly

___somewhat bashful

___extremely shy

How does your child usually behave toward children who are strangers to him/her?

___passive (ignores them)

___friendly

___assertive (directs activity, tells others what to do, stands up for own rights)

___aggressive (pushes others around, curses, yells, fights)

___compliant (does what he/she is told, takes direction from others without comment)

___fearful

___reserved, but friendly

___somewhat bashful

___extremely shy

Environmental Changes

Has there been a recent death in the family?

___No ___Yes If Yes, what happened? _____

_____

How did this affect your child? _____

_____

Has your family moved recently?   ___No ___Yes

How long has your family lived at your present address? _____

How many times has your family changed residences in the past two years? _____

Has your child changed schools recently? ___No ____Yes

If Yes, explain: _____

How many schools has your child attended in all? _____

Has there been a severe accident or illness in the family recently?
___No   ___Yes   If Yes, explain: _____
_____
_____

Has there been a recent divorce, separation, marriage or other
change in who is living in the home?   ___No   ___Yes
If Yes, explain: _____
_____
_____

School Adjustment

Does _____ like school ____   dislike school ___   Not
really care one way or the other ____

How often is _____ absent from school: once a month ____
several days a month ____   2-3 times a year ____   other
(explain) _____
_____
_____

Does _____ ever complain of headache, stomach ache,
nausea or other illness prior to school?   Yes ___No. ____   If Yes,
how often? _____
If yes, does he/she usually start feeling better and become playful
by noontime or early afternoon?   Yes ____   No ____

Does _____ sometimes leave school during the day?

___yes   ___no

If yes, where does he/she usually go? _____

Does_____sometimes express fear of school or school mates?

___Yes   ___No

Does _____ sometimes express the need to stay home to help parent, to prevent parent from being ill, or to help care for ill parent?

___Yes   ___No

_____

NOTES

ADAPTIVE BEHAVIOR ASSESSMENT
Autonomous Activities Subscale

1. When it is time for a bath or shower, _____
   - 2 is responsible for starting the water, washing and drying himself/herself without help.
   - 1 washes himself/herself, but needs help in starting the water and getting in and out of the tub.
   - 0 must be bathed by someone else.

2. When _____is hurt or ill, he/she
   - 1 recognizes that the wound or illness needs attention and asks for help.
   - 2 cares for the cut or wound with soap, antiseptic and/or bandages or asks for the proper medicine: aspirin, cough syrup, etc.
   - 0 ignores it/ does not recognize the need for medical attention.

3. When_____'s hair needs washing
   - 2 he/she does it without help
   - 1 he/she washes it, but someone must check to see if it has been done properly.
   - 0 someone must do it for him/her.

4. When _____ needs to go to the bathroom, does he/she
   - 1 go by himself/herself, but need some assistance.
   - 2 go alone.
   - 0 have to be taken by someone else.

5. When his/her fingernails or toenails need cutting or cleaning, does _____
   - 0 let you or someone else do it or does he/she bite or chew them.
   - 2 do it himself/herself.
   - 1 ask you or someone else to do it.

6. Does _____
   - 2 dress himself/herself completely, including buttoning and tying.
   - 1 dress himself/herself except for buttoning and tying.
   - 0 require assistance in getting clothes on and off.

7. Does _____
   - 1 show concern for his/her appearance by combing/brushing hair, refusing to wear dirty or torn clothes, etc.
   - 0 show no concern for his/her appearance.
   - 2 show concern for his/her appearance by selecting clothes carefully, "primping," caring for skin (applying make-up or simple cream), asking how he/she looks, etc.

8. When eating, does _____
   0 have to be fed.
   1 feed himself/herself adequately with some assistance in cutting meat.
   2 feed himself/herself correctly using spoon, fork, and knife.

9. When _____ wants a drink, he/she
   2 pours from a bottle or pitcher into a glass or cup and drinks unaided.
   1 drinks unaided but requires assistance in pouring.
   0 must hold glass or cup with both hands, or someone else must hold it for him/hr.

10. When opening a bottle or can, does _____
    2 use an opener without assistance.
    1 use an opener with assistance.
    0 asks someone to open it for him/her.

11. Does _____
    1 prepare sandwiches for himself/herself or someone else by spreading something on bread.
    2 prepare sandwiches using luncheon meat, lettuce, tomato, etc.
    0 let someone else prepare sandwiches or similar foods.

12. When cookies are baked in your home, does _____
    2 mix the batter, place cookies in oven, and remove them when ready.
    1 receive some assistance or assist you or someone else in preparing the cookies.
    0 let someone else bake the cookies.

13. Does _____ ever cook eggs, soup, hot cereal or other simple foods
    1 with your supervision or the supervision of another person.
    2 by himself/herself
    0 or doesn't he/she cook.

14. Does _____ ever cook an entire meal for the family
    2 by himself/herself.
    1 with your supervision or the supervision of another.
    0 or doesn't he/she cook an entire meal.

15. At mealtime does _____
    1 set the table with some assistance.
    0 let someone else set the table.
    2 set the table without help.

16. After a meal does _____
    2 clean off the table and/or wash the dishes without help.
    1 clean off the table and/or wash the dishes with some assistance.
    0 let someone else clean up

17. Is _____ responsible for
    2 making his/her bed and keeping his/her room neat.
    1 picking up toys, but not making bed.
    0 or does someone else clean the room and make the bed.

18. When his/her bed linens need changing, does _____
    0 let someone else change them.
    2 change them himself/herself.
    1 change them with some assistance.

19. In his/her room has _____
    2 decorated the walls with favorite pictures, posters, or other items.
    0 shown no interest in decorating his/her room.
    1 shown interest but let you or someone else choose the decorations.

20. After the clothes have been washed, does _____
    1 help you or someone else fold and put them away.
    2 fold and put them away himself/herself.
    0 let someone else fold and put them away.

21. When it is time to clean the family's clothes, does _____
    2 sort the clothes into loads for washing, place them in the machine, and dry them or hang them out.
    1 let someone else wash the clothes, but help out by putting clothes in dryer or on line—or help out in some other way.
    0 let someone else wash the clothes.

22. Does _____
    2 do small household tasks such as dusting, sweeping, straightening up or carrying out trash without help.
    1 do small household tasks with some help or help someone else do them.
    0 let someone else do small tasks.

23. Does _____
    2 perform major household chores such as vacuuming, mopping, cleaning the bathroom, cleaning the oven, etc. without help.
    1 perform major chores with assistance or assist someone else in doing them.
    0 let someone else do major chores.

24. In the yard does _____
   1 rake, sweep or pick up debris.
   2 mow the lawn or do heavy pruning.
   0 let someone else do the yardwork.

25. If there are pets in the family, does _____
   2 care for the pets by feeding and watering them.
   1 assist someone else in caring for the pets.
   0 let someone else care for them.

26. Is _____
   2 aware of items that may cause accidents—toys on stairs, fire hazards, improper storage of poisons, etc.—and tries to prevent them.
   1 aware that some things may cause accidents, but doesn't know how to prevent them.
   0 unaware of items that cause accidents.

Mechanical Skills

1. When watching television, does _____
   - 2 turn the TV set on and off and select channels without supervision.
   - 1 turn set on and/or off but cannot select channels.
   - 0 always let others operate the television.

2. Does _____ turn light switches and faucets on and off
   - 1 with assistance.
   - 0 not at all.
   - 2 without assistance.

3. Does _____ plug and unplug electrical appliances
   - 1 with assistance.
   - 2 without assistance.
   - 0 not at all.

4. When the bulb in a lamp or light fixture burns out, does
   - 0 let someone else replace the bulb.
   - 2 change the bulb himself/herself.
   - 1 help someone else change the bulb.

5. When a flashlight or some other battery-operated toy or appliance stops working, does _____
   - 2 change the batteries by himself/herself.
   - 1 ask you or someone else to change the batteries.
   - 0 fail to realize what is wrong with the flashlight.

6. Does _____ use electrical appliances or power tools
   - 1 electric mixer, hairdryer, toaster, etc.
   - 2 skill saw, drill, sewing machine.
   - 0 not at all.

7. Does _____ lock and unlock doors and other things with a key
   - 0 not at all.
   - 2 without assistance.
   - 1 with assistance.

8. When things around the house get broken or quit operating, does _____
   - 1 repair small appliances such as kitchen aids , clocks.
   - 2 repair large appliances such as washing machines, sewing machines, etc.
   - 0 let someone else make repairs.

9. Does _____ sew
   1 on buttons, hem, or make small items without a machine or with a toy machine.
   2 using a machine to make clothes or other items.
   0 not at all.

10. Does _____ iron clothes and/or perform minor carpentry with nails and hammer, saw
   2 without supervision.
   1 with supervision.
   0 not at all.

11. Does _____ paint the exterior or interior of houses, cabinets, furniture, etc.
   1 with assistance.
   2 without assistance.
   0 not at all.

12. Does _____ use a screw driver, wrench, pliers
   0 not at all.
   2 without supervision.
   1 with supervision.

13. Does _____ drive a car, truck, or motorcycle
   1 with a licensed driver along.
   2 alone.
   0 not at all.

14. Does _____ make repairs
   1 on tricycles, bicycles, or other riding toys only.
   2 on motorcycles and/or automobiles.
   0 only on smaller items.

15. Does _____ take care of the maintenance of a car or motorcycle by changing tires, plugs, oil, etc. when necessary, filling with gasoline, water, etc.
   2 without supervision.
   0 not at all.
   1 with supervision.

16. Does _____ assemble toys, shelves, objects, etc. from diagramed or written instructions
   2 without assistance.
   1 with assistance.
   0 not at all.

Play and Recreation

1. To amuse himself/herself at home does _____
   1 play alone with boxes, pots and pans or other accessible objects.
   2 build things with blocks, tinkertoys, or other building toys; read, watch television, play games, etc.
   0 have to have you or someone to play with or amuse him/her.

2. Does _____
   2 play games using imaginary or made-up foes, weapons, comrades, etc.
   1 play games requiring actual objects.
   0 not play much at all.

3. Does _____ pretend to be a TV or movie hero or heroine, an animal, etc.
   1 only when he/she is alone.
   2 when playing with other children.
   0 not at all.

4. When playing with other children does _____ play "house," "school," "doctors," "cowboys," "soldier," etc.
   2 a lot of the time.
   1 some of the time.
   0 none of the time.

5. Does _____ play games like tag, chase, hide and seek
   1 only with brothers and sisters.
   2 with neighborhood children or schoolmates.
   0 not at all.

6. Does _____ ride a tricycle, bicycle, "Big Wheel," skateboard or other riding toy
   2 around the block or a few blocks from your house.
   1 only in the yard or in front of your house.
   0 not at all.

7. Does _____ ride a minibike or motorcycle
   0 not at all.
   2 several miles from your home.
   1 only in your immediate neighborhood.

8. When _____ takes part in table games requiring cooperation between two or among more players, does he play
   2 games like checquers, scrabble, monopoly; complex card games like poker, bridge, etc.
   1 games like checkers, chinese checkers, marbles, dominoes, simple card games like Old Maid, Slap Jack, etc.
   0 or doesn't he/she play at all.

9. Does _____ have a hobby, such as drawing, painting, singing, dancing, playing a musical instrument, sewing, crocheting, etc.
   2 that he/she engages in regularly.
   1 that he/she engages in every once in a while.
   0 or doesn't he/she have a hobby.

10. Does _____ play
   1 with children's wooden or cardboard puzzles.
   2 with complex jigsaw puzzles, crossword puzzles, or other complicated puzzles.
   0 with no puzzles of any kind.

11. When he/she is at home, does _____
   2 make objects or pictures using modeling clay, "Pla-dough," paste/glue and/or scissors, paint, etc.
   1 draw simple pictures using pencil or crayons or color in coloring books.
   0 not use pencils, crayons, clay, scissors or paste.

12. With his/her friends, classmates, or family, _____
   1 plays unorganized games with rules created as the game progresses.
   2 plays organized games with set rules.
   0 does not play games.

13. Does _____ take part in sports such as baseball, football, soccer, basketball, golf, tennis, racquetball, etc.
   2 as a member of an organized team.
   1 in a physical education class or with friends/family.
   0 not at all.

14. Does _____ fish, hunt, swim or go camping
   0 not at all.
   2 alone or with friends/siblings.
   1 as an organized family outing.

15. Does _____ roller skate, ice skate, bowl, play miniature golf
   2 alone or with friends/siblings.
   0 not at all.
   1 as an organized family outing.

16. Does _____ attend movies, dances, or parties
   1 with adult supervision.
   2 without adult supervision.
   0 not at all.

Communication and Social Skills

1. When he/she is communicating with you or someone else, does _____
   0 use only gestures or sounds.
   1 talk using single words or phrases.
   2 talk using sentences.

2. When talking, does _____
   2 use complex sentences containing clauses and prepositional phrases.
   0 use simple sentences with subject and verb (he goes).
   1 show an understanding of words like on, in, behind, in front of, etc.

3. Does _____ tell you about things that have happened at school or things that he/she has seen on TV or at the movies
   0 not at all.
   1 only when you ask him/her.
   2 whenever something
interesting happens.

4. Does _____ write letters or cards to friends or relatives
   1 only when asked.
   0 not at all.
   2 whenever the occasion arises.

5. Does _____ ask questions and respond to questions appropriately
   0 not at all.
   1 some of the time.
   2 most of the time.

6. When he/she is asked, does he/she respond
   2 with his/her full name, address and/or telephone number.
   1 with his/her name only.
   0 not at all.

7. Does _____ know
   0 his/her parents only as "mama" and "daddy".
   1 his/her parents' full names.
   2 his/her parents' full names and occupations.

8. When he/she causes a problem for you or someone else, does _____
   2 realize that he/she has caused a problem and try to correct it.
   1 realize that he/she has caused a problem, but not why.
   0 not realize that he/she has caused a problem.

9. Does _____ know
   0 no shapes at all.
   2 the differences between geometric shapes—square, triangle, rectangle, circle.
   1 only the difference between a square and a circle.

10. Does _____ use the telephone
   0 not at all or by answering it only.
   1 by making calls and taking messages.
   2 for calling long distance and/or as a large part of his/her social activity.

11. When he/she is around several adults who are talking, does

   _____

   2 join in the conversation.
   1 listen but does not join in.
   0 ignore them or seem unaware of them.

12. When he/she is around several children who are talking, does _____
   1 listen but does not join in.
   0i ignore them or seem unaware of them.
   2 join in the conversation.

13. Does _____ interact or play
   0 only at home by himself or with brothers and sisters.
   1 with children at school and/or with children who live in the same block or close by.
   2 with children who live several blocks away or in a different area of town.

14. Does _____
   2 have a best friend or group of friends that he/she interacts with almost exclusively.
   1 play or interact with several different individuals or groups at different times.
   0 interact very little with others.

15. Does _____ invite friends or relatives to spend the night and/or does he/she spend the night with friends or relatives
   2 frequently.
   1 only on occasion.
   0 not at all.

16. Does _____ attend birthday parties or other parties
   0 not at all.
   1 only on occasion.
   2 frequently.

17. Does _____ share his/her belongings with others
    2 of his/her own accord.
    1 only when told to do so.
    0 not at all.

18. Does _____ participate in clubs, on teams, or in other organizations
    0 not at all.
    2 as one of the leaders of the group.
    1 as one of the rank and file members.

19. Does _____
    0 show no interest in members of the opposite sex.
    2 have dates with members of the opposite sex.
    1 show interest in members of the opposite sex, but does not date.

20. Does _____ plan parties or other events
    0 not at all.
    2 without assistance.
    1 with assistance.

21. Does _____ arrange his/her social affairs—where he/she will go, when, and with whom
    2 without the input of his parents or someone else.
    1 with the input of parents or others.
    0 not at all.

Responsibility

1. At home does _____
   2 move about the house and yard without supervision.
   1 move about the house, but not the yard without supervision.
   0 require supervision in the house and yard.

2. Does _____ walk or drive to school or to the bus stop
   2 without supervision.
   1 with supervision.
   0 or does someone drive him/her to school.

3. Does _____ walk or drive to the grocery or convenience store
   2 without supervision.
   1 with supervision.
   0 not at all.

4. Does _____ go to movies, social events, the park, library, etc.
   0 not at all.
   2 without supervision.
   1 with supervision.

5. Does _____ use public transportation such as a bus, taxi, train, airplane, etc.
   0 not at all.
   1 with supervision.
   2 without supervision.

6. Is _____ ever left alone in the house
   0 for a few minutes or not at all.
   1 for 30 minutes to an hour.
   2 for several hours.

7. When _____ makes a mistake, does he/she
   1 blame someone else for the mistake.
   2 admit that he/she made a mistake.
   0 fail to recognize that a mistake has been made.

8. When he/she has homework to do, does _____
   2 do it without prodding.
   1 do it at your insistence.
   0 put it off or not do it at all.

9. When _____ is supposed to perform a chore around the house, does he/she
   1 do it at your insistence.
   2 do it without prodding.
   0 put it off and/or not do it at all.

10. Does _____ take care of younger children or care for the elderly
   2 often.
   1 anytime the opportunity arises.
   0 never.

11. If _____ is supposed to be somewhere at a given time, how often does he/she arrive on time
   0 almost never.
   2 almost every time.
   1 some of the the.

12. Does _____ know what to do in case of emergency—accident, fire, theft, etc.
   2 so that he/she could handle the situation himself/herself.
   1 so that he/she could handle the situation with your help or someone else's.
   0 not at all.

13. When _____ sees a person in need of help, such as a person who is carrying heavy grocery bags, does he/she
   1 offer to help after you or someone else tells him to.
   0 not offer to help.
   2 offer to help.

14. When _____ tells someone he will do something or signs a contract agreeing to do something, does he/she fulfill his/her obligation
   2 almost always.
   1 some of the time.
   0 almost never.

Economic Activity

1. When playing with family members or friends, does _____
   1 sometimes use play money or pretend to buy or sell items at a store.
   2 sometimes play board or card games in which money (real or play) is exchanged.
   0 never use real or play money.

2. Does _____ use money
   0 not at all.
   1 to buy only candy, cokes, etc.
   2 to buy toys, records, sports equipment, clothes.

3. Does _____ understand
   1 that a penny is 1¢, that 5 pennies are a nickel and 10 pennies are a dime.
   2 how to make change for at least one dollar.
   0 no money equivalents.

4. When _____ goes to the movies, sports events, etc. does he/she pay his/her own way
   2 almost always.
   1 sometimes.
   0 almost never.

5. Does _____ run errands to purchase food—a loaf of bread, carton of milk, or other items
   2 without supervision.
   1 with supervision.
   0 not at all.

6. When _____ gets some money, does he/she
   0 spend it right away, almost immediately.
   1 put it in a piggy bank or some place at home so that he/she can add to it and buy something later on.
   2 put it in a savings account.

7. Does _____ get his/her own money
   1 from an allowance that you or someone else give him.
   0 a little at a time whenever someone gives it to him/her.
   2 from a job.

8. Does _____ have a checking account
   2 upon which he/she writes checks and makes deposits independently.
   1 which is co-signed by you or someone else who carries out transactions on the account.
   0 not at all.

9. Does _____ buy groceries (enough for several days) for the family
   0 not at all.
   2 without assistance.
   1 with assistance.

SCORE SHEET FOR THE
TEXAS ENVIRONMENTAL ADAPTATION MEASURE
ADAPTIVE BEHAVIOR ASSESSMENT

Child's Name: School:

Address: Grade: Teacher:

Telephone No.:   Date of Interview:

Date of Birth: Interviewer:

Age: ____ Yrs. ____Mos. ____   Respondent:

                                                          (relationship)

Directions: Circle the appropriate numerical or "NO" response for each question. Comments, notations, etc. may be recorded in the space provided following each question. Total the responses in the space provided at the end of each subscale.

Scoring

Subscale	Raw Score	
		TOTAL RAW SCORE: _____
		MEAN RAW SCORE (EXPECTED): _____
Autonomous Activities	_____	$S.D. =$
Mechanical Skills	_____	$\dfrac{\text{Total Raw Score} - \text{Expected Mean Raw Score}}{s.d.}$
Play and Recreation	_____	
Communication & Social Skills	_____	
Responsibility	_____	$S.D. = \dfrac{}{14}$
Economic Activity	_____	
TOTAL	=========	$S.D. = $ _____

Leigh S. Scott and Alan T. Fisher

Autonomous Activities

1. Bathes _____ 2 1 0 NO	15. Sets table _____ 2 1 0 NO
2. Cares for injuries ____ 2 1 0 NO	16. Washes dishes _____ 21 0 NO
3. Washes Hair _____ 2 1 0 NO	17. Cleans room_____ 2 1 0 NO
4. Bathroom use _____ 2 1 0 NO	18. Changes linens _____ 2 1 0 NO
5. Cuts fingernails _____ 2 1 0 NO	19. Decorates room _____ 2 1 0 NO
6. Dresses self 2 1 0 NO _____	20. Folds clothes_____ 2 1 0 NO
7. Cares for appearance 2 1 0 NO	21. Washes clothes _____ 210 N O
8. Feeds self _____ 2 1 0 NO	22. Does minor chores _____ 2 1 0 NO
9. Gets drink _____ 2 1 0 NO	23. Does major chores _____ 2 1 0 NO
10. Opens bottles, cans 2 1 0 NO	24. Mows, rakes yard _____ 2 1 0 NO
11. Prepares Sandwiches 2 1 0 NO	25. Cares for pets _____ 2 1 0 NO
12. Bakes _____ 2 1 0 NO	26. Prevents accidents ____ 2 1 0 NO
13. Cooks simple foods _2 1 0 NO	
14. Cooks meal _____ 2 1 0 NO	

# of 2's = _____ X 2 = _____
# of 1's = _____ X 1 = _____
# of 0's = _____
# of No's = _____
(26)

Autonomous Act. Score _____

184

Mechanical Skills

1. Operates TV set _____ 2 1 0 NO

9. Sews _____ 2 1 0 NO

2. Operates faucets____ 2 1 0 NO

10. Irons, hammers   2 1 0 NO

3. Plugs in appliances __ 2 1 0 NO

11. Paints _____ 2 1 0 NO

4.Changes light bulbs __ 2 1 0 NO

12. Uses tools_____ 2 1 0 NO

5. Change batteries____ 2 1 0 NO

13. Drives car 2 1 0 NO

6. Uses appliances _____ 2 1 0 NO

14. Repairs vehicles 2 1 0 NO

7. Unlocks with key_____ 2 1 0 NO

15. Cares for car 2 1 0 NO

8. Repairs appliances __ 2 1 0 NO

16. Assembles items 2 1 0 NO

# of 2's = _____X 2 = _____

# of I's = _____X 1 =

# of 0's = _____

# of NO's= _____

(16)

Mechanical Skills Score _____

NOTES

Play and Recreation

1. Plays alone _____ 2 1 0 NO	9. Has a hobby _____ 2 1 0 NO
2. Plays games	
using imagination _____ 2 1 0 NO	10. Plays with puzzles _____ 2 1 0 NO
3. Pretends to be TV,	
movie hero _____ 2 1 0 NO	11. Plays with art materials _____ 2 1 0 NO
4. Plays "house' "school" _____ 2 1 0 NO	12. Plays unorganized games ____ 2 1 0 NO
5. Plays tag, chase _____ 2 1 0 NO	13. Plays sports _____ 2 1 0 NO
6. Rides tricycle, Bicycle _____ 2 1 0 NO	14. Fishes, hunts, swims _____ . 2 1 0 NO
7. Rides minibike _____ 2 1 0 NO	15. Skates, bowls, golfs _____ 2 1 0 NO
8. Plays table games _____ 2 1 0 NO	16. Attends movies, dances, parties 2 1 0 NO

# of 2's = _____ X 2 = _____
# of 1's = _____ X 1 = _____
# of 0's = _____
# of No's = _____
(16)

**Play & Recreation
Score** _____

Notes

Communication and Social Skills

1. Talks phrases, sentences ___ 2 1 0 NO

2. Uses complex sentences ___ 2 1 0 NO

3. Tells about school, TV _____ 2 1 0 NO

4. Writes letters, cards _____ 2 1 0 NO

5. Asks questions _____ 2 1 0 NO

6. Knows name, address ____ 2 1 0 NO

7. Knows parents' names ____ 2 1 0 NO

8. Recognizes behavior ____ 2 1 0 NO

9. Recognizes shapes _____ 2 1 0 NO

10. Uses telephone _____ 2 1 0 NO

11. Talks with adults _____ 2 1 0 NO

12. Talks with children _____ 2 1 0 NO

13. Plays with neighbors _____ 2 1 0 NO

14. Has a best friend _____ 2 1 0 NO

15. Has overnight guests _____ 2 1 0 NO

16. Attends parties _____ 2 1 0 NO

17. Shares belongings _____ 2 1 0 NO

18. Participates in clubs _____ 2 1 0 NO

19. Dates _____ 2 1 0 NO

20. Plans partie _____ 2 1 0 NO

21. Arranges social affairs ___ 2 1 0 NO

# of 2's = _____ X 2 = _____

# of 1's = _____ X 1 = _____

# of 0's = _____

# of No's = _____
         (21)

Communication & Social Skills
Score _____

NOTES

Responsibility

1. Moves about house, yard __ 2 1 0 NO

2. Walks, drives to school ____ 2 1 0 NO

3. Walks, drives to store_____ 2 1 0 NO

4. Goes to social events_____ 2 1 0 NO

5. Uses bus, taxi_____ 2 1 0 NO

6. Is left alone _____ 2 1 0 NO

7. Admits mistakes _____ 2 1 0 NO

8. Does homework_____2 1 0 NO

9. Does chores_____2 1 0 NO

10. Cares for children, elderly ___2 1 0 NO

11. Is punctual _____2 1 0 NO

12. Handles emergencies _____2 1 0 NO

13. Helps others_____2 1 0 NO

14. Fulfills obligations _____2 1 0 NO

# of 2's = _____ X 2 = _____

# of 1's = _____ X 1 = _____

# of 0's = _____

# of No's = _____
(14)

Responsibility Score _____

Notes

Economic Activity

1. Plays games using money__ 2 1 0 NO

2. Uses money for purchases _ 2 1 0 NO

3. Makes change_____ 2 1 0 NO

4. Pays for entertainmen _____ 2 1 0 NO

5. Runs errands _____ 2 1 0 NO

6. Saves money_____2 1 0 NO

7. Earns money _____2 1 0 NO

8. Has checking account_____2 1 0 NO

9. Buys groceries_____2 1 0 NO

# of 2's = _____ X 2 = _____

# of 1's = _____ X 1 = _____

# of 0's = _____

# of No's = _____
                (5)

Economic Activity
Score _____

Notes

Part 3
Behavioral Assessment

THE BEHAVIORAL ASSESSMENT OF CONDUCT DISORDER IN A BLACK CHILD

William H. Anderson, Jr.

The Concern for Fairness and Objectivity in Child Assessment

When parents receive phone calls from the school complaining of a child's poor conduct in the classroom or when they receive a letter from the principal suggesting that their child is out of control and should receive evaluation for special educational services, concerns about bias may immediately come to mind. They may respond with reticence or express doubts about the objectivity of both those making the referral and those conducting the assessment. The educational professionals involved may also have concerns that their decisions and recommendations should be impartial and based on unbiased evaluations. This chapter focuses on ways in which concerns for assessment objectivity may be addressed by behavioral approaches to assessment.

Anti-Minority Bias in Traditional Assessment

Bias in assessment often plagues minority children who stand in need of psychological evaluation, but some forms of bias are problematic in the assessment of all children regardless of their cultural or ethnic backgrounds. For example, all children to varying degrees run the risk of misevaluation due to assessor bias in the assessment instruments being used. To some extent, all children may suffer from shortcomings inherent in diagnostic systems currently in use. Among these shortcomings, problems of reliability and validity figure prominently. O'Leary and Johnson (1979) have observed that "all assessment devices for evaluating social problems of children have their methodological shortcomings..." In their review, which examines the advantages and disadvantages of some of the major assessment methods, they show that none is totally without fault. Similarly, Nathan and Harris (1980) have observed that two of the greatest weaknesses in psychiatric diagnosis are the problems of reliability and validity. Citing the investigations of Greenberg (1977) and Spitzer and Fliess (1974), they argued that reliability for measuring height, weight and circumference is high, reliability for measuring intelligence is only moderately high, and the reliability of measures of personality and of psychopathologic diagnosis is comparatively low. Thus, assessment methodologies with low validity and reliability may lead to the misapplication of diagnostic labels to children.

Whether or not a diagnostic label has been misapplied, there is always the chance that such labeling will lead to stigmatization and distortions in the subsequent perceptions of professionals and other significant individuals in the child's environment. Such stigmatization may go so far as to distort the child's own perceptions of himself (Guskin, Bartel, & Macmillan, 1975). These hazards of assessment, while problematic for children in general, may be especially problematic for minority youngsters such as black children who are too often the victims of this society's racial prejudices (Comer, & Poussaint, 1975; Wilson, 1978).

Research has revealed the presence of racial and anti-minority bias in various forms of child assessment, ranging from the use of psychometric measures such as personality inventories, ability scales and intelligence tests to the use of informal non-standardized techniques such as unstructured clinical interviews. Issues concerning the discriminatory effects of standardized tests have been hotly debated. Although some have argued that certain standardized tests can provide fair assessments of minority children (e.g., Lambert, 1981), others have argued that these tests discriminate against minority children (e.g., Gonzales, 1982; Kamin, 1974; Mercer, 1975a,b; Williams, 1974; Wright & Isenstein, 1975). Individuals taking the latter point of view have argued that blacks and other minorities have not been included in normative samples and that the selection of test content and processes have been more accessible to children in advantaged groups. They have gone on to argue that when minority children are assessed with such instruments, they are unfairly evaluated as being less adequate or actually deficient.

The failure to make tests more fair by including diversity of culture, language, race, and socioeconomic background in standardization groups may have a far-reaching impact on the lives of minority children assessed with these instruments. Gelfand, Jenson, and Drew (1982) have argued that "selecting the standardization group sets the norm for use in schools, clinics, and government agencies. The effects of these judgments can range from limiting educational opportunities and damaging self-esteem to sterilization programs which rob people of opportunities for parenthood." (p. 381)

Specific cultural and racial bias has also been shown to exist in non-standardized tests and other forms of clinical assessment (Nathan & Harris, 1980). Examples of bias in clinical assessment may be found in studies by DeHoyos and DeHoyos (1965), and Singer (1967). In these studies, white psychiatrists were observed to record fewer symptoms for black patients than for corresponding white patients. They also focused on the most dramatic symptoms in the black patients and perceived them as being more disturbed and more pathological than white patients displaying the same symptoms. Moreover, when 2,279 outpatient cases coming into a psychiatric institute at the University of Maryland were studied by Gross, Herbert, Knatterud and Donner (1969), they found that the same symptoms which led to hospitalization and a label of neurosis in a group of white patients led to hospitalization and diagnosis of schizophrenia in a corresponding group of black patients. These studies demonstrate that bias can influence diagnostic and assessment decisions.

Outside of the clinic and in the schools where many assessments and referrals for assessments are made, racial bias can especially influence the evaluation of minority children. Anti-minority bias in the classroom has been reported in a study by the U.S. Civil Rights Commission (1973). In a study of interactions between teachers and their students in 429 classrooms throughout the southwest, the authors found that teachers made a significantly larger number of positive evaluations and responses to the Anglo students than to those from Mexican-American backgrounds. Lietz and Gregory (1978) conducted a study exploring teacher referrals of black and white elementary school pupils for diagnosis and discipline. They compared the number of black and white behavior problem pupils who were referred to the principal's office for disciplinary action with those referred to a multidisciplinary team for evaluation as candidates for exceptional education services. They found that exceptional education referrals did not differ with regard to race but significantly more black children were perceived by their teachers as requiring disciplinary action and were sent to the principal's office.

Further evidence for racial bias in the assessment of black school children can be found in a study by Kaufman, Swan, and Wood (1980). In examining whether parents, teachers, and psychoeducational diagnosticians agreed in their evaluations of problem behaviors in emotionally disturbed children, they found a significant difference in the reliability of ratings for black and white children. Raters reached high levels of agreement in their perceptions of white children, but interrater agreement was very low with regard to the problems of black children. Particularly low was the agreement between teachers and the parents of the black children. Although the reason for this racial difference is not clear, the authors speculate that one of several factors have come into play. Among these, cultural differences may have caused a disparity in judgments of appropriate and inappropriate behavior. It is also possible that the SES differences which existed between the black and white families caused the less educated participants to have more difficulty understanding terms used in the evaluation (e.g., distractibility, perseveration, self-derogatory).

The possible presence of racial or cultural bias in an evaluation may cause many minority members to hesitate when one of their children is recommended for assessment and evaluation. But despite their reluctance to place much confidence in traditional methods of assessment, minority parents and professionals are hard pressed to seek alternative methods. In seeking evaluation procedures which are less subjective, inferential and bias prone, they might do well to consider behavioral approaches to assessment.

Behavioral Assessment as a Strategy for Minimizing Racial and Cultural Bias

Development and Characteristics of Behavioral Assessments

Behavioral assessment is a social learning approach to psychological evaluation which focuses on objective and measurable responses. Because there is currently no single and universally accepted definition of child behavior assessment (O'Leary, 1979; Mash, 1979; Mash, & Terdal, 1981), this approach to assessment is best described and recognized in terms of characteristically occurring concepts which distinguish it from traditional diagnostic assessment (Nathan, & Harris, 1980). In contrast to traditional assessment which indirectly measures personality constructs (e.g., those which use verbal responses to projective tests in measuring ego strength or achievement motivation), behavioral assessment directly samples and measures observable responses which are closely linked to the presenting problem. Traditional assessment often focuses heavily on remote historical events for which the accuracy of the information is difficult to determine (e.g., early toilet training or sibling rivalry). Behavioral assessment focuses primarily on current situational determinants. It focuses on past history only insofar as it is verifiable and directly contributory to the present behavior under consideration (Nelson, & Hayes, 1979). Perhaps the most important way in which behavioral assessment differs from traditional forms of assessment is its direct relationship to treatment formulation and evaluation.

A feature which recommends behavioral assessment as an alternative approach to evaluating minority children is its basis in empirical research. This emphasis on empiricism can be detected throughout the history and development of behavioral assessment. In its earliest stages, behavior assessment (and modification) grew out of operant learning theory and research (Ullman, & Krasner, 1965). Procedures for obtaining frequency, rate, and duration measures of target responses provided straightforward methods for clearly delineating clinical problems and establishing therapeutic effectiveness. Following this operant tradition, studies such as those of Baer, Wolf, and Risley (1968) expanded behavioral assessment strategies beyond the simple measurement of frequency, rate and duration of behaviors to an examination of the events which immediately preceded and followed these responses (Bijou, & Peterson, 1971). This has come to be called the ABC approach to assessment, where B stands for the behavior of interest and A and C respectively symbolize the behavior's antecedents and consequences. According to Mash and Terdal (1981), a number of early workers have made contributions resulting in the development of broadly empirical approaches to child clinical problems (Cooper, 1974; Gelfand, & Hartmann, 1975; and Sulzer-Azaroff, & Mayer, 1977). These approaches have necessitated the development of assessment methods having high face validity (Kanfer, 1979; O'Leary, 1979).

As the field has continued to evolve, so have the uses of behavioral assessment; and many of these are directly relevant to the types of problems which so often confront black children. Clinical researchers such as Patterson (1976) and Wahler (1976) have placed greater emphasis on the social context of the child behavior they assess. By examining behavior in different settings (e.g., home and school), they have underscored the importance of interactions between the child and significant others (e.g., parents, siblings, teachers, and peers). Thus, behavior assessments now often evaluate the child as part of a larger network of interacting systems. They have revealed that problems or behavior changes assessed in one environment (e.g., school) may not exist in another (e.g., home). It would appear from these characteristics of behavioral assessment that its emphasis on objectivity might have the practical effect of overcoming or at least limiting some of the distortions which have characterized traditional assessments of minority children.

The most recent and perhaps most exciting development in behavior assessment has come with the development of cognitive behavioral therapeutic approaches for children. Behavioral assessment allied with these treatments has focused on the role of cognitions and affect as mediators of children's responses (Bandura, 1969, 1977; Kanfer, & Phillips, 1970); Karoly, 1981; Meichenbaum, 1977; Mischel, 1973, 1979). Mash and Terdal (1981) have observed that recent developments such as these have changed the quality of behavior assessment from the simple measurement of target behavior "to a more general problem solving strategy based upon ongoing functional analysis and encompassing a greater range of independent and dependent variables." (p. 7) The broadened conceptualization of behavioral assessment as it exists today is best described and summarized by Evans and Nelson (1977) who have written:

> Behavioral assessment of children can best be considered an exploratory strategy rather than a routine application of specific procedures. The elements of the strategy are complex, but they include an emphasis on the psychology of child development and an extension of the experimental method, although in practice the latter is often more reminiscent of Piaget's *méthods clinique* than a controlled experiment in the formal sense. (p. 610)

Observers might surmise from this description that behavior assessment would be strongly preferred by educational professionals (and others concerned about bias) as a highly desirable method of assessment of minority children. After all, its foundations are strongly empirical and its methods are highly objective. However, Turner (1982) has suggested that in some cases, members of the black community, rather than advocating the use of behavioral approaches, have actually argued against their use. This antipathy may be due in part to concerns that behavioral methods "threaten autonomy and self-determination." Such concerns are not exclusively confined to minority members. The use of behavioral procedures has often been the victim of widely publicized abuses and bad press. The helpfulness of behavioral assessments and therapies to blacks and other minority people has often been ignored outside the domain of the research literature and state hospitals.

Some Uses of Behavioral Assessment in Helping Minority Children

That behavioral assessment procedures can be used to the advantage of clients from different backgrounds is supported by the research literature. However, studies investigating the effectiveness of behavioral procedures with minority populations have been difficult to isolate due to the frequent omission of data which describe the subjects' ethnicity. The lack of inclusion of such data is more than likely due to the authors' belief in the universal applicability of behavioral principles. Although one would not expect black people to function under different laws of behavior, racial information about the subjects would strengthen claims that behavioral principles are the same for all people. A study which does not omit this important information is one by Madden, Russo, and Cataldo (1980). It reports the use of behavior assessment and modification in eliminating pica (the ingestion of inedible substances such as paint chips) which threatened the lives of three black two year old girls. Although the literature is not replete with evidence clearly documenting client race, current studies are attempting to correct this deficiency.

A book edited by Turner and Jones (1982) examines studies specifically focusing on the use of behavioral procedures in black populations. A chapter by Jones in this volume cites several studies which demonstrate the usefulness of behavioral assessment and therapy in remediating academic problems in black school children (e.g., Hayes, 1978; Masters, & Peskay, 1972; Miller, & Schneider, 1970; Rollins et al.. 1974; Sibley et al., 1969; Ward, & Baker, 1968; Wasik et al., 1969).

Not included in Jones' review are two studies which provide additional examples of ways in which behavioral assessment can be used to help black school children. Fantuzzo, Harrell, and McLeod (1979) worked with two black third grade boys who had problems attending in class. Using a self-regulation procedure which required that the target child observe, evaluate, and reinforce his own behavior, they assessed the degree of generalization across the two subjects with an ABAB design. In the first phase (A), the frequencies of attention in the target child and the control subject were assessed for a 10-day base line period. In the next phase (B), the self-regulation procedure was instated for the target child. During this 12-day period, a change in attention was observed in both the target child and the control subject. In order to establish that the behaioral intervention was responsible for this change, the baseline phase (1) was reinstated for five days. During this period, the unobtrusive recording procedure revealed that the level of attentiveness in both boys returned to baseline frequency. Finally, the treatment condition (B) was reinstated. This ABAB design which demonstrated the efficacy of behavioral treatment for these boys is often used to establish the effectiveness of behavioral therapeutic procedures.

A study by Noland, Arnold, and Clement (1980) reports that two black sixth grade girls were exhibiting problems which included breaking school rules, academic underachieving and coercing other children with threats and the use of violence. Behavioral assessment in this intervention required the girls to record their own behavior and reinforce themselves when their behavior changed in the contracted direction. Independent observers provided further assessment by tracking three classroom behaviors approximately every day of each phase for each subject. This self-monitoring and self-reinforcement led to an improvement in the children's behavior.

The studies reviewed above suggest that there is specific and strong evidence of behavioral assessment's utility for black children, especially in educational settings. The importance of systematic assessment of target behaviors within environmental contexts is underscored in each study. Accurate observations and objective recordings are of primary significance. In each case, the child is approached as an individual so that both assessment and therapy can be tailored to his or her unique needs. These characteristics of behavioral assessment have served to attract an ever widening following among practitioners and those seeking evaluation services. Although it has already been mentioned that behavioral assessment is closely tied to behavioral therapy, Adams and Turner (1979, in Mash, & Terdal, 1981) have argued that behavioral assessment is not restricted to situations in which behavioral treatments are being considered or used. Indeed, these authors have pointed out that behavioral approaches have enjoyed increasing popularity among therapists who have not identified themselves as being particularly behavioral in their therapeutic orientations. This increased popularity and demonstrated efficacy of behavioral assessment is bound to have an influence on members of the black community (perhaps in spite of aforementioned reservations and protestations). The present author (Anderson, 1982) and others (e.g., Hayes, 1980; Jackson, 1976; Turner, 1982) have argued that it would be advantageous for black people to utilize these approaches. Indeed, such an argument might be made for all people, regardless of culture. Turner has gone so far as to say that "the behavioral approach is the only one within psychology that has properly recognized subcultural differences in its assessment strategies." (p. 17) Whether or not one believes this statement to be hyperbolic, it suggests that behavioral assessments are valid to describe the needs of individuals in a nondiscriminatory manner, especially those who do not fit into the middle class Euro-American mold.

The Structure of a Comprehensive Behavioral Assessment

To insure that a behavioral assessment will meet the needs of the individual child, it must be structured for comprehensiveness. Several schema for structuring the assessment process systematically have been proposed. One proposed by Kanfer and Saslow (1965, 1969) serves to alert the clinician to variables maintaining the response in question. It includes the following:

(1)   a detailed description of the problem behavior giving an accurate account of the behavior's frequency and intensity;
(2)   clarification of the behavior's context by obtaining information with regard to the setting and associated environmental factors;
(3)   an analysis of motivational factors including an identification of stimuli which maintain and strengthen the response;
(4)   an analysis of developmental processes including the specification of biological, sociocultural, and personal historical factors when relevant to treatment;
(5)   an analysis of self-control indicating the extent to which a client can participate in a treatment which requires him to manipulate his own behavior;
(6)   an analysis of social relationships providing information about those social resources (family, teachers, peers) which may facilitate or interfere with treatment;
(7)   an analysis of the sociocultural-physical environment to reveal ways in which the child's current environment and a potentially more supportive future environment may be harmonized.

Not only may this format be used to guide the clinician in the selection and sequencing of specific assessment procedures before and during the assessment process, it may also be used as a guide in the conceptualization of the problem which precedes treatment formulation.

Another structuring schema particularly helpful for conceptualizing the presenting problem has been outlined by Goldfried and Pomeranz (1968, p. 82). First, the assessor attempts to account for antecedent stimulus variables which either elicit or set the stage for the behavior. Second, organismic variables (whether psychological or physiological) are taken into account. Third, an examination is made of the behavior itself. This may include response topography, intensity and frequency. Fourth, the changes in the environment which are a consequence of the behavior are considered.

The tasks outlined in the above proposed structures are demonstrated in the execution and conceptualization of behavioral assessment in the case illustration which follows.

A Case Illustration of Behavioral Assessment

Assessing Conduct Disorder in a Black Child. Roland was a black six year old whose misconduct in his first grade class made assessment and intervention imperative. The only son of middle-aged professional parents, he was well above average in his intellectual and academic abilities. His teacher and principal complained, however, that he habitually disrupted classroom activities with a number of bad behaviors. They made these complaints in a series of letters, phone calls, and conferences with Roland's parents. In these letters and conversations, the school authorities threatened to start procedures to suspend Roland from school unless some change could be brought about. His classroom teacher lamented that Roland's behavior problems were costing Roland, his classmates, and his teacher, valuable academic time. The teacher asked if there were any problems at home which might be setting off problems at school. The parents countered by asking if something might not be going on in the classroom since Roland always left home in a cheerful mood.

After a school conference in which they learned of tentative plans to have their son evaluated by the school psychologist for possible placement in a class of emotionally disturbed youngsters, Roland's parents decided to seek outside help. They expressed to one another fears that the school professionals might be racially biased against Roland. They also told each other that they did not want their son to be labeled or stigmatized as emotionally disturbed or maladjusted. These concerns led them to seek someone who, they thought, would better understand their own cultural perspective. Because they believed that the school professionals were racially biased against Roland, they sought the help of black professionals who were not connected with the school.

The parents first asked a black educational specialist to visit Roland's classroom and observe his behavior. However, the parents were not convinced that the child had a problem even when the educator told them that Roland's classroom behavior was highly disruptive. Instead, they concluded that the teacher, in addition to being racially biased, lacked adequate classroom management skills. They decided to seek the help of someone who would be able to provide the teacher with classroom management training and help her to focus directly on Roland's behavior rather than on some presumed deep emotional problem. When they finally made phone contact with a black behavior therapist with these skills, the parents had kept Roland out of school for six days. The mother stated that she had become so frustrated with the "negative messages" from Roland's teacher that she had stopped sending him to school. During the initial phone contact, the parents agreed with the therapist to send Roland back to school. They met with the therapist on the following day.

Initial Screening and Parent Interview. The therapist asked Roland's parents to come to the first sessions without Roland. The therapist asked the parents for information regarding their perceptions of Roland's behavior, his developmental history, and the development and current situational determinants of the problem behaviors.

While they sat in the waiting room, the parents were each asked to fill out the Eyberg Behavior Inventory (Eyberg & Ross, 1978) separately. This 36 item checklist assessed the parent's perceptions of Roland's behavior as they experienced it. Although this instrument is easy to administer and provides normative data for children between two and seven years of age, it does not provide normative data with regard to race. The Eyberg yields two scores: A Problem Score (Is this behavior a problem for you?) and an Intensity Score (How often does this behavior occur?) For normal non-clinic children, no more than seven items are usually identified as problem areas and the total score does not exceed 130 on the intensity scale. Roland's father identified no problem areas and a total score of 73 on the intensity scale. Roland's mother identified no problem areas and a total intensity scale score of 67. It appeared from this initial screening that Roland's parents did not think of him as being a problem child at home.

In the interview itself, an attempt was made to assess the developmental and current situational determinants of the problem. Roland's development had been normal, but his mother (who recalled his speaking simple words before he was nine months old) thought that he had always been more verbal than other children his age. Both parents were proud of his high intelligence and academic abilities. (Assessment on the WISC-R produced a full scale IQ of 130; his teacher had indicated that he was the top reader in his class.) They related that they both always spent a lot of time with Roland and had never witnessed the kind of behavior problems described to them by his teachers. They did admit that a year earlier, Roland's kindergarten teacher had complained to them of excessive attention seeking and disruptive classroom behaviors. These included speaking out of turn and disrupting group activities by making noises and walking around on all fours. However, the parents hastened to add that the kindergarten teacher had brought these responses under control without extraordinary consultation or help. They expressed dismay that the present teacher was unable to do this. The parents also disclosed their hypothesis that the present teacher and the principal might be racially biased against such an exceptionally intelligent black boy.

The therapist next attempted to use the interview to determine if there were any problematic parent-child interactions which had not shown up on the checklist. For any problem behaviors uncovered, an attempt was made to examine the antecedent conditions (What happens just before the problem interaction?), the child's behavior (What does Roland do then?), the parent's response (What do you do in response to his response?), and the child's reaction to the parent's intervention (What does Roland do then?). Relevant information such as frequency (How often...), duration (How long...), and the developmental history of each specified problem was obtained.

This procedure uncovered only one behavior which approached being a problem: at the announcement of bedtime, Roland would sometimes whine and say he did not want to go. One of the parents would promise to read him a bedtime story; this was always enough to get him to go to bed. They reported that Roland often fell asleep before the story was finished. This behavioral sequence was estimated to occur four times a week and had been a habit since Roland was two and a half. Having obtained this information, the therapist received the parents' permission to continue the assessment by interviewing Roland's principal and teacher.

Behavior Rating and Teacher Interview. Interviews with Roland's teacher and principal were structured like the interview with his parents. In preparing for his interview with the teacher, the therapist mailed her the Walker Problem Behavior Identification Checklist (Walker, 1970) so that he could get an idea of her perceptions of Roland. The Walker Problem Behavior Identification Checklist consists of 50 descriptors of overt behavior on which a child can be rated with a minimum of inference. The child being assessed on this rating scale receives a score on each of five factors which include: (1) acting out, (2) withdrawal, (3) distractibility, (4) disturbed peer relations, and (5) immaturity. There are T-score norms for each of these factors by sex, but there are none for age or race. The teacher's responses on this 50-item checklist indicated that Roland exhibited problems on two of five scales. The T-score of 61 on the distractibility scale and 78 on the acting out scale suggested that Roland's teacher perceived him as exhibiting overt, attention seeking, disruptive and aggressive behaviors in the classroom.

The subsequent interview with Roland's teacher provided information concerning the antecedents, consequences, frequency, intensity, and topography of each problem behavior emitted by Roland in the classroom. These included (1) interrupting the teacher as she worked individually with other pupils by calling out to her or by going over to her and making requests or demands which distracted both her and the pupil with whom she was working; (2) disrupting the activities of the class as a group by speaking out of turn and making noises, sometimes while being out of his seat; (3) refusing to comply with the teacher's demands to cease engaging in disruptive behaviors; and (4) physically aggressing (i.e., hitting, biting and/or kicking) against the teacher or other children when frustrated or when corrected by the teacher. In addition to revealing the current situational determinants of the behavior, the interview was used by the therapist to assess some ways in which the teacher was currently using rewards and punishments to control Roland's behavior. The therapist was also able to form an impression of the teacher's motivation, her willingness to work with him, and her ability to carry out a treatment program skillfully and conscientiously. It must be acknowledged, however, that such impressions are subjective and open to bias.

Behavior Observation and Recording by Teacher. At the end of the assessment interview, the therapist asked the teacher to observe Roland's behavior and note the problem responses in a log with three columns. Under Column A, she described the antecedent conditions which preceded the behavior. Under Column B, she listed the specific problem response which had occurred, and under Column C, she described the consequent events which followed the response. This form of log keeping helped to confirm and validate impressions formed during the interview. While providing additional data concerning situational determinants and response topography, it also provided base line data (i.e., a record of the frequency of the conduct problem behaviors occurring under existing classroom conditions before any treatment intervention was undertaken). Six days of such baseline data collection by the teacher indicated that Roland was making an average of 25.5 problematic responses per day. Because this type of behavioral log keeping is both tedious and energy and time consuming, it was discontinued at the end of baseline data collection. From then on, the teacher kept a tally of problem behaviors by using a golf counter. At the end of each day, she recorded the total number of problem responses on a data sheet provided by the therapist.

Classroom Observation by the Therapist. Information from the parents and teachers was supplemented by the therapist's own observation of classroom behavior. It will be noted that up to this point, the therapist and Roland had never met. When Roland or another pupil asked about the identity and purposes of the observer, they were told simply that the gentleman was a visitor who had come to work in the classroom for a short while. No further explanation was given.

In observing Roland's interactions with his teacher, the therapist noted the presence or absence of the conduct disordered behaviors which the teacher had identified in the interview. He also observed and recorded the teacher's responses to Roland.

During the 45 minutes of observation, Roland got out of his seat three times and walked over to his teacher to ask her for help when she was working individually with another student. Twice, he called out to her from across the room, once when she was working at her desk, and once when she was giving individual attention to another student. Although he did not hit her, Roland drew his hand back as if to strike his teacher when she walked over to his desk and angrily warned him not to call out from across the room any more. A little later, when he was on task, the teacher came to work with him at his desk. While the teacher gave him this individual attention, his behavior was appropriate and cooperative.

Even as she worked with him at his desk, Roland's teacher praised him infrequently (only once during the 45-minute observation and that was at the end of her individual work with him). Although she did not glance in his direction or attend to him during the times he was working quietly, she did speak to him and try to correct his behavior when he was disruptive. A total of six disruptive episodes were recorded. Prorating this to the full day would yield a negative incident rate of 30 versus the teacher count of 25. On the average, Roland's disruptions lasted 1.1 minutes each and took up a total of 7 minutes time during the observation period. Two other classroom observations were made with similar results.

Child Interview. Three days after the classroom observations were completed, the therapist had an interview with Roland in an effort to determine how the child perceived his own problems. Although Roland was reluctant to speak at all about his interactions with his teacher at school, he did provide valuable information about his favorite activities, pets, toys, and treats. This information was later used by the therapist in his suggestions to the parents and teacher concerning the development of a treatment program.

Summary of Behavioral Treatment and Ongoing Assessment

The interview with Roland completed the initial assessment phase of the program. At this point, the therapist organized all the data and presented the parents and teacher with a conceptualization of the problem. This enabled him to work with the teacher in delineating appropriate behaviors as targets for change.

Focusing on the relevant environmental antecedents (such as subjects and classroom activities), the therapist suggested to the parents that Roland did indeed exhibit problems at school. He hypothesized to the teacher that Roland was most likely to misbehave when he was not the direct focus of her attention. Problem behaviors became highly likely when teacher attention was off of him for more than a few minutes. Misbehaviors such as calling for the teacher, interrupting, speaking out of turn, non-compliance, and physical aggression, all resulted in more prolonged teacher attention. Even when this attention involved negative consequences, Roland was still getting what he had been accustomed to getting most of his life as an only child: exclusive adult attention. Teacher attention, therefore, served two purposes: it reinforced misconduct as a means of attention-getting and when negative, it served to maintain a cycle of negative and coercive interaction. Roland's persistence, perhaps shaped by the teacher's intermittent reinforcement, along with the pattern of mutual frustration, contributed to the negative and coercive nature of these classroom interactions.

The historical setting events were presented along with the current situational determinants to help the teacher to see Roland not as a naughty manipulative child, but as a child who had not yet learned to share the attention of significant adults with others. The therapist helped the parents to understand that although Roland was accustomed to a great deal of individual attention at home, his expectations and demands for teacher time and attention had to be moderated due to the needr of others.

The presentation of this conceptualization was followed by the selection of the most relevant targets for change. In this case, the observable maladaptive responses of calling out to the teacher in the classroom and making distracting noises seemed to be most appropriate. Non-compliance and physical aggression were hypothesized to be more likely when the teacher used coercive means to stop these behaviors. The teacher collaborated with the therapist in developing a program which essentially required her to ignore inappropriate behavior and to praise desirable behavior. Time out (a procedure which required Roland to sit alone in an empty room for five minutes) was used for physical aggression. Attention was withheld for noise making and calling out to the teacher. In addition to praising Roland for quiet, cooperative, and on-task behaviors, the teacher continued to tally misbehaviors unobtrusively with her golf counter and to record the total number of responses daily. She was warned that the ignoring would likely produce an initial increase in the problem behaviors before they would improve.

It can be seen on the graph that during the time the teacher praised good behavior and ignored bad behavior, the total number of maladaptive behaviors decreased from an average of 26 per day during baseline to 17 per day during the first phase of the modification program. Roland's teacher expressed satisfaction that the time out was effective in eliminating the aggression, but she complained that he was still disruptive in the class. When the therapist showed her a graph of the data she had collected, she was greatly encouraged that it indicated a decrease in disruptions. Thus, the continued assessment helped to maintain the teacher's morale and motivation to continue using the procedure during the next phase of the intervention.

In the next phase, the teacher continued to give praise and withheld attention, but in addition, she gave Roland the task of monitoring his own behavior. At the beginning of each day, she taped a single chart to his desk. At the end of each activity period, she gave him a star (which he could place in the appropriate square on the chart) if he had exhibited the criterion cooperative behaviors during the activity (e.g., working quietly and speaking in turn). If he interrupted (or physically aggressed), he forfeited the opportunity to earn a star for that activity. The teacher's direction in this "self-monitoring" process was gradually lessened as Roland began to show that he could reliably tell the teacher if he deserved a star at the end of an activity.

At the end of the day, Roland took his chart home and discussed his progress with his parents. These daily charts would then be posted on the refrigerator door. At the end of the week, Roland received a special reward if he had been able to obtain a criterion number of stars on his charts during the five days. It can be seen on the graph that when the teacher modification program was backed up with contingencies at home, the frequency of conduct disorder decreased from an average of 17 to 6 responses per day. Even though this improvement in Roland's behavior took place, Roland's parents decided to have the school authorities transfer him to a classroom with a black teacher. They argued that they had more confidence in this teacher, and that she would have a better relationship with Roland. The behavioral intervention was discontinued with the change in teachers. In follow-up phone conversations, the parents reported to the therapist that Roland was getting along well with his new teacher and was not showing behavioral problems in the classroom. No quantitative data were reported in these communications and the therapist never got an opportunity to do a follow-up observation in the classroom.

Discussion

Behavioral Interviews. The first step in child behavioral assessment usually involves interviewing significant adults in the child's life. In addition to providing important information relevant to the strength, severity and extent of problematic behaviors, interviews with significant adults provide some indication of the adults' motivation and ability to implement behavioral programs. In Roland's case, the most significant adults were his parents and his teacher. Because the etiology of child conduct problems is conceptualized in terms of coercive interactions between the child and adults, these interviews focused on identifying

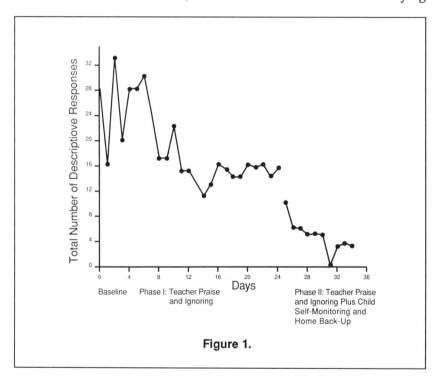

Figure 1.

those behaviors (both child and adult) which typified Roland's interactions. Even though the initial referral had indicated that the problem behaviors were occurring at school, it was still necessary to talk with the parents first. The parent interview allowed the therapist to determine how they perceived the current situational determinants maintaining the problematic behaviors. It also provided important historical and developmental data directly relevant to the problem. The teacher interview gathered equally important information, since the classroom was

209

the setting in which the problems occurred. In addition to providing information concerning the variables maintaining the behavior, the interview gave the therapist an opportunity to assess the adults' motivation and ability to participate in the treatment program (cf. Atkeson, & Forehand, 1981).

Interviews, even when behavioral, are subject to certain biases, however. Gelfand, Jenson, and Drew (1982) have observed that the degree of reliability of the information obtained in an interview will depend on the type of information gathered and characteristics of the individual being interviewed. For example, Evans and Nelson (1977) have noted that information related to emotions, feelings, attitudes, and child rearing practices have been found to be less accurate than the facts concerning the child's development. Although mother information has been shown to be more accurate than that of fathers, the information is more likely to be valid if both parents agree about the details of the problem. Mash and Terdal (1981) have observed that there are no data to indicate the validity of parent interview information for predicting treatment or treatment outcome. The responses of Roland's parents in the interview may have presented an overly favorable picture of his behavior at home, but this possibility did not seem to be directly relevant to the presenting problem which took place at school. For this reason, the therapist felt comfortable in moving quickly to an interview with the teacher once he had established that the parents did not perceive any behavioral problems at home.

Mash and Terdal (1981) have pointed out that "situation-specific views within behavioral assessment suggest that different interview informants may be appropriate for information related to different child settings." (p. 47) Because the setting for the problem was the classroom, a behavioral assessment of Roland's problem required an interview with his teacher. Most of the information directly relevant to the problem behaviors was provided in the interview with the teacher. But an interview with Roland was also scheduled. In behavioral assessment, the child interview does not typically focus on target problems since the child (especially when young) does not usually provide much information about target problems (O'Leary, & Johnson, 1979). Instead, the interview with the child is used to get an impression of the child's physical attributes as well as some of his cognitive and behavioral characteristics (e.g., verbal and social skills), his view of the problem, and his preference for reinforcers (Gelfand et al., 1982; O'Leary & Johnson, 1979; Mash & Terdal, 1981).

A number of efforts have been made to improve the validity and reliability of behavioral interviews. Evidence reviewed by Ciminero and Drabman (1977) suggests that more accurate information can be obtained when interview questions are specific. Structured interviews have been shown to produce more reliable information (Herjanic, Herjanic, Brown, & Wheatt, 1975) and may be clinically more useful than non-structured interviews (O'Leary & Johnson, 1979). Several behavior modifiers have devised structured interview formats which are useful in interviewing the parents and teachers of conduct disordered children (e.g., Gelfand & Hartmann, 1975; Holland, 1970; Patterson et al., 1975. Atkeson & Forehand (1981) have suggested that an interview format used by Hanf (1970) is extremely useful in structuring interviews with the parents of conduct disordered children.

Although these developments in behavioral interviewing have been very useful and hold great promise, the present empirical base on which the practice rests is somewhat limited and requires that interviewing be used in conjunction with other behavioral assessment procedures in order to provide a valid functional analysis of the referred problem (Atkeson & Forehand, 1981).

Behavioral Questionnaires and Inventories. In Roland's case, the information gathered in the interview was supplemented by data from parent and teacher questionnaires. Two instruments were chosen from among several available behavior checklists and rating scales. The Eyberg Child Behavior Inventory (Eyberg & Ross, 1978) was used to provide supplemental information regarding parental perception of Roland. The Walker Problem Checklist (Walker, 1970) was used to supplement the teacher's interview. The latter was especially designed for use by teachers (Walker, 1967), but it has also been used by parents to indicate conduct disordered child behaviors occurring at home. A study by Green, Forehand, and McMahon (1979) reported differential ratings for non-clinic and conduct disordered clinic-referred children on the acting-out and distractibility scales. It is interesting to note that Roland's highest scores were for these two scales. Although the Walker Behavioral Problem Checklist is clinically useful, there are other behavioral rating scales and checklists which have been used to assess conduct disorders.

Three which are frequently found in the research literature include the Becker Bipolar Adjective Checklist developed by Becker (1960), the Parent Attitude Test developed by Cowen, Huser, Beach, and Rappaport (1970), and the Behavior Problem Checklist developed by Peterson (1961). Ciminero and Drabman (1977) indicate that the Behavior Problem Checklist is the most extensively researched of these; but like the others, it has not been used extensively in assessing the effectiveness of behavioral treatment for conduct disorders. It is unfortunate that the therapist did not readminister the Walker at the end of

Roland's behavior modification program to see if changes in his behavior were accompanied by changes in the teacher's perceptions of
him on this particular instrument. As a means of substantiating that a
therapeutic change in behavior has occurred, any instrument, such as
the Walker, administered prior to use in behavior modification should
be readministered after its use.

Behavior Observation. The last, but perhaps most behavioral of all the
procedures employed in assessing this case, was the use of observational data. Ross (1981) has asserted that assessment, if it is to be behavioral,
"cannot be limited to second hand information provided by the child's
parents or teachers..." Rather it must involve direct observation of the
child in his natural environment. The observation of Roland's behavior
in his classroom provided important information regarding antecedents
and consequences of his disruptive responses.

Before the direct observation (first by the teacher and later by the
therapist) got under way, precise definitions of the target behaviors
were required. Such definitions served to maximize agreement while
minimizing inferences, misinterpretations, and guess work about what
problems were being assessed. (For example, it was agreed that behaviors defined as "disruptions" in the classroom involved Roland's
speaking out of turn, making noises, calling out to the teacher or going
over to her to make requests or demands of her while she worked with
someone else.)

Once the problem behaviors had been defined, one of several
methods for collecting observational data was chosen. Both the teacher
and therapist used the ABC method of assessment in making the initial
observations. The ABC method tallies the target behaviors along with
antecedents and consequences. Later, the teacher kept a simple tally of
all the defined behaviors occurring each day. These procedures for
recording ongoing observational data are examples of what is called the
tally method or event sampling. Sulzer and Mayer (1972) define event
sampling as a "procedure in which the frequency or duration of a
specific behavior is recorded over a specific period" (p. 263). They go on
to point out that the specific interval may, for instance, be a classroom
period (as in the observation by Roland's therapist) or a day (as in the
observations of Roland's teacher). This method was particularly suited
for use by Roland's teacher in recording her classroom observations because it was easy to use (i.e., she could keep her tally with a golf
counter). Sometimes event sampling is supplemented with observations of the response's duration. This was done when the therapist observed Roland's classroom behavior, but it was not practical to include

recordings of response duration as part of the teacher's daily observation.

Event sampling and recordings of response duration are best used when a discrete response which has a clear beginning and a clear ending is being recorded. Although they were useful in assessing Roland's behavior, most conduct disorder behaviors are not easily broken down into discrete units (i.e., it is difficult to discern where an episode of off-task behavior begins and ends). In such cases, it is better to use a time sampling or an interval method of recording. In time sampling, the observation period is broken up into equal blocks of time and the observer notes the occurrence or nonoccurrence of the target response (or responses) for that interval. Whether one uses an event sampling or an interval method in making direct observations of a child's behavior problems, these procedures can yield important quantitative data. In the process of collecting the data, important qualitative data can also be gathered. For example, had the therapist relied only on second hand reports of Roland's behavior such as that reported in the teacher's log, he would have known about particular responses emitted by the teacher in response to Roland's disruptive and noncompliant behaviors, but he would have missed the rage communicated in her demeanor during these interactions.

Despite its advantages, direct observation, like other behavioral assessment procedures, has its limitations. Among these are the greater expense, time, and energy required in comparison to traditional clinical assessment. Although direct observation is highly objective and noninferential, there is research indicating that it can be biased by both observers and those being observed. Kent and Foster (1977) in reviewing this research have observed that such data do not prove that such potential biases are the norm, only that they can occur. It is important to be ever mindful of the subjectivity involved in the behavioral observation process. Although behavioral observation is more objective than some other assessments, there still exist cultural differences which come with each individual. Every observer should be aware of this.

Gelfand et al. (1982) have suggested that observer bias in direct observation may be minimized by keeping observers as naive as possible about the child's background, but they acknowledge that this solution is not practical in most clinical settings. Concerning bias in those being observed, they have asserted that perhaps the greatest threat to the validity of direct observation is subject reactivity to it. In other words, the observation may influence the very behaviors it is meant to assess. The fact that Roland knew he was being watched by his teacher on a daily basis and that he might have known that he was being observed by the therapist in his classroom visit could have caused Roland to alter his behavior in a more or less favorable direction. However, there are studies suggesting that students (and teachers) are minimally reactive to classroom observation (Dubey, Kent, O'Leary, Broderick, & O'Leary, 1977; Mercatoris & Craighead, 1974; Nelson, Kapust, & Dorsey, 1978; Weinrott, Garrett, & Todd, 1978). Atkeson and Forehand (1981) have concluded that "although not without its own limitations, behavioral observation is the most accepted procedure for obtaining valid and reliable data pertaining to the child's problem behaviors and to the child's relevant interactions with others in his or her environment."

Behavioral observation does not always involve the assessment of the child by his teacher, therapist, or independent observer; increasingly, behavioral assessments have used data collected by the child himself (Gelfand et al., 1982). Such self-monitoring was a part of Roland's treatment and continuing assessment. As is the case with the behavioral observations mentioned above, reactivity can also result from self-observation. But the reactivity which is the result of self-monitoring is usually in the direction of desirable responses so that the observed inappropriate behaviors are likely to decrease while observed appropriate responses are likely to increase (Gelfand, et al., 1982). Mash and Terdal (1981) have cited a number of reviews studying the uses of self-monitoring in child assessment. They have observed that in most instances, child self-monitoring used in these studies has served mainly as a subset of procedures used to modify the behavior being monitored rather than as a source of information to be used in diagnosis, treatment formulation, or therapy evaluation. As a consequence, there has been little elaboration of the assessment functions of child self-monitoring (p. 53).

Behavioral Assessment Batteries. It can be seen from this discussion of Roland's case that it, in many ways, typifies the use of behavioral assessment procedures in clinical settings. In assessing Roland's problem behavior, the therapist made use of data sources which minimized inference and relied more heavily on objective data. Although direct observation, which Johnson and Bolstad (1973) have called the *sine qua non* of behavioral assessment, played a central role in the assessment of Roland's behavior, it was used in conjunction with other sources of data such as interviews and behavioral questionnaires. In the past, "secondary" sources of information such as verbal reports were looked at askance by those doing behavioral assessments, but Mash and Terdal (1981) have observed that there is now a lessening of emphasis on direct observation as an exclusive procedure. Rather, behavioral assessors have begun to rely more and more on combinations of behavioral assessment devices realizing that each may tap a different dimension of the same problem and, when taken together, may provide a more valid assessment of the problem than when used alone. No assessment procedure is equally applicable to every case. The combination of behavioral assessment procedures used to evaluate Roland was tailored to his unique needs and circumstances.

Social Validation of Behavioral Assessment and Therapy. How helpful were the assessment procedures used in Roland's case? There are several ways in which this question may be answered. If the therapist had readministered the Eyberg Behavior Inventory and the Walker Problem Behavior Checklist, he would have been able to detect whether there had been a change in parent and teacher perceptions of Roland at the end of the intervention. A follow-up classroom observation would have provided particularly useful information regarding changes in the target teacher-child interactions.

However, Atkeson and Forehand (1981) have questioned the sufficiency of the aforementioned treatment assessment strategies. They have argued along with Wolf (1978) that behavioral assessment procedures "must be expanded to include social validation of behavioral interventions." In this regard, several questions must be answered. First, what was the social significance of the intervention; how much were the assessment and treatment needed? In Roland's case, the immediate need was clear. Valuable time had been lost in class due to his misbehavior, and there is a possibility that he would have been taken out of the class if his behavior there had not changed. The long term significance of the problem also underlined the need for treatment and assessment. Roland's parents were concerned about him being stigmatized and labeled. Research has shown that children with severe conduct disorders are likely to exhibit similar patterns of behavior as adults if they are left untreated (Morris, 1956).

A second question which must be answered in socially validating the intervention relates to the social appropriateness of the intervention. How acceptable was the approach to those involved? In Roland's case, the use of behavioral assessment seemed clearly appropriate since it had been specifically requested by his parents, was accepted by his teacher, and led to the establishment of a treatment program which reduced the frequency of the problem behaviors. However, the approach was not endorsed without reservation. From the beginning, the parents had difficulty accepting reports of conduct problems in their child. They never fully accepted reports of the teacher and principal as being without prejudice. Even when a black educator observed Roland in class and reported disruptive behavior, the parents concluded that the problem was with the teacher rather than with their child. They then sought the intervention of a behavior therapist, but after accepting and participating in the behavioral assessment and treatment, and even after obtaining feedback of improved behavior, the parents chose to transfer their child to the class of a black teacher.

The third question which must be answered in the social validation process relates to the social importance of the treatment effects. How satisfied are the child and significant others with the results of the intervention? Roland's behavior did change after assessment and treatment. The results of the intervention did not leave the family content, however. The parents' removal of Roland to another class and their subsequent reports suggest that their own solution made them happier. The parents reported that Roland's new teacher was having no problems with him. One might hypothesize that the parents' solution and perceptions were correct, or one might hypothesize that they were rationalizing. Still another hypothesis is that Roland's behavior under the new teacher was appropriate because this bright child realized that there would be no excuse if his behavior was inappropriate with this last teacher. Whether or not this indicates Roland's satisfaction with the program is debatable. Kazdin (1977) has suggested that the third question can be answered in terms of subjective evaluation and social comparison. Roland's parents and teacher at first seemed to make their subjective evaluation clear in their expressions of satisfaction with the assessment and treatment results. But the subsequent actions of the parents contradicted this. Social comparison of the boy's behavior with that of his peers before and after treatment would have provided important information in evaluating the efficacy of Roland's assessment and treatment.

The relevance of the social evaluation process in assessing the efficacy of treatment seems particularly relevant to cases of minority child assessment. If such a process became a standard procedure in the evaluation of every behavioral assessment and treatment, many of the fears which some minority people have expressed about behavioral approaches to assessment might be allayed.

Both strength and weakness are evident in the application of behavioral assessment to this case. The case shows that even when evaluations are well done and as objective as possible, minority members may still feel mistreated. Behavioral assessments may be preferred because they yield relatively objective data to which all parties can be witness, but this alone may not be enough to restore the trust of minorities who have been so badly abused by past discrimination. The behavioral approach produced a relatively objective assessment of Roland's problem, but it did not completely overcome the fears and prejudices of his parents. Herein is underscored the need for assessors to look beyond the assessment instruments to the social context of the individuals being assessed. Such is the case regardless of the socioeconomic or minority status of the particular client. Such is also the case whether or not the assessment is behavioral.

Conclusions

That children can, and often do, find ingenious ways to get into trouble at school is not seriously debated by those familiar with child behavior and development. No one would argue that minority children never have problems and never need help. Controversy begins when a decision has to made about what can be done to remedy the problems. The author has shown in this chapter that those concerned about fairness and objectivity in the assessment of minority children's problems are not alone in their concerns. However, for minority children, the untoward effects of diagnostic imprecision, bias, and labeling may be compounded by racial bias in assessment. These biases often show up in psychological evaluations conducted at schools, where decisions about the disposition of a child in the early grades may affect the rest of his or her academic career and even life after leaving school.

The author has argued here that behavioral approaches in assessment, by virtue of their objectivity and noninferential empirically derived procedures, may be less prone to bias than other assessment procedures. To date, studies have not shown that behavioral assessment or behavioral assessors are immune to bias. But there are a number of studies showing that behavioral assessment approaches can be used to the advantage of black and other minority school children. Generally, these approaches are designed to meet the particular needs of the individual child. By virtue of this fact, each example of behavioral assessment may be less likely to discriminate against a child to whom it has been tailored.

The parents in the case illustration presented in this chapter expressed concerns which are shared by many minority parents whose children stand in need of assessment. They did not want their son to be labeled or stigmatized by a diagnostic assessment which might categorize him as being emotionally disturbed or as having some deepseated emotional problem. Their decision to contact a behavioral psychologist did not mean that all bias against their son would be eliminated. The psychologist they contacted was acutely sensitive to these bias issues and attempted to use techniques designed to be objective and to minimize the inferences which might reflect bias.

217

The case illustration along with the studies reviewed in this chapter show the promise and potential which behavioral assessment may have for helping minority children. The fact that behavior assessment can be tailored to the characteristics and needs of individual clients bodes well for the minority child who too often has been straight jacketed into assessment (and therapeutic procedures) standardized on and designed for non-minority children. Nevertheless, before these procedures can be unreservedly recommended to the use of those working with minority children, research is needed which will provide clear evidence of each procedure's efficacy and its nondiscriminatory nature. Such evidence is beginning to be collected. Normative data are also increasing in the field of behavioral assessment. As behavioral procedures become increasingly standardized, an effort must be made to insure that such standardization will help and not discriminate against minority children who will be assessed by them. Although hazards attend the use of behavioral assessment, they seem to be reduced in comparison to other forms of assessment. Future applications of behavioral approaches in assessing the problems of black and other minority children may demonstrate that this form of psychological assessment, rather than being a hazard, can be a great help.

References

Adams, H.W., & Turner, S.M. (1979). Editorial. *Journal of Behavioral Assessment,* *1,* 1-2.

Anderson, William H. (1982). *Ways in which the cognitive-behavioral therapist may assist parents and teachers in helping black children.* Paper presented at the annual meeting of the Association of Black Psychologists, Cincinnati, Ohio.

Atkeson, B.M., & Forehand, R. (1981). Conduct disorders. In E.J. Mash & L.G. Terdal, *Behavioral assessment of childhood disorders* (pp. 185-219). New York: Guilford Press.

Baer, D.M., Wolf, M.M., & Risley, T.R. (1968). Some current dimensions of applied behavior analysis. *Journal of Applied Behavior Analysis, 1,* 91-97.

Bandura, A. (1969). *Principles of behavior modification.* New York: Holt, Rinehart, & Winston.

Bandura, A. (1977). Self-efficacy: Toward a unifying theory of change. *Psychological Review, 84,* 191-215.

Becker, W.C. (1960). The relationship of factors in parental ratings of self and each other to the behavior of kindergarten children as rated by mothers, fathers, and teachers. *Journal of Consulting Psychology, 24,* 507-527.

Bijou, S.W., & Peterson, R.F. (1971). Functional analysis in the assessment of children. In P. McReynolds (Ed.), *Advances in psychological assessment* (Vol. 2). Palo Alto, CA: Science and Behavioral Books.

Ciminero, A.R., & Drabman, R.S. (1977). Current developments in the behavioral assessment of children. In B.B. Lahey, & A.E. Kazdin (Eds.), *Advances in clinical child psychology* (Vol. 1). New York: Plenum.

Civil Rights Commission (1973). *Teachers and students. Report V: Differences in teacher interaction with Mexican-American and Anglo students.* Washington, D.C.: U.S. Government Printing Office.

Comer, James P., & Poussaint, A.F. (1975). *Black child care.* New York: Simon & Schuster.

Cooper, J.O. (1974). *Measurement and analysis of behavioral techniques.* Columbus, Ohio: Charles E. Merrill.

Cowen, E.L., Huser, J., Beach, D.R., & Rappaport, J. (1970). Parental perceptions of young children and their relation to indexes of adjustment. *Journal of Consulting and Clinical Psychology, 34,* 97-103.

DeHoyos, A., & DeHoyos, G. (1965). Symptomatology differentials between Negro and white schizophrenics. *International Journal of Social Psychiatry, 11,* 245-255.

Dubey, D.R., Kent, R.N., O'Leary, S.G., Broderick, J.E., & O'Leary, K.D. (1977). Reactions of children and teachers to classroom observers: A series of controlled investigations. *Behavior Therapy, 8,* 887-897.

Evans, I.M., & Nelson, R.O. (1977). Assessment of child behavior problems. In A.R. Ciminero, K.D. Calhoun, & H.E. Adams (Eds.), *Handbook of behavioral assessment* (pp. 603-681). New York: Wiley.

Eyberg, S., & Ross, A.W. (1978). Assessment of child behavior problems: The validation of a new invntory. *Journal of Clinical Child Psychology, 7,* 113-116.

Fantuzzo, J., Harrell, K., & McLeod, M. (1979). Across-subject generalization of attending behavior as a function of self-regulation training. *Child Behavior Therapy, 1*(4), 313-321.

Gelfand, D.M., & Hartmann, D.P. (1975). *Child behavior analysis and therapy.* New York: Pergamon.

Gelfand, D.M., Jenson, W.R., & Drew, C.J. (1982). *Understanding child behavior disorders.* New York: Holt, Rinehart & Winston.

Goldfried, M., & Pomeranz, D. (1968). Role of assessment in behavior modification. *Psychological Reports, 23,* 75-87.

Gonzales, Eloy (1982). A cross-cultural comparison of the developmental items of five ethnic groups in the Southwest. *Journal of Personality Assessment, 46,* 26-31.

Green, K.D., Forehand, R., & McMahon, R.J. (1979). Parental manipulation of compliance and non-compliance in normal and deviant children. *Behavior Modification, 3,* 245-266.

Greenberg, J. (1977). How accurate is psychiatry? *Science News, 112,* 28-29.

Gross, H.S., Herbert, M.R., Knatterud, G.L., & Donner, L. (1969). The effect of race and sex on the variation of diagnosis and disposition in a psychiatric emergency room. *Journal of Nervous and Mental Disease, 148,* 628-642.

Guskin, S.L., Bartel, N.R., & MacMillan, D.L. (1975). Perspective of the labeled child. In N. Hobbs (Ed.), *Issues in the classification of children* (pp. 189-212). San Francisco: Jossey-Bass.

Hanf, C. (1970). *Shaping mothers to shape their children's behavior.* Unpublished manuscript, University of Oregon Medical School.

Hayes, C.S. (1978). Effects of race, success, and failure on children's self-reward. *The Journal of Genetic Psychology, 133,* 301-302.

Hayes, W.A. (1980). Radical black behaviorism. In R.L. Jones (Ed.), *Black psychology* (pp. 37-47). New York: Harper & Row.

Herjanic, B., Herjanic, M., Brown, F., & Wheatt, T. (1975). Are children reliable reporters? *Journal of Abnormal Child Psychology, 3,* 41-48.

Holland, C.J. (1970). An interview guide for behavioral counseling with parents. *Behavior Therapy, 1,* 70-79.

Jackson, G.C. (1976). Is behavior therapy a threat to black clients? *Journal of the National Medical Association, 68,* 362-367.

Johnson, S.M., & Bolstad, O.D. (1973). Methodological issues in naturalistic observation. Some problems and solutions for field research. In L.A. Hamerlynck, L.C. Handy, & E.J. Mash (Eds.), *Behavior changes: Methodology, concepts and practice.* Champaign, Ill: Research Press.

Kamin, L.J. (1974). *The science and politics of IQ.* New York: John Wiley & Sons.

Kanfer, F.H. (1979). A few comments on the current status of behavioral assessment. *Behavioral Assessment, 1,* 37-39.

Kanfer, F.H., & Phillips, J.S. (1970). *Learning foundations of behavior therapy.* New York: Wiley.

Kanfer, F.H., & Saslow, G. (1965). Behavioral diagnosis. *Archives of General Psychiatry, 12,* 529-538.

Kanfer, F.H., & Saslow, G. (1969). Behavioral diagnosis. In C.M. Franks (Ed.), *Behavior therapy: Appraisal and status* (pp. 417-444). New York: McGraw-Hill.

Karoly, P. Self-management problems in children. (1981). In E.J. Mash, & L.G. Terdal (Eds.), *Behavioral assessment of childhood disorders* (pp. 79-126). New York: Guilford Press.

Kaufman, A.S., Swan, W.W., & Wood, M.M. (1980). Do parents, teachers and psychoeducational evaluators agree in their perceptions of the problems of black and white emotionally disturbed children? *Psychology in the Schools, 17*(2), 185-191.

Kazdin, A.E. (1977). Assessing the clinical or applied importance of behavior change through social validation. *Behavior Modification, 1,* 427-452.

Kent, R.N., & Foster, S.L. (1977). Direct observation procedures: Methodological issues in naturalistic settings. In A.R. Ciminero, K.S. Calhoun, & H.E. Adams (Eds.), *Handbook of behavioral assessment* (pp. 279-328). New York: Wiley.

Lambert, N.M. (1981). Psychological evidence in Larry P. v. Wilson Riles: An evaluation by a witness for the defense. *American Psychologist, 36*(9), 937-952.

Lietz, J.J., & Gregory, M.K. (1978). Pupil race and sex determinants of office and exceptional educational referrals. *Educational Research Quarterly, 3*(2), 61-66.

Madden, N.A., Russon, C.D., & Cataldo, M.D. (1980). Behavioral treatment of pica in children with lead poisoning. *Child Behavior Therapy, 2*(4), 67-81.

Mash, E.J. (1979). What is behavioral assessment? *Behavioral Assessment, 1,* 23-29.

Mash, E.J., & Terdal, L.G. (1981). *Behavioral assessment of childhood disorders.* New York: Guilford Press.

Mash, E.J., & Terdal, L.G. (1981). Behavioral assessment of childhood disturbances. In E.J. Mash, & L.G. Terdal, *Behavioral assessment of childhood disorders* (pp. 3-76). New York: Guilford Press.

Masters, J.C., & Peskay, J. (1972). Effects of race, socioeconomic status, and success or failure upon contingent and non-contingent self-reinforcement in children. *Developmental Psychology, 7,* 139-145.

Meichenbaum, D. (1977). *Cognitive-behavior modification: An integrative approach.* New York: Plenum.

Mercatoris, M., & Craighead, W.E. (1974). The effects of non-participant observation on teacher and pupil classroom behavior. *Journal of Educational Psychology, 66,* 512-519.

Mercer, J.R. (1975, a). Psychological assessment and the rights of children. In N. Hobbs (Ed.), *The classification of children* (Vol. 1) (pp. 130-158). San Francisco: Jossey-Bass.

Mercer, J.R. (1975, b). Sociocultural factors in educational labeling. In M.J. Begab & S.A. Richardson (Eds.), *The mentally retarded and society: A social science perspective.* Baltimore: University Park Press.

Miller, L.K., & Schneider, R. (1970). The use of a token system in project Head Start. *Journal of Applied Behavior Analysis, 3,* 213-220.

Mischel, W. (1973). Toward a cognitive social learning reconceptualization of personality. *Psychological Review, 80,* 252-283.

Mischel, W. (1979). On the interface of cognition and personality: Beyond the person-situation debate. *American Psychologist, 34,* 740-754.

Morris, H.H. (1956). Aggressive behavior disorders in children: A follow-up study. *American Journal of Psychiatry, 112,* 991-997.

Nathan, P.E., & Harris, S.L. (1980). *Psychopathology and society.* New York: McGraw-Hill.

Nelson, R.O., & Hayes, S.C. (1979). Some current dimensions of behavioral assessment. *Behavioral Assessment, 1,* 1-16.

Nelson, R.O., Kapust, J.A., & Dorsey, B.L. (1978). Minimal reactivity to overt classroom observations on school and teacher behaviors. *Behavior Therapy, 8,* 695-702.

Noland, D.A., Arnold, J., & Clement, P.W. (1980). Self-reinforcement by underachieving under-controlled girls. *Psychological Reports, 47*(2), 671-678.

O'Leary, K.D. (1979). Behavioral assessment. *Behavioral Assessment, 1,* 31-36.

O'Leary, K.D., & Johnson, S.G. (1979). Psychological assessment. In H.C. Quay, & J.S. Werry (Eds.), *Psychopathological disorders of childhood* (2nd ed.) (pp. 210-246). New York: Wiley.

Patterson, G.R. (1976). The aggressive child: Victim and architect of a coercive system. In E.J. Mash, L.A. Hamerlynck, & L.C. Handy (Eds.), *Behavior modification and families* (pp. 267-316). New York: Brunner/Mazel.

Patterson, G.R., Reid, J.B., Jones, R., & Conger, R.E. (1975). *A social learning approach to family intervention: Families with aggressive children* (Vol. 1). Eugene, Oregon: Castalia.

Peterson, D.R. (1961). Behavior problems of middle childhood. *Journal of Consulting Psychology, 25*, 205-209.

Rollins, H.A., & McCandless, B.R., Thompson, M., & Brassell, W.R. (1974). Project success environment: An extended application of contingency management in inner-city schools. *Journal of Educational Psychology, 66*, 167-178.

Ross, A.O. (1981). *Child behavior therapy: Principles, procedures and empirical basis.* New York: John Wiley.

Sibley, S., Abbott, M., & Cooper, B. (1969). Modification of the classroom behavior of a "disadvantaged" kindergarten boy by social reinforcement and isolation. *Journal of Experimental and Child Psychology, 7*, 203-219.

Singer, B.D. (1967). Some implications of differential psychiatric treatment of Negro and white patients. *Social Science and Medicine, 1*, 77-83.

Skinner, B.F. (1953). *Science and human behavior.* New York: Macmillan.

Spitzer, R.L., & Fliess, J.L. (1974). A reanalysis of the reliability of psychiatric diagnosis. *British Journal of Psychiatry, 125*, 341-347.

Sulzer, B., & Meyer, G.R. (1972). *Behavior modification procedures for school personnel.* New York: Holt, Rinehart & Winston.

Sulzer-Azaroff, E., & Meyer, G.R. (1977). *Applying behavior-analysis procedures with children and youth.* New York: Holt, Rinehart & Winston.

Turner, S.M. (1982). Behavior modification and black populations. In S.M. Turner and R. Jones (Eds.), *Behavior modification in black populations: Psychosocial issues and empirical findings* (1-19). New York: Plenum.

Turner, S.M., & Jones, R. (Eds.) (1982). *Behavior modification in black populations: Psychosocial issues and empirical findings.* New York: Plenum.

Ullman, L.P., & Krasner, L. (Eds.) (1965). *Case studies in behavior modification.* New York: Holt, Rinehart & Winston.

Wahler, R.G. (1976). Deviant child behavior in the family: Developmental speculations and behavior change strategies. In H. Leitenberg (Ed.), *Handbook of behavior modification and behavior therapy* (pp. 516-543). Englewood Cliffs, NJ: Prentice Hall.

Walker, H.M. (1967). Construction and validation of a behavior checklist for identification of children with behavior problems. *Dissertation Abstracts, 28*, 978-979.

Walker, H.M. (1970). *The Walker Problem Behavior Identification Checklist.* Los Angeles: Psychological Services.

Ward, M.H., & Baker, B.L. (1968). Reinforcement therapy in the classroom. *Journal of Applied Behavior Analysis, 1*, 323-328.

Wasik, B.H., Senn, K., Welch, R.H., & Cooper, B.R. (1969). Behavior modification with culturally deprived children: Two case studies. *Journal of Applied Behavior Analysis, 2*, 181-194.

Weinrott, M.R., Garrett, B., & Todd, N. (1978). The influence of observer presence on classroom behavior. *Behavior Therapy, 9*, 900-911.

Williams, R.L. (1974). The problem of match and mismatch in testing black children. In L. Miller (Ed.), *The testing of black students: A symposium* (pp. 17-30). Englewood Cliffs, NJ: Prentice Hall.

Wilson, A.N. (1978). *The developmental psychology of the black child.* New York: Africana Research Publications.

Wolf, M.M. (1978). Social validity: The case for subjective measurement or how applied behavior analysis is finding its heart. *Journal of Applied Behavior Analysis, 11,* 203-214.

Wright, J.B., & Isenstein, V.R. (1975). *Psychological tests and minorities.* U.S. Dept. of HEW.

BEHAVIORAL ASSESSMENT AND SPECIAL EDUCATION EVALUATION: A SUCCESSFUL AND NECESSARY MARRIAGE

John M. Taylor

In recent years, there has been considerable discussion on the part of parents, professionals, and governmental agencies regarding a disproportionate overinclusion of minority children in special education programs (Cleary, Humphreys, Kendrick, & Wesman, 1975; Dunn, 1968; Heller, Holtzman & Messick, 1982; Hobbs, 1975; Jones, 1978; Mercer, 1973; Reschly, 1980; Tucker, 1980). The magnitude of this concern was highlighted in a recent United States General Accounting Office (GAO) report entitled "Disparities Still Exist in Who Gets Special Education."

> Black special education students are clearly overrepresented in programs for the educable mentally retarded. Over 40 percent of these (black special education) students are in educable mentally retarded programs. They are also the top proportion (6 percent) participating in programs for the emotionally disturbed and the trainable mentally retarded (4.7 percent). (U.S.G.A.O., 1981, pp. 61-63)

Other findings of this report indicate that Asian American children are overrepresented in programs for the speech impaired, and that the proportion of American Indian children in programs for the learning disabled is greater than for any other racial/ethnic group. In light of the findings of the many studies reviewed in the GAO report, the authors concluded that "the forecast for success of congressional safeguards against the overclassification of disadvantaged and minority group children as handicapped seems guarded." (p. 81)

This brings us to the issue of evaluation procedures and the contribution of inappropriate and less than comprehensive procedures in the misidentification of handicapped children, and the disproportionate placement of minority children in special education programs. Efforts to reduce assessment bias have included attempts to develop new "non-biased" instruments (Mercer, 1979), or to extend the breadth of evaluation procedures so that more instruments which purport to control for cultural/ethnic differences are utilized as part of the evaluation process (CORRC, 1979; Louisiana S.D.E., 1978; Michigan D.E., 1981; Nazzaro, undated; New Jersey S.D.E., 1980). Others have developed local or state norms for existing instruments (Reschly, Grimes, & Ross-Reynolds, 1981). Whether or not such efforts will ultimately result in less disproportionate placement or more effective services for children is questionable, however. Many noted critics contend that the development of "fair" tests will not result in non-discriminatory assessment (Duffy, Salvia, Tucker, & Ysseldyke, 1981; Salvia & Ysseldyke, 1978; Ysseldyke, 1978; Ysseldyke & Regan, 1979).

They suggest instead an assessment process which includes direct classroom intervention as an essential first component of the evaluation process (Heller, Holtzman, & Messick, 1982; Louisiana S.D.E., 1981; Tucker, 1977; Ysseldyke & Regan, 1979). Referred to by some as psychosituational assessment (Bardon, Bennett, Bruchez, & Sanderson, 1976; Bersoff & Grieger, 1971; Dickinson, 1978; Ellett & Bersoff, 1976), such practices in recent years have been subsumed under the broader label of behavioral assessment.

A behavioral assessment approach emphasizes the specification of problems in measurable terms, the identification of controlling variables, the selection and implementation of a treatment (intervention) for problem resolution, and the measurement of the effectiveness of the treatment (Ciminero, Calhoun, & Adams, 1977; Nelson & Hayes, 1979). This approach has found widespread acceptance in the clinical treatment of individual and group problems as evidenced by the numerous books (Ciminero, Calhoun, & Adams, 1977; Hayes & Wilson, 1979; Hersen & Bellack, 1976; Mash & Terdall, 1980), and journals (*Behavioral Assessment; Journal of Behavioral Assessment*) now available. While behavior therapy techniques have been frequently utilized as a treatment procedure in various settings, behavioral assessment has been suggested as a recommended procedure for use in routine assessment practices in schools only recently.

Gresham (1982) described a useful behavioral assessment approach for the identification of behavior disorders in school children which focused on the measurement rather than intervention component of the process. Tombari (1981) clearly and concisely presented a comprehensive approach to the nonbiased assessment of emotionally disturbed children which included as essential components the identification, measurement, treatment/intervention, and follow-up evaluation of problem behaviors *prior* to the classification of the child as handicapped. The Louisiana State Department of Education (1981) has taken this recommended approach one step further by *requiring* behavioral assessment activities (e.g., observation, problem specification, measurement, intervention, measurement) as a component of the state mandated comprehensive special education evaluation criteria for suspected mildly handicapped students.

The obvious reasoning behind such requirements is that direct efforts to modify the inappropriate behavior in the classroom as part of the overall evaluation process may result in a reduction in the misidentification of handicapped children, the improvement of behavior in the regular classroom, a decrease in the unnecessary "labeling" of children in order for them to receive helpful services, direct assistance to both teachers and students, reduced costs for education and, coupled with the recent changes in traditional testing practices, an even more "non-biased" assessment.

The need for a behavioral approach has been recently expressed in a comprehensive treatise on the assessment and placement of children in special education prepared by the Panel on Selection and Placement of Students in Programs for the Mentally Retarded (Heller, Holtzman, & Messick, 1982). The panel's recommendations, following an in-depth review of assessment practices and special education, included a "two-phase" assessment process which begins first with an assessment of the child's learning environment (Phase 1), and proceeds to a comprehensive individual child assessment (Phase 2) "only after it has been established that he or she fails to learn in a variety of classroom settings under a variety of well conceived instructional strategies." (p. 69)

By first exhausting the resources of the current educational setting, the case described below is an example of "psychosituational" or "behavioral" assessment conducted in an effort to determine whether or not a minority student required more restrictive special education services.

Case Study

Student and Setting

The student, Raymond, was a deaf, nine year old black boy enrolled in a self contained program for elementary age hearing-impaired children in north Florida. An intellectual assessment (Leiter) conducted solely because it was "typically" done resulted in an IQ of 96.

Raymond was referred by his teachers in the hearing-impaired program because of his extreme acting-out and off-task behaviors in the classroom. He had been a disruptive factor in the school for the past two years, with reported inappropriate behaviors such as: punching, hitting, and pushing peers; running uncontrolled through the class and school; employing disruptive "silly" behaviors in seat; failing to complete work assignments; destroying property; and striking his teachers.

Attempts at controlling Raymond in the past included isolating him in a time-out room, restraining him in a chair, using praise and candy, and various token systems. A referral to a physician had been submitted by the school earlier in the school year with the expectation that medication would be prescribed to reduce his hyperactivity.

All previous efforts had failed. Raymond could outlast any punishment program; and reinforcing systems, such as praise and tokens, typically had not been utilized in a consistent or contingent manner. The majority of the staff at the school had given up on Raymond; they thought he was emotionally disturbed, and they were convinced that he could only be taught and controlled in a special institutionalized program. The school was considering recommending Raymond's transfer to a special education program for the emotionally disturbed, and requested the support of the school psychologist in the recommendation, since Raymond was enrolled in an exceptional student program.

Because Raymond lived in another county and was bused to this regional center, direct involvement with Raymond's home was limited. A decision was arbitrarily made that since time was short, home intervention efforts would not be possible; instead, we would focus on school-based intervention efforts.

Procedure

An agreement was reached with school personnel, all of whom were extremely cooperative and eager to help Raymond, that the school psychologist would support the recommendation for placement in a more restrictive setting if the teachers felt this recommendation was still necessary after first cooperating fully in the development of a behavioral intervention program during a two-month probationary period.

Anecdotal observations in the classroom and further conversation with Raymond's teacher resulted in agreement being reached on the "target behaviors" for intervention focus. The object of the intervention was to increase the percent of time spent engaged in "on-task" behavior. On-task was defined as paying attention to instructions and activities, working at appropriate times, and not engaging in aggression, destruction or refusals.

A simple observation system was then developed using an interval recording technique. Raymond was observed for approximately 45 minutes during each observation session. Each minute was divided into alternating 10 second "observe" and 10 second "record" intervals. Raymond was considered "on-task" only if he was on-task for the full 10 second interval. The observer (either the author—the school psychologist—or a school psychology intern) made simple observation forms to assist in data recording and analysis.

Baseline observation in Raymond's afternoon class, as shown in Figure 1, revealed that he was on-task an average of only 34% of the observation intervals. Raymond's off-task behaviors were frequently quite aggressive (striking or pushing others, throwing objects) or active (jumping on tables, running in and out of the room). The analysis of the classroom observation data suggested that Raymond's inappropriate behaviors were being maintained by the attention he received from his classmates. They laughed when he ran around the room and threw things, hit back when he struck them, and generally shifted their attention from the teacher to him. Raymond appeared to continue in his acting out behaviors until he received attention from his peers.

Our plan was to try and increase both peer and teacher approval for appropriate social as well as academic behaviors, and similarly, to decrease all forms of attention for misbehavior. A small box was constructed which contained two houselights, one red and one blue. The box was prominently located in the front of the room and was remotely controlled first by a psychological assistant and later by a teacher aide. The lights were used to cue Raymond and the class as to whether his behavior was acceptable or not.

As long as Raymond was on-task, the blue light was turned on. At the end of every continuous minute of appropriate social and academic behavior, the light operator would signal the teacher with a blue card to reinforce Raymond. This was done by displaying a token on the blackboard in the front of the room for all to see and by praising Raymond for his good behavior. If Raymond was not on-task, the red light was activated and if it remained on for 10 seconds or longer, the teacher was cued, and a token loss resulted. If at the end of the class period, Raymond had earned 30 or more tokens, the class as a whole received some reward, candy the first three days, and 15 minutes of free play time thereafter.

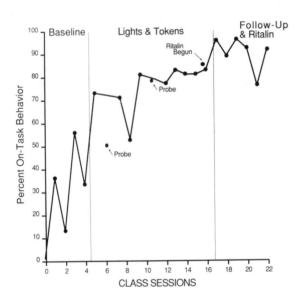

Figure 1.

Results

As Figure 1 indicates, on the very first day of the Light and Token Condition, Raymond's on-task behavior increased to 73% of the observation intervals and remained high throughout this condition, with an average on-task level near 75%. As a quick check to determine whether or not the lights and praise were responsible for this jump so soon, a probe was instituted on the next session, and a quick return to baseline level resulted. In the probe, lights and tokens were discontinued, and there was no reward at the end of class. On session 10, another probe was instituted. Here, the increased on-task was still evident, suggesting some maintenance of this behavior was occurring. With a substitute teacher present on session 13, Raymond's good behavior still continued to be displayed.

Beginning with session 17, lights, tokens, and rewards were discontinued and only observations were conducted, so it was in a sense a return to the baseline condition. Figure 1 clearly demonstrates that Raymond's behavior change was being maintained during this last condition. This may have been due first to increased teacher attention for good behavior as a reinforcer, since praise was paired with each token in the lights and token condition. Raymond received much more approval and contact from the teacher once his behavior was under control. In fact, Raymond probably received more attention now than did any other student as he was, both subjectively and objectively, the best behaved student in the class.

A dramatic decrease in peer approval for inappropriate behaviors also appeared to have helped maintain this change, and was perhaps itself under the control now of teacher approval and instructions. Also of possible importance is the fact that Raymond began taking the paradoxical stimulant Ritalin for his purported hyperactivity on session 16. The data presented here suggest a possible effect of Ritalin as evidenced by a nearly 10% increase in on-task behavior in the Follow-up and Ritalin Condition, but this increase is clearly minor when compared to the amount of change in the Lights and Tokens condition. As such, these results were shared with Raymond's physician and the Ritalin was eventually discontinued.

As a result of this intervention, a change in placement was no longer deemed necessary. Standardized testing was not needed, and all parties involved were pleased with the outcome. Raymond continued to advance in school with his classmates in the hearing-impaired program, and at last report, was making satisfactory progress in high school as a "mainstreamed" hearing-impaired student.

Discussion

More often than not, non-biased assessment means the use of appropriately standardized tests, a measure of adaptive behavior, and an interpretation of results which takes into account the socio/political climate of the educational system and community. While such practices are followed with all referrals, they may still result in biased assessment practices and disproportionate placement.

Duffy, Salvia, Tucker, and Ysseldyke (1981) reviewed the major attempts to alleviate problems associated with bias in assessment and concluded that all efforts to date have failed because "the use of test data has been the biasing factor rather than the tests themselves" (p. 433). If we are to improve upon current practices, additional data are needed as part of the evaluation process. Rather than continuing to make placement decisions solely on the basis of "test scores," we must operationalize the assessment process to include attempts at direct intervention prior to conducting a formal individual evaluation.

The traditional evaluation of a child suspected of being emotionally disturbed (as was true in this case study) usually includes the "psychologist's observations of the student at the time of testing, an IQ test, norm-referenced achievement test, human figure drawing, and other projective techniques, such as the TAT, CAT, or Rorschach." (Tombari, 1981, p. 126) Such an evaluation conducted with this subject would have yielded little if any information useful for eliminating the behavior problems. Instead, the evaluation would have led to placement in a program for the emotionally disturbed (since the school was determined to have the student removed if his problem behavior continued).

In this case, a behavioral assessment approach to the resolution of the problem was attempted. The foci of the measurement were the problem behaviors identified by the teacher and verified through classroom observation. By systematically observing in the classroom setting, the behaviors of concern were specified and measured, and the possible controlling variables were identified. An intervention which involved the manipulation of the suspected controlling variables (peer and teacher attention) was designed and implemented, and the results of the intervention were closely monitored. The intervention was successful, and placemnt in a more restrictive setting and classification as emotionally disturbed were avoided. If the intervention had failed, the more traditional assessment would have been completed. "Following a genuine effort at classroom intervention, school psychologists can be more confident in judging whether a student is emotionally disturbed than if no interventions were tried and no data were gathered." (Tombari, 1981, p. 120) While previous "intervention" efforts had been attempted by the school staff, the inconsistencies in application and failure to utilize a systematic procedure in the classroom did not convince this author that the previous efforts had been "genuine."

While this case study illustrated the application of behavioral assessment procedures to the evaluation of a student already identified as handicapped who was being recommended for placement in a more restrictive setting, the process is just as applicable to newly referred students. Heller, Holtzman, and Messick (1982) articulated the utility of this approach on behalf of the Panel on Selection and Placement of Students in programs for the mentally retarded:

> A concern with disproportion per se dictates a focus on bias in assessment instruments and a search for instruments that will reduce disproportion. A concern with instructional utility leads to a search for assessment procedures and instruments that will aid in selecting or designing effective programs for all children. We believe that better assessment and instruction will in fact reduce disproportion, because minority children have disproportionately been the victims of poor instruction. We believe also that the problem should be attacked at its roots, which lie in the presumption that learning problems must imply deficiencies in the child and in consequent inattention to the role of education itself in creating and ameliorating these problems. (p. 72)

The inclusion of behavioral assessment procedures in the required comprehensive evaluation of suspected handicapped children will greatly reduce the bias inherent in our current practices, will result in more specific recommendations to teachers of the subsequently identified handicapped children, and will in many cases result in the successful modification of academic and social/personal difficulties such that a transfer to a more restrictive educational placement will no longer be necessary.

References

Bardon, J.I., Bennett, V.C., Bruchez, P.K., & Sanderson, R.A. (1976). Psychosituational classroom intervention: Rationale and description. *Journal of School Psychology, 2,* 97-104.

Bersoff, D.N., & Grieger, R.M. (1971). An interview model for psychosituational assessment of children's behavior. *American Journal of Orthopsychiatry, 41,* 483-493.

Ciminero, A.R., Calhoun, K.S., & Adams, H.E. (Eds.) (1977). *Handbook of Behavioral Assessment.* New York: Wiley Interscience.

Cleary, T.A., Humphreys, L., Kendrick, A., & Wesman, A. (1975). Educational uses of tests with disadvantaged students. *American Psychologist, 30,* 15-41.

CORRC (Coordinating Office of Regional Resource Centers) (1979). *With bias towards none: Volume III, A national survey of assessment programs and procedures.* Lexington: University of Kentucky.

Diana v. State Board of Education, C.A. No. C-70-37 (N.D. Cal. 1970); C.A. No. C-70-37 (N.D. Cal. 1973).

Dickinson, D.J. (1978). Direct assessment of behavioral and emotional problems. *Psychology in the Schools, 4,* 472-477.

Duffy, J.B., Salvia, J.A., Tucker, J., & Ysseldyke, J.E. (1981). Nonbiased assessment: A need for operationalism. *Exceptional Children, 47,* 427-434.

Dunn, L. (1968). Special education for the mildly retarded: Is much of it justifiable? *Exceptional Children, 35,* 5-22.

Ellett, C.D., & Bersoff, D.N. (1976, Nov). An integrated approach to the psychosituational assessment of behavior. *Professional Psychology,* 485-494.

Gresham, F.M. (1982). A model for the behavioral assessment of behavior disorders in children: Measurement considerations and practical application. *Journal of School Psychology, 2,* 131-144.

Haynes, S.N., & Wilson, C.C. (1979). *Behavioral assessment: Recent advances in methods, concepts, and applications.* San Francisco: Jossey-Bass.

Heller, K.A., Holtzman, W.H., & Messick, S. (Eds.) (1982). *Placing children in special education: A strategy for equity.* Washington, D.C.: National Academy Press.

Hersen, M., & Bellack, A. (Eds.) (1976). *Behavior assessment: A practical handbook.* New York: Pergamon.

Hobbs, N. (Ed.) (1975). *Issues in the classification of children.* San Francisco: Jossey-Bass.

Jones, R. (1978). Protection in evaluation procedures: Criteria and recommendations. In L. Morra (Ed.), *Developing criteria for evaluation of the protection in evaluation procedures of Public Law 94-142* (pp. 16-86). Washington, D.C.: U.S. Office of Education, Bureau of Education for the Handicapped.

Journal of Behavioral Assessment. New York: Plenum Press.

Larry P. et al. v. Wilson Riles et al., 343 F. Suppl. 1306 (N.D. Cal. 1972); 502 F. 2d 963 (8th Cir. 1974); 495 F. Supp. 926 (N.D. Cal. 1979); appeal docketed No. 80.4027 (9th Cir., Jan. 17, 1980).

Louisiana State Department of Education (1978). *Non-discriminatory intellectual assessment procedures.* Baton Rouge, LA.

Louisiana State Department of Education (1981). *Pupil appraisal handbook: Bulletin 1508.* Baton Rouge, LA.

Mash, B., & Terdal, L. (1980). *Behavioral assessment of childhood disorders.* New York: Guilford.

Mattie T. et al. v. Charles E. Holladay et al., C.A. No. DC-75- 31-S. (N.D. Miss. 1975).

Mercer, J.A. (1973). *Labeling the mentally retarded.* Berkeley, CA: University of California Press.

Mercer, J.A. (1979). *Technical manual: SOMPA: System of Multicultural Pluralistic Assessment.* New York: Psychological Corporation.

Michigan Department of Education (1981, June). *Invitational conference on non-biased psychological assessment for handicapped students: Conference proceedings.* Lansing, MI.

Nazzaro, J. (undated). *Non-discrimination in testing and evaluation: A CEC training institute.* Reston, VA: The Council for Exceptional Children.

Nelson, R.O., & Hayes, S.C. (1979). Some current dimensions of behavioral assessment. *Behavioral Assessment, 1,* 1-16.

New Jersey State Department of Education (1980, Nov). *The status of minority group representation in special education programs in the State of New Jersey: A summary report.* Trenton, NJ.

(PASE) Parents in Action on Special Education v. Joseph P. Hannon, No. 74-C-3586 (N.D. Ill. 1980).

Reschly, D. (1980). Nonbiased assessment and the mildly retarded. In T. Oakland, *Nonbiased assessment* (pp. 97-122). National School Psychology Inservice Training Network, University of Minnesota-Federal Bureau of Education for the Handicapped.

Reschly, D., Grimes, J., & Ross-Reynolds, J. (1981, June). *State norms for IQ, adaptive behavior, and sociocultural status: Implications for nonbiased assessment.* State of Iowa Department of Public Instruction, Des Moines, Iowa.

Salvia, J., & Ysseldyke, J. (1978). *Assessment in special and remedial education.* Boston: Houghton Mifflin.

Tombari, M.L. (1980). Nonbiased assessment of emotionally disturbed students. In T. Oakland, *Nonbiased assessment* (pp. 123-140). National School Psychology Inservice Training Network, University of Minnesota-Federal Bureau of Education for the Handicapped.

Tucker, J. (1980). Operationalizing the diagnostic-intervention process. In R.R. DeBlassie (Ed.), *Testing Mexican American Youth: A nondiscriminatory approach* (pp. 37-54). Hingham, MA: Teaching Resources Corporation.

Tucker, J.A. (1980). Ethnic disproportions in classes for the learning disabled issuing on non-biased assessment. *Journal of Special Education, 1,* 93-105.

(U.S.G.A.O.) (1981, Sept 30). United States General Accounting Office. *Disparities still exist in who gets special education.* Report No. IEP-81-1. Washington, D.C.: U.S. Government Printing Office.

Ysseldyke, J. (1978). *Implementation of the non-discriminatory assessment provisions of Public Law 94-142.* A position monograph prepared for the Bureau of Education for the Handicapped. Washington, D.C.: U.S. Government Printing Office.

Ysseldyke, J., & Regan, R.R. (1979). *Non-discriminatory assessment and decision making: Embedding assessment in the intervention process. (Monograph No. 7.)* Minneapolis: University of Minnesota, Institute for Research on Learning Disabilities.

Part 4
Bilingual Assessment

NONDISCRIMINATORY ASSESSMENT AND INFORMAL DATA GATHERING: THE CASE OF GONZALDO L.

Hermes T. Cervantes

Introduction

Since the early 1950s, there has been a growing awareness that linguistically different children need a unique type of academic assistance if they are to have an opportunity to succeed in school. Such children, along with ethnic minority children, are frequently excluded from participation in academic programs because they do not possess skills necessary to achieve in schools which reflect Anglo middle class attitudes, values, and characteristics. Many of these children have been relegated to special education classes because of assessment procedures that are unable to identify accurately handicapping conditions or to determine when academic failure is due to linguistic and culturally related characteristics which have not been taken into consideration in program offerings.

Overrepresentation of linguistically different children in special education has been attributed to traditional assessment procedures as well as the decision-making process used to diagnose handicapping conditions. The negative effects of inappropriate identification, programming, and placement on children's learning, social, and psychological development are significant (Dunn, 1968; Hobbs, 1975; Jones, 1972).

The assessment procedure is further complicated when the child being tested is non-English speaking, has limited English language proficiency, or is bilingual. There is, frequently, a lack of trained assessment personnel who can administer tests in the child's primary language and who can interpret test results in light of the child's linguistic and cultural characteristics. In addition, there is a lack of reliable and valid assessment instruments and strategies which have been normed on linguistically different children (Archuleta & Cervantes, 1981; Baca,

Cervantes, & Torres, 1978; Oakland, 1977; Silverman, Noa, & Russell, 1976).

However, Ysseldyke (1979) argues that assessment difficulties are a function of the people who administer them. He states:

> The discrimination occurring in assessment is as much a people problem as it is a problem specific to the use of tests. In an effort to eliminate bias and discrimination in assessment, it is high time we reject the practice of blaming tests and quit trying to find the fair test. We can more constructively and profitably address our efforts to the identification of ways to modify or eliminate human bias, both in and following assessment. (Ysseldyke, 1979, p. 102)

Ysseldyke goes on to suggest that the inappropriateness of assessment with linguistically, culturally, and ethnically different individuals may be more accurately viewed in terms of the way in which the assessment and decisionmaking process is carried out than in terms of the tools used in assessment. More specifically, this point of view of bias recognizes a variety of points in the assessment and decisionmaking process during which bias can occur. They include:

1. **Referral**—the possibility that students are not referred for special education consideration in the same ethnic, linguistic, cultural, or sex proportions as those that are representative of the school district population. Findings of disproportionate referral exist and have been reported by Greenleaf (1980) and Mercer (1973, 1979).

2. **Instrument Selection**—the possibility that special services personnel select inappropriate instruments for evaluating the abilities and skills of handicapped and language minority children referred for evaluation. An example of bias in instrument selection might be the selection of an English language achievement test for evaluating a Vietnamese child's language ability. Bennett (1979), Bernal (1975), Hilliard (1976), Laosa (1975), Lennon (1970), and Oakland (1977) indicate that instrument selection poses significant difficulties in assessment.

3. **Instrument Administration**—the possibility that tests, interviews, observations, etc., are administered or conducted in a manner that disadvantages handicapped or linguistically different children. This type of bias might result, for example, when assessment is conducted in a way that is inconsistent with the child's culture or socioeconomic background. Such inconsistencies are thought to affect the child's desire to respond positively to the task. Findings of this type of bias have been reported by Laosa (1975), and Miller and Chansky (1972).

4. **Instrument Interpretation**—the possibility that the results of assessment are inappropriately interpreted. An example of bias in inter-

pretation would be the interpretation of an intelligence test score as an indication of a child's inherited capacity. Results indicating that tests have been inappropriately interpreted have been reported by Bernal (1975), Warren and Brown (1973), and Ysseldyke, Algozzine, Regan and Potter (1980).

5. **Decision Making**—the possibility that decisions are biased by pupil characteristics such as ethnicity, socioeconomic status, sex, attractiveness, linguistic background, or disability label. An example of such bias would result if two students with similar test protocols but from different socioeconomic backgrounds, with one judged more attractive by some scale, had an unequal likelihood of being diagnosed as handicapped by special services staff. Laosa (1975), Ross and Salvia (1975), Salvia, Algozzine, and Sheare (1977), and Ysseldyke (1973), have reported such biases in decisionmaking.

The Bilingual Diagnostic-Intervention Process Used in the Case of Gonzaldo L.

With these above five points in mind, Ysseldyke and others (Cromwell, Blashfield & Strauss, 1975; Mercer, 1979; Ysseldyke, 1973, 1979; and Ysseldyke & Salvia, 1975; 1975) have developed a diagnostic-intervention process that was the model utilized in the case of Gonzaldo L.

Essentially, the diagnostic-intervention process includes the following: (a) Historical-etiological information, (b) Assessment of present behavior, (c) Defined treatments or interventions, and (d) Predictive outcomes or prognosis. To enhance its applicability to culturally, ethnically, and linguistically different individuals, Ysseldyke and his associates have further defined the assessment process based upon five conceptual models: (1) The Medical Model, (2) Social System Model, (3) The Psychoeducational Process Model, (4) The Task Analysis Model, and (5) The Pluralistic Model.

A schematic flow-chart was developed by Tucker (1977) and modified by Baca and Cervantes (1984) for linguistically different students. This schematic flow-chart is presented in Figure 1.

As can be seen from Figure 1, the bilingual diagnostic-intervention process used in the Gonzaldo L. case is a thorough and comprehensive assessment program that involves a team effort. Such a team must include the student's parents or guardians, the student's teacher (including the bilingual education resource teacher), a school administrator as well as other designated personnel.

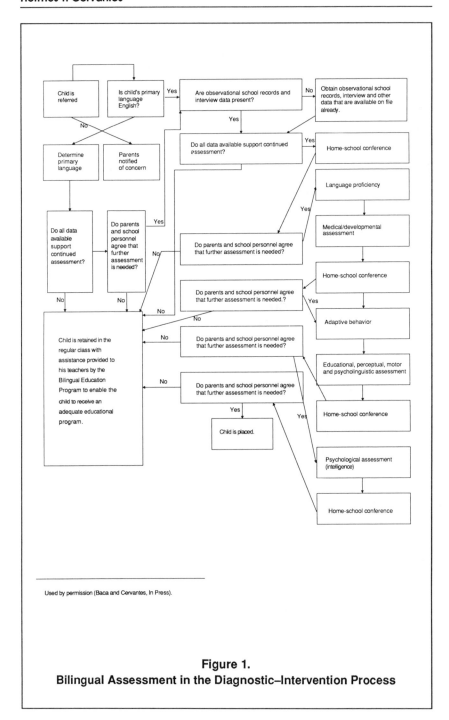

Figure 1.
Bilingual Assessment in the Diagnostic–Intervention Process

It should be clear from Figure 1 that the child's parents are an integral part of this process and at no time are school staff members allowed to make decisions about special education placement and programming without direct involvement of the parents or guardians in each step of the process.

Is Gonzaldo L. Severely Learning Disabled?

The schematic flow-chart provided in Figure 1 is followed in most cases and was used in the case of Gonzaldo L. Gonzaldo was an eleven year old student in fourth grade at Weston Elementary School which is located in a predominantly Hispanic community. Of the 484,000 people residing in the City and County of Denver, Colorado, 121,000, or 25%, are Hispanic. The Hispanic population resides throughout the city; however, there are considerable concentrations in the west side of Denver, where neighborhoods range between 40 and 75 percent Hispanic.

Weston Elementary School is located in this area. The community is described as fairly transient, and socioeconomic conditions are low by state standards. Median family income levels range from $4,484 to $7,693, whereas the median family income for all Denver families is $9,654. Educationally, 42% of the adults in this area have completed high school compared with 82% for the Denver metropolitan area.

After about a month in school, Gonzaldo was referred by the classroom teacher and bilingual resource teacher to the diagnostic team at Weston Elementary School. He was described by the referring teacher as quiet, soft-spoken, and shy. His primary language was Spanish although he could not read or write in Spanish according to the Bilingual Education teacher. She pointed out that he understood very little English. She also revealed that Gonzaldo had extremely poor visual-motor coordination and was unable to draw geometric shapes such as squares, diamonds, or triangles. He was unable to print his name. He was suspected of being severely learning disabled or possibly mentally retarded. A referral form was completed for Gonzaldo (see Table 1).

The Referral

Following the assessment diagram presented in Figure 1, the child was referred (see Table 1). An examination of the Student Referral Form reveals that Gonzaldo is a bilingual Spanish-speaking student with Spanish being the primary language spoken in the home according to

243

Table 1
Student Referral Form

Referring Person Dina A. Carlson   Title Teacher   Date Oct. 6, 1981
Parent Contacted by Carolyn Valdez   Title Bil. Ed. Res. Tchr.
Date 10/15/81
Pupil's Name Gonzaldo L.   Birthdate July 13, 1970   Age 11
Address 1123 E. Rio Grande St.   Phone # None
          Denver, CO 80204   Reachable by: _X_ day   __evening
Parent/Guardian Mother, Mrs.L.
School Weston Elementary   Grade 4th   Room # 117
Teacher Dina Carlson
Primary language spoken in home Spanish
Is student bilingual _X_ yes   ____no   ____barely

Basis for determination of bilingualism: Ms. Valdez spoke with Mrs. L and with Gonzaldo. Ms. Valdez states Gonzldo cannot read or write in Spanish. He understands very little English.

Health problems known: According to Ms. Valdez mother did not report severe health problems. An informal visual motor test by Ms. Valdez revealed extremely poor visual motor skills. He was unable to draw basic geometric images. He could not print his name.

Academic History (includes schools attended, grade levels, and most recent grades earned.)

Ms. Valdez and I visited with mother about his schooling. Mom states he attended K-3rd grade in Mexico and was doing well in school. She does not have any report cards but said he enjoyed school. It sounds like he might have attended a school in a small town.

Academic Functioning Level (be specific) Testing by Ms. Valdez (Boehm Test of Basic Skills) in Spanish:
Reading - 1.2 grade level
Math - 1.3 grade level

Student's Strengths (be specific and examine academic, social, emotional and other areas)

Gonzaldo does try to complete his assignments. He sits in his chair, does not bother anyone, is not abusive or disruptive in class socially, he keeps much to himself and does not interact much with the other students. He can follow simple and direct directions when given in Spanish.

Behavioral Functioning Level (be specific)
He appears overly quiet, soft spoken and shy. Much of his time is spent by himself. He does not talk to other children and on the playground; I have been told by the gym teacher that he just walks around the field. This behavior is also observed at lunch time, both in the lunchroom and on the playground.

Describe the Presenting Problem (be specific and include information when it was first observed, the situation in which it occurs, and how classmates respond)

Gonzaldo's primary problems are academic. Even in Spanish his skills in reading and math are at first grade level. He is unable to print his name and is awkward just holding a pencil. He is primarily Spanish-speaking and according to Ms. Valdez his visual-motor skills are erratic. He suspect that he is severely learning disabled or possibly mentally retarded.

Describe the measures you have taken to solve this problem (be specific examining possibly: changes in seating, assignments classes, tutoring by peers, adults or paraprofessional; conferences with pupil, parent or support staff; alternative programs)

Gonzaldo was moved next to a bilingual Spanish-speaking student that I used to explain things to him. With assistance from Ms. Valdez, academic assignments have been adjusted for him so that he could complete them. I referred him to the Bilingual Education Program for extra help the Bilingual Education Resource teacher who spoke with his mother. No health problems were reported.

Gonzaldo's academic history is cloudy, at best; his previous school records were unavailable. A conference with Ms. Carlson, Ms. Valdez, and Gonzaldo's mother, revealed that he had attended school in a small town in Mexico.

Academic testing, conducted in Spanish by the Bilingual Education Resource teacher, indicated that his reading and math skills were at beginning first grade level. Gonzaldo does appear to have some strengths. He sits in his chair and attempts to complete his academic assignments. In addition, he is not disruptive, abusive, or a problem in class. He can follow directions fairly well (if given in Spanish) when the directions are simple and direct and not primarily academic in nature. His behavior appears to be of some concern as he is seen as quiet, soft-spoken, and shy. The teacher also indicates that he keeps much to himself, and does not play with other children at gym time or during the lunch period.

According to the classroom teacher, Gonzaldo's primary difficulties have to do with learning. For an eleven year old student in fourth grade, she points out, he cannot write his name and has trouble just holding his pencil. Some preliminary screening by the Bilingual Education Resource teacher revealed that his primary language was Spanish and his language skills in Spanish were simple and concrete. He was unable to read or write in Spanish. A cursory visual-motor screening test indicated that his eye-hand coordination was quite immature.

The classroom teacher has exerted some effort on behalf of Gonzaldo. She has placed him next to a bilingual student who can explain things to him and answer questions he might have. She has adjusted academic assignments for him with assistance from the Bilingual Education Resource teacher. Gonzaldo was referred to the Bilingual Education Program for additional assistance.

Primary Language Determination

Following notification to the parents of the teacher's concern, the question of the child's primary language was addressed according to Figure 1. Although it appeared that Spanish was the primary language, an informal sociolinguistic measure was administered individually to Gonzaldo's parents. The Home Bilingual Usage Estimate (HBUE) was selected as it appeared to be technically adequate according to Silverman, Noa, and Russell (1976). The HBUE is designed to measure Spanish language usage of the parents and other household members, in the home. It is important to note that this initial phase differs from a later phase where actual primary language proficiency is determined. At the latter phase, the domains of linguistic structures (grammar, phonology, semantics, and vocabulary) are evaluated more comprehensively.

The HBUE clearly indicated that Spanish was used exclusively by Gonzaldo, his parents, and other family members in the home. A subsequent meeting with his parents and members of the Weston Elementary School diagnostic team resulted in a recommendation for continued assessment. Diagnostic team specialists explained to Mr. and Mrs. L. in Spanish that Gonzaldo's present difficulties could be possibly related to a learning disability, previous school experiences, second language acquisition, or a combination of these factors.

All parties agreed that observational and school records as well as interview and other data should be obtained. According to Cervantes and his associates (Baca & Cervantes, 1984), these informal, observational data are extremely critical in the accurate diagnosis of severe learning disability. There is considerable evidence that standardized assessment procedures which rely excessively on achievement test performance tend to ignore the importance of the child's functioning in his particular sociocultural, economic, and linguistic environment (Archuleta & Cervantes, 1981; Baca & Cervantes, 1984; Cervantes & Baca, 1979; Laosa & Oakland, 1974; Mercer, 1974; Oakland, 1973; and Thorndike & Hagan, 1969). For this reason as well as for the safeguards included in Public Law 94-142, the Handicapped Children's Act (*Federal Register*, August 4, 1982) considerable effort is exerted in obtaining this informal data.

Thus far, information obtained suggests that Gonzaldo's current academic difficulties could be rlated to one or a combination of factors that include (1) situational problems related to adjustment to a new environment, (2) limited previous educational experiences, (3) emotional and/or behavioral problems, (4) second language learning, (5) learning disability, (6) sociocultural differences, (7) linguistic differences, and (8) physical and/or health problems. Without additional information, it is not possible to determine specifically which factor(s) are involved.

Observational and Interview Data

Table 2 and Table 3 contain observational and interview data on Gonzaldo. During the observation, Gonzaldo was working individually with the bilingual classroom teacher aide, Ms. Armijo. The classroom

Table 2
Classroom Observation

Student's Name Gonzaldo L.
School Weston Elem.
Grade 4th   **Room** #117
Teacher Name Dina Carlson

Student's needs as seen by referring person: Gonzaldo is significantly behind academically. As a fourth grader, his reading and math skills are at a first grade level. He seems to have visual motor problems.

Time of day morning
Length of Observation in Minutes 60

Classroom setting (be specific, including approximate number of students, seating, organization of classroom, daily schedule, etc.)

There are 28 students in this class seated at seven table groups of four each. The classroom reflects a warm, comfortable and relaxed atmosphere. On the walls around the room were many examples of the children's school work as well as on the bulletin boards.

Specific activity (reading, math, etc. - size of group, etc.)

Reading was in progress. Mrs. Carlson had a group of six students and the rest of the classroom was working independently. Ms. Joyce Armijo, a bilingual teacher aide, was working individually with Gonzaldo with the materials provided by Ms. Valdez.

Management and instructional techniques of teacher (be specific, including use of positive or negative reinforcement, verbal and non-verbal cues, etc. NOTE teacher-child interaction. How does teacher present materials, use of questioning, student answering, etc.)

Ms. Carlson is a very positive teacher and positive reinforcement in the form of praise was noted frequently. The classroom is well organized and there is a schedule (by hour) of things to be done that day. Ms. Armijo was observed to be sitting near Gonzaldo. He did not appear interested and was not paying attention. Ms. Armijo called his name several times for him to pay attention.

Observation of student's behavior with independent seat work assignments (be specific, including how well student completes work, attending to tasks, etc.)

At his seat he held his pencil awkwardly. A check of his printing showed it to be quite immature and primitive. He seemed self conscious and his his work with his left hand so others could not see his writing.

Observation of student's behavior in group situation (be specific, including group size, types of interactions between student and group members)

At his table there was minimal communication between Gonzaldo and the other three children around the table. He seemed san and did not smile much. He did not bother anyone and vice versa. Students who talked to him got short answers of just a few words.

Observation of student's interactions with peers as they relate to the classroom or other education setting (be specific, including how conversations are initiated, who initiates, how student responds, etc.)

Much of the interactions appear initiated by other students. They seem friendly to him but he responds with few words and seldom looks at them. He doesn't appear very happy.

Additional comments:

Child appears out of place.

Does the classroom teacher believe that the student's behavior during the observation period was typical of student's everyday school performance?

_X_ yes ___no

Observer Hector Ruybal
Title Social Worker
Date October 20, 1981

was described as warm, comfortable and relaxed. The walls and bulletin boards were decorated with the children's work.

During the time he was working with Ms. Armijo, Gonzaldo was apparently having difficulty. He did not appear interested and was not paying attention to the instruction being provided. A check with Ms. Armijo indicated that the reading material being used with Gonzaldo was at first grade level and had been provided by Ms. Valdez, the Bilingual Education Resource teacher.

Later, at his seat, Gonzaldo was seen to interact minimally with other children seated around his table. He did not appear happy and seldom smiled or laughed. He did not appear to be bothered by the other children and was pretty much left alone during the observation period. Conversation initiated by other bilingual Spanish-speaking students appeared only briefly to bring a smile to his face. Responses by Gonzaldo to his classmates were quite brief.

During a seat work assignment, Gonzaldo was observed holding his pencil awkwardly. His printing was immature and primitive. He appeared self-conscious and used his left hand to shield his scribblings from the view of other students as well as the observer.

Information gathered in the interview with the classroom teacher, the Bilingual Resource teacher, the student, and parents, is provided in Table 3. The classroom teacher thinks that Gonzaldo's academic difficulties are severe and not just related to his linguistic background. She feels that his extremely poor visual-motor coordination is significantly interfering with his classroom learning and would best be remediated in a special education program for students with severe learning disabilities. In addition, she believes that Gonzaldo should receive continued assistance through the Bilingual Education Program.

The student interview reveals that Gonzaldo is aware he is not doing as well as the other children in class; he is quite embarrassed by this fact. When asked whether he enjoys school, Gonzaldo indicated that he did not enjoy it and felt out of place there. However, Gonzaldo stated that he only attended his previous school for part of the academic year as he had to work and assist his parents. At present he prefers to return to their hometown in Mexico where he has friends and relatives.

The most revealing data were acquired through the interview with Gonzaldo's parents. They saw no significant academic problems and felt comfortable with his skills and abilities. However, when asked about previous schooling, the information obtained idicated that Gonzaldo had attended school sporadically and had missed much of third grade; he had to help his parents on the farm.

Mrs. L. indicated that Gonzaldo was born and raised in Aguililla, a small rural community located in the southwestern portion of the Sierra

Table 3
Referral Interview Summary

Student's Name Gonzaldo L.
School Weston
Grade 4th   **Room** #117

Teacher's Name Dina Carlson

Interviewer for teacher Hector Ruybal
Student Hector Ruybal

Parent H. Ruybal

Date of interview for teacher 10/19/81

Teacher interview (ask general open-ended questions such as, what is your major concern about the student? What could be done to help the student? etc.)

Ms. Carlson feels that Gonzaldo has severe academic problems that are more involved than just being bilingual. She feels he has poor visual motor problems that are interfering with his learning and thinks he belongs in a learning disabled program. Also, he should continue in the Bilingual Education Program.

Student interview (ask general open-ended questions such as, what do you enjoy doing at school on the playground, at home? What subjects are most fun or enjoyable? What makes them enjoyable or fun? What subjects are most difficult? What makes them difficult? etc.)

Gonzaldo says he knows he has problems and that he does not do as well as the other children. This is embarrassing to him. He says he does not enjoy school and feels out of place at school. He said he missed some school last year (third grade in Mexico) because he had to work and help his mom and dad. He would prefer to return home to Mexico with his parents where he has all his friends and relatives.

Parent interview (ask general open-ended questions such as, how do you see your child's progress at school? What subjects do you think your child enjoys most? Least? How does your child get along at home? School? Neighborhood? etc.)

Mr. and Mrs. L do not see any severe academic problems with Gonzaldo and think his skills and abilities are OK. When asked about school in Mexico, Mrs. L said he attended school off and on and missed much of third grade. He had to help them on the farm.

Mrs. L. said he was born and raised in Aguililla, a small rural community in Michoacan, Mexico. Gonzaldo, she stated, was responsible for herding twelve goats on their small farm. He would rise early on most days, take his goats to pasture and return at nightfall. He knew the names of each of his goats and their names came from their color, walk or disposition.

Neither she nor her husband could read or write in Spanish. Also, none of his eight brothers or sister could either. Three of his older brothers were employed as laborers in Coalcoman, a small town about 50 kilometers away. Two older sisters remained in Aguililla along with a younger brother and a grandmother to care for the farm. Gonzaldo had arrived in Denver with his parents and his sister, age 2.

Madre mountain range in the state of Michoacan, Mexico. His inconsistent school attendance was due to necessity, she said. Gonzaldo was responsible for herding twelve goats they had on their small farm. On most days, he would rise early in the morning, take his herd to pasture and return home only at dusk. Gonzaldo's mother fondly pointed out that Gonzaldo had names for each of his goats. Their names, she said, were taken from some particular characteristic such as their color, walk, or disposition.

Neither she nor her husband could read or write in Spanish. In addition, none of Gonzaldo's eight brothers and sisters could read or write. Three of his older brothers were employed as laborers in Coalcoman, a small town about fifty kilometers away. Two older sisters remained in Aguililla, along with a younger brother and a grandmother to care for the farm. Gonzaldo had arrived in Denver with his parents and his sister, aged two.

Diagnostic Team Conference

A diagnostic team conference was held at Weston Elementary School where the observational and interview data were presented. Although the possible existence of a severe learning disability was unresolved, significant information on Gonzaldo's background and previous experiences were obtained in the informal interview. Limited previous educational experiences, sociocultural differences, linguistic differences, and situational problems related to adjustment to a new environment were prominent factors. Because it would be impossible to show that the discrepancy between his achievement and ability was ""not primarily the result of environmental, cultural or economic disadvantage," (*Federal Register*, August 4, 1982, p. 33858), continued assessment was not recommended.

However, the diagnostic team recommended that Gonzaldo receive additional and intensive remediation through the Bilingual Education Program at the school. They further suggested that Gonzaldo be given additional time to adjust to a different and foreign environment and be given support to his developing a feeling of"comfortableness." English as a second language (ESL) instruction was not recommended until Gonzaldo appeared more adjusted to his new setting and until he was making considerable progress in Spanish oral language instruction.

A three month follow-up indicated that Gonzaldo was making progress both in adjustment and in his Spanish oral language skills. By early spring, he began Spanish reading instruction and basic penmanship.

Conclusions

The case of Gonzaldo L. demonstrates the importance of obtaining informal data such as primary language spoken in the home, observational data, and interview data. Although one could argue that such information would be routinely obtained at the school at the time of the student's registration, this is not generally the case. For the most part, all registration requires is that parents complete a variety of forms.

It is possible that the referral would have been questioned earlier if the classroom teacher or other bilingual staff member had interviewed Gonzaldo's parents. The assumption is that such individuals are experienced interviewers and know how to probe in sensitive areas. As the author has noted elsewhere, interviewing is best left to skilled professionals (Baca & Cervantes, 1984).

Over the period of time that the Bilingual-Diagnostic-Intervention Process has been in use, the number of linguistically different children placed in special education programs has decreased significantly. This state of affairs is not due entirely to this process but to P.L. 94-142, Colorado State legislation, and lawsuits, as well as to general community concern regarding linguistically different students.

Whether legislation, litigation, and related activities are having a detrimental effect on linguistically different, severely handicapped children who are not placed in special education programs can be debated (the assumption is the academic deficiencies of bilingual children are most appropriately remediated by special education placements). As the author and others have noted, this does not appear to be clearly the best course of action (Baca & Cervantes, 1984; Carlbrg, 1979; Carlberg & Kavale, 1980; Dunn, 1968; and Mercer, 1979, 1973).

Author's Note

This project was supported in part by the Center for Bilingual-Multicultural Research and Service, Boulder, Colorado. The opinions, procedures, and conclusions in this case do not necessarily reflect the policy of this agency or of the named school district. All the names of the participants have been changed.

References

Archuleta, K., & Cervantes, H.T. (1981). The misplaced child: Does linguistically different mean learning disabled? In P.C. Gonzales (Ed.), *Proceedings of the Eighth Annual International Bilingual Bicultural Education Conference* (pp. 292-295). Roslyn, VA: National Clearinghouse for Bilingual Education.

Baca, L.M., & Cervantes, H.T. (1984). *The bilingual special education interface.* St. Louis: C.V. Mosby Co.

Baca, L.M., Cervantes, H.T., & Torres, D.S. (1978). Uses of bilingual testing instruments in Colorado. *The Bilingual Journal, 3*, 10-14.

Bennett, R. (1979). *Basic measurement competence in special education teacher diagnosticians.* Unpublished doctoral dissertation, Teachers College, Columbia University.

Bernal, E.M. (1975). A response to educational uses of tests with disadvantaged students. *American Psychologist, 30*, 93-95.

Carlberg, C.G. (1979). Meta-analysis of the effects of special classes, resource rooms and other treatments on exceptional children. *Dissertation Abstracts, 40*, 1998-1999.

Carlberg, C.G., & Kavale, K. (1980). The efficacy of special versus regular class placement for exceptional children: A meta-analysis. *Journal of Special Education, 14*, 295-309.

Cervantes, H.T., & Baca, L.M. (1979). Assessing minority students: The role of adaptive behavior scales. *Journal of Non-White Concerns, 7*, 122-127.

Cromwell, R.L. (1975). Blashfield, R.K., & Strauss, J.S. Criteria for classification system. In N. Hobbs (Ed.), *Issues in the classification of children* (Vol. 1) (pp. 148-153). San Francisco: Jossey-Bass.

Dunn, L. (1968). Special education for the mildly retarded—Is much of it justifiable? *Exceptional Children, 35*, 5-22.

Federal Register, Wednesday, August 4, 1982: Part II, Department of Education, Office of Handicapped Children; Assistance to States for Education of Handicapped Children, Proposed Rules, Vol. 47, #150,33836-33860.

Greenleaf, W. (1980, May). *Work with SOMPA.* Paper presented at the BEHNIE-IEL Conference, Toward equity in the evaluation of children suspected of educational handicaps. Washington, D.C.

Hilliard, A.G. (1976). *Alternatives to IQ testing: An approach to the identification of gifted minority children.* Sacramento, CA: California State Department of Education.

Hobbs, N. (1975). *The futures of children.* San Francisco: Jossey-Bass.

Jones, R. (1972). Labels and stigma in special education. *Exceptional Children, 38*, 553-564.

Laosa, L.M. (1975). Bilingualism in three United States Hispanic groups: Contextual use of language by children and adults in their families. *Journal of Educational Psychology, 67*, 617-627.

Laosa, L.M. (1977). Nonbiased assessment of children's abilities: Historical antecedents and current issues. In T. Oakland (Ed.), *Psychological and educational assessment of minority children* (pp. 310-314). New York: Brunner/Mazel

Laosa, L.M., & Oakland, T.D. (1974, April). *Social control in mental health: Psychological assessment and the schools.* Paper presented at the 51st annual meeting of the American Orthopsychiatric Association, San Francisco.

Lennon, R.T. (1970). Testing: The question of bias. In T.J. Fitzgibbon (Ed.), *Evaluation in the inner city* (pp. 156-161). New York: Harcourt, Brace and World.

Mercer, J.R. (1973). *Labeling the mentally retarded.* Berkeley: University of California Press.

Mercer, J.R. (1974). A policy statement on assessment procedures and the rights of children. *Harvard Educational Review, 44,* 125-141.

Mercer, J.R. (1979). *System of multicultural pluralistic assessment.* New York: The Psychological Corporation.

Miller, C., & Chansky, N. (1972). Psychologists' scoring of WISC protocols. *Psychology in the Schools, 9,* 144-152.

Oakland, T.M. (1973). Assessing minority group children: Challenges for school psychologists. In T.M. Oakland & B.N. Phillips (Eds.), *Assessing minority group children,* (pp. 294-303). A special issue of the *Journal of School Psychology.* New York: Behavioral Publications.

Oakland, T.M. (1977). *Psychological and educational assessment of minority children.* New York: Brunner.

Ross, M., & Salvia, J. (1975). Attractiveness as a biasing factor in teacher judgments. *American Journal of Mental Deficiency, 80,* 96-98.

Salvia, J., Algazzino, B., & Sheare, J. (1977). Attractiveness and school achievement. *Journal of School Psychology, 15,* 60- 67.

Silverman, R.J., Noa, J.K., & Russell, R.H. (1976). *Oral language tests for bilingual students: An evaluation of language dominance and proficiency instruments.* Portland, ORE: Northwest Regional Educational Laboratory.

Thorndike, R.L., & Hagen, E. (1969). *Measurement and evaluation in psychology and education.* New York: John Wiley and Sons.

Tucker, J.A. (1977). Operationalizing the diagnostic intervention process. In T. Oakland (Ed.), *Psychological and educational assessment of minority children,* (pp. 91-111). New York: Brunner.

Warren, S., & Brown, W. (1973). Examiner scoring errors on individual intelligence tests. *Psychology in the Schools, 10,* 118- 122.

Ysseldyke, J.E. (1973). Diagnostic-prescriptive teaching: The search for aptitude-treatment interactions. In L. Mann, & D. Sabatino (Eds.), *The first review of special education* (pp. 23-33). Philadelphia: Buttonwood Farms.

Ysseldyke, J.E. (1979). Issues in psychoeducational assessment. In G.D. Phye, & D. Reschly (Eds.), *School psychology: Methods and role* (pp. 266-273). New York: Academic Press.

Ysseldyke, J., Algazzino, B., Regan, R., & Potter, J. (1980). Technical adequacy of tests used by professionals in simulated decision making. *Psychology in the Schools, 17,* 202-209.

Ysseldyke, J.E., & Salvia, J. (1974). Diagnostic-prescriptive teaching: Two models. *Exceptional Children, 41,* 181-186.

Ysseldyke, J.E., & Salvia, J. (1975). *Methodological considerations in aptitude treatment interaction research with intact groups.* University Park, PA: Mimeographed.

GLORIA: A BILINGUAL LANGUAGE/LEARNING DISABLED STUDENT

Henriette W. Langdon

Introduction

Four important mandates of Public Law 94-142 are: 1) modification of the regular school curriculum prior to referral to special education; 2) active participation of the parent(s) in the process of referral, assessment, and program planning; 3) assessment of a Limited-English-Proficient (LEP) student in his/her primary language when a learning/language handicap is suspected; and 4) initial placement in the least restrictive learning environment.

The case described below illustrates the application of these mandates in reference to an 10 year old female Mexican-American youngster. The use of language sampling in the school setting and home is utilized to further specify the degree of linguistic proficiency of the student.

Review of Current Practices

Despite a recent increase in the number of published studies on bilingual language development and instruction (summarized in Hatch, [1978]; Carrow-Woolfolk & Lynch [1982]; and McLaughlin [1982], to name a few), several questions are unresolved, especially: what should be expected, linguistically, of a youngster living in a bilingual environment at a given age, and what are the best techniques to enhance the learning of a second language? Research from Canadian studies offers some answers. Yet, they are not always applicable to minority language groups in the United States. Some of the differences are attributed to the teaching models utilized and the motivation of the students as well as the expectations of teachers (Tucker, 1975).

At the same time, there have been an increasing number of published assessment materials for primarily Spanish-speaking students which report normative data. However, they must be used cautiously since they were normed on a relatively small sample size within a limited geographic location (Del Rió Language Screening Test, 1975), they have been developed at an experimental stage (Spanish version of the Illinois Test of Psycholinguistic Abilities, 1980), or they have been normed on a specific geographic population (Pruebas de Expresión Oral y Percepción de la Lengua Española, 1981). Also, language assessment tools for bilingual students older than 10 years of age are virtually non-existent with the exception of the Ber-Sil Receptive Vocabulary Test, (1972) and the Spanish version of the Woodcock Language Proficiency Battery (1982). Similar tests for English-speaking students are also limited, although the number is increasing (e.g., Clinical Evaluation of Language Functions, 1980, and the Word Test, 1981).

Determination of the native language proficiency of a LEP student becomes important when advancement in the second language is slower than that of students with similar bilingual backgrounds. Thus, normative data need to be interpreted with caution; more reliance should be placed on the linguistic process involved. Also, a complete linguistic history gathered from previous records and parental input is crucial. The final diagnosis of a language disability needs to be completed with supplementary data from teachers who have actively worked with the student. In addition, a psychological assessment may be needed to determine the discrepancy between the student's present level of performance and general learning ability.

Recent studies indicate that a LEP student may need up to two years to gain conversational skills in English and up to seven to reach academic skills equivalent to his/her native English-speaking peers (Cummins, 1981). The present writer feels that a LEP student could be assessed prior to the two years, inasmuch as learning problems may exist from the beginning and thus could hinder the acquisition of the new language. As a matter of fact, it has been her experience that an assessment in the second language *as well as* in the native language is very beneficial in program planning and has intercepted student problems of potentially greater magnitude.

The Student's Background Information

Reason for Referral

Gloria is a 10 year old Mexican-American child enrolled in an all-English third grade program. Her teacher is concerned because Gloria is excessively quiet. She seldom speaks with other children (in either English or Spanish) and her classroom participation is limited. Gloria was dismissed from the bilingual program at the end of the prior year as her skills in the second language were judged adequate to qualify for an all-English program. Despite good decoding skills in English, Gloria has difficulty comprehending what she reads. Similar problems had been noted in Spanish reading in the previous grades. Her math computation skills are grade level appropriate.

Developmental History

Gloria's general motor and speech developmental milestones were reported by her mother as occurring within age level expectancy. No serious health problems were reported other than frequent ear infections which persisted throughout childhood and continue to recur occasionally. (Her last pure tone hearing test prior to the initial testing was normal for both ears.)

Social and Educational History

Gloria is an only child. Both parents are Spanish-speaking and their English is limited; they need interpreters during parent conferences. Their education was terminated after the second grade and they are employed as farm workers. Gloria was born in the United States and has resided in this country most of her life. She spent one year in Mexico when she was in the first grade. She did not attend school while in Mexico and was, therefore, enrolled in the first grade upon her return to the United States. Mrs. R. reports that because the family lives on an isolated farm, Gloria has had limited peer interaction prior to entering school.

Gloria attended a bilingual kindergarten, first, and second grades at the same school she is presently attending.

Modification of the Regular Program

Despite Gloria's "graduating" from a bilingual class, her teacher had noticed learning difficulties not apparent in other youngsters of similar language backgrounds. Gloria had been receiving intensive English as a Second Language instruction and individualized reading while in the third grade. Her progress had been slow.

Initial Testing (May of 1981—End of Third Grade)

Prior to testing, Mr. and Mrs. R. were invited for a conference to discuss Gloria's progress and the reason for language and academic testing. The interview was translated into Spanish. Mrs. R. reported that Gloria was very talkative at home and speculated that she did not talk very much at school due to shyness. Mrs. R. reported that Gloria had no language difficulties in Spanish. Permission was obtained to conduct a bilingual language assessment by two Speech and Language Specialists, native speakers of English and Spanish respectively, as well as academic testing in English (since this had been Gloria's main language of instruction).

Tests Administered

A variety of tests were utilized to assess Gloria's receptive and expressive language skills in both English and Spanish and present academic skills.

Language Assessment

Results

Gloria is still Spanish language dominant. (Her overall language performance in that language was slightly better than in English.) However, her proficiency in either language was significantly below age expectancy. She had the greatest difficulty with tasks that required the processing of material presented orally. This included remembering specific sentence structures, making auditory associations and com-

Language Assessment

Area Tested	Names of Tests	
	English	Spanish
Receptive Vocabulary	Peabody-Picture Vocabulary Test (Form B)	Ber-Sil
Verbal Opposites	Dos Amigos Detroit subtest	Dos Amigos
Sentence Repetition	Del Rió Detroit subtest	Del Rió
Auditory	Illinois Test of Psycholinguistic Abilities (ITPA)	ITPA (Spanish version)
Language Sample	Carrow Elicited Language Inventory. Conversation with examiner	Conversation with examiner, with parents (at home) and a relative.

Academic Assessment

Math		
Reading (decoding)	Peabody Individual Achievement Test (PIAT)	Not administered
Reading (comprehension)		
Spelling		
General Information		
Math computation and Concepts	Key Math	
Other	Informal assessment of writing skills	

prehending material that was presented verbally. Her discrimination at the word and sentence level was weak. She often misinterpreted what she heard (despite normal pure tone testing at that time). The discrepancy was 4 to 5 years in English and 2 to 3 years in Spanish. When this material was paired with visual stimuli, the discrepancy was one to two years in either language. This included tasks such as visual association, visual reception and visual closure.

Gloria used very short sentences to express herself in either language. Often her answers were one to two words long with minimal elaboration. She used short sentences to describe pictures or a show she had seen on TV. Frequent pauses were noted during which she appeared to search for words to express her thoughts. Also, there were repetitions of words and phrases. However, most of her comments were appropriate. These results were reported to Mr. and Mrs. R. prior to the Individualized Program Planning (IEP) meeting. Because they were dissatisfied with the evaluation of Gloria's expressive language, they were asked to tape record their conversations with her at home. The transcription of Gloria's conversation with each parent separately and a relative (parents' initiative) yielded similar results. The review of the transcribed tape assisted the parents in understanding the teachers' concerns and provided information on Gloria's language skills in various contexts.

The results of academic testing indicated Gloria could decode what she read at close to grade level expectancy in English. However, she had difficulty comprehending what she had read. Although her spelling was slightly below grade level (when she had to choose the best spelling among four alternatives as required with the PIAT), she had great difficulty generating words when they were dictated. She could not write more than one or two simple sentences when asked to write a short composition. She could perform simple computations but could not remember tables beyond the 2s and 3s and was unable to solve math word problems. Overall, her academic achievement was between the first and second grade levels.

Discussion

Gloria is a case of a youngster who is bilingual but does not have sufficient linguistic proficiency in either language to be successful in communicating her ideas beyond a very concrete level or to achieve in academic subjects which require the processing and synthesis of complex language. Her history of ear infections has very likely contributed to a slower language development in her primary language and interfered with a normal second language acquisition process. Middle ear pathology has an important impact on auditory perceptual skills. Brandes and Ehinger (1981) reported that the performance of a matched sample of children with and without middle ear pathology did not differ for nonverbal tests and visual perception tasks, but their performance differed on tasks which required the processing of auditory material. These findings stress the important implications middle ear pathology can have on the educational achievement of youngsters. Additionally, Gloria had to learn a new language upon entering school, become acquainted with a new environment (more contact with peers), and overcome a one year interruption of formal schooling. However, the individual help offered in the third grade was insufficient to enable her to catch up with peers of similar linguistic backgrounds. It is interesting to note that Gloria did not have strong language skills in either language. Hence, there was little possibility for a positive transfer from one language to the other. Thus, it appeared that a language disability was a contributing factor in her slow acquisition process of the second language and academic skills.

Development of the IEP and Program Placement

Upon the review of the above results with Gloria's parents, teacher, and assessment specialists, IEP participants decided that Gloria needed assistance in expanding her concepts and vocabulary knowledge as well as building her memory and expressive language skills. She also needed assistance in developing reading comprehension skills. To meet these goals, Gloria was enrolled in daily language therapy sessions offered by a Speech and Language Specialist as well as daily sessions with a Resource Specialist. All assistance was to be given in English since this had been her primary language of instruction during the past year. The parents were encouraged to continue speaking Spanish at home to enhance the language further and foster bilingualism.

Progress Review (May of 1982—End of Fourth Grade)

Gloria's progress was judged to be slow. Approximately one year's progress had been made in reading comprehension. She had gained some further skills in vocabulary and concepts. She was able to express some of her ideas with longer sentences and seemed more confident. She had acquired some friends and was "more talkative."

However, her gains did not seem substantial enough to warrant continuing progress in an upper grade class where greater skills in abstract vocabulary and ideas are needed. Her parents had also noted progress in her confidence and ability to express her ideas in Spanish. Assessment personnel suggested that Gloria should be placed in a special class within her school where most of her instruction would be conducted by a teacher and an aide in a class of approximately 10 students. She would be integrated in the regular classroom for non-academic subjects (P.E., art). Psychological assessment conducted by a school psychologist substantiated the existence of a gap between Gloria's achievement and her potential. Gloria performed at the average range on the Leiter International Performance Scale and the Performance section of the Wechsler Intelligence Test-Revised.

Present Status (November 1982— Upper Elementary Grade Special Day Class)

The classroom teacher reports Gloria feels more secure in this environment. She initiates conversation quite frequently. Because her academic skills are greater than those of other children in the class, she feels more confident about herself. She does have difficulty remembering verbal information and integrating what she reads. However, these skills are continually reinforced during the day. Gloria's progress will be reviewed at the end of the academic year. She may be able to acquire sufficient skills to warrant returning to the regular classroom (a sixth grade) with further assistance in language and reading comprehension.

Conclusions

The cited case illustrates one of many instances of bilingual students who experience learning difficulties. It illustrates the need for careful assessment of the student's language skills in both the native and second language, including the parents' input. The case also describes the steps followed in programming for a student when attempting to serve her needs in the least restrictive environment and it indicates that a restrictive educational environment may be the best learning situation for some bilingual students having language disabilities. However, placement needs to be made carefully and should involve the cooperation of several professionals and the skills of staff proficient in the student's native language. Such cases require considerable staff time. The need for parent participation and cooperation is also of utmost importance. Continual improvement in research and testing methodology should aid in providing the best possible program for such students.

References

Books and Articles

Brandes, P.J., & Ehinger, D.M, (1981). The effects of early middle ear pathology on auditory perception and academic achievement. *Journal of Speech and Hearing Disorders, 46,* 301-307.

Carrow-Woolfolk, E., & Lynch, J.I. (1982). *An Integrative Approach to Language Disorders in Children.* New York: Grune and Stratton.

Cummins, J. (1981). The role of primary language development in promoting educational success for language minority students, in D.P. Dolson (Ed.), *Schooling and Language Minority Students: A Theoretical Framework.* Los Angeles, CA.: California State University, Los Angeles.

Hatch, E.M. (1978). *Second Language Acquisition: A Book of Readings.* Rowley, Mass.: Newbury House.

McLaughlin, B. (1982). *Children's Second Language Learning.* Washington, D.C.: Center for Applied Linguistics.

Tucker, R. (1975). The acquisition of knowledge by children educated bilingually, in D. Dato (Ed.) *Developmental Psycholinguistics: Theory and Applications.* Washington, D.C.: Georgetown University Press.

Tests

(English)

Carrow Elicited Language Inventory. (1974). Austin, TX: Learning Concepts.

Clinical Evaluation of Language Functions. (1980). Columbus, Ohio: Charles E. Merrill Publishing Company.

Detroit Tests of Learning Aptitude (Revised). (1967). Indianapolis, Indiana: Bobbs-Merrill Company.

Illinois Test of Psycholinguistic Abilities. (1968). Urbana, Ill.: University of Illinois Press.

Key Math Diagnostic Arithmetic Test. (1971). Circle Pines, MN: American Guidance Service.

Leiter International Performance Scale. (1960). Chicago, Ill.: C.H. Stoelting Company.

Peabody Individual Achievement Test (PIAT). (1970). Circle Pines, MN: American Guidance Service.

Peabody Picture Vocabulary Test (PPVT). (1965). Circle Pines, MN: American Guidance Service.

Wechsler Intelligence Scale for Children—Revised (WISC-R). (1974). New York, New York: The Psychological Corporation.

Word Test. (1981). Moline, Ill.: LinguiSystems.

(Spanish)

Batería Woodcock de Proficiencia en el Idioma. (1982). Hingham, Mass.: Teaching Resources.

Ber-Sil Spanish Test. (1972). Ranchos Palos Verdes, CA.: The Ber-Sil Company.

Pruebas de Expresión Oral y Percepción de la Lengua Española (PEOPLE). (1981). Los Angeles, CA.: Office of the Los Angeles Superintendent of Schools.

Prueba Illinois de Habilidades Psicolingüísticas (Spanish Version). (1980). Tucson: Department of Special Education, University of Arizona.

(Spanish and English)

Bilingual Syntax Measure (BSM I and II). (1975, 1980). San Francisco, CA.: Harcourt Brace and Jovanovich.

Del Rio Language Screening Test. (1975). Austin, TX: National Education Laboratory.

Dos Amigos Verbal Language Scales. (1974). San Rafael, CA.: Academic Therapy Publishers.

Language Assessment Scales (LAS I and II). (1977). Corte Madera, CA.: Linguametric Group.

Appendix

Parent–Child Interaction at Home.
Fragment of tape recorded conversation.

Parent	Gloria
¿Gloria, que hiciste ahora, que trabajo te dieron ahora?	Una historia una historia
Gloria, what did you do today, what kind of work did they give you today?	A story (pause) a story
¿Historia de que?	De un perro
A story about what?	About a dog (pause)
¿Y que hizo el perro?	Corría . . . y era color cafe.
What did the dog do?	It would run and it was brown.
¿Y el perro, por que corría?	(No response)
Why did the dog run? (long pause before Gloria would answer)	
¿Por que corría el perro?	Porque todos los perros corren.
Why did the dog run?	Because all dogs run.
Si, pero tenía que correr por algo.	Porque asi corren todos los perros. Asi saltan y corren.
Yes, but it had to run for some reason.	Because all dogs run—they hop and run.
¿Que, iba correteando algo?	Asi nada mas le puse en la historia.
Was it trying to reach something or what?	That's all, I put in the story.

Si la historia es de un perro que iba corriendo. Tenía que corre tras algo, correteando algo, por algo tenía que correr.

Si.

So the story is only about the dog that was running? It must have run for something, for some reason.

Yes.

A bit further

Parent	**Gloria**
¿Cuando te acaban de platicar una lecture, y te preguntan sobre ella, se te olvida lo que te platicaron?	A veces.
When they ask you something they have just told you, like a story, or they have read you something and then they ask you, do you forget what they say?	Sometimes.
¿Se te olvida lo que te acaban de decir o tienes vergüenza?	A veces se me olvida.
Do you forget what they just said or are you ashamed?	I forget sometimes.
¿Y las otras veces?	(No answer)
And what about other times?	
¿Te da verguenza hablar con ellos, con los maestros?	No.
Also are you ashamed to speak with them, with the teachers?	No.

¿Entonces se te olvida lo que te acaban de decir?

So you forget what they just told you?

No, pero a veces si se me olvida.

No, but sometimes I forget.

¿Cuando no te olvidas de la lectura, te apenas al pensar que no hablas bien?

And when you don't forget the work the things they have just read you, do you feel ashamed you may not speak well?

Pienso que no voy hablar bien.

I am afraid I won't speak well.

¿Entonces habla, responde a lo que digo, contesta a lo que sepas, no tengas vergüenza de hablar. Que te gustaría ser cuando crescas?

So say, respond to everything I say, everything you know, don't be ashamed of speaking. What would you like to be when you grow up?

(No answer)

¿Que te gustaría ser?

What do you like doing?

(No answer)

¿Que te gustaría ser cuando seas grande?

What would you like to be when you grow older?

Una maestra.

A teacher.

Note: This conversation was done with Gloria's awareness that the tape recorder was on

Part 5
Group Methods

AN ALTERNATIVE MODEL FOR IDENTIFICATION OF POTENTIALLY GIFTED STUDENTS: A CASE STUDY

Margaret G. Dabney

Introduction

Richmond Community High School is a demonstration site for the Secondary School Experiential Learning Community (SSELC) Project. It is a full time alternative school which was created to develop, demonstrate, and disseminate models of identification, curriculum, governance, and evaluation for the education of academically gifted students from disadvantaging circumstances, including many under-achievers. It is a cooperative project of the Richmond Public Schools, Virginia State University, and a group of private citizens from the City of Richmond, Virginia, who serve on an Advisory Board.

Every group engaged in planning a program for gifted students must ask early in the process: Who makes up the population to be served? The characteristics which are identified and accepted by the planners will contribute to the conceptualization of the program. Academically gifted children, for purposes of the SSELC program, are those identified by professionally qualified persons, through a variety of appropriate assessments, as having superior intellectual and creative potential, and functional abilities for academic performance.

Children having these potentials or abilities should meet one or more of the criteria listed in each of the three groups below:

Category I—Aptitude and achievement
Category II—Outstanding creative ability
Category III—Outstanding leadership, motivation, and
  adaptability

Tests which have been most useful in identification of certain academic talents, for example, the Stanford-Binet, consist chiefly of two components: verbal/linguistic and quantitative/mathematical. They do not measure all of the dimensions of academic talent. The two components of the Stanford-Binet measure "developed abilities" which appear to be clearly related to academic achievement. However, such indices of "developed ability" may be more a product of opportunity than of native ability. Thus, such tests are often biased against members of some ethnic and socioeconomic groups.

During the last few years, aspects of academic talent other than those measured by intelligence tests have received considerable attention. Revisions in the concepts of intelligence owe much to the work of J.M. Hunt (1961), who defines intelligence as consisting of strategies for learning and information processing, concepts, skills, and motivations. These characteristics are developed as the individual interacts with the environment. Guilford (1956) suggests that "intellect can be meaningfully defined as the system of thinking and memory factors, functions or processes." The work of Piaget relates to both Hunt and Guilford through its demonstration of the evolution of intelligence as the child interacts with the environment, and in the process of that interaction, develops a set of characteristic mental operations.

Conventional intelligence tests fail to recognize many of the intellectual components of talent such as divergent thinking, openness to ideas, and tolerance of ambiguity and complexity as well as non- intellectual factors, such as motivation and strength of self-concept. This is not to argue against the use of tests entirely. However, many factors of giftedness are not amenable to assessment through the kind of question which requires a single correct answer. Group tests are useful primarily for preliminary screening. Individual intelligence tests come closest to providing a reliable and valid measure of some *facets* of intellectual functioning, but they are costly and time consuming. Torrance (1979) found that children scoring high on creativity tended to perform as well as children scoring high on IQ. Beyond an IQ of 120, the ability to think creatively appears to add significantly to school achievement. Psychologists such as Torrance are only now beginning to learn to measure creativity by providing evidence of an intellectual factor of divergent thinking, i.e., seeing many ways of restructuring data, many solutions, etc. Instruments are now being tested which attempt to assess some of the factors which relate to divergent thinking, such as fluency of response, flexibility, originality, and elaboration.

There are many gifted underachievers. Comparison of gifted underachievers and high achievers shows a significant difference in self-concept, school attitudes, and out-of-school pursuits (Gallagher, 1975). The junior high school often marks the point of consistent underachieving, especially for children who fall within the category of the disadvantaged gifted. What people become, however, is largely a function of what they have experienced. In this sense, notes Elliot Eisner, "our minds are a product of the tools that are made available to us during maturation" (1980, p. 466-471). There may be a difference between one's potential and one's performance.

Traditional methods of assessment are too often based upon an assumption of genetic deficits in disadvantaged or culturally different populations (Kamin, 1974; Gould, 1981; Chase, 1977; Feuerstein, 1971). Thus, they have not always been predictive of real-life abilities to cope with mainstream society. Education has discriminated against children with needs different from the norm. The historical emphasis upon capacity for learning has been to perceive school learning as primarily dependent upon the presumed ability of the student, rather than upon the quality of the learning environment. This emphasis has served the political function of supporting social categorizing in the culture, and creating and maintaining artificial social distance between groups. However, there appears to be a growing recognition that school failure and student underachievement are socially determined. Even so, as John and Leacock (1979) note, such recognition has not prevented new interpretations of these failures which blame the victims and, often, coexist with arguments about innate or class deficiencies. The gifted, or potentially gifted, minority adolescent is probably the most frequent casualty of persisting myths about the differential educability of children from varying ethnic, racial, and socioeconomic backgrounds.

There is abundant evidence to suggest that current tests have low predictive value/validity for estimating cognitive potential in persons whose previous experience and environment have lacked the stimulation appropriate for certain types of cognitive development and conceptual modeling (Feuerstein, 1971; Hunt, 1979; Gordon, 1979; and Ginsberg, 1972).

Some writers suggest that intellectual functioning and social class differences are the result of adaptation to the environment (Feuerstein, 1980, p. 17; Cronbach, 1975; Chase, 1977). Poor and minority children live in unique environments, often characterized by oppression and deprivation, which present problems to be solved which cannot be imagined by affluence and/or majority children. That reasonable adjustments are created to meet these problems should lead us to ask, as Ginsberg suggests (1972), "not why are poor children deficient, but why do they develop as well as they do?"

In light of the present evidence, the position of SSELC is that educability is a universal human characteristic and that special gifts and talents are distributed proportionately in all ethnic, racial, and class groups.

275

The SSELC Model

The mandate of the SSELC Project is to provide an alternative secondary school for students who are identified as gifted, or potentially gifted, and economically disadvantaged. The mandate guarantees that a significant number of the students will come from low income homes and will be drawn from the majority group in the secondary school population of Richmond, i.e., black adolescents of low economic status.

The focus of the curriculum is upon the development of academic talent. Students attend school for eleven months and are generally accelerated by one year. However, curriculum developers understand that personal development, content mastery, and skills development proceed simultaneously. A rigorous academic program is combined with a variety of guidance activities in order to meet the challenge of compensating for the disadvantages which often accompany economic and/or minority status in our society. The curriculum is process oriented, designed to motivate students to explore, to question, to reason, to think, and to care. (See Figure 1) We expect that some students identified as potentially gifted will develop and begin to demonstrate the appropriate characteristics as they participate in the program (Dabney, 1980).

The nature of academic giftedness is described through items listed below. These items are derived from the research literature dealing with characteristics of gifted and/or talented persons, especially the literature dealing with disadvantaged or culturally different gifted and/or talented (Bruch & Curry, 1978; Witty, 1978; Gay, 1978; Torrance, 1977; Tuttle & Becker, 1980; Torrance, 1979). Many of the qualities listed, the reader should note, may be demonstrated through behaviors which may be negatively defined within the school, family, or community setting.

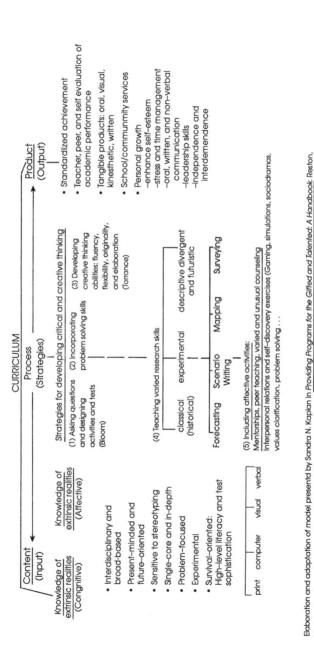

RICHMOND COMMUNITY HIGH SCHOOL
Differentiated Curriculum Design for Gifted Students

The following structured overview graphically defines curriculum as the interaction of content or subject matter and experiences with the process or strategies for learning which results in an outcome or product.

CURRICULUM

Content
(Input)

Knowledge of extrinsic realities
(Cognitive)

• Interdisciplinary and broad-based
• Present-minded and future-oriented
• Sensitive to stereotyping
• Single-core and in-depth
• Problem-focused
• Experimental
• Survival-oriented: High-level literacy and test sophistication

print   computer   visual   verbal

Knowledge of extrinsic realities
(Affective)

Process
(Strategies)

Strategies for developing critical and creative thinking

(1) Asking questions and designing activities and tests (Bloom)

(2) Incorporating problem solving skills

(3) Developing creative thinking abilities: fluency, flexibility, originality, and elaboration (Torrance)

(4) Teaching varied research skills

classical (historical)   experimental   descriptive divergent and futuristic

Forecasting   Scenario Writing   Mapping   Surveying

(5) Including affective activities:
Mentorships, peer teaching, varied and unusual counseling interpersonal relations and self-discovery exercises (Gaming, simulations, sociodramas, values clarification, problem solving . . .

Product
(Output)

• Standardized achievement
• Teacher, peer, and self evaluation of academic performance
• Tangible products: oral, visual, kinesthetic, written
• School/community services
• Personal growth
  –enhance self-esteem
  –stress and time management
  –oral, written, and non-verbal communication
  –leadership skills
  –independence and interdemendence

Barbara-lyn Morris, 1980–81

Figure 1

Elaboration and adaptation of model presentd by Sandra N. Kaplan in *Providing Programs for the Gifted and Talented: A Handbook.* Reston, Virginia: The Council for Exceptional Children, 1977.

Category I. Aptitude and Achievement (Learning characteristics)
Retains and recalls information well
Reads widely and well above grade level
Possesses high mathematical ability
Enjoys problem situations, deals easily with complexity
Is intelligently playful
Takes risks
Creates outstanding products or performance
Can tolerate ambiguity
Has insight into cause—effect
Is a good elaborator
Uses a lot of common sense
Works independently

Category II. Outstanding Creative Ability (creativity characteristics)
Displays great curiosity
Displays divergent thinking
Displays flexibility and/or fluency
Displays originality and/or ability to elaborate
Displays nonverbal fluency and originality
Is able to redefine and rearrange ideas
Displays creativity in movement and physical activity
Displays language rich in imagery
Displays keen sense of humor
Displays high creative productivity in small groups
Invents things, plays, poetry, pictures, etc.

Category III. Outstanding Leadership Characteristics, Duration, and
Adaptability
    a.   Leadership characteristics
        Is sociable
        Excels in athletic and movement activities
        Is self-confident
        Is perceptive about social situations
        Assumes leadership responsibilities easily
        Is able to express feelings and emotions
    b.   Motivational characteristics
        Is highly motivated by games, music, sports, concrete objects
        Is easily bored with routine
        Has the courage of his/her convictions
        Is interested in adult problems
        Evaluates and passes judgment
    c.   Adaptability characteristics
        Handles outside responsibilities and meets school demands

Learns through experience and is flexible and resourceful in
solving day-to-day problems
Deals effectively with deprivations, problems, frustrations, or
obstacles caused by the complexities of living conditions
Overcomes lack of environmental structure and direction
Needs emotional support and sympathetic attitude
Displays high degree of social reasoning and/or behavior
and shows ability to discriminate
Uses limited resources to make meaningful products
Displays maturity of judgment and reasoning beyond own
age level
Is knowledgeable about things of which others are unaware
Can transfer learning from one situation to another

Selection Criteria

Since characteristics signifying giftedness are the product of interaction of underlying competencies and nurturing environments, some
students identified as potentially gifted may be expected to develop and
begin to demonstrate the appropriate characteristics as they participate
in a program tailored to their unique needs.

The selection process is guided by the following principles:

1. No student is excluded solely on the basis of achievement or
ability scores.
2. The selection pool must be broadly representative of the entire
student population in terms of race, sex, socioeconomic status,
and ethnic group.
3. If there are errors in selection, they should be in the direction of
inclusion rather than exclusion; i.e., those who may need special
services to achieve exceptional potential should not be excluded.

The identification of gifts and talents, including some types of cognitive skills, is still a relatively unrefined diagnostic skill; therefore, multiple means of identification are called for. The functional definition of
academic giftedness for SSELC includes measures of ability and
achievement, creativity, and psychosocial characteristics of motivation
and leadership. Thus, multiple means of identification are required. The
ideal of incorporating these multiple factors into a matrix was suggested by the work of Alexinia Baldwin (see Figure 2). The concept of a
matrix recommends itself since the focus is upon the various facets of
one type of giftedness, academic, which facets are presumed to interact
with one another. One assumption underlying the use of the matrix is
that academic potential is often masked by sociocultural differences.

Name_____

Date_____

Identification Matrix*
Indicate points after each test or other score
Add total number of points earned by students
Divide total by number of level

Evidence	Scores				
	5	4	3	2	1
		90-94	85	80	75
	95%tile	94%tile	89%tile	84%tile	79%tile
1. Ability Test**	( )	( )	( )	( )	( )
2. SRA or other Reading score	( )	( )	( )	( )	( )
3. SRA or other Math or Science score	( )	( )	( )	( )	( )
4. STEA	( )	( )	( )	( )	( )
5. Torrance Test of Creativity	( )	( )	( )	( )	( )
6. RAP	( )	( )	( )	( )	( )
7. Writing Sample	( )	( )	( )	( )	( )
8. Renzulli-Hartman Scale Motivational Characteristics, Activities	36 ( )	32-35 ( )	28-31 ( )	24-27 ( )	18-23 ( )
9. Renzulli-Hartman Scale Leadership Characteristics	40 ( )	36-39 ( )	32-35 ( )	28-31 ( )	27-30 ( )
	Superior	Very Good	Good	Average	Below Average
10. Interviews	( )	( )	( )	( )	( )

Total Score _____

* See Alexinia Baldwin, *The Baldwin Matrix*. Buffalo, N.Y.: DOK Publishing Company, 1978.

**Please specify test.

Figure 2

Note that this adapted Baldwin Identification Matrix is designed to give a good deal of weight to procedures that will reveal characteristics not revealed by standardized tests, summarize a variety of data, and provide an estimate of learning potential referenced in part to local norms.

The three factors of the definition of giftedness have been translated into assessment variables which are expected to predict the expected growth and development of students. These variables are shown in Figure 3 which illustrates their interplay with program components and assessment techniques in the identification, assessment, and program planning model.

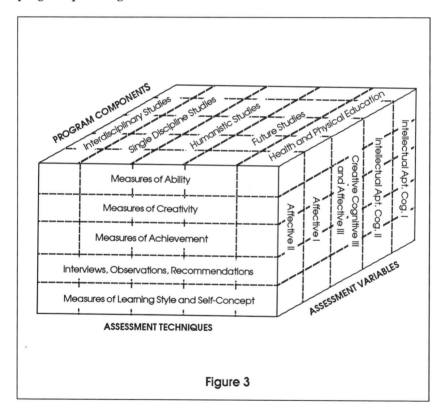

Figure 3

The assessment variables are:

1. *Intellectual aptitude and abilities*—a certain level of mental power, ability to abstract, analyze, generalize, etc., i.e., the basic capacities to acquire the skills and abilities associated with academic and career success. These factors are identified as

Cognitive I and II. They are measured by an Otis- Lennon Ability Test, the Short Test of Education Ability (STEA) and SRA Achievement Tests.

2. *Creativity*—a special quality involving divergent thinking, originality, fluency, imagination, and transcendence. The ability to find and solve problems. Creativity is an important factor in giftedness. It permits the production of new ways of doing things, of performing, or of producing unusual products. These factors are identified as Cognitive III and Affective III and are measured by the Torrance Test of Creativity, Figural Form B, a Writing Sample, and through the interviews.

3. *Psychosocial characteristics*—these are the characteristics that help persons to become what they are capable of being. They include motivation, leadership, energy, etc. They are identified as Affective I and II and are measured by a survey instrument, Relevant Aptitude Potential (RAP), by a writing sample, and by interviews and Renzulli-Hartman Scales for motivation and leadership characteristics which are submitted by teachers.

Data resulting from a particular measure or technique are translated into a scale score and entered on the Matrix. The Matrix used for a selection of the 1981 Freshman class contained ten factors, compared with a 14-factor matrix which was used to select the 1979 Freshman class. (Whole classes are admitted every two years. In the intermediate years, a few students have been admitted to replace transfers.)

The reduction in the number of factors in the Matrix came about because analysis of student performance suggested that of achievement test scores, reading and mathematics or science were the reliable predictors of performance. Thus, the entire SRA battery of subtest scores need not be used. The STEA has many limitations but had been used in the selection process throughout the first cycle (four years). The committee decided to introduce a more reliable instrument in 1981 under circumstances which would permit comparisons to be made of the predictive ability of the two years. Limited funds have prevented the use of individual ability tests for each child, the most desirable procedure. (All forms and instruments except standardized tests are included in the Appendix.)

Identification and Selection Process

Identification and selection are managed by the principal and counselor. They are assisted by the Virginia State University and Richmond Public Schools Coordinators, students, parents, and Advisory

Board members. Counselors from the middle school provide SRA test data, teacher responses to the Renzulli-Hartman instrument, and arrange for testing and interview sessions. Parents are asked to respond to a questionnaire.

Stage I—Referrals from teachers, administrators, guidance counselors, other personnel, peers, parents, citizens, and self are solicited. Nominations and referrals may be by staff, members of the Board, students, etc. Notices are circulated within the school system, encouraging referrals to be sent to counselors at the middle schools. The assistance of churches, social agencies, community groups, and community leaders is sought to identify potential students.

Stage II—The interest of parent/guardian and child is determined by their responses to a short questionnaire. Only interested candidates are maintained on the active list. A developmental profile of each student is begun and includes items listed below:

Aptitude Scores—STEA and Otis-Lennon.
Achievement Scores—Reading and mathematics or science.
Products—including essays, projects, art work, etc., which may have been submitted by the students. These were not used in 1981, but may be reinstated.
Creativity—Torrance Test of Creativity, Figural Form B, Writing Sample and Interview.
Motivation and Leadership—Renzulli-Hartman Scale and Interview.
Parent Questionnaire

Prospective students are interviewed in small groups or individually. Interview teams consist of staff persons, members of the Advisory Board, and Richmond Community High School students. (Teams are provided an orientation to the purpose and procedures.) Interviews are structured around a series of questions (see Appendix). Students receive an interview score which is the average of scores assigned by all interviewers. Scale scores are determined by calculating a mean score of all interview scores and the standard deviation. The mean score is assigned a value of 3 on a 5-point scale. Scale scores of 4 or 5 are equal to the mean score plus 1 or 2 standard deviations. For a score of 1 or 2, the standard deviation is subtracted from the mean score. This procedure is also used to scale the Relevant Aptitude Potential scores, the Torrance scores and the Writing Sample scores.

The Writing Samples are generally scored by university composition teachers who take into account organization and structure, mechanics, originality, and unusual elements. Scores for all variables are entered on the Matrix.

Stage III—The school staff conducts a first review of the developmental profile using criteria approved by the school system and the Advisory Board as indices of socioeconomic status, intellectual functioning, and potential, creativity, and psychosocial characteristics. Both black and white high socioeconomic status students are over-represented in the pool. High SES parents are eager for their children to participate and are aggressive in their efforts to have them considered. Parents of poor children are often unaware of such opportunities, unaware of the value of such opportunities in the future lives of their children, or unwilling to submit their children to experiences which might cause them to feel or become different from family or peers. The SSELC Committee has observed that in the Richmond area, young people from lower socioecnomic circumstances do not apply for other special academic activities as often as those from higher socioeconomic circumstances, even when eligible.

Selection Guidelines

Guidelines which have evolved during the first phase of the project are listed below and are applied for a first screening:

1. SES—

    The student should be eligible for free or reduced lunch.
    The student should be a member of a family whose annual income falls within the following guidelines:

Family Size	Income
2	up to $12,057.
3	14,985.
4	17,908.
5	20,832.
6	23,766.
8	27,790.

Other indicators of interest may be:

The student lives with relatives or guardians other than parents, including foster parents.
The student's parent(s) pursue a blue collar occupation.

The student is a member of a family which receives public assistance.
The student comes from a low-income single parent family.

2. Racial/Ethnic Composition
    The RCHS population must approach the multiethnic, multiracial composition of RPS. Selection of each class should take into consideration the present composition of the school. Following is the desirable proportionate breakdown:

Race		Sex		SES	
B	W	M	F	Low	Middle
65%	35%	50%	50%	75%	25%

Also, members of other racial/ethnic groups are encouraged to apply.

3. Definitions of Giftedness
    a. Intellectual functioning—one or more of the following:
    –Aptitude Score(s) within upper 10% of RPS
    –SRA reading above 90th percentile (national norms)
    –SRA science or math above 90th percentile (national norms)
    In addition, students may submit a product in science, the social studies, etc., which is judged by an expert in the field to be excellent.

    b. Creativity
    –A Torrance Test of Creativity Scale Score of 3 or above

    c. Psychosocial Factors, i.e., leadership, motivation, etc.
    –RAP Scale Score of 3 or above
    –Renzulli-Hartman Scale Score of 3 or above

This first screening results in three rough categories, i.e., clearly eligible, questionably eligible, and clearly not eligible. Members of the questionably eligible group are referred to the school system for individual psychological testing, generally the Wechsler Intelligence Scale for Children. Additional information about the student may be sought from parents, teachers, social agencies, counselors, etc.

Stage IV—Staff persons conduct a final review of the updated developmental profiles of each student. The Matrix profiles are presented to the members of the Selection Committee taking the required steps to protect confidentiality. Final selections take into account the total profile of the student. An example of the results of the selection process may be found in the information provided below about aspects of entering status of the September, 1979 Freshman class.

Median Percentile Standing
SRA Achievement and STEA Aptitude Tests—
National Norm
RCHS Entering Class—September, 1979

	Boys	Girls
STEA (Ability)	95	89
SRA (Composite)	88	89
SRA (Reading)	91	89
SRA (Science)	90	84
SRA (Social Studies)	90	87
SRA (Mathematics)	83	84
SRA (Language Arts)	88	89

The scores reported above are those to be found at the mid-point of the distribution of each set of scores. They indicate that on the average, the prformance of boys as measured by these tests is somewhat better than that of girls. The lowest performance areas are to be found on the mathematics test and on the science test (girls). However, the individual profiles of the students are of greatest interest. Shown below are the percentile scores of four students, two boys and two girls.

	Student A	Student B	Student C	Student D
STEA	99	87	99	87
SRA (Composite)	96	93	84	94
SRA (Reading)	91	85	84	96
SRA (Science)	96	99	88	99
SRA (Mathematics)	86	97	81	78
SRA (Lang. Arts)	94	90	81	98
SRA (Soc. Studies)	96	96	81	93

Students A and C, a boy and a girl, have the highest possible STEA percentile scores, but quite different performance profiles. Students B and D have the same STEA scores, somewhat below the median for girls and considerably below the median for boys. However, the performance of student D compares favorably with that of student A. The performance record of student A is consistent with his STEA score. The performance records of students B and D are better than might be predicted, and the performance record of student C is not what might be predicted by the STEA score. The weakest area for three of the four students is mathematics. This has implications for curriculum.

Examination of the profiles reveals that the student with the lowest entering STEA score earned the highest entering score on the test of Relevant Aptitude Potential. On a scale of 1-5, this student earned a 4 on the Torrance Test of Creativity and was awarded a score of 4 on the interview and on three of the four Renzulli-Hartman scales by his teacher. His Composite SRA score is at the 80th percentile. These profiles serve to indicate the necessity of using a variety of factors to predict the potential gifts of students.

Discussion

Comparison of the 11th grade SRA scores of the 1981 graduating class with a local group matched for Short Test of Educational Ability scores, sex, race, and socioeconomic status indicated a difference in performance in favor of the SSELC group ($p \leq .05$). Such a comparison has not yet been completed for the 1983 graduating class. However, for the 39 students admitted in 1979, data from the Torrance Test of Creative Thinking, the Survey of Relevant Aptitude Potential, the Science Research Associates battery, the Preliminary Scholastic Aptitude Test, the Scholastic Aptitude Test, and grade point averages were submitted to a series of Pearson Product Moment correlations (one-tailed test).

Creativity is one of three major factors in the SSELC definition of giftedness. Torrance has suggested that 25 percent of the variance in ability scores of high ability children (beyond an IQ of 120) may be explained by creativity. Thus, it was expected that the measures of creative aptitude would correlate with scholastic aptitude and achievement to the extent that they would account for approximately 25 percent of the variance. Since psychosocial factors such as motivation and leadership are generally thought to be significant factors in giftedness, these factors as measured by the RAP were expected to be significantly correlated with achievement and ability to the extent that they would account for about 25 percent of the variance. (The RAP represents the psychosocial factor since it correlates at the .001 level with Renzulli-Hartman scores.) With an N of 39, an r of at least .35 was needed to be significant at the .001 level. A correlation below .35 indicates that less than 25 percent of the variance in the two measures is common to both.

Predictions for a group may not be of great value if the correlations fall below this point. However, they may point the way to additional avenues of research exploration. If the expected predictions were supported by the data analysis, a regression equation could then be developed for selection which would include factors in addition to those measured by achieveent and group ability tests.

The tables below reveal generally higher correlations of the RAP with a set of selected variables than of the Torrance subtests with the same factors. Table 1 displays correlations of the Torrance with both standardized achievement and ability tests and grade point averages in a number of subject areas.

Table 1
Correlation of RAP and Torrance
With Selected Achievement Scores and with EAS

	Cum. GPA	EAS**	SRA COMP.	Cum. Eng.	Cum Hist.	Cum Sci.	Cum. Math.
RAP	.50*	.16	.42	.57*	.54*	.38	.63*
Torrance Factors							
Fluidity	-.26	-.58*	-.33	-.01	.05	-.32	-.23
Flexibility	-.32	-.59*	.39	-.06	.04	-.29	-.29
Originality	-.33	-.26	-.48	-.15	-.27	-.21	-.43
Elaboration	.42	.01	.40	.30	.36	.04	-.38

*P<.001
**EAS - Educational Ability Scores

Elaboration is the only Torrance subtest which correlates positively with all of the grade point averages and with SRA Composite. However, none of the coefficients reaches the .001 level of significance. On the other hand, the RAP correlates positively at the .001 level with cumulative grade point averages in English, history, and mathematics, as well as with total GPA. The association of the RAP with the EAS is statistically nonsignificant.

Table 2 permits an examination of the relationship of the Torrance subtests with PSAT and SAT scores. One may note that each succeeding year and score produced a lower correlation with the PSAT and SAT, though the mean scores for the SAT and PSAT have not declined. This decline of scores raises several intriguing questions:

- Do the Torrance Tests measure creativity?
- Does the SSELC Program emphasize convergent thinking whereas creativity implies divergent thinking?
- Are the achievement tests so heavily weighted toward convergent thinking that divergent thinking can be counterproductive?

Table 2
Correlation of Torrance Sub-test Scores
with PSAT and SAT

	1980 PSAT-V	1980 PSAT-M	1981 PSAT-V	1981 PSAT-M	SAT-V	SAT-M
Fluidity	.61*	.58*	.17	.18	-.13	-.19
Flexibility	.51*	.60*	.15	.24	-.12	-.16
Originality	.32	.43	.12	.34	-.22	-.09
Elaboration	.38	.02	.36	.29	.11	.09
	x̄–420	x̄–420	x̄–508	x̄–492	x̄–523	x̄–552

*P<.001

Table 3
Correlation of Cumulative Math GPA
with Selected Veriables

	Corre.	Sig.
SAT Math	.24	.063
SAT Verbal	.53	.001
Cumulative English GPA	.69	.001
Cumulative History GPA	.73	.001
Cumulative Language Arts GPA	.48	.001
Cumulative GPA	.76	.001
SRA Reading	.65	.001
RAP	.63	.001
EAS	.31	.026
Torrance Factors		
Fluidity	-.23	.012
Flexibility	-.39	.030
Originality	-.43	.335
Elaboration	.38	.413

Table 3 demonstrates that cumulative math GPA is an excellent predictor of performance in a variety of areas of the school curriculum. The Table shows the degree of relationship of the mathematics GPA to a sample of test scores representing all facets of the SSELC definition of giftedness. It is apparent that the math GPA is even significantly associated with related activities.

Findings and Implications

The two major findings of this stage of our investigation are (1) that the subtests of the Torrance Test of Creativity do not appear to be potentially predictive of academic success as measured by the SRA subtests, the SAT, or grade point average and (2) the RAP appears to be potentially predictive of academic success as measured by grades, at least in this program. It is much less reliable if the measures are SAT or SRA/EAS.

Finally, the author notes that if students were to be admitted to the program on the basis of standardized test scores which have a rigid cutoff point, a number of successful student candidates would have been rejected. Students in the first graduating class with profiles comparable to students B and D mentioned earlier have sccessfully matriculated at many prestigious colleges and universities. This program is contributing to the evidence which suggests that many of the commonly used standardized instruments have low predictive value for estimating cognitive potential and academic performance in persons whose previous experiences have not stimulated certain types of cognitive development.

References

Baldwin, Alexinia (1978). *The Baldwin Matrix.* Buffalo, NY: Dok Publishing.

Bruch, C.B. (1978). Recent insights on the culturally different gifted. *The Gifted Child Quarterly,* 22:3, 374-393.

Bruch, K., & Curry, J. (1978). Personal learnings: A current synthesis on the culturally different gifted. *The Gifted Child Quarterly,* 22:33, 313-321.

Chase, A. (1976). *The legacy of Malthus: The social costs of the new scientific racism.* New York: Knopf.

College Entrance Examination Board (1973). *Scholastic Aptitude Test (SAT).* Princeton: Educational Testing Service.

Cronbach, L.J. (1975). Five decades of controversy over mental testing. *American Psychologist, 30,* 1-14.

Dabney, M.G. (1980). *Report of an experiment: Gifted education at Richmond Community High School.* Petersburg, VA: Virginia State University.

Eisner, E. (1980, Spring). The role of the arts in the invention of man. *New York University Education Quarterly,* (211:3, 2-7.

Feuerstein, R. (1972). *Studies in cognitive modifiability.* Proposal for extension of the learning potential model for applied individual and group assessment. Ford Foundation Trustees.

Feuerstein, R. (1980). *Instrumental enrichment.* Baltimore: University Park Press.

Gallagher, J.J. (1975). *Teaching the gifted child* (2nd ed.) (pp. 341-34). Boston: Allyn & Bacon.

Gay, J. (1978, Fall). A proposed plan for identifying black gifted children. *The Gifted Child Quarterly,* 22:3, 353-360.

Getzels, J.W., & Jackson, P.W. (1962). *Creativity and intelligence.* New York: Wiley.

Ginzberg, H. (1972). *The myth of the deprived child.* Englewood Cliffs, NJ: Prentice Hall.

Gordon, E.W. (1979). New perspectives on old issues. In Wilkerson, D.A. (Ed.), *Educating all our children* (pp. 52-73). Westport, CONN: Mediax.

Gould, S.J. (1981). *The mismeasure of man.* New York: Norton.

Grant, T.E., & Renzulli, J.S. (1974). *Relevant aptitude potential (RAP).* Marlborough, CONN: RAP Researchers.

Guilford, J.P. (1956). The structure of intellect. *Psychological Bulletin, 53,* 267-293.

Hunt, J.McV. (1961). *Intelligence and experience.* New York: Ronald Press.

Hunt, J.McV. (1979). Recent concern with early education. In Wilkerson, D.A. (Ed.), *Educating all our children* (pp. 76-91). Westport, CONN: Mediax.

John, V.P., & Leacock, A. (1979). Transforming the structure of failure. In Wilkerson, D.A. (Ed.), *Educating all our children* (pp. 16-50). Westport, CONN: Mediax.

Kamin, L. (1974). *The science and politics of IQ.* Potomac, MD: Lawrence Erlbaum Associates. Distributed by Halsted Press. New York: Wiley.

Kaplan, S.R. (1977). *Providing programs for the gifted and talented: A handbook.* Reston, VA: The Council for Exceptional Children.

Otis, A.S., & Lennon, R.T. (1970). *Otis-Lennon Mental Ability Test.* New York: Harcourt Brace Jovanovich.

Preliminary Scholastic Aptitude Test/National Merit Scholarship Qualifying Test (PSAT/NMSQT) (1973). Princeton: Educational Testing Service.

Renzulli-Hartman Scales for Rating Behavioral Characteristics of Superior Students. See *Exceptional Children* (1971), *38,* 211-214, 243-248.

Renzulli, J.S. (1973). *An evaluation of project gifted.* Storrs, CONN: University of Connecticut.

SRA (1972). *Short Test of Educational Ability.* Chicago: Science Research Associates.

Torrance, E.P. (1966). *Torrance Test of Creative Thinking.* Research Edition. Columbus, Ohio: Personnel Press.

Torrance, E.P. (1977). *Discovery and nurturance of giftedness in the culturally different.* Reston, VA: The Council for Exceptional Children.

Torrance, E.P. (1979). Creative positives of disadvantaged children and youth. In J.C. Gowan, J. Khatena, & E.P. Torrance, *Educating the ablest* (pp. 341-451). Ithaca, ILL: Peacock.

Tuttle, F., & Becker, L.A. (1980). *Characteristics and identification of gifted and talented students.* Washington, D.C.: National Education Association.

Wechsler, D. (1949). *Wechsler Intelligence Scale for Children—Revised.* New York: The Psychological Corporation.

Witty, E. (1978, Fall). Equal educational opportunity for gifted minority children. *The Gifted Child Quarterly,* 22:3, 344- 352.

Appendix: An Alternative Model for Identification of Potentially Gifted Students—A Case Study

Richmond Community High School
Identification of Academically Gifted Students
Preliminary Teacher Check List

Name_____

Please describe the student whose name appears above by checking the most accurate description. Rating scales are subjective at best, but they provide opportunities for the persons who know students as individuals to contribute information from their perceptions. Your responses will be reviewed along with several other kinds of information to assist us in the preliminary screening process. Thanks for your help.

1. With regard to motivation, this student:

_Must be prodded to get work done	_Requires occasional reminders	_Usually completes work promptly	_Often does more than is required	_Consistently works creatively and on a high level

2. With regard to work attitude, this student:

_Does not like to tackle new ideas	_Has difficulty following established class procedures	_Applies established classroom procedures capably	_Occasionally employs a new approach	_Finds many ways to solve problems

3. With regard to curiosity, this student:

_Is seldom curious enough to get all the facts	_Accepts facts and situations as presented	_Asks some questions for better understanding	_Wants reasons and clarification; expresses doubts	_Investigates further and arrives at conclusions

4. With regard to creativity, this student:

_Never has a new idea	_Tends to use only familiar ideas	_Sometimes has original ideas	_Often has good suggestions and original ideas	_Sees new relationships, uses materials in unusual ways

5. This student is unusually resourceful in coping with responsibilities: (Check as many as apply)

_at home   _school   _work   _community   _other, please specify

6. This student is unusually resourceful in coping with deprivations: (Check as many as apply.)

_economic   _social   _cultural   _educational   _expression, information, communication

7. This student is unusually resourceful in coping with problems, frustrations, obstacles:

_in school   _at home   _social   _other, please specify

8. This student is unusually resourceful in coping with:

_new resources   _free or unstructured time   _new environments   _new experiences   _other, please specify

9. This student shows poor or irrational organization of:

_time   _work tasks   _learning experiences   _social experiences

10. This student is playful with:

_materials   _people   _ideas   _other things

11. This student is often: (check as many as apply)

_critical or skeptical   _observant   _well-informed   _logical

Richmond Community High School
Student Selection Interview Scale

Date_____

Name of Applicant _____

Rating

1. Please describe your ideal school.

Be sensitive to:

Goals   Cognitive style

Achievement orientation   Preferences/values, etc.

2. In your view what is the most important news event of the last two weeks? Why?

Be sensitive to:

Organization of ideas

Breadth and depth of knowledge, etc.

3. How do you spend your out-of-school time?

Be sensitive to:

Values   Degree of task commitment

Hobbies   Achievement orientation, etc.

4. Describe yourself in the year 2000.

Be sensitive to:

Goals   Values

Achievement orientation

5. What do you think is the most pressing problem to be solved in the world today?

Be sensitive to:

Organization of ideas   Fluency

Breadth & depth of knowledge   Cognitive style, etc.

Your general comments:

	Superior	Very Good	Good	Avg.	Below Avg.
	5	4	3	2	1

Overall Rating

Content

Depth, breadth, accuracy of information, values, goals, intensity of interests

Originality

Fluency, imagination, creativity, style

Organization

Clarity, unity, development of thought

Mechanics

Structure, grammatical usage

Total _____ _____ _____ _____ _____

Name of Interviewer _____

Richmond Community High School
Richmond, Virginia
SSELC
Evaluation Scale for Writing Sample

Name _____ Date _____

Evaluator _____

Total Score _____

	Low		Moderate		High	
	1	2	3	4	5	6
I. Organization Unity, developoment, clarity						
II. Mechanics Structure, grammar, usage Skills: spelling, punctuation						
III. Originality Creative fluency, emotional quality, imagination, style, theme						
IV. Unusual/Other Elements Dialogue, special format, mood/setting, character development						
Column Total						
Weight	1	2	3	4	5	6
Weighted Column Total						
	TOTAL SCORE					

From: Renzulli, J.S. *An Evaluation of Project Gifted.* Storrs, University of Connecticut, 1973.

SCALE SCORES
RCHS SELECTION 1981

	1	2	3	4	5
1. Ability Test	75–70%	80–84%	85–89%	90–94%	95% plus
2. Torrance Test	1	2	3	4	5
(Flex) $\overline{X}$ = 7.7 sd = 3.63	1.0	4.1	7.7	11.3	14.9
(Flux) $\overline{X}$ = 10.9 sd = 5.34	–1.0	5.6	10.9	16.2	21.5
(Orig) $\overline{X}$ = 7.6 sd = 3.62	–1.0	4.0	7.6	11.2	14.8
(Elab) $\overline{X}$ = 45 sd = 22.6	–1.0	20.4	45.0	67.6	90.2
3. RAP $\overline{X}$ = 102 sd = 15	72	87	102	117	132
4. Writing Sample $\overline{X}$ = 8.0 sd = 3.39	1.22	4.61	8.0	11.39	14.78
5. Renzulli–Hartman					
(Motivation)	18–23	24–27	28–31	32–35	36 plus
(Leadership)	27–30	28–31	32–35	36–39	40 plus
6. Interview $\overline{X}$ = 14.9 sd = 2.80	9.3	12.1	14.9	17.7	20.5

Richmond Community High School

Screening and Selection Form
for Identifying Gifted Students

Name _____ Date of Birth _____

School _____ Grade _____

Teacher _____ Sex/Race Code _____

Referral—Self _____

       Teacher or Counselor _____

       Parent-Guardian _____

       Peer _____

       Other _____

Section A: Intelligence Test Information

I. Group Intelligence Tests

Date	Grade	Name of Test	Verbal Score	Non-Verbal Score	Total Score	%tile

The following action is recommended:

    ____ Further consideration for placement is recommended.

    ____ An individual intelligence test should be administered.

2. Individual Intelligence Tests

Attach report of examiner.

Comments:

Section B. Achievement Information

I. Achievement Tests

Date	Grade	Name of Test	Reading G.E. %tile	Lang. G.E.	Total %tile	Math G.E.	Total %tile

Soc. Stud. G.E. %tile	Science G.E. %tile	Use of Sources G.E. %tile

G.E. = Grade Equivalent

Circle all scores that are two or more years above grade level and/or above the 90th percentile.

Student's best area(s) of achievement _____

Student's poorest area(s) of achievement _____

2. Grades—last two years

Date	Grade	Teacher	Reading	Math	Lang. Arts	Social Studies	Science

Attach relevant comments regarding achievement from permanent record.

Student's best area(s) of performance _____

Student's poorest area(s) of performance _____

Section E: Torrance Test of Creativity

Date _____

_____

Myers-Briggs _____

Date _____ Results _____

_____

Section F: Motivation and Leadership

1. Relevant Aptitude Potential

Date _____ Score _____

Remarks _____

_____

_____

_____

2. Renzulli Scales

Date _____ Grade _____ Teacher _____

_____

Leadership _____ Raw Score _____ Scale Score _____

Motivation _____ Raw Score _____ Scale Score _____

Section G: Other information which should be considered:
Parent Survey, products, etc.

Based on the above information, the following action is recommended:

____ Placement in the program is recommended.

____ Additional information is needed in the form of:

_____

____ Placement is not recommended at this time.

RICHMOND COMMUNITY HIGH SCHOOL
Parent Questionnaire

Date _____

1. Student's Name _____

2. School Currently Attending _____

3. Sex (circle)   M   F   4. Grade _____

5. Birthday _____   6. Age _____

7. City of Birth _____

8. Describe any early indication of superior ability: _____

_____

9. Brothers & Sisters:	Name	Age
	_____	_____
	_____	_____
	_____	_____

10. Hobbies of:	Father	Mother
	_____	_____
	_____	_____

11. If money were no problem, what career would you prefer for your son or daughter? _____

12. Has your son or daughter had music lessons?   ___yes   ___no

   Dancing lessons?   ___yes   ___no

   Lessons of Other Kinds?   ___yes   ___no Please specify

_____

13. Trips your son or daugher has taken: (place & age) _____

_____

14. What do you do together as a family? _____

_____

ADAPTATION OF THE LEARNING POTENTIAL ASSESSMENT STRATEGY TO SPECIAL EDUCATION DIAGNOSTIC CLASSROOM SETTINGS

Ralph M. Hausman

In 1972, the present writer used Budoff's learning potential procedures (Budoff, 1965) to assess elementary-age Mexican-American students (Hausman, 1972). This exploratory study examined relationships among a variety of tests, including tests administered in English and Spanish, and several learning potential assessment instruments. As an outgrowth of the project, followed by additional experience applying Budoff's learning potential versions of the Kohs Block Designs Test (Kohs, 1923) and Raven's Coloured Progressive Matrices Test (Raven, 1956) with differing ethnic groups, the writer has been developing a learning-potential assessment based structure within diagnostic class-rooms for mildly involved, culturally and/or experientially atypical, school age children. The purpose of this chapter is to describe the over-all classroom structure utilized and present some of the data obtained from a Mexican-American student in one diagnostic classroom.

Diagnostic Classroom: Learning-Potential-Assessment Version

While the original conceptualization of such a classroom structure came from the writer's doctoral dissertation (Hausman, 1972), there were several pragmatic reasons for the development of such a classroom structure: First, the teachers' verbal responses to data ob-tained by the writer on the learning potential versions of the Kohs and Raven tests typically have been less than enthusiastic, since most tradi-tionally trained teachers have reportedly found generalization to the classroom situation difficult. Second, direct translation by the author of the specific data obtained (i.e., either Budoff's LP status or the original, raw gain scores) to the prediction of students' actual performance within the academic courses was found to be highly variable and thus, not particularly reliable. Third, few school psychologists or diagnosticians are trained in the application and interpretation of either Feuerstein's LPAD (Feuerstein, 1979) or Budoff's LP versions of the Kohs or Raven tests. Rather than continue to invest extensive time and energy in orienting teachers to clinical and experimental approaches used in assessing the ability of students to profit from instruction, the writer developed the learning-potential assessment based diagnostic classroom described herein.

Classroom: Overview

The final class structure evolved in a slow yet systematic manner. Initially, the concept was examined in a series of pilot or "mini" projects conducted informally within various special education settings. These pilot projects involved the application of a test-teach-retest strategy within a single academic area with each teacher-in-training structuring his or her instructional procedures within the basic parameters established. The structure that evolved over a span of several years consists of sectioning each 50 minute "teaching hour" into a short pretest, a structured teaching unit, and a short posttest.

Regardless of the content area, each class period is initiated by the administration of a teacher-made, wide-range pretest of approximately five minutes duration. The pretest includes 15 to 25 test items (depending on the specific content area targeted.) One-fourth to one-third of the items relate to content covered in previous sessions and three-fourths to two-thirds cover information to be taught during the impending session. The pretest is immediately followed by a 45 minute, group-oriented instructional session.

The teacher systematically varies the modality of instruction in a session (e.g., employing in one session a primarily visual approach, in the next session a primarily auditory approach, in yet another session a multi-dimensional approach, etc.), the type of classroom participation required of the students (oral, multiple choice, written response to essay questions, short written answers, etc.) and the type of reinforcement system. The term "primarily" acknowledges that no single modality is presented in "pure" form; the presentations have, however, been constructed to emphasize a specific modality, essentially following Neville's original approach (1968). When a task is referred to as "primarily visual" in nature, it simply means that the stimuli are represented on the blackboard or overhead projector and are visually emphasized, e.g., through outlining the overall shape of the word and/or component letters, through the use of high value stimuli like colored letters or numbers, etc. Ideally, the teacher should structure each session to permit systematic analysis of the effects of changing single instructional dimensions.

A posttest, structured in the same manner as the pretest, is then administered during the last five minutes of the class period. The measure of a student's ability to profit from a specific set of instructional procedures is then defined as the obtained gain score (or, the score resulting from subtracting the pre and posttest scores). Depending on the overall time available, when evaluating the student's preference for type of presentation modality, each alteration should be presented on three consecutive days. When evaluating the student's preferred response modality, a five-day sequence is usually required (i.e., to evaluate the following conditions: oral responses, pictorially presented worksheets, traditional graphic or symbolic worksheets, multiple choice responses, written short answers, and written essay responses).

Persons interested in implementing the approach should begin the process with five three-day sequences in which the student's presentation modality preference is evaluated, followed by two or three five-day sequences in which the student's response modality preference is determined. During this time, with one exception, all except the single selected dimension should remain constant. The exception to this rule is the reinforcement schedule. Because of a variety of problems, including time constraints, student responses, and teacher preferences, the analysis of the student's preferred type of reinforcement has usually overlapped the other two dimensions.

Specifically, the three approaches commonly tried (i.e., use of tangible, edible rewards, use of natural rewards earned within a token economy system, and the use of social rewards) have been presented in two-week blocks during the typical six-week period. This approach permits overlapping several "sequences" within the other strategies. The order of presentation recommended is that listed above. Admittedly, while such an approach is not consistent with accepted laboratory style research, it allows teachers to obtain a rough estimate of the students' preferences within an ongoing classroom setting.

At this point in program development, several difficulties continue to exist. Due to the nature of the classroom setting, the specific content presented during each session must vary according to the curriculum design. While the provision of different, although sequentially related content, may be beneficial in some ways, e.g., maintaining the student's interest level and preventing the possibility of a "learning-to-learn" set or cumulative effect that would cloud data interpretation, it may also be deleterious in that the specifics involved in the different materials may naturally result in a differential learning pattern for different students. However, this writer believes any deleterious effects would be "washed out" or minimized through the repetitive process.

Ideally, each student would be presented a series of different presentations, with the specific "alternations" (i.e., the use of a primarily visual approach, etc.) repeated with different content over a period of four to six weeks. To avoid the establishment of a "learning-to-learn" set or cumulative effect, teachers have found it beneficial to vary the order of presentation so that, for example, when presentation modality is the variable under scrutiny, the primarily visual approach does not always occur initially in the three-day sequence. Also, students vary according to how they best learn different academic subject matter; thus, implementation of the approach described would require systematic application in several major academic areas at the same time. Finally, a major problem is that the teacher effectiveness variable is, as yet, uncontrolled.

In spite of these difficulties, this writer believes, based on personal experience and evaluations of implementing teachers, that systematic variation of critical instructional dimensions can be examined in specific content areas in three to six weeks.

Illustrative Case Study: Johnny

Johnny, an eleven year and two months old Mexican-American boy, was assigned to an elementary-level generically-oriented resource room containing students manifesting a variety of handicapping conditions when the "Learning Potential" (LP) classroom structure was implemented by his classroom teacher (a graduate student completing her special education practicum while employed as a full time teacher). Johnny was then receiving resource assistance for two fifty-minute periods each day. According to available records, he lived at home with his natural mother, his stepfather and three siblings. His stepfather was a maintenance worker and his mother a housewife. Although Johnny and his siblings were considered functionally bilingual, his parents were reported to prefer speaking in Spanish. He was placed in the resource room on the basis of a WISC-R Verbal IQ of 65, a Performance IQ of 77, and a Full Scale IQ of 69 (with Scaled Scores of 21, 33 and 54, respectively). On the Wide Range Achievement Test he was functioning two or more years below his expected grade level in reading, spelling and arithmetic.

During a three-week period in early Fall, Johnny's teacher implemented the LP teaching strategy while he attended the resource room for remedial mathematics and spelling assistance. In both classes the mode of academic content presentation was systematically altered every third day to examine the students' preferred learning modality as well as preferred method of response. In both classes, the material taught was presented in three different modes (i.e., primarily visual, primarily auditory and primarily multisensory, as previously defined.)

In the mathematics class, students were asked to respond to either an abstract worksheet (where the numbers were displayed on traditional worksheets) or a pictorially oriented worksheet (where the problems were presented in cartoon or picture format). The students' method of response in the spelling class was somewhat different in that they were required either to write out the words as dictated on a straight line (in the traditional manner) or to choose which of three spellings was the correct word. In both classes, the first nine days focused on the use of the traditional style (i.e., primarily abstract) worksheet while presenting the information in each of three modalities. During the next six days, the pictorial or multiple choice worksheets were employed in each of three presentation modalities. An examination of reinforcement systems, e.g., the use of a token economy system compared with the use of social rewards, was not undertaken due to temporal limitations.

Since the data were collected in a field-based classroom setting, the modes of presentation were, of necessity, only primarily oriented. In both classes, for example, while some written work was involved in almost all activities, the primarily visual presentation involved the use of stimuli presented on either the blackboard or the overhead projector (visually structuring the math problems or outlining the visual configuration of the spelling words); the primarily auditory modality involved teacher lecture and/or discussion; and the primarily multi-sensory modality involved the use of concrete objects (e.g., Cuisenaire Rods and dominoes in math and three-dimensional letters or writing on clay tablets in spelling).

Mean gain scores are reported in Table 1. Inspection of scores revealed that in mathematics, Johnny appeared to perform better when the content was presented multisensorily and when he was allowed to respond in a less traditional manner (i.e., when provided with pictorial cues on the worksheets). In spelling, however, he appeared to profit most from visually presented materials. Johnny still seemed to need partial cues (i.e., seeing three different word spellings) to enable him to produce accurate responses.

Two points concerning Johnny's performance are noteworthy. First, he appeared to manifest different preferred presentation

Table 1
Mean Gain Scores

Mathematics (Abstract Worksheets; 12 items each):
Primarily Visual Presentation   4.0
Primarily Auditory Presentation   4.3
Primarily Multisensory Presentation   7.7

Mathematics (Pictorial Worksheets; 12 items each):
Primarily Visual Presentation   4.5
Primarily Auditory Presentation   5.5
Primarily Multisensory Presentation   8.0

Spelling (Traditional Worksheets; 12 words each):
Primarily Visual Presentation   6.7
Primarily Auditory Presentation   3.7
Primarily Multisensory Presentation   4.7

Spelling (Multiple Choice Worksheets; 12 words each):
Primarily Visual Presentation   7.5
Primarily Auditory Presentation   3.5
Primarily Multisensory Presentation   4.5

modalities in the different academic areas. When comparing the data reported for Johnny with data obtained on other students in similar situations, this result has been observed often enough to be considered typical rather than uncommon. Second, Johnny's relatively high gain scores (which appear higher than would be predicted by his traditionally determined IQ scores) were interpreted as indicative of "functional" retardation at best. Indeed, it would appear that the scores produced on the traditionally administered psychometric as well as academic tests were spuriously low in this particular case. In the event that this is an accurate interpretation, use of the LP diagnostic strategy may prove preferable to the traditional diagnostic approach, at least with students similar to Johnny.

Program Evaluation

The development of a diagnostic classroom based on the learning potential strategy occurred, for the most part, while the author served as a special education "teacher trainer" in a private, parochial university in central Texas. At the time, Diagnostic Classes were being funded to allow local systems to temporarily place mildly involved students within diagnostically oriented special education classes for a maximum of 90 days. The LP version of the Diagnostic Classroom was specifically designed to produce a systematic approach to the in-class, dynamic assessment of such children. Because of the lack of external funds as well as the emphasis on teacher training rather than research activity, the program evolved, of necessity, through the use of undergraduate and graduate students who initially volunteered to implement the strategy in their practice placements. Later, some of these individuals actively continued the practice in their own classroom settings. As a consequence, most of the early program evaluation consisted of subjective evaluations. As the overall strategy solidified, data were collected on individual students within differing settings.

In view of the nature of the state-funded Diagnostic Classrooms, the subjects involved consisted of mildly handicapped students tentatively under consideration for placement within Learning Disabilities, Emotionally Disturbed (Behavior Disorders) or Educable Mentally Retarded resource room programs. According to the guidelines in force at the time, students could be placed in such diagnostically oriented classes for a maximum of 90 days, after which they had either to be returned to the regular program or recommended for special education placement. While the author's ultimate goal was the development of a diagnostic classroom in which the entire day consisted of similarly structured class periods, the majority of the implementing teachers agreed that the most efficacious approach has been to restrict the use of the test-teach-retest strategy to a maximum of three major content areas at a time. Because of the extensive preparation time and paperwork involved in initiating such a program, the employment of more than three periods structured in this fashion has proved unacceptably fatiguing. The academic areas in which the LP approach has proven particularly successful are mathematics, reading and spelling; the procedures have enjoyed limited success in science and social studies.

Early in the development of the system, an attempt was made to improve both Feuerstein's clinical approach (Feuerstein, 1967, 1968, 1970, 1979, and 1980) and Budoff's molecular tack (Budoff, 1965, 1967; Budoff, Meskin, & Harrison, 1971; Gimon, Budoff, & Corman, 1974) through the construction of a standardized set of specific instructional packets to be used by all diagnostic teachers. The rationale is that if the content is presented in a consistent manner by controlling the teacher's personal input, comparable results will be produced. Such results would then, conceivably, permit the development of age-related, interpretive norms. Unfortunately, although standardized approaches were repeatedly tested, all attempts to construct sets of instructional units that negated the effects of teachers' instructional styles failed. Regardless of the approach used, each of the implementing teachers or teachers-in-training indicated that they felt uncomfortable as well as restricted when employing the standardized instructions. In addition, when they attempted to employ instructional strategies other than their own, their students failed to demonstrate clearly discernible preferred learning modalities or response patterns. As a result of the early attempts to control instructional input, subsequent efforts focused on the development of an overall instructional strategy that allowed each teacher to develop his or her own materials and use his or her teaching strengths while still employing a highly similar test-teach-retest approach.

References

Budoff, M.(1965). Learning potential among the educable retarded. Progress report. Unpublished manuscript. Cambridge, Mass.: Mental Health Clinic.

Budoff, M.(1967). Learning potential among institutionalized young adult retardates. *American Journal of Mental Deficiency*, 72, 404-411.

Budoff, M., Meskin, J., & Harrison, R.H.(1971). Educational test of the learning potential hypothesis. *American Journal of Mental Deficiency*, 76, 159-169.

Feuerstein, R.(1967). *Problems of Assessment and evaluation of the mentally retarded and culturally deprived child and adolescent: The Learning Potential Assessment Device.* Unpublished manuscript. Presented at the First Congress of the International Association for the Scientific Study of Mental Deficiency, Montpelier, Vermont.

Feuerstein, R.(1968). *The Learning Potential Assessment Device: A new method for assessing modifiability of the cognitive functioning of socioculturally disadvantaged adolescents.* Unpublished manuscript. Presented to Israel Foundations Trustees, Tel Aviv, Israel.

Feuerstein, R.(1970). A dynamic approach to the causation, prevention and alleviation of retarded performance. In H.C. Haywood (Ed.), *Social-cultural aspects of mental retardation* (pp. 341-377). New York: Appleton-Century-Crofts.

Feuerstein, R.(1979). *The dynamic assessment of retarded performers: The Learning Potential Assessment Device, theory, instruments and techniques.* Baltimore: University Park Press.

Feuerstein, R.(1980). *Instrument enrichment: An intervention program for cognitive modifiability.* Baltimore: University Park Press.

Gimon, A., Budoff, M., & Corman, L.(1974). *Applicability of learning potential measurement with Spanish-speaking youth as an alternative to IQ.* Final report, Grant OEG-1-72-0020(509). Washington, D.C.: Office of Education.

Hausman, R.M.(1972). *Efficacy of three Learning Potential Assessment procedures with Mexican-American educable mentally retarded children.* Unpublished doctoral dissertation. Nashville, TN: Peabody College for Teachers.

Kohs, S.C.(1923). *Intelligence measurement.* New York: Macmillan.

Neville, D.(1968). *Peabody Differentiated Learning Test(PDLT).* Nashville, TN: George Peabody College for Teachers.

Raven, J.C.(1956). *Guide to using the Coloured Progressive Matrices.* London, England: H.K. Lewis & Co.

Part 6
Other Methods/Procedures

NONBIASED ASSESSMENT OF THE PRESCHOOL CHILD

Marcia L. Mc Evoy and David W. Barnett

Assessment and intervention of preschool children have received considerable recent attention (e.g., Bagnato & Neisworth, 1981). At the same time, evidence suggests a lack of preparation in this area for school psychologists (Goh, Teslow, & Fuller, 1981). For children of all ages, implementing procedural guidelines for assessment (Barnett, 1983; Oakland, 1977, 1980), avoiding clinical assessment errors (e.g., Nay, 1979), and being concerned with social outcomes of test usage (Messick, 1980; Reschly, 1979) are critical. Problems with preschool assessment and intervention result from the following: (a) a lack of consensus in theory about child development, especially cognitive and emotional development; (b) the neglect of key constructs of importance to young children (e.g., play, social-cognition); (c) instability and rapid change in cognition, language, and motor skills; (d) concerns about unnecessary or harmful labeling; and (e) inadequate, unnecessary intervention, or treatment having unintentional, negative long term consequences (e.g., Willems, 1977). In addition, a comprehensive multicultural approach to assessing minority groups has been at best unevenly represented in the coursework, practica, and research requirements of professional psychology programs (e.g., Bernal & Padilla, 1982). Only recently are references available which attend to the wide range of necessary professional skills and attitudes (e.g., Bass, Wyatt, & Powell, 1982).

The following two cases were selected to help illustrate the application of nondiscriminatory assessment with young minority children. They were brought to the attention of the second author as a mental health consultant to a Head Start program serving a primarily black and Appalachian population.

Rafael, a black child, was identified at eighteen months because of a severe language delay as indicated by his guardian. By the time he reached Head Start at age four, he was described by a social case worker as "possibly" mentally retarded and emotionally disturbed. In the classroom, his preschool teacher described him as being aggressive, destructive, sometimes violent, distractible, very active, and noncommunicative. Observed behaviors included kicking, punching, and hitting objects. An evaluation was conducted and assessment information was used to plan several intervention strategies. He was then reevaluated a year later at age five.

Danny, also a black child, began Head Start at age four. He was referred at age five because both his teacher and his mother were concerned about his high activity level, impulsivity, and distractibility. He had difficulty following directions, sustaining attention on required tasks, working in a small group without constant supervision, or sitting quietly for more than a very short period of time. Prior to the evaluation, Danny's mother and grandmother had made an appointment with their family physician for the prescription of medication to control his hyperactivity. They and their physician agreed to wait until after the evaluation before proceeding with medical intervention. The following are the psychological reports written for Rafael and Danny, including the recommendations and mutually agreed upon intervention strategies. The reports are about actual children referred for psychological services and are presented almost verbatim. For purposes of confidentiality, all dates and identifying information were modified or excluded.

Case I: Rafael

Name: Rafael Armstrong
Birthdate: 6-15-76
Sex: Male
Age: Five years, five months
Grade: 5 year old class
School: Head Start
Dates of Evaluation: 11-16-81; 11-18-81; 11-30-81; 12-2-81; 12-9-81; 12-16-81

Reason for Referral. Rafael was referred in the fall of 1980 because of behavioral problems associated with adjustment to school. A reevaluation was recommended after a suitable period of time during which intervention strategies would be implemented. In addition, in the fall of 1981, Rafael's teacher referred him for psychoeducational assessment because of her concerns that he was experiencing difficulty in following directions, communicating with peers and adults, and getting interested in preacademic work.

Background Information. Rafael has been enrolled in the Head Start program since September, 1979, and is currently enrolled in a class of five year olds. He was initially referred for evaluation by his teacher when he was four years, five months old because of her concerns about his aggressive behavior, activity level, and lack of communicative abilities. At that time, the multidisciplinary team determined that Rafael's most prevalent needs were for intervention strategies aimed at assisting with the acquisition of self-control and reducing impulsivity and aggressive behaviors. They also determined that Rafael could benefit from help in relating positively to peers, increasing his attention span, reducing his activity level, and participating in and completing activities. A behavior management program was implemented aimed at the above areas with very successful results. A staff conference was held on 5-11-81 with the consensus that Rafael had made remarkable progress with the aforementioned concerns and that he could now benefit from assessment of his educational needs.

Rafael's communication skills were evaluated by the Speech Pathologist in November, 1981. The test results indicated a significant delay in both receptive and expressive language processes. The Speech Pathologist also noted that Rafael failed both his pure tone hearing and middle ear impedence screening. This failure indicated possible auditory difficulties which could have contributed to his delayed language development.

Completion of the Learning Accomplishment Profile (LAP) by Rafael's teacher in October, 1981, showed his development to be approximately the following: Gross and fine motor skills (four years), social skills (four years), self-help skills (three years, six months), cognitive skills (three years, six months), and language skills (two years).

Evaluation Techniques. Stanford-Binet Intelligence Scale; Wechsler Preschool and Primary Scales of Intelligence (nonverbal section only); Developmental Test of Visual-Motor Integration (VMI); Developmental Profile (with mother); Test of Language Development (TOLD); Boehm Test of Basic Concepts; Burks' Behavior Rating Scale (with mother and teacher); Classroom Observations; Interview with teacher.

RESULTS

Intellectual. Rafael was administered the Stanford-Binet and the WPPSI (in part), both measures of general cognitive skills. Because of Rafael's serious receptive and expressive language difficulties, the test results represented only a *minimal estimate* of his current functioning and were

319

used primarily as a tool to achieve insights into areas of cognitive development and learning style.

On the Binet, Rafael was able to receive credit for passing all items at the three year, six month level and achieving a scattering of successes through age level five. All of Rafael's successes at the four year and four year-six month levels were on tasks which required either a nonverbal or one word response. For example, he was able to name pictures of objects, identify objects by description, visually discriminate various geometric forms, and carry out three verbal directions in the correct sequence. At the five year level, Rafael was able to provide functional definitions of objects such as ball and stove.

On the WPPSI and Binet, Rafael's language difficulties interfered with his ability to respond correctly to both items of a verbal nature and items requiring comprehension of lengthy instructions. However, on the WPPSI, during the administration of a nonverbal task requiring comprehension of only short directions, his performance improved significantly and was in the average range.

Testing of limits procedures was utilized by repeating questions, altering question formats, providing extra modeling and prompts, and removing time limits. These modifications resulted in some improvement in Rafael's performance. Several of the items missed by Rafael during standardized procedures were initially repeated verbatim at the beginning of the testing of limits session, and he was able to answer a few of these items correctly on the first attempt. On other items, Rafael could provide the correct answer if the question was rephrased, but he did not comprehend the original question as stated. It appeared that Rafael could perform more adequately when repetitions and modifications were made, suggesting the need for similar strategies to be utilized in the classroom. Part of Rafael's language problems may be the result of suspected auditory difficulties.

Personal-Social. During the evaluation sessions, rapport was established by engaging in play activities with Rafael. Once rapport was established, Rafael was cooperative and seemed to work best when testing sessions were relatively short and followed by a play activity of his choice.

Personal and social areas of concern were identified during the individual sessions with Rafael, teacher interviews, and on the Burks' Behavior Rating Scale, which was filled out separately by Rafael's mother and teacher. In general, Rafael was seen as needing assistance in (a) the pragmatics of communication in order to facilitate positive social interactions, (b) self-control regarding impulsive behaviors, and (c) other specific skills related to play and social interaction with his peers (e.g., taking turns, identifying feelings, learning ways to resolve conflicts, associating one's behaviors with the actions and reactions of others, etc.). Many of the concerns expressed by Rafael's teacher last year were not apparent this year because of his positive responses and resultant growth when interventions aimed at those particular areas of difficulty were implemented. Similarly, an assumption can be made that Rafael has the same potential for growth in the present areas of concern when instructional methods directed toward those problem areas are applied.

Language. The Test of Language Development (TOLD) was administered to survey Rafael's language skills over a range of areas including receptive and expressive vocabulary, grammatical understanding, sentence completion and imitation, and word articulation. This instrument was not sensitive enough to assess the present extent of Rafael's language abilities as the norms did not extend downward to the necessary degree. However, Rafael's performance indicated that his skills were at least one year, six months below his age level with difficulties in both receptive and expressive processes.

Rafael was also administered the Boehm, which measures the child's understanding of language concepts in the areas of space, quantity, and time. Rafael scored in the 35th percentile and displayed an uneven scattering of successes across the measured areas, demonstrating the most difficulty with concepts of time and quantity. During the testing sessions, Rafael often had trouble selectively attending to just one set of pictures on the page. He also frequently responded beore instructions were completed. When pictures not being examined were covered, and firm limits were set concerning when to begin, Rafael's performance improved. When limits were assessed after test completion, Rafael demonstrated understanding of a significant number of the language concepts missed with the paper and pencil format when concrete objects were used to test his knowledge. For example, although he missed the concepts "below" and "alike" during standard administration, he was able to point to the place below the table, as well as hand the examiner two blocks that were alike in color from five possible choices.

Perceptual-Motor. On the VMI, a task requiring the child to copy geometric forms of increasing difficulty, Rafael's performance was equivalent to the performance of a child of about four years, one month. After standard administration of the VMI, the examiner tested the limits of Rafael's current ability by having him imitate the examiner's drawings. In this manner, he was able to improve the quality of his reproductions.

Developmental. Rafael's mother was interviewed using the Developmental Profile to help evaluate his growth in five major areas. The following age levels approximate Mrs. Armstrong's perceptions of Rafael's development: physical development (six years, two months), self-help skills (four years, four months), social skills (four years, two months), academic skills (three years, six months), and communication skills (three years, ten months).

According to Mrs. Armstrong, Rafael's physical abilities were well developed for his age. He could perform many age appropriate tasks as well as tasks estimated above this level. Rafael's difficulties with social interaction, language, and fine motor coordination significantly affected his functioning in the other developmental realms.

The LAP, which reflected the teacher's perceptions of Rafael's development, corroborated the results of the Developmental Profile in the areas of social and academic development. In the areas of gross and fine motor, self-help and language skills, the mother perceived Rafael's skills to be more highly developed than did the teacher. These differences might be explained as an indication that Rafael responded differently in the home and school setting, there were greater opportunities to observe certain behaviors in different settings, or bias existed in one or both sets of observations. The different estimates may require further exploration.

RECOMMENDATIONS.

1. Rafael should be referred for an audiological examination for further diagnostic testing of suspected auditory difficulties.

2. Rafael should be referred to the Head Start Speech/Language Clinician for therapy in both receptive and expressive language processes.

3. The following activities are suggested for Rafael's mother and teacher as general methods to improve his expressive and receptive language skills:

    A. A specific time could be set aside daily when Rafael is encouraged to talk about his school experiences (i.e., after school, during dinner). Assisting him to order his experiences sequentially in time would be beneficial for teaching concepts such as first, second, third, before, last, etc.

    B. Rafael should be encouraged to respond in whole sentences. An adult could model appropriate responses by recasting

Rafael's two or three word utterances into more complete phrases or sentences, and then encouraging him to repeat them after the adult. Rafael should be praised for successive approximations.

C. Rafael's vocabulary could be improved by having an adult leaf through a magazine or picture book with him, and then assist him to identify objects or actions (such as running, cooking, playing).

D. Reading and discussing stories, sharing television programs, teaching jingles and short poems, and retelling past experiences are all activities that promote communication skills.

E. When going shopping, objects could be named for Rafael as they are placed in the shopping cart. Next, he could be asked to "Say it the way I do." This activity might also be applied to common objects found in and around the home, and approached as a game.

F. Language concepts such as around, through, between, next to, away from, in front of, alike, different, etc., could be introduced by using everyday objects (blocks, pencils, chairs, pictures) and common situations (standing in line, taking turns on the playground, eating lunch).

G. Rafael could be paired for classroom activities with a friend of his choice to provide an appropriate language and social skills model and increase the opportunities for engaging in conversation and appropriate play.

4. Rafael may be eligible to participate in the Resource Room program to receive assistance in developing readiness skills. Activities might include:

A. Using concrete materials like blocks, pennies, buttons, or an abacus to learn number concepts.

B. Learning number songs such as Three Little Indians, One, Two, Buckle My Shoe, etc.

C. Building and counting block towers; counting and clapping games.

D. Using geometric forms, letters, and numbers in an adapted form of the game *Concentration* to assist Rafael in identifying, sorting, and matching skills.

E. Developing auditory recognition of letter sounds using concrete objects or magazine pictures; this might be accomplished by using shoe boxes, each representing a particular letter sound, and collecting toys, pictures, or other objects for Rafael to place in the appropriate box.

5. A combined program for academic and fine motor skills could be employed using the chalkboard in assisting Rafael with writing letters, numbers, and copying geometric shapes. First, he could begin by tracing large letters, numbers, and shapes on the board with his index finger either with or without the help of the teacher. Second, he could be physically guided by his teacher(s) in first tracing over, then copying, the letters with chalk until he could make fair approximations of the shapes by himself. Third, Rafael could move to a paper and pencil task where he would draw outlines of the shapes with a pencil using stencils or templates. Finally, he could practice the shapes by copying models.

6. Rafael can be assisted by both his regular and resource room teacher in learning how to follow directions. An appropriate activity might include playing Simple Simon games in which Rafael must listen carefully for what "Simon says." At first, only one short direction should be given, with gradual increases in the number and complexity of the directions as Rafael's performance improves. In the beginning, verbal directions could be combined with visual directions. If errors are made, Rafael should be asked to repeat the directions and helped to locate his errors. When Rafael is required to do seat work in which he must attend to and follow directions, the following techniques can be implemented: (a) the teacher should use visual aids whenever possible; (b) focus Rafael's attention before beginning verbal directions (if this is a problem, rearrange seating, move closer to him, redirect his attention, and have him repeat the directions or explain in his own words); (c) once work is started, check frequently to help Rafael stay on-task; and (d) if he has difficulty, repeat directions and help Rafael locate his errors by modeling error correcting behaviors (i.e., self-monitoring, comparing, and correcting responses).

7. Rafael can be provided with situations conducive to social interaction. Examples of such situations might include giving Rafael tasks that involve coordinated efforts and cooperation of at least two children, such as doing puzzles, playing catch, teeter-totter, or games for two such as pick-up sticks.

Case II: Danny

Name: Daniel Sanders
Birthdate: 8-28-75
Sex: Male
Age: Five years, six months
Grade: 5 year old class
School: Head Start
Dates of Evaluation: 2-19-81; 2-23-81; 2-26-81; 3-2-81; 3-4-81; 3-9-81

Reason for Referral. Danny was referred for psychoeducational assessment because of his teacher's concerns about his activity level, impulsivity, and disinterest in preacademic work.

Background Information. Danny has been enrolled in the Head Start program since September, 1979, and is currently enrolled in a class of five year olds. Completion of the Learning Accomplishment Profile (LAP) by Danny's teacher in January, 1981, showed his development to be approximately the following: gross motor skills (five years), fine motor skills (four years, six months), social and self-help skills (five years), cognitive and language skills (four years, six months).

Valuation Techniques. Stanford-Binet Intelligence Scale; Basic School Skills Inventory (BSSI); Peabody Picture Vocabulary Test-Revised (PPVT-R); Boehm Test of Basic Skills; Developmental Test of Visual-Motor Integration (VMI); Draw-A-Person; Burks' Behavior Rating Scale (with teacher); Developmental Profile (with mother and grandmother); Interview with Teacher; Classroom Observations.

Results

Intellectual. Danny was administered the Stanford-Binet, a measure of general cognitive skills. During the testing session, Danny was easily distracted and exhibited difficulty staying on task or in his seat for more than a few minutes. His overall approach to tasks suggested that he had an "impulsive" cognitive style; he offered his answers quickly, without critically examining the potential accuracy of his responses, and would often begin tasks before directions were given. For these reasons, the test results represented only a *minimal estimate* of Danny's current functioning and were used primarily to help select domains for instruction and to serve as a baseline for evaluating progress after a sufficient time for intervention.

Danny passed all subtests at the four year level and achieved a scattering of successes through age level five. No significant strengths or weaknesses were detected.

Danny responded well to praise, but worked for only short periods of time before losing interest in the tasks. Throughout the testing sessions, he continually asked for reassurances about his performance and attempted to seek the examiner's approval. Many avoidance techniques were noted such as trying to distract the examiner's attention; getting out of his seat; and requesting permission to go to the bathroom, play with toys, or go back to the classroom. When firm limits were set, Danny's behavior improved. He seemed to work best when testing sessions were short and followed by a play activity of his choice or a small reward, e.g., Cracker Jack surprise toys.

Testing of limits procedures were utilized by rephrasing and repeating questions, providing guided prompts, and giving explicit feedback. These modifications resulted in a substantial improvement in Danny's performance, placing him in the average range of intellectual functioning. It appeared that Danny could perform adequately when modeling and specific feedback were provided.

Personal-Social. Through classroom and assessment observations, a teacher interview, and the teacher's perceptions on the Burks' Behavior Rating Scale, several significant personal and social areas seemed to warrant attention in terms of Danny's adjustment to school.

Danny's teacher described him as a very active child who had difficulty waiting his turn, concentrating on one task at a time, and engaging in structured activities without a great deal of guidance and supervision. She stated that he sought a large amount of her attention and approval. Danny's mother and grandmother expressed many of the same concerns regarding Danny's behavior at home.

In general, Danny was seen as needing assistance in the following areas: (a) learning how to follow directions and to wait his turn; (b) increasing his attention span and controlling his impulsivity; (c) being cooperative as, for example, when taking instruction; and (d) learning how to work efficiently in small group settings. Further, his responses to discipline as well as the various discipline strategies used required attention. Danny's teacher observed that his performance on structured activities improved when these tasks were followed by an unstructured activity of his choice. He also responded well to teacher praise and peer approval.

Academic. The Basic School Skills Inventory was administered to Danny to assess his academic readiness in the areas of basic information, self-help and oral communication skills, handwriting, reading and number readiness, and classroom behavior. The results indicated above average performance in oral communication and basic information. In the other areas, Danny was seen as benefiting from instruction in: (a) recognizing and naming letters of the alphabet; (b) recognizing letter sounds; (c) understanding concepts of quantity; (d) counting to twenty; (e) recognizing the numbers one through ten; (f) printing from left to right; (g) drawing common shapes; (h) printing his first and last name; (i) sharing toys and games with other children; and (j) following classroom rules.

Language. Danny's receptive vocabulary, as measured by the Peabody Picture Vocabulary Test-Revised, was within the average range. On the Boehm, which measures a child's understanding of language concepts in the areas of space, time, and quantity, Danny scored in the 50th percentile, indicating average functioning. On both the PPVT-R and the Boehm, Danny was reminded throughout to examine all possible choices before responding because of his tendency to answer quickly without carefully considering each potential response. These reminders helped Danny to be more reflective, and resulted in improved performance.

Perceptual-Motor. On the VMI, a task requiring the child to copy geometric shapes of increasing difficulty, Danny's performance was below that expected of his chronological age. After standard administration of the VMI, the examiner tested limits by having Danny imitate the examiner's drawings and self-instructions. In this manner, Danny was able to improve the quality of his reproductions significantly. Danny's teacher reported that he could benefit from additional practice and instruction in fine motor activities such as cutting, tying shoes, printing letters, and copying shapes.

Developmental. In order to help evaluate Danny's growth in five major areas, his mother and grandmother were interviewed, using the Developmental Profile. The following age levels approximated their perceptions of Danny's development: physical development (six years), self-help skills (five years, six months), social skills (four years, two months), academic kills (four years, ten months), and communication skills (five years, six months). On measures of academic and social skills, his performance was affected by his fine motor difficulties and his tendency to be impulsive and very active.

RECOMMENDATIONS

1. Danny should receive a complete physical examination by the staff pediatrician at Head Start. In addition, consultation regarding his diet would be beneficial.

2. A teacher-managed, school and home-based reward program for reducing Danny's impulsivity can be implemented. The program may also indirectly help Danny identify appropriate activity levels for different settings. Included in the program will be the following components:

    A. At the beginning of each school day, the teacher specifies Danny's classroom goals for that day. Such goals might include eating breakfast without spilling, playing with one other child without fighting, waiting his turn, listening to instructions, and completing structured tasks.

    B. The teacher awards Danny a checkmark on a card and praises him for each correct academic or behavioral response. These checkmarks could be exchanged later in the day for a choice among a variety of rewards.

    C. At the end of the day, the teacher evaluates Danny's behavior relevant to his goals and sends Danny's mother a daily report card on Danny's progress toward his goals.

    D. His mother, in turn, rewards Danny for progress toward his goals.
    Danny's classmates can be reinforced whenever Danny meets his goals in order to facilitate their encouragement and cooperation in the plan. Ongoing consultation with Danny's mother, grandmother, and teacher in terms of monitoring and evaluating the plan will be implemented.

3. Danny's educational program can include opportunities for developing a more effective problem-solving approach that could be applied in many situations. He needs to "Stop, Look, Listen, and Think." This could be done in the following manner:

    A. First, an adult could solve a problem while verbalizing his/her problem-solving strategy logically, step-by-step.

    B. Danny could then perform the same task, using the step-by-step apprach as he is guided and directed through the process.

C. Next, he could be required to go through the problem- solving steps alone, verbalizing each step aloud as the adult listens.

D. Finally, inner speech is used.

4. The following activities can be used to help Danny develop the academic skills necessary for next year.

A. Help Danny identify letters and numbers by playing letter/number bingo with him. Cards with different letters or numbers can be passed to each player. The adult or child covers the appropriate letter/number when it is called. The first person to fill a card is the winner.

B. Have Danny establish counting through large and small muscle activities such as clapping, jumping, stringing beads or buttons, building block towers, and counting aloud when going up or down stairs.

C. Play the card game "War" with Danny to develop his understanding of quantity (more than, less than). Playing this game could also facilitate recognition of numbers through repeated exposure.

D. Teach the alphabet song.

E. Develop auditory recognition of letters by teaching letter sounds, using concrete objects or pictures of objects. This might be accomplished by identifying the initial sounds of varied illustrated objects in books or magazines.

F. Utilize dot-to-dot activity books which connect letters, numbers, and shapes.
In order to increase Danny's willingness to participate in structured academic activities, these activities should be of short duration at first, then gradually lengthened and interspersed with play activities of Danny's choice contingent on adequate performance.

5. Danny can be assisted in learning how to follow directions. Activities which could be utilized with several children at once include games whereby the number and complexity of the directions are increased as performance improves. If errors are made, Danny could be asked to repeat the directions to help him locate his errors.

Significant or Innovative Nature of the Practices

Certain procedures are common to both the cases of Rafael and Danny. First, an attempt was made to utilize multifactored assessment techniques to provide a broad variety of information and to avoid bias and labeling. Both evaluations included cognitive, language, social/emotional, adaptive, academic, and gross and fine motor areas. Both norm and criterion-referenced tests were used for the purposes of establishing long- and short-term instructional objectives. An ecologically based, psychosocial/situational framework for assessment and intervention was also utilized. Direct observations of the children were made in a variety of settings (classroom, resource room, playground, hallway). In addition, the time of the evaluations was intentionally extended over a period of one month to provide a more reliable and valid framework for decision making. The assessment process for both children included frequent contact with significant persons in their lives. Rafael's mother and social workers and Danny's mother and grandmother were seen on many separate occasions to discuss their children's educational and developmental histories and consult about changes occurring at school or home. Both mothers' concerns, and their degree of correspondence with school concerns, were explored via rating scales, interviews, and the Developmental Profile, a technique designed specifically to reduce bias.

Another significant procedure in both cases was the advocacy rather than clinical perspective of the psychological report (Zins & Barnett, 1983). Maladaptive behaviors were recast in terms of barriers to adjustment and needs to be met by social and educational systems and personal resources. Further, healthy mechanisms both within the children and within their social systems were assessed and used to develop interventions. Contrasts in performance during standard administration of tests and during testing of limits sessions were used for describing optimal versus usual functioning and assessing emerging skills. Both were important in setting realistic but high expectations. Rafael was not prematurely labeled mentally retarded, behavior disordered, or emotionally disturbed, nor was Danny labeled hyperactive or mentally retarded. Each of these labels would have been possibilities at different times during the evaluation given conventional test interpretation, or because of the evaluation techniques selected.

In the assessment of minority children, an attempt should be made to incorporate a model of ethnic validity (e.g., Savage & Adair, 1980). In both cases, the settings were culturally diverse at administrative and service levels; a minority director, social workers, and teachers, as well as the children's mothers, were collaborative participants in decision making. The purpose of the evaluations, and the potential positive and negative outcomes were clarified. Interventions were mutually agreed upon by all involved.

Other significant practices in both cases included the nontraditional interpretation of traditional measures, and a consistent emphasis on a process-oriented approach to evaluation procedures. For both children, tests could not be administered in a strictly standardized manner. In the case of Rafael, his severe behavior problems during the first evaluation, and his severe language difficulties during the second evaluation a year later, would probably have led to underestimated abilities and would have precluded any further attempt to obtain a fair estimate of cognitive skills. In Danny's case, his high activity level, impulsivity, and distractibility interfered with test procedures and accurate test interpretation. Therefore, specific IQ scores or ranges were *not* reported for either child and test results were described only in terms of tools to (a) provide baseline information for later reevaluation' (b) help select domains for interventions; (c) achieve insights into areas of cognitive development and learning style; and (d) estimate the extent of intervention possibly needed (e.g., in-class program, resource room, or special class).

Issues related to test bias with minority children were viewed in terms of the criterion of outcomes for individuals:

> If assessment activities result in needed services, effective interventions, or expanded opportunities for individuals, then assessment is useful, and by the definition proposed here, unbiased. If the assessment activities do not lead to appropriate services and are not related to effective interventions, then the assessment activities must be regarded as useless for the individual, and biased or unfair if members of minority groups are differentially exposed to inappropriate services or ineffective interventions as a result of assessment activities. (Reschly, 1979, pp. 215-216)

Reschly's emphasis on the social consequences of test use and interpretation provides a broader perspective for the psychologist assessing minority children. Whether cultural bias does or does not exist in a test coexists with the important issue of ensuring effective educational outcomes.

In the cases of Rafael and Danny, adhering to strictly standardized procedures and reporting test scores would have resulted in unnecessary labeling. The dangers of labeling have been widely discussed (e.g., Becker, 1963; Hobbs, 1975; Mercer, 1973; Scheff, 1966). Labels can be stigmatizing, dehumanizing, self-fulfilling, and limiting in known or unknown ways. With young children, the following hazards should be considered: labels may restrict parental, teacher, or self-expectations, and the outcome of labeling may not necessarily bring about more effective treatments. Especially in the area of emotional disturbance, there may be little consensus about appropriate diagnosis or treatment. Further, recent studies have addressed the "self-righting" tendencies of young children (Werner, 1982), suggesting minimal or no intervention if informal familial or community support systems are available to the child. In the two cases presented, the children's behavior had been of concern to their parents for several years. Sufficient resources were available to attempt interventions without formal labels. Classification for the provision or organization of services to children is not necessarily harmful or unconstitutional (Bersoff, 1979). However, if appropriate and successful services can be provided without classification, potential and needless dangers can be circumvented.

Diagnosis and remediation were influenced by the conceptual models of Vygotsky (1978) and Feuerstein (1979, 1980), stressing a dynamic approach to the assessment process. Vygotsky stated that normative data obtained in traditional testing are oriented toward developmental stages already completed, and that the examiner assumes that skills indicative of mental ability are reflected only by what children can perform independent of assistance. In contrast, Vygotsky theorized that "what children can do with the assistance of others might be in some sense even more indicative of their mental development than what they can do alone" (Vygotsky, 1978, p. 85). A new role for testing is illustrated within the framework of Vygotsky's concept of the zone of potential development defined as:

> the distance between the actual developmental level as determined by independent problem solving and the level of potential development as determined through problem solving under adult guidance or in collaboration with more capable peers... The zone of potential development defines those functions that have not yet matured but are in the process of maturation... (p. 86)

The zone of potential or proximal development is used as a gauge for measuring cognitive potential. Children with the same IQ score may often vary greatly in terms of their learning potential. A major difference among children with progressive degrees of retardation lies in the width of their potential zone (Brown & French, 1979).

Feuerstein (1979, 1980) has developed a program in Israel that parallels Vygotsky's theory and has resulted in a comprehensive system of assessment and intervention. He has created an instrument called the Learning Potential Assessment Device, which measures cognitive modifiability. In Vygotsky's terms, it is a concrete way of measuring the zone of potential development, as it distinguishes between the level of present functioning of the child and the potential capacity for modifiability.

The ideal testing situation ascribed to by both Feuerstein and Vygotsky, then, would include a supportive adult in an "active and cooperative role" who guides the child to the limits of his current ability. The examiner may ask for repetitions, and may assist the child in anticipating difficulties. An active goal is to create "reflective insightful thinking in the child" (Feuerstein, 1979, p. 102). The degree of improvement which results from interventions is the significant variable, not the original performance. The child's ability to employ and benefit from adult guidance is consistent with the theory that children will eventually incorporate into their own actions what they are able to do only with such help (e.g., Meichenbaum, 1977). This kind of dyadic problem-solving has begun to be systematically researched by a number of psychologists interested in the process by which children acquire self-regulatory skills (Brown & DeLoache, 1978; Mahoney, 1974; Meichenbaum, 1977; Ross, 1981) and interpersonal problem-solving abilities (Spivack, Platt, & Shure, 1976). In earlier efforts, intervention with preschoolers stressed external control rather than the enhancement of internal mechanisms. It seems likely that efficacy expectations and self-regulatory processes may be modified in either a positive or negative way by the child's participation in an intervention (e.g., Bandura, 1981), and these effects should be monitored.

Until more theoretical and empirical verification has been completed on these newer assessment concepts, and until some become commercially available or widely disseminated, the practitioner must rely on his or her own creativity and willingness to experiment with present assessment tools. These attempts are contraindicated by many established conventions in our field but are an aspect of exemplary practice in our view. In the absence of formal statistical or technical solutions to the complexities of test bias, the best contemporary responses seem to lie with a careful consideration of professional practice issues, as well as assessment and intervention within an N=1 framework (Kratochwill, 1977).

In the cases of Rafael and Danny, the evaluation emphasis was changed from the performance outcome to a concern with the process variables—the "why" and "how" of assessment (Meichenbaum, 1977). Both children became the subject of an experimental investigation utilizing a test-teach-retest paradigm, whereby the distinction between assessment and intervention becomes far less significant. After standardized procedures were followed, an attempt was made to provide additional information about each child's abilities by trying to facilitate his performance through a variety of methods and techniques. Testing of limits is one such technique of gathering less biased assessment information for minority group children (Aliotti, 1977). These sessions included rephrasing, repeating, and altering question formats, providing extra modeling and guided prompts, giving explicit feedback, removing time limits, offering leading questions, and providing one or more steps in the problem-solving process. (For a more detailed explanation of these techniques, see Brown & French, 1979; Lidz, 1981; and Sattler, 1982.)

Testing sessions were kept short (six over a period of one month) to sustain interest in the tasks, reduce distractibility, and provide a more reliable and valid framework for drawing conclusions. Because of avoidance behavior displayed by both children, firm limits were set during assessment, and small rewards or play activities of the children's choice were made contingent on completion of items. In this manner, successful techniques for lengthening attention span and establishing reward preferences were discovered. As a result, both children's behavior improved over successive sessions. Because both Rafael and Danny had difficulty with selective attention, items on the Boehm, VMI, PPVT-R, and BSSI that were not being examined were covered. To reduce impulsive behavior (e.g., responding before screening each item), the examiner held the children's hands and pointed to each of the items before completing instructions. Familiar objects, such as blocks and other toys, were utilized to test for language concepts missed in response to the paper and pencil format of the Boehm. Cognitive-behavioral techniques (e.g., Camp & Bash, 1981; Meichenbaum & Goodman, 1971; Meichenbaum, 1977) were used to help the children imitate the examiner's drawings on the visual-perceptual designs missed. The process orientation resulted in a series of hypotheses for possible intervention.

In summary, the authors attempted to utilize ecologically based, multifactored assessment techniques and process-oriented procedures to establish interventions and to avoid bias and labeling. Both reports were written from an advocacy viewpoint. The authors also attempted to incorporate a model of ethnic validity. Assessment was ongoing and interventions were mutually agreed upon through continuing consultation with parents, teachers, and related professionals.

Despite these similarities, there were significant points of divergence in the two cases. With Danny, a formal diagnosis of hyperactivity and mental retardation was avoided, and instead the treatment of his attentional deficit and off-task behavior was addressed. Medication was avoided through the following: (a) dietary management; (b) a teacher-managed, school and home-based behavioral program for reducing activity level and increasing on-task academic behavior; (c) cognitive self-instructional techniques for developing self-control and reflective problem solving; and (d) specific skills training in academic readiness. As a result of the above interventions, Danny's problem behaviors decreased dramatically, and he began to make significant social and academic gains which brought him up to age level in several important areas of his functioning within six months.

Danny's mother and grandmother were interested in and capable of using specific principles of behavior management. Games and techniques were demonstrated using ordinary household items and activities to help teach Danny educational skills at home. These were received well and applied to a moderate extent.

Finally, Danny made significant gains in cognitive skills during the process-oriented approach to assessment. A distinction was made between Danny's actual developmental level (e.g., his completed development as measured on a standardized test—IQ = 73) and his level of proximal development (the degree of competence he achieved with aid—IQ = 94). The results were dramatic and exciting. The change of 21 IQ points took him from the educable mentally retarded range (in his state) to the average range of intellectual functioning. Self-instructional techniques (e.g., Camp & Bash, 1981), when applied to visual-perceptual designs, also resulted in a rapid improvement in Danny's performance.

In the case of Rafael, labeling issues were particularly salient. Because of the variability in behavior of young children and the importance of the interrelationships among language, cognition, and behavior, a low score on an IQ test would be uninterpretable except as measured performance. At various times, Rafael could have been labeled in the following ways: educable mentally retarded in his state (IQ = 69), severe behavior disordered or emotionally disturbed, and/or specific language disabled. A formal diagnosis was avoided in the preschool setting. Because of the nature of Rafael's difficulties, a multidisciplinary assessment was appropriate. In addition to the psychological evaluation, Rafael was referred to a pediatrician, language, speech, and hearing clinician, and social case worker. Bizarre behaviors (e.g., drawings of snakes for family members and for self in the Human Figure Drawing) were monitored for increasing or decreasing trends. Such behaviors can be highly stigmatizing when framed by a psychologist through unnecessary interpretation or when reported as an "interesting" finding, and can create barriers to helping by alarming teachers and assistants. The behaviors were spontaneously terminated in Rafael's case.

During the first year, an in-class behavioral program was developed to reduce aggressive behaviors and to increase on-task behaviors, important prerequisites to learning. Use of primary reinforcers (food, drink) was necessary at first. Gradually, Rafael responded to secondary reinforcers such as being held, having a story read to him, and being allowed to play with glue and clay. A contingency contract for completion of required activities was developed, and a "private" desk was established to reduce distractibility during structured academic tasks. Time out was used for inappropriate behavior. Other children were verbally reinforced for successfully ignoring him when he was acting inappropriately. As a result of these interventions, a great improvement was seen in Rafael's behavior over the course of the year.

Rafael also participated in language therapy for two years where he made significant gains in both expressive and receptive language processes. In a resource room program, and in consultation with his teachers, the following skill areas were also addressed: listening skills, academic skills, and social skills (e.g., turn-taking, cooperative play, self-expression, communication of feelings).

Finally, whereas Danny made dramatic gains in all cognitive areas during the process-oriented approach to assessment, Rafael made only small gains in a few specific areas. Even so, a danger not often discussed when using the test-teach-test format or any similar paradigm to estimate potential is that the intervention of the examiner may disconfirm low potential, but logically cannot assess an absence of or limited potential for change. The type of intervention(s) used by the examiner may not be appropriate. There is no way of directly measuring potential outside of eliciting higher than usual performance from an individual.

In Rafael's case, his performance on the nonverbal subtests of the WPPSI ranged from average to random; his total score would have been misleading, descriptive of neither level, and would have served to disguise the variability of performance. However, the variation in scores and low performance in the verbal areas suggest the likelihood of continued difficulty in school. In later years, his schooling may require special education services. Since services were provided in the preschool setting, premature labeling was prevented. In general, over the two-year span, Rafael's major changes were behavioral, rather than cognitive or academic, therefore avoiding a "diagnosis" of emotional disturbance.

Conclusion

We have attempted to describe some innovative, non-discriminatory assessment practices for use with minority preschool children. Much work needs to be completed before legal, social, conceptual, and empirical problems associated with test usage and interpretation are adequately addressed. There appear to be no easy answers or uniform panaceas for the complexities of test bias. With the increasingly diverse social and cultural characteristics of school children, there is a need for establishing a broader base from which to evaluate a child's potential and reducing inappropriate labeling or ineffective interventions.

In a time of economic retrenchment, within a context of complex social and political issues, an individual's professional and theoretical orientation, skills, and values seem paramount but are often neglected or minimized. The diagnostic testing procedures advocated by Feuerstein and Vygotsky, with emphasis on process dimensions, appeared to be one useful way of obtaining fairer, more accurate assessment information in the two cases presented. In addition, viewing the cases from the ecological, cognitive-behavioral perspective implicit in Bandura's social learning theory seemed to provide a heuristic framework for creating hypotheses and establishing interventions. Social learning theory allows for a complex analysis of cognition within a consistent theoretical orientation. While it is likely that conventional assessment techniques will continue to be used for pragmatic reasons, the authors hope that additional procedures will be implemented based on new knowledge in the areas of cognition and information-processing, neuropsychology, and learning theory. In particular, more systematic and comprehensive research is needed in the modification of existing tests, creation of new instruments, and development of conceptual models which challenge the current thinking about the dimensions of assessment and intervention.

Epilogue

We were unable to respond to many of the concerns and criticisms that resulted from the analysis given by the reviewers since we had reported work that had already been completed. However, our critics have encouraged us to reflect upon and reevaluate our practices, attitudes, and knowledge base. One reviewer failed to see where either of these evaluations is an example of alternative approaches to nonbiased assessment. Another made us reconsider a response to the question, "How do you avoid test bias when biased tools are employed?" A third reviewer made us consider more carefully the role of the teacher in the assessment process and suggested using actual materials found in the classroom as diagnostic aids. We perhaps should modestly mention that many comments were quite positive, lest the reader wonder why we did not, logically, withdraw our contribution. However, we would like to use this opportunity to highlight our reactions to our own work, and to offer a response to our most severe critics.

Any discussion of psychological practices with culturally different individuals is embedded within a context and history of racism. Such feelings and attitudes are impossible to ignore and include both anti-white and anti-black (or minority) sentiments. Recent reviews suggest contradictory findings at first glance: (a) some evidence of improved public acceptance; (b) some evidence of innovativeness with respect to public policy; (c) continued evidence of overt racism; (d) widespread covert racism; and (e) the possibility of substantial variance in interracial acceptance (e.g., reviews by Barnett, 1982; Crosby, Bromley & Saxe, 1980). The review by Crosby, Bromley and Saxe is especially important for a number of reasons. Their findings strongly suggest "covert anti-black racism" as a central theme underlying black-white encounters. Further, their findings underscore what appears to be an inconsistent trilogy of expressed attitudes, private sentiments, and overt behavior in interracial interactions. The only positive outcome, if it can be called that, is a "shift" from blatant to subtle racism among whites. As discussed by Barnett (1982), the research has significant practical ramifications in that it suggests the probability of a rather brittle alliance in situations where trust and mutual goals are prerequisites for change. Majority expressions of concern may seem "pseudoliberal," or embarrassingly suspect. The highly emotional issues and pessimistic findings are likely to deter efforts in innovation and practice in the development of community-based models of mental health and educational intervention in ethnically diverse communities. A related issue is the relative lack of minority psychologists. Cynicism and skepticism abound; daily evidence suggests this to be the case, but evidence for increased acceptance and opportunities for mutual goals also exist.

The reports reflect our philosophical and professional views, in part substantiated by research, but certainly not carved in stone. When we reviewed the research relating to developmental and social constructs, including that of intelligence, we found evidence of substantial change in both theory and practice over the past 70 years. A number of longitudinal studies have permanently modified the view of intelligence as a fixed or immutable quality established at birth. When one extends the recent theoretical developments and research in cognitive psychology into its logical future, it is clear that much more change will be forthcoming (Barnett, 1983). The future of cognitive assessment promises to be rich, exciting, and far more optimistic than implied by contemporary practice with the Wechsler Scales or the Binet (e.g., Flavell, 1982; Lidz, 1983; Rosenthal & Zimmerman, 1978; Sternberg & Detterman, 1979). Simply put, our reports illustrate the application of recent research and theory about psychosocial change and advocacy in order to extend contemporary practice. Perhaps our title is a misnomer. We would like to go on record as saying that "nonbiased" assessment is a poorly understood and multifaceted construct. It is probably best restated as a goal. Any study of bias should include, as a major focus, the specific purposes and social outcomes of the assessment process (Messick, 1980).

Our use of the Binet and WPPSI created a negative stimulus for some of our readers, understandable within a broader context. IQ tests carry so much emotional baggage that we would have been naive to expect anything less. We are in no way accepting the status quo by endorsing their use. The pros and cons of even the traditional usage of IQ tests have been widely debated and disseminated. Our "innovativeness' was to bring the interpretation, process, and outcomes of test use more into line with current research. Numerous studies with diverse populations have found that the "bias" inherent in IQ tests is much more limited than widely accepted beliefs would suggest (for a comprehensive review, see Reynolds, 1982). Further, Ysseldyke and Algozzine (1982) point out that significant sources of bias may result from (a) the statement of the referral problem, (b) the physical characteristics of a child (e.g., race, sex, attractiveness), and (c) the decision making process.

This is not the place for a literature review, nor do we wish to rehash obvious points. However, we do want to point out that the scales are best used as a screening tool for identifying *severe* developmental disabilities with young children. Most of the controversies have related to children with suspected mild handicaps and the subsequent outcomes of special class placements or tracking systems (e.g., Dunn, 1968). In the two cases cited, parents and professionals alike (including minorities) had more limiting opinions about the children than indicated by the results of the testing. The tests disconfirmed more negative, intuitive, or private hypotheses held by individuals working with the children.

The predictive power of the major scales for a child's subsequent few years in school is far from trivial, even though some of the individual questions on the tests themselves may lack intrinsic interest. Flaugher (1978) has warned us that an incorrect interpretation of tests may yield a conclusion to rid ourselves of those "lying" tests, rather than to apply needed resources. Children will not profit from the denial that their school-related skills, as measured by such tests, differ as a result of ethnicity (Scarr, 1981). A well constructed test seems stronger, although far from perfect, than an intuitive approach, as suggested by one of our critics, of applying actual classroom materials as diagnostic aids. Questions remain as to who is to select the materials and to what end? Might a "bias" be involved in this decision also? The many parents we have worked with clearly want their children to succeed in school, and the use of the scales may functionally serve to indicate a need for intervention or support. Unfortunately, special classes have not been the needed remedy. We want our clients to make more informed choices and deliberate decisions, and we want them to develop programs for children tied to validated research whether their role is that of parent or teacher. We have discovered real problems with respect to parents' and teachers' feelings of powerlessness. These often have impeded the development of mutually agreed upon procedures, even though this remains our goal.

We have not attempted to address every relevant issue related to nonbiased assessment within this chapter. As implied earlier, we failed to cast our reports within the realities of political, social, and economic problems, all facets of cross-cultural issues. We do not deny their existence as we face them on a daily basis. Another neglected issue is that of sex role. By far, the vast majority of our clients have been poverty mothers without adequate support systems or finances, raising children under perilous circumstances. For a small number of children, no clearly identifiable "family" seemed to exist, bringing into clarity the implications of Feuerstein's (1979) definition of "sociocultural deprivation or disadvantage." Recast, it may apply to a child "that has become alienated from [his/her] *own culture*" (p. 39). Feuerstein emphasizes the outcomes of alienation, produced by a variety of economic, geographic, and sociological causes which affect the teaching of culture to children. The significance of the mediational processes that adults use to enhance all learning is forcefully demonstrated in such cases.

We cannot attempt to solve all of these difficulties with the processes outlined in our reports, nor do we recommend that anyone try (see Barnett, 1986, for a review of broader issues related to preschool psychological services). All parents have questions and concerns in raising children. Cultural differences may be minimized when mutual goals can be established. Research supports a number of future possibilities (e.g., Laosa & Sigel, 1982). We think that we have helped individual parents and teachers to provide for young children in a responsible and committed manner.

References

Aliotti, N.C. (1977). Alternative assessment strategies in a pluralistic society. *School Psychology Digest, 6,* 6-12.

Bagnato, S.J., & Neisworth, J.T. (1981). *Linking developmental assessment and curricula.* Rockville, MD: Aspen Systems.

Bandura, A. (1981). Self-referent thought: A developmental analysis of self-efficacy. In J.H. Flavell, & L. Ross (Eds.), *Social cognitive development: Frontiers and possible futures* (pp. 200-239). Cambridge, England: Cambridge University.

Barnett, D.W. (1982). Some issues and findings related to interracial acceptance. *Psychological Reports, 51,* 27-37.

Barnett, D.W. (1983). *Nondiscriminatory multifactored assessment: A sourcebook.* New York: Human Sciences Press.

Barnett, D. (1986). School psychology in preschool settings: A review of training and practice issues. *Professional Psychology, 17,* 58-64.

Bass, B.A., Wyatt, G.E., & Powell, G.J. (1982). *The Afro-American family: Assessment, treatment and research issues.* New York: Grune & Stratton.

Becker, H.S. (1963). *Outsiders: Studies in the sociology of deviance.* New York: Free Press.

Bernal, M.E., & Padilla, A.M. (1982). Status of minority curricula and training in clinical psychology. *American Psychologist, 37,* 780-787.

Bersoff, D.N. (1979, Sept). *Legal and psychometric critique of school testing litigation.* Paper presented at the meeting of the American Psychological Association, New York.

Brown, A.L., & DeLoache, J.S. (1978). Skills, plans, and self-regulation. In R. Siegler (Ed.), *Children's thinking: What develops?* (pp. 3-35). Hillsdale, NJ: Lawrence Erlbaum Associates.

Brown, A.L., & French, L.A. (1979). The zone of potential development: Implications for intelligence testing in the year 2000. In R.J. Sternberg & D.K. Detterman (Eds.), *Human intelligence: Perspectives on its theory and measurement* (pp. 217-235). New Jersey: Ablex Publishing.

Camp, B.W., & Bash, M.S. (1981). *Think aloud: Increasing social and cognitive skills—A problem-solving program for children.* Champaign, ILL: Research Press.

Crosby, F., Bromley, S., & Saxe, L. (1980). Recent unobtrusive studies of black and white discrimination and prejudice: A literature review. *Psychological Bulletin, 87,* 546-563.

Dunn, L.M. (1968). Special education for the mildly retarded—is much of it justifiable? *Exceptional Children, 35,* 5-22.

Feuerstein, R. (1979). *The dynamic assessment of retarded performers: The Learning Potential Assessment Device, theory, instruments, and techniques.* Baltimore: University Park Press.

Feuerstein, R. (1980). *Instrument enrichment: An intervention program for cognitive modifiability.* Baltimore: University Park Press.

Flaugher, R.L. (1978). The many definitions of test bias. *American Psychologist, 33,* 671-679.

341

Flavell, J.H. (1982). Structure, stages, and sequences in cognitive development. In W.A. Collins (Ed.), *The concept of development: The Minnesota symposia on child psychology* (Vol. 15) (pp. 1-28). Hillsdale, NJ: Erlbaum.

Goh, D.S., Teslow, C.J., & Fuller, G.B. (1981). The practice of psychological assessment among school psychologists. *Professional Psychology, 12,* 696-706.

Hobbs, N. (Ed.) (1975). *Issues in the classification of children* (Vols. 1 & 2). San Francisco: Jossey-Bass.

Kratochwill, T.R. (1977). N=1: An alternative research strategy for school psychologists. *Journal of School Psychology, 15,* 239-249.

Laosa, L.M., & Sigel, I.E. (Eds.) (1982). *Families as learning environments for children.* New York: Plenum.

Lidz, C.S. (1981). *Improving assessment of school children.* San Francisco: Jossey-Bass.

Lidz, C.S. (1983). Dynamic assessment and the preschool child. *Journal of Psychoeducational Assessment, 1,* 59-72.

Mahoney, M.J. (1974). *Cognition and behavior modification.* Cambridge, MASS: Ballinger.

Meichenbaum, D. (1977). *Cognitive-behavior modification: An integrative approach.* New York: Plenum.

Meichenbaum, D.H., & Goodman, J. (1971). Training impulsive children to talk to themselves: A means of developing self-control. *Journal of Abnormal Psychology, 77,* 115-126.

Mercer, J.R. (1973). *Labeling the mentally retarded.* Berkeley: University of California.

Messick, S. (1980). Test validity and the ethics of assessment. *American Psychologist, 35,* 1012-1027.

Nay, W.R. (1979). *Multimethod clinical assessment.* New York: Gardner Press.

Oakland, T. (Ed.) (1977). *Psychological and educational assessment of minority children.* New York: Brunner/Mazel.

Oakland, T. (1980). Nonbiased assessment of minority group children. *Exceptional Child Quarterly, 1,* 31-46.

Reschly, D.J. (1979). Nonbiased assessment. In G.D. Phye & D.J. Reschly (Eds.), *School psychology: Perspectives and issues* (pp. 215-156). New York: Academic Press.

Reynolds, C.R. (1982). The problem of bias in psychological assessment. In C.R. Reynolds & T.B. Gutkin (Eds.), *The handbook of school psychology* (pp. 178-208). New York: Wiley.

Rosenthal, T.L., & Zimmerman, B.J. (1978). *Social learning and cognition.* New York: Academic Press.

Ross, A.O. (1981). *Child behavior therapy: Principles, procedures, and empirical basis.* New York: John Wiley & Sons.

Sattler, J.M. (1982). *Assessment of children's intelligence and special abilities.* Boston: Allyn & Bacon.

Savage, J.E., & Adair, A.A. (1980). Testing minorities: Developing more culturally relevant assessment systems. In R.L. Jones (Ed.), *Black psychology* (2nd ed.) (pp. 196-200). New York: Harper & Row.

Scarr, S. (1981). Dilemmas in the assessment of disadvantaged children. In M.J. Begab, H.C. Haywood, & H.L. Garber (Eds.), *Psychosocial influences in retarded performance* Vol. II: *Strategies for improving competence* (pp. 3-16). Baltimore, MD: University Park Press.

Scheff, T.J. (1966). *Being mentally ill.* Chicago: Aldine.

Spivack, G., Platt, J.J., & Shure, M.B. (1976). *The problem-solving approach to adjustment.* San Francisco: Jossey-Bass.

Sternberg, R.J., & Detterman, D.K. (Eds.) (1979). *Human intelligence: Perspectives on its theory and measurement.* Norwood, NJ: Ablex.

Vygotsky, L.S. (1978). *Mind in society: The development of higher psychological processes.* Cambridge, MASS: Harvard University Press.

Werner, E.E. (1982). Sources of support for high-risk children. In N.J. Anastasiow, W.K. Frankenburg, & A.W. Fandal (Eds.), *Identifying the developmentally delayed child.* Baltimore: University Park Press.

Willems, E.P. (1977). Steps toward an ecobehavioral technology. In A. Rogers-Warren & S.F. Warren (Eds.), *Ecological perspectives in behavioral analysis.* Baltimore: University Park Press.

Ysseldyke, J.E., & Algozinne, B. (1982). *Critical issues in special and remedial education.* Boston: Houghton Mifflin.

Zins, J.E., & Barnett, D.W. (1983). Report writing: Legislative, ethical and professional challenges. *Journal of School Psychology, 21,* 219-227.

Appendix

The following is a list of instruments used in the psychological reports:

Alpern, G.D., Boll, T.J., & Shearer, M.S. (1980). *Developmental Profile II.* Aspen, CO: Psychological Development Publications.

Beery, K.E. (1967). *Developmental test of visual-motor integration.* Chicago: Follett.

Boehm, A.E. (1971). *Boehm test of basic concepts.* New York: Psychological Corp.

Burks, H.F. (1977). *Burks' behavior rating scales: Preschool and kindergarten edition.* Los Angeles: Western Psychological Services.

Dunn, L.M., & Dunn, L.M. (1981). *Peabody Picture Vocabulary Test— Revised.* Circle Pines, MN: American Guidance Service.

Goodman, L., & Hammill, D.D. (1975). *Basic Schools Skills Inventory.* New York: Follett.

Newcomer, P.L., & Hammill, D.D. (1977). *The test of language development.* Austin, TX: ProEd.

Terman, L.M., & Merrill, M.A. (1973). *Stanford-Binet Intelligence Scale: 1972 norms edition.* Boston: Houghton Mifflin.

Wechsler, D. (1967). *Manual for the preschool and primary scales of intelligence.* New York: Psychological Corp.

CASE STUDY OF AN "EMOTIONALLY DISTURBED" ESKIMO BOY—UTUK

Debra L. McIntosh and Herbert G.W. Bischoff

Child study teams are frequently challenged by the task of determining a student's eligibility for special services under the "emotionally disturbed" classification. Most professionals would agree that a consensus has not been reached regarding the etiology and behaviors characteristic of an emotional disturbance. Efforts to clarify this category have resulted in the acknowledgment that unique cultural conditions are significant determinants of behavior. These factors must, therefore, be evaluated and appropriately integrated into any assessment. We have observed that the probability of making an inappropriate placement decision is greatly increased if this integration of cultural considerations does not occur.

Utuk is an Eskimo student who was labeled "emotionally disturbed." Soon after the evaluation he transferred to another school within the same district. At the time of the annual review, the decision was made that Utuk no longer qualified for services under this classification. This conclusion was reached despite the fact that his behavior had not changed appreciably from one school setting to the other. The major difference between the two evaluations was that in the second, but not in the first, behavior was judged in terms of local cultural, as well as educational, expectations. This judgment was made to ascertain if conflicting values and standards for behavior were contributing to Utuk's inappropriate classroom behavior.

Our approach to the assessment of cultural influences on behavior and the integration of these into the total evaluation process evolved during our frequent visits to schools in rural Alaska. When we first began servicing these schools in the capacity of consulting school psychologists, the severe environmental conditions impressed us with the necessity of utilizing caution when interpreting the results of standardized tests with this student population. For example, villages generally are isolated and economically depressed. Until the recent acquisition of television, most Eskimos had only limited knowledge of the outside world. Most Eskimo students have never been outside of Alaska; in fact, many have never even traveled to the larger Alaskan communities. Daily activities continue to be consistent with subsistence living (e.g., carrying water, collecting firewood, hunting for food, sewing skins for clothing). Going to a movie, shopping in a large department store, eating in a restaurant and the associated "appropriate" behaviors, are experiences completely foreign to many Eskimos.

Through extended visits, overnight stays in homes, discussions with residents, and participation in community activities, our knowledge and understanding of village life and cultural traditions increased. It became increasingly clear that cultural expectations, as well as the more obvious environmental factors, are powerful determinants of behavior and must be considered in a comprehensive evaluation of the behaviors and abilities of students native to Alaska. These various considerations are elaborated further in the Case Presentation section.

The tools we usually use to conduct a comprehensive evaluation are not unique in themselves. Standardized tests, interviews, observations, and informal polls are used to obtain the information needed to identify emotionally disturbed students. The uniqueness of our approach lies in the fact that every step of the evaluation process, including each component of assessment, is examined for the possible influence of the cultural conditions that permeate the local environment. In order to do this accurately we do not rely on a general, undefined awareness of cultural considerations. Instead, we place a unique emphasis on community input to obtain specific and local information regarding the cultural expectations and standards which impact on the individual student's behavior. Research in this area is rather limited and often dated by the time of its publication.

The assessment process includes an evaluation of the student, home, community, and classroom. More specifically, the student's academic functioning and behavior are assessed by administering a traditional battery of such procedures as standardized intelligence and academic achievement tests, projectives, behavior rating scales, and observation of the student in a number of school settings such as the classroom, playground, and cafeteria. Although Eskimo students were not included in national standardization samples, several widely used tests have been renormed for this population (Robinson, 1978). Included in Robinson's normative sample were the Wechsler Intelligence Scale for Children -Revised, the Bender Gestalt Test, and the Draw-A-Person. Since village schools typically adopt the same curricula utilized in schools outside Alaska, national norms are useful for predicting a student's ability to be successful with this curricula and determining appropriate instructional levels. Local norms minimize the cultural bias present in the general interpretation of these instruments and allow a more accurate estimate of ability to be made based on local experiences. The norms simultaneously provide a standardized procedure for comparing a student with his cultural peers although some specific test items may not be locally relevant.

Information pertaining to the student's home life is obtained by making a home visit and talking to the parent(s). The visit clarifies whether the home environment, parenting styles, and expectations for child behavior are typical of this family, as we have come to understand these behaviors as being predominant within this cultural group. The visit also affords us the opportunity to determine if additional considerations, whether or not culturally-related, are influencing a student's behavior. A description of the home environment, accompanied by a statement detailing the cultural factors that could account for the child's behavior, minimizes inappropriate assumptions being made about the home situation.

Many community standards and related values are identified through informal conversation with local residents. This is not a formidable task because many village people are friendly toward outsiders as well as curious about our reason for visiting the village; in fact, they frequently initiate the conversation. Many questions are answered about the community as well as questions related to specific behaviors exhibited by the identified student. General questions provide information about the expectations of the community members. These answers provide information regarding the best/worst thing an individual could do in the village, appropriate/inappropriate after-school activities for students, situations in which fighting is acceptable (if ever), and things parents do when children disobey. Questions regarding specific student behaviors provide a local standard by which to judge their appropriateness (e.g., when is it acceptable for children to fight, are students responsible for their own attendance at school, should students obey their teachers, etc.)

The learning environment is assessed via teacher interview and classroom observation. In addition to the information traditionally obtained using these procedures, practices that could produce cultural conflict for the student are identified. This is accomplished by obtaining information regarding such specific factors as types of positive reinforcement delivered, method of discipline utilized, amount of competitiveness built into learning situations, teaching method most frequently used to present new material, and teacher expectations regarding the student's ability to work independently. This list results from knowledge of both cultural mores and values and educational methods and philosophy. In addition, teachers are asked to compare informally the functioning of the identified student with the other students in the classroom.

While the consideration of unique cultural conditions is an essential element of the assessment process, it is also instrumental in designing interventions that are culturally appropriate for the student. A concerted effort is made to assure that recommendations are feasible in the context of the classroom and suited to the cultural requirements of the student.

Before presenting the case study, we reiterate that with limited research available, our knowledge of Eskimo cultural traditions and expectations is based on first-hand experience in the villages we serve. While the comprehensive assessment procedures we have described can be utilized to evaluate students from any minority group and are designed to minimize cultural bias, we caution that bias may actually be increased if examiners use the stereotyped descriptions of behavior commonly associated with various cultural/racial groups; each examiner must make certain that his/her information regarding cultural influences is current and applicable to the student being evaluated. As Henderson (1981) succinctly states:

Although an understanding of the cultural background of children with whom we work is important, blanket descriptions sometimes are more harmful than helpful because the social science research base for the cultural description of ethnic groups is suspect in several aspects... Many descriptions start with the acceptance of dated assumptions without the benefit of first-hand study of the communities in question. (p. 41)

We suggest that if time constraints hinder an examiner from acquiring knowledge personally of the cultural considerations relevant for a particular student, a representative from the community who is familiar with the student (and preferably understands the educational process) should be included as a member of the Multidisciplinary Evaluation or Child Study Team.

Case Presentation

Utuk, an Eskimo (Inuit) boy, is an eight year old third grader from an isolated Alaskan "bush" village. He attends a village school with an enrollment of 40, preschool through grade twelve. We first saw Utuk at the time of his second annual review.

Background

A review of Utuk's records revealed that until recently he lived in a relatively large Eskimo community and had attended a highly structured school serving approximately 300 students. He resided with his alcoholic father; his mother is deceased. Utuk's home appeared to offer little guidance or supervision. He reportedly wandered freely around the village and frequently slept at the homes of neighboring families. He was often tardy or absent from school. Two years ago, he had been referred by his classroom teacher for psychological testing. The referral problem involved frequent fighting with peers and difficulty controlling his temper. When not fighting, he was described as being extremely quiet and frequently refusing to participate in classroom activities and discussions. Fighting had resulted in repeated visits to the principal's office and his placement in a behavior management program. His behavior did not change appreciably and continued to affect his performance in the classroom adversely. It is unclear why the intervention was unsuccessful. His academic achievement remained below the level of his classmates.

An evaluation was conducted by the district school psychologist which included cognitive, academic readiness and developmental tests, a parent conference, classroom observation, and interviews with Utuk's teacher. Constraints on the psychologist's time prevented him from making a home visit or consulting with community members regarding standards for appropriate behavior. Utuk's behavior was evaluated according to standards established by the school system. He was subsequently certified under the "emotionally disturbed" classification. Past records contain no mention of psychological interventions attempted prior to certification, no mention of parent or family contacts made, and no mention of whether Utuk's behavior problems extended beyond the school grounds.

As a result of the evaluation, Utuk was scheduled for individual sessions with the school counselor to help control his fighting. Records indicate that counseling was discontinued because Utuk would not discuss his feelings and did not appear to be benefiting from therapy. One year later, various circumstances resulted in Utuk moving to his former village home under the custody of his grandfather.

Assessment

The task at the annual review was to determine his continued eligibility for services under the "emotionally disturbed" classification.

349

Only two years had elapsed since the initial evaluation; cognitive ability (WISC-R) test results were considered current and not repeated during this review. The primary emphasis was placed on reviewing the success of the Individual Education Program (IEP) interventions. Utuk was at home with an ear infection during the visit to his village. Even though he lived several miles from the village, a home visit was made via snowmobile. His grandfather transports him to and from school each day. The home visit was conducted to allow the psychologist to interact with Utuk in a more familiar and "safe" setting. Information was obtained regarding cultural traditions influencing his home life and their possible effects on Utuk's school behaviors.

The one-room home contained two beds and a small table. A lantern provided light, subsistence meals were cooked on the propane stove, and a caribou hide partially covered the floor. Clothing and blankets were piled on the two beds which also served as chairs. Grandfather, a 75 year old village elder, is visually impaired, single, and lives on a meager income. He has assumed custody of two grandchildren, including Utuk. The condition of Utuk's home did not appear to differ significantly from that of other Eskimo families and was considered consistent with the traditional, subsistence lifestyle followed by his grandfather. Survival in this environment, required that Utuk be well disciplined, supportive and cooperative, thereby allowing family functions to go smoothly.

An interview-based assessment was adopted for the review. Utuk was attentive and cooperative throughout the home visit. Although initially shy, he quickly relaxed and readily engaged in conversation with the examiner, particularly when discussing locally relevant topics such as hunting caribou, animals that live close to the village, and weather conditions. An examination of Utuk's mental status was conducted through the use of projective stories and drawings and revealed no significant pathology.

The grandfather, who primarily speaks the native language, was questioned through the assistance of a local interpreter. It quickly became clear that he provides a traditional home environment for his grandchildren. To control Utuk's behavior, he stated that he uses stories and legends, which are culturally sanctioned methods for rearing children. For example, if you wander away from the village at night (or during the dark days of the Arctic winter) the "Black Hands" will get you. The legend of "The Enchanting Aroma" (Frost, 1972) reinforces this lesson by telling of a mouse who wandered away from home following a delicious odor. He finally reached the source which was a large container of seal oil. The mouse immediately jumped in, only to find that the oil made his fur so heavy that he could not climb out. He sank to the bottom and died.

In addition, when his grandchildren misbehave, the grandfather uses diversion tactics to terminate the behaviors; he does not punish them. For example, if Utuk were playing with a loaded gun, the grandfather would shift Utuk's attention to something else rather than telling him directly to leave the gun alone. Tradition specifies that new skills are most often acquired by observing village elders. The grandfather, therefore, expects Utuk to learn to handle a gun appropriately by watching him and the other hunters in the village. Until that occurs, he will keep Utuk from mishandling the gun through diversion rather than punishment. It becomes evident that modeling is an important strategy for behavioral change. By contrast, "discovery" learning techniques and assertive discipline strategies are not common.

Informal interaction among the village residents yielded information regarding behaviors deemed acceptable (and unacceptable) by local standards. We learned that it is acceptable for children to wander around the village because everyone looks out for them and will come to their aid if trouble occurs. Likewise, it is not uncommon for children to sleep on the floor of the home they happen to be visiting rather than going to their own home. Partly because of the long months of darkness in the winter and the constant daylight of summer, people sleep when they are tired rather than according to a fixed schedule. This notion often plays havoc with the school's attempts at scheduling classes. Fighting among young people is often viewed as an outlet for hostile feelings although fighting with a child younger than oneself is not tolerated. Emotions are not often openly discussed with outsiders, and feelings are generally expressed immediately and with minimal regard to future consequences. Killing someone would be considered unacceptable under most conditions while cooperating with others is viewed as highly desirable since it facilitates subsistence level tasks.

Interviews with Utuk's teachers and observation in he classroom revealed that the personnel in this school, although non-native, work to make the educational process an integral part of village life. The school emphasizes cooperation among students, which is consistent with cultural tradition. A warm, "friendly" atmosphere pervades this school rather than the formal, competitive climate found in Utuk's previous school. There, as in many American schools, most school personnel teach using a lecture format, encourage competition, and enforce strict discipline and attendance policies. Although regular attendance is encouraged in his present school, life patterns are taken into account and the students are not punished for tardiness or absenteeism. It is recognized that children frequently have to miss school to perform chores

351

consistent with subsistence living. Teachers incorporate as many demonstrations and projects as feasible in their presentation of new material and minimize lectures. They seek to integrate as much cultural information into the curricula as possible.

Utuk's teachers report that fighting still occurs more frequently than with the other students, appearing to be caused by teasing from classmates or frustration with classwork. They do not consider this a major problem. They stated that although the school does not have a counselor, they have tried to follow Utuk's IEP by providing informal counseling and support at times when fighting occurs. A more specific behavioral management program was introduced to reduce aggressive behavior. Teachers also report that since attending their school, he has been willing to participate in class projects and discussions. Maintaining attention and on-task behavior are areas that continue to be difficult for Utuk.

The integration of cultural and educational considerations when evaluating Utuk's behavior resulted in the decision that sufficient grounds were no longer present to justify continued certification as "emotionally disturbed." It was determined, however, from interviews with Utuk's teachers, examination of work samples, results of criteria-referenced achievement tests recently administered by the teacher, and analysis of his perceptual-motor development from drawings obtained during the home visit, that learning difficulties rather than any emotional disturbance were hindering Utuk's academic progress. Both psychometric data and informal comparisons with cultural peers indicated that, additionally, a significant discrepancy existed between Utuk's cognitive ability and academic achievements. The decision was made to shift emphasis from behavior management to differentiated instructional techniques which addressed academic deficits.

Intervention

Cultural factors were closely considered when providing recommendations and intervention strategies. We have observed that the tendency of Native parents to use story-telling and diversion as disciplinary techniques can create in their children a greater dependency on adults (or others) to set limits and standards of behavior. In school, teachers expect a certain amount of independence and internal control from students. Seatwork and individualized assignments can be difficult, however, for students who appear to need continual input from adults. It was, therefore, suggested that Utuk be given short assignments to complete and that directions be stated so as to involve only one or two steps at a time. It was further recommended that his ability to work independently be increased by providing tangible positive reinforcement (such as a sticker) for completing assignments without help. This recommendation was supported by the grandfather as teaching self-sufficiency, provided the reinforcer was to become an internalized value as opposed to the external reward or payoff. Furthermore, each week that Utuk earned a designated number of stickers, a "culturally-appropriate" reward was to be provided, such as being allowed to spend time Friday afternoons assisting in the Early Childhood Education classroom. He would be helping others while being rewarded for his own good work.

Basketball was recently introduced to this village and students now enjoy shooting baskets during their spare moments. Utuk is no exception. We suggested that shooting baskets, rather than fighting, could be used as an outlet for expressing anger.

It was determined that Utuk would spend two hours per day in the Resource Room for reading and math. We encouraged his resource teacher to continue using culturally related materials whenever possible to increase his interest in academic subjects.

Outcome

One year later, Utuk underwent a comprehensive third-year reevaluation to determine his continued eligibility for special services (see Appendix). Many changes had occurred in his village in the space of that year. The village moved to a new site, the population grew due to construction of new homes, and television and telephone service were introduced. Interviews with his teachers indicated that in spite of these unsettling changes, Utuk's behavior continues to be appropriate. He still fights occasionally but only when excessively provoked. Basketball has proven to be an effective activity for venting feelings. Reports from community members reveal that Utuk is accepted and well-liked.

Learning difficulties, including a perceptual-motor processing deficit, continue to affect Utuk's academic progress significantly. His teachers report that Utuk's work in the Early Childhood Education classroom has been both enjoyable and beneficial for him. They note increased confidence in his own ability and more tolerance for provocation from his peers. His attention span and on-task behavior have also increased.

Conclusion

Utuk's case brings clarity to why local/cultural conditions must be taken into consideration when identifying and intervening on behalf of exceptional children. Here is an example of an Eskimo boy who finds himself well-trained in the ways of his community, yet when placed in a foreign school environment, he is identified as emotionally disturbed. Intervention was provided to take into account, to the extent possible, the needs of the school system and the realities of the local community situation.

Although his behavior continued to be within acceptable limits, Utuk was placed in a residential care facility because his aging grandfather could no longer care for him. He appears to be adjusting well to his temporary placement and hopes to return to his village soon under the protective care of a relative or foster home.

Authors' Note

This case study was completed in 1981 and written in early 1982.

References

Frost, O.W. (1972). *Tales of Eskimo Alaska*. Anchorage, Alaska: Alaska Methodist University.

Henderson, R.W. (1981). Nonbiased assessment: Sociocultural considerations. In T. Oakland, *Nonbiased assessment* (pp. 34-55). Minneapolis: The National School Psychology Training Network.

Robinson, M.L. (1978) *Inuit norms for five clinical tests*. Barrow, Alaska: North Slope Borough School District.

APPENDIX
Summary of Third Year Reevaluation Results

Wechsler Intelligence Scale for Children–Revised (WISC–R):

(national/local)

Subtest	Score	Scaled Subtest	Scaled Score	IQ Score	
Information	6/10	Picture Completion	10/9	Verbal	79/95
Similarities	7/9	Picture Arrangement	11/11	Performance	87/87
Arithmetic	7/10	Block Design	9/8		
Vocabulary	7/11	Object Assembly	8/8	Full Scale	81/89
Comprehension	6/9	Coding	3/4		
Digit Span	8/10				

Woodcock–Johnson Psycho–Educational Battery Tests of Achievement:

Reading	1.7 (grade equivalency score)
Mathematics	1.7
Written Language	1.1
Knowledge	1.0
Skills	1.5

These results were substantiated by curriculum-based assessment procedures.

Bender Visual–Motor Gestalt Test:

Koppitz error score—8 (including perseveration, integration and distortion errors)

National norms—2 to 2-1/2 years below age level

Local norms—greater than 1-1/2 standard deviations below the mean

INFORMAL ASSESSMENT OF INTELLECTUAL ABILITY USING PIAGETIAN TASKS

Lorraine Taylor

The approach to be described in this chapter is based upon Piaget's view of intellectual development in children and adolescents. My emphasis is upon the selection and administration of Piagetian- derived tasks within the context of informal assessment procedures. The tasks provide the opportunity for students to demonstrate characteristics of their thinking. The developmental view of intelligence described by Piaget and Inhelder (1958) includes characteristics of thinking at different ages and stages of development. Thus, careful observation of a child's performance and questioning by the examiner to determine how the child arrives at an answer can indicate ability to think at the appropriate developmental level.

According to Piaget and Inhelder (1958), adolescents are at the stage of formal operations, a stage attained in the 12 to 15 age period. This stage is characterized by the ability to solve complex verbal and other types of problems and to think scientifically (Wadsworth, 1978). Combinatorial thinking, hypothetical thinking, and logical thinking are descriptions of thinking that differentiate children from adolescents. Children of different cultures vary in the ages at which they reach the stage of formal operations. Piaget attributes this variation to the influence of experience and social interactions. However, the important role of maturation in Piaget's theory makes his approach distinctly different from the traditional, additive view of intelligence on which most traditional tests are based (Inhelder, 1968). A Piagetian-based approach to assessment is more optimistic and less biased.

Because Piagetian measures are less influenced by formal school learning and mainstream cultural experiences, De Avila and Havassy (1974) compared Mexican-American and white middle class children on Piagetian and non-Piagetian measures. They found significant differences between the groups in achievement and intelligence on traditional measures, but not on Piagetian measures. De Avila and Havassy indicated that language, cultural, and school learning experiences influenced traditional scores but these factors did not influence Piagetian scores.

The original inspiration for my use of Piagetian tasks as an informal measure of intellectual assessment of adolescents came from the work of Furth (1966, 1974; Furth & Youniss, 1969) and Elkind (1966, 1974; Elkind, Barocas & Rosenthal, 1968; Elkind & Johnson, 1969). In his work with deaf children, Furth found that linguistic competence was not a prerequisite for intellectual development. He was able to verify propositional thinking in deaf adolescents who had severe language handicaps (Furth, 1971). Furth used such tasks as combinations, probability, and displaced volume. Elkind compared combinatorial thinking in students from graded and ungraded classes (his use of the combinations task will be described later as part of my informal assessment approach). Other studies by Elkind (1966, 1969) verified differences in the thinking of adolescents as compared with that of children.

Piagetian tasks were explored with black adolescents because of the author's responsibility to plan curriculum and instruction in an alternative high school program for dropouts and students at risk for dropping out. Students enrolled in the program had low scores on traditional achievement and intelligence tests, restricted verbal language, and hostility toward school and teachers. Many of the students had been enrolled in special education classes in public, inner city schools. However, informal observations revealed that a significant number of them had far more potential than was evident in their formal test scores, which ranged from second to sixth grade in reading and math. Their mastery of chess, management of family affairs, informal responses in discussion, and problem-solving at school functions indicated such potential. As a curriculum planner, I needed to identify measures which could accurately distinguish individual differences in ability in order to provide realistic guidance and counseling for curriculum choices and post-secondary educational planning.

Samples of Piagetian tasks were collected from various sources. They were selected on the basis of the type of thinking elicited, ease and simplicity of administration, wide use in the literature, and interest in the tasks—as demonstrated by black adolescents' performance in preliminary trials. The tasks represent only samples of the many possible choices available. (See Wadsworth [1978], for example, for additional tasks to be used.)

The combinations task, for example (Elkind, et al., 1968), assesses the student's ability to explore all possible combinations when presented with red, blue, black and white poker chips. Variations of this task include combining four playing cards, and short girl, tall girl, short boy, and tall boy. The response is evaluated in terms of the number of combinations found and the process by which the student arrives at his answer. The student who demonstrates the use of formal operational thinking will systematically explore all possible combinations. This involves holding one or more elements constant while combining it with others. There are sixteen possible combinations (see Appendix).

The second type of task assesses the student's understanding of probability. A recent description of this task can be found in Wadsworth (1978). This author has also used coins instead of small blocks. Ninety-six coins of four types—pennies, nickels, dimes and quarters—are divided into two groups. One group is used as a reference set and is placed on the table in view of the student. The second set is placed in a bag (or box). Two coins at a time are withdrawn after the bag has been shaken. The student is asked to predict what the coins will be each time. The use of the reference set which increases the accuracy of the predictions is indicative of the understanding of probability (see Appendix).

The third type of task includes a set of formal reasoning items. In order to avoid penalizing students with reading difficulties, the items are read to the subject. This task assesses the adolescent's ability to reason and to do hypothetical thinking. The items are based on several models. One of these is described by Wadsworth (1978) and another is based upon the work of Morf (1973).

The adolescent's response on formal reasoning tasks, as well as well as the other Piagetian measures, must be interpreted cautiously. Success is interpreted as age-appropriate thinking. Failure is more difficult to explain since it may be due to normal stage mixtures, inadequate assessment, and age variations in the acquisition of certain concepts (Wadsworth, 1977). The influence of interest also is important. However, Bart (1971), for example, examined the effect of interest on horizontal decalage. He explains that this is similar to "the notion of generalizability of formal operational skills." Interest was doubtful as a key factor in his study. Racial/cultural background may also influence development of the stages, but there is little research on such influence. Piaget has stated that cultural/environmental influences are important determinants of the age at which a given stage is reached.

Two important problems in the interpretation of performance on Piagetian tasks are discussed by Siegel and Brainerd (1978). In their preface to *Alternatives to Piaget: Critical Essays on the Theory*, the editors introduce the performance-competence problem with the question, "When a child fails a certain Piagetian test that is supposed to tap some given underlying concept, what does this mean" (p. xii)? The competence explanation favored by Piaget is that the child does not possess the concept. The performance explanation is that failure was a result of task difficulty or that Piagetian tests invariably measure attributes other than the intended ones. Failure, therefore, should not be interpreted to mean the respondent does not possess the underlying concept.

The role of cognitive development in learning involves readiness. Piaget's pessimistic view dictates that children must be developmentally ready to learn what we want to teach. Therefore, we should not attempt to teach content or concepts for which the cognitive structures are not present. When the Piagetian test is failed, do we refuse to teach adolescents content which requires the use of formal operations? The reverse question should also be considered. When there is evidence that the student is ready, based on successful completion of Piagetian tasks, can we refuse to teach the appropriate level of content? Can we refuse to teach content which requires the use of formal operations? Siegel and Brainerd describe Piaget's ideas about learning as a "classic readiness model in which learning is subordinated to development. Some incipient competence (concept, operation, structure, etc.) is supposed to develop before learning occurs"(p. xiii).

Wadsworth (1978), who discusses the readiness problem, points out that there is a difference between memorizing and learning. Children can memorize correct responses even when they do not have the underlying structures of necessary readiness, but they cannot truly learn. Ennis (1978) also challenges Piaget's propositional logic. He provides an excellent discussion which includes valuable clarification of the nature of such tasks. Questions are raised about the validity of characteristics which separate the thinking of children from that of adolescents. Ennis' evidence supports the use of abstract thinking and logic by children while Piaget reserves this ability for adolescents. However, this author's experience, and that of many others, supports Piaget's differentiation. Feuerstein (1981), for example, is optimistic with respect to readiness. His *Instrumental Enrichment Program* has led to cognitive gains in mentally retarded performers.

A variety of criticism of Piaget's theories is found in the research literature. They include discussions of the adequacy of his logical model (Isaacs, 1951), inadequacies in his discussion of adolescents' thinking (Parsons, 1970), and insufficient explanation for the shift from concrete to formal operational equilibrium (Ausubel, 1956).

In using Piagetian tests for practical purposes, a decision must be made about the number of tasks that must be successfully completed. Some students will complete one, others will complete all. The criterion for passing is open to discussion. Furth and Youniss (1969) accept a single task. This author accepts two of the three informal assessment tasks. Because combinatorial thinking has been identified as an early stage of formal operations (Martorano, 1973), it appears that this task must be passed. However, some students in my graduate classes have had difficulty in their approach and have not "passed" combinatorial thinking items.

The number of tasks to be included in an informal assessment is another practical consideration. The number included in this approach has been developed on an empirical basis. Trials with difficult students have indicated that the time, attention, and thinking involved in this group of three tasks have been close to the limit of tolerance.

Despite criticism of the theory and its application, I have found that Piagetian tasks can reveal distinct differences in the nature and quality of thinking among black adolescents. The characteristics of their thinking can closely resemble characteristics identified and described by Piaget at the stage of formal operations—and the dimensions of mental ability tapped by these tasks are not available on traditional intelligence tests.

The informal approach described in this chapter represents initial work involving the author's efforts to use Piagetian tasks to assess evidence of age-appropriate intellectual capability in black adolescents. There is much work to be done, but the author believes application of the results from informal assessment using Piagetian tasks in educational planning and curriculum decisions can be made at the present time.

The problem of readiness discussed earlier represents a dilemma for curriculum areas important to adolescents. Curriculum content in this area is difficult to justify until certain "stage-related" evidence is available. The problem of failure also is difficult. If Inhelder's (1968) conclusion that mentally retarded individuals do not reach the stage of formal operations is accepted, success on Piagetian measures offers important contributions to the entire special education decision-making process. Can we justify a label of educable mentally retarded for an adolescent who succeeds on these tasks as well as more formal Piagetian measures? If Piagetian measures are failed, can we accept mental retardation with confidence?

The focus on how the student arrives at his answer represents a major value of the Piagetian approach. The teacher can learn important information about how the student thinks and how the student can be taught. Incorrect responses are better understood when the explanation is provided by the student in his process of finding the answer. When the response is correct, the teacher learns about the strategies used in the process; when it is incorrect, the teacher learns what can go wrong, detract, or distract the student from the correct outcome in the thinking process. Some students will explain their choice of a name as correct because "You said it last." Others, in response to some of the formal reasoning items, have responded to questions about "Who is tallest?", "None of them because I don't know any boys named Sam or Mike."

This focus on the answer and its explanation is most needed by teachers to understand better the nature of thinking and learning and to differentiate ultimately among students and their needs. Correctives may then be more appropriately and effectively selected.

Interestingly, the responses quoted above are from students classified as educable mentally retarded. Other students in their classes correctly responded to all of the tasks administered. Piagetian measures, which can supplement scholastically-based measures comprising most test batteries, offer black students the unique opportunity to express intellectual capability in different and important dimensions. The developmental view of intelligence appears particularly useful in evaluating black school-aged children and youth.

Two case studies are presented. Both are male adolescents who attend a public middle school. One student was classified educable mentally retarded and placed in a departmentalized special education program with mainstreamed art, music and physical education. The second student was enrolled in a regular sixth grade program but was being considered for referral because he was very slow and completed little schoolwork each day. The special education student was described by his teachers as "having behavior problems". The regular class student was described as polite, courteous, and likeable.

Case 1

Name: Johnny
Age: 13
Birthdate: 5/19/70
Sex: Male
Grade: 6—regular classes, departmentalized program
School: public, middle school

Reason for Referral

This student has not been referred for formal evaluation. Rather, his mother was referred to me by the reading teacher, for outside evaluation and tutoring. The student is failing all of his sixth grade classes except physical education. His teachers complain that he is "slow," has poor work habits, daydreams, and completes little work each day. The reading teacher commented that he has not been referred for formal evaluation or retained thus far because his behavior is exemplary.

Educational Evaluation

Because his formal school records were not available, the author administered the following tests in addition to the Piagetian tasks: Wide Range Achievement Test (WRAT); Key Math Test; and Slosson Intelligence Test. Informal classroom work samples were collected. The results were as follows:

Slosson—83
WRAT Reading: Grade 3.5
Spelling: Grade 1.7
Key Math Grade Level—5.3

Johnny was cooperative and pleasant during testing. However, distraction was a problem; several times he yawned and complained that the tests were difficult. He was encouraged to continue and was praised. While most students require about 30-40 minutes to complete the Key Math test, Johnny completed it in 90 minutes. The examiner allowed him as much time as he required to complete the test. Because he counts on his fingers for all of his computation problems, this section required most of the total testing time. However, given the time he required, few computation errors occurred. In regular classes of 45 minutes, it is easy to understand that a student who works slowly will have great difficulty. Johnny's failing math grade in the regular sixth grade math class is due to his minimal completion of assignments.

Johnny's low reading and spelling scores reflect poor word attack skills. Even when his responses are correct, he expresses uncertainty. He explains his difficulties in reading, spelling, and pronunciation as resulting from the fact that he is "half from the South and half from the North." Since he spends vacations with relatives of his mother in the South, perhaps this is what he is describing. Many of the grammatical forms which he uses appear to be modeled by his mother.

Health

Johnny's health is described by his mother as excellent. He has had no serious illnesses. However, he did recently have a growth removed from his neck and an obvious scar remains from the surgery. His mother reported that Johnny has normal vision and hearing although he has a hearing impaired sister. The sister, who is non-verbal, attends a special school. The mother did not reveal in the interview whether or not the sister is also mentally retarded.

363

Family History

Johnny resides with his mother and ten year old sister. His sister is transported each day by special bus to a special school. Johnny's father died when he was seven years old. His mother is employed full time at a post office. She has made provision for the management of her daughter in the after-school period during the hours when she is at work.

Interviews in the home revealed the mother has provided encyclopedias, games, dictionaries, and outside tutoring to help Johnny. She describes her son as "slow" and disinterested in school. With respect to school during the past six years, she described him as "having problems." She also noted that teachers are too quick to decide that Johnny should be in special education when they learn about his sister.

Student Interview

Johnny's perceptions of his school problems were explored in an interview. He described school as being difficult. He views his problems as due to not completing his work and, sometimes, to not understanding his teachers. He reported that his average in his classes is 50 and that 50 is the lowest grade most teachers will give. He also described the grouping of students in his school in the following manner: "There are the smart kids at the top. Then there are the kids who are half smart and half dumb. They are called the "academics'. Then there are the kids who are dumber than they are smart, or just dumb. They are callethe "generals'. That's the group that I am in. Then there are the special education kids at the bottom and they are "all dumb', the dumbest." He explains much of his school problems as caused by his "slowness". His favorite subject is Math Lab where he receives extra help. The subject he dislikes most is English. He worries a great deal about discipline problems at his school and also about being retained next year in sixth grade.

Recent Report Card Grades and Comments:

Social Studies	65	
Math	50	
Science/Health	65	
Reading	65	(Teacher comment: word attack skills are below grade level)
Math Lab	75	(Teacher comment: wastes time and performs inconsistently)

Band	78	(Teacher comment: insufficient practice time)
Exploratory	6P	
Physical Education	100	(Teacher comment: outstanding; a pleasure to have in class)

The sixth grade students attend classes in ability groups. Johnny is in the lowest group (an informal spelling test, an example of his performance, is included in the Appendix. In oral reading of a grade 6 paragraph from the Durrell Analysis of Reading Difficulty, Johnny did not recognize the following words: yield, substance, drying, gradually, sort, determined, pure, ever, weighed. Recognition is based on the correct pronunciation of the word. He appears to comprehend through the skillful use of context clues. In several comic books which he read to the author, the vocabulary appeared quite difficult. However, Johnny's use of picture and context clues facilitated his reading of several of the stories.

Personal-Social Observations

Johnny is described by all his teachers as courteous, pleasant, and likeable . The author also found him to be cooperative, humorous and eager to please. Since his mother is employed full time, Johnny shares many of the management chores of their home. He must carefully record telephone mesages, and he must phone his mother at work if an emergency arises concerning any member of the family, particularly his sister who is cared for by a baby sitter after school. Johnny must also start dinner according to his mother's directions. Saturday is devoted to routine household tasks. He must remember when his mother will work late, when he is to report to the baby sitter, when he must care for his sister (if the baby sitter is unavailable), and many other family matters. Preparations for a recent trip to the South required that he plan for his necessary clothing, school books, hobby materials, and the special activities that he would engage in during his visit there.

He is frequently in charge at home. He describes the "worst day in my life" as the day that his sister was born. He must frequently manage her when his mother is at work, and he must share his mother's time and attention with his sister. On a recent visit to his home, the author waited while Johnny made several calls to his mother, wrote messages received for his mother, prepared a cup of tea for the author, checked the date on a kitchen calendar, and reviewed the week's events at school.

Classroom Observation

Johnny was recently observed in his reading class. The teacher asked the class to wrie an imaginary story about "the worst day in my life". Johnny wrote 42 words in 32 minutes. He lost time when he retrieved a pencil from the floor, stared at the ceiling, listened to other students as they read their stories aloud before he had finished, and asked the teacher for the date. His handwriting appeared labored and difficult. This product is included in the Appendix.

Summary

Johnny is a 13 year old black male adolescent who is in regular sixth grade in a public middle school. He has been placed in the lowest group on the basis of achievement and "ability". His basic skills are approximately at the third grade level, and his school grades are usually from 50 to 65. He appears to be easily distracted and slow in his classroom responses compared with his peers. He has problems completing tasks, handwriting assignments, and activities which involve short-term memory. He often forgets dates, books, papers, recent events and important messages. Some of his teachers believe he is more capable than his performance and grades indicate; others disagree. His teachers and parent are at a loss to explain the nature and cause of his problems and the means to correct them. His IQ score obtained on the Slosson is 83. Formal school data are not yet available. There is increasing pressure by some of his teachers for a formal referral to evaluate Johnny for a handicapping condition. His mother continues to refuse consent.

PIAGETIAN TASKS—
Combinatorial Thinking

As a variation of the combinations task, Johnny was asked to find all the possible combinations of: tall girl, short girl, tall boy, short boy. He was given an example of making all possible combinations using four colors. "For example, I could combine red and white or red, white and blue." The colors were identified as red, blue, black and white. (The author usually provides four poker chips, but they were not available on this occasion.)

Four circles at the top of the page were labeled in this way:

tall girls   tall boys   short girls   short boys

The author wrote Johnny's responses as he dictated them. His responses were as follows:

short boys, short girls
tall boys, tall girls
short boys, tall boys
tall girls, short girls
tall boys
tall girls
short boys
short girls
tall boys, short girls
tall girls, short boys

Results

Johnny neither systematically explored all possible combinations nor identified all 16 possible combinations. He used contiguity mainly as the basis for completing this task. That means the choices were made on the basis of position—what was close to, next to, or near. Thus, "short boys" is next to/contiguous with "short girls". "Tall girls" and "tall boys" are contiguous. Some students use this approach when combining poker chips. They will place them and then name the combination on the basis of what is closest to what other color. This is not considered systematic exploration of all possible combinations in which one or more elements are held constant and systematically paired with others.

Probability

In order to assess Johnny's understanding of probability, he was asked to tell what he thought the coins were going to be each time the examiner first shook the bag and withdrew two coins.

For the first five predictions, he made wild guesses. He appeared to be distracted, looking at the ceiling and a light fixture. He observed neiter the referencgroup nor the group of coins as they were withdrawn and placed on the table. Upon making an error, guessing the wrong coins, he expressed disappointment in "Oh, wrong again", etc... After the examiner observed him staring at the opposite wall, she asked Johnny, "Are you looking at the table?" He responded, "Yes," although

it was obvious that he was not looking. He made two more wild guesses, and suddenly, as if realizing what the task involved and what he
should do, he looked carefully at the coins which had been withdrawn
from the bag and counted each type—pennies, nickels, dimes and
quarters. Then he examined the reference group and counted all of the
coins in the reference group. He then examined the reference group
after each drawing. Sometimes he counted the coins of each type in the
withdrawn group before making his predction. His predictions improved dramatically. He continued to predict based upon observations
and counting. He accurately predicted the final four coins as pennies
since his count probably indicated that there were more pennies in the
bag. The examiner sat quietly through the observations and counting.
When asked, "How did you get the answer?" he did not respond verbally. However, the answer was obvious. Johnny performed well on
this task once he began to attend to the reference group and count the
coins. He demonstrated an understanding of probability.

The same question posed to other children, "Are you looking at
the table, or the coins?" will not result in this type of performance if they
have no understanding of probability. The author uses this question
routinely for that assurance.

Reasoning Items

The following series of items comprises the third type of task administered in this informal assessment. The purpose is to assess the
student's ability to reason, to do hypothetical thinking. A piece of
scratch paper is provided. Each item was read to Johnny and, when
necessary, he was asked to explain (or draw) how he arrived at his
answer.

Johnny appeared to enjoy these tasks. His responses came quickly
and easily. When given the first item, "Jane is taller than Susie. Jane is
shorter than Mary. Who is tallest? Who is shortest?" Johnny quickly
sketched three stick figures and responded correctly. For each of the
other items, his response was based on the sketch. There were six items
based on this model. The seventh item involves hypothetical thinking:
"Suppose I ask you to agree that if an animal has long ears, it can be
either a donkey or a mule; and if an animal has a big tail, it can be either
a mule or a horse. If I want an animal with long ears and a big tail, what
can it be?" Johnny quickly answered, "A mule."

The author also administered the *Cartoon Conservation Scales* (De
Avila, 1980) in order to compare the results with that of the informal assessment. (See Appendix for results and interpretation.)

Interpretation and Recommendations

Johnny demonstrated evidence of formal operational thinking on the probability task and the formal reasoning items. His thinking appears to be age-appropriate. He is distractible and must be constantly reminded to stay "on task." He wastes a great deal of time getting started. Johnny describes his poor achievement as "due to not completing much work". His problems appear to be due less to lack of ability than to lack of organization and concentration. This author has recently begun to tutor him and to work with his regular teachers in order to identify informal assessment techniques and strategies which can be used by the regular teachers. Thus far, teachers have been pleased by his performance on the *Cartoon Conservation Scales* and Piagetian tasks and now are concerned about motivating him to do more. Since he enjoys comic books, his reading teacher will try to identify materials in that format for reading.

A simple behavior modification technique has been implemented to try to increase the percentage of tasks he completes each school day. Each week a report is required on the number of tasks completed in each class. If the figure represents an increase of at least 20% over the previous week, he earns a free Saturday. A recommendation for the use of a program such as the Glass Analysis for Decoding Skills was made to his reading teacher. However, it is difficult for the regular reading teacher to obtain special materials or to find time to use them with individual students. Perhaps a "skills center" can be organized in her room for independent work in this area. The author suggested that a timer be placed on Johnny's desk as a reminder of the time available to complete his tasks. Curriculum activities which may challenge and stimulate him in math and science can be planned and developed as learning activity packets to individualize his instruction. Learning centers in the regular classrooms can facilitate this individualization. Johnny's teachers hope he can remain in the mainstream classes without retention and improve his performance. They are shifting their interest from the cause of his "problem" to stimulation and motivation. Other simple behavior modification techniques will be tried to increase the percentage of tasks completed and the rate of responses. Johnny will continue to receive after school tutoring. Thus far, we have avoided referral for formal evaluation, the first step in removal from the mainstream and placement in special education classes.

Case 2

Name: B.P.
Age: 14.5
Birthdate: 11/24/68
Sex: Male
School Status: Grade 7, special class.

B.P. is classified educable mentally retarded and has been in a departmentalized program within the special education classes. Four special education teachers share the schedule, which consists of math, science, social studies and English. The students are mainstreamed for art, music and physical education. He is enrolled in a self- contained special class.

Reason for Referral

The parents consented to a special assessment for a school project conducted by this author. According to his current teacher, the original referral was based on severe behavior problems.

Available Test Scores:

Reading: Grade Level 4.0, Stanford Achievement Test
Key Math Test—3.7 grade level
Full Scale WISC-R IQ: 76

Reasoning Items

The verbal reasoning items were read to B.P. and he was asked to answer each question and tell how he decided on his answer. On the first item, "If Jane is taller than Susie... Jane is shorter than Mary. Who is tallest? Who is shortest?" B.P. first responded, "Susie is tallest." He had a question mark in his voice and asked that the item be repeated. He was told that he could draw the problem to show how he figured it out and also to help remember what was said. He sketched the three stick figures and quickly corrected his responses. "Mary is tallest. Susie is shortest." B.P. then sketched each of the reasoning items and quickly responded without questions in his voice. He was alert and his responses were accurate.

Several authors have pointed out that children at the stage of concrete operations cannot correctly respond to these items. They have also noted that it is more difficult to answer, "Who is shortest?" than "Who is tallest?" I have found that students who are able to answer one form of this question do not have difficulty with the reverse. Nevertheless, in an effort to be certain that the use of formal operational thinking is being tapped, both forms are administered. Obviously, B.P. is able to figure out these problems. Although his verbal responses consisted of "Na," "Yeh," "Uh-uh," "Huh?", his drawings and quick responses communicated his understanding. He would either repeat his answer or shrug his shoulders and smile when asked, "How do you know? Prove it." Disadvantaged black students have often been unable to verbalize how they get their answers on Piagetian tasks (La Rue, 1974).

Probability

To assess B.P.'s understanding of probability, 96 coins were divided into two equal groups and the same procedure was followed as in the case of Johnny. B.P. was asked to predict what he thought the two coins were going to be each time the examiner withdrew them. Before the first coins were withdrawn, B.P. counted all the coins on the table. As the coins were withdrawn each time, he would check the reference group and those coins already taken from the bag. Occasionally the examiner would say, "I'll bet that it's going to be a penny and a nickel," or some other combination. This was done to maintain interest and also to maintain friendly rapport. Since it is possible to predict coins which are most unlikely, if not impossible, it also serves to verify the student's understanding. For example, after the quarters were withdrawn (there are only 2), the examiner said, "I'll bet that it's going to be a quarter and a dime." B.P. replied, "It can't be because there's no more quarters in there. It's going to be two pennies because there are more pennies." B.P. predicted very well as he carefully observed and counted from the beginning of the procedure. He matched the group of drawn coins constantly with the reference group. At one point he said, "All the dimes are out, all the pennies are out, it must be nickels." Thus he accurately predicted the last two coins before the examiner shook the bag to withdraw them. He was alert, involved, and accurate throughout this task. His responses came quickly and with confidence.

When the student is allowed to draw or sketch his/her understanding of the problem, it offers several advantages. First, the task's memory requirements are reduced; the student does not have to remember the details once they are drawn. Second, the verbal aspects of the task are reduced for the student of limited expressive language, particularly limited standard vocabulary. The sketching aspect of the tasks

371

has only created a problem when the student has been so interested in the artwork that too much time was invested in the details of the "picture".

Combinations

In order to assess ability to do combinatorial thinking, the student is asked to find or make all possible combinations of four items. The student is given four poker chips—red, blue, black and white—and may manually place them in patterns or arrangements or combinations or simply keep them in view. Older students usually write their combinations on a piece of paper; younger students dictate them and the list is kept in view so they can refer to it. Combinations cannot be repeated. There are 16 possible combinations if "none" is included as a choice. The systematic, orderly exploration of all possible combinations as well as the number made are two aspects of the performance which are evaluated.

B.P. was asked to do two examples of this task. First, he was asked to make all the different combinations possible of the four poker chips. Secondly, he was asked to combine four playing cards. B.P. dictated the following combinations for the cards:

diamond, club   heart, spade   spade, club   heart, diamond
heart, club   diamond, spade   spade, heart, club
spade, club, heart, diamond

Although B.P. found eight of the 16 possible combinations, he did not use a systematic, orderly exploration of all possible task combinations. The combinations do show some organization, however, in that the same card appears to be held constant through some of the combinations above, for example, the diamond with the club and then with the heart. The heart is paired with the spade and then with the club. When this task is performed easily and competently, systematic exploration is obvious. Students who possess good verbal ability can provide an explanation such as, "I took the heart and used it with each of the others, one by one."

Interpretation and Recommendations

B.P.'s performance on the Piagetian-derived tasks supported teachers' perceptions that he was brighter than his test scores revealed. His special education math teacher believed B.P. was more capable than the educable mentally retarded label implied. The main question raised by the special education teachers was, "How could the results of Piagetian tasks be applied in their classrooms?" The math and science teachers expressed the opinion that it was probably going to be easier to derive curriculum applications in those areas than in other content areas. It was decided that we would explore the "Finding Out" curricula developed by De Avila, et al. (1981) in the areas of math and science and select instructional objectives at the level of formal operations which appeared appropriate for B.P. Although B.P.'s Key Math Score of 3.7 is considerably below grade level, his teachers believed it was possible to attempt to enrich his math program with "thinking or word problems" which involved the use of reasoning or hypothetical thinking. The teachers were also interested in the possible use of Feuerstein's (1981) Instrumental Enrichment Program for students like B.P. who appear to be more capable than his standardized scores indicate. These teacher discussions took place at the end of the previous school year. Several additional resources were recommended to the teachers for their use in selecting learning tasks which were designed for students at the formal operational stage.

Several months into the next school year, the author visited the school to check on B.P.'s progress and his possibilities for being mainstreamed. B.P.'s behavior was described as deteriorating. He had been removed from the departmentalized special education arrangement with mainstreamed art, music, and physical education classes. He is now in a self-contained, special class for educable mentally retarded students. The specific incident which precipitated this decision appears to be that B.P. threw a chair in the classroom. In discussions concerning B.P.'s academic needs and intellectual potential, teachers remarked that "His behavior is unmanageable in a mainstreamed situation" and that recommendations concerning his academic needs must wait until his behavior improves.

B.P. appears to be a student who could have remained in the mainstream classes if a behavior management plan had been available to his regular teachers. B.P.'s previous special education teachers agree that he appears to have more ability than his test scores reveal. His problem does not appear unique. The likelihood of removal from the mainstream classes is much greater if disruptive behavior is involved (teachers' reports). Although his achievement scores are below grade level, they are not too different from those of students who remain in the mainstream classes at his school.

While neither B.P. nor Johnny was successful on the combinations task, they were both successful on the reasoning task and the probability task. B.P., in particular, whose verbal language was restricted to "yeah" and "na" and shrugs and other nonverbal gestures, was very alert and enthusiastic in his performance on the Piagetian tasks (other disadvantaged black students have also performed well on the combinations task). The author has found these tasks to be simple, easy and dependable in the differentiation of the characteristics of thinking in the adolescents with whom they have been used.

Further research and development are needed. Evaluation of this informal assessment approach on a broader scale is important. Since individual administration is required, time is an important factor in the use of Piagetian assessment. Questions concerning the number of tasks to be included and the criteria for passing are also important, practical issues. Nevertheless, the important contribution that this type of assessment can make in the evaluation of intellectual capability in black and other minority students deserves special attention and effort.

Followup

Although several of his teachers last year insisted on referral for a possible handicapping condition, he continues to function in the mainstream. His current average in math is 80 and in English 85. Improvement in reading and spelling have occurred as well as in math. He continues to have difficulty in social studies and science. These averages are currently 60 and 50 respectively. Again, there are mainstream teachers who insist that he is a candidate for special education. Johnny describes his problems in science and social studies as due to boredom. The informal Piagetian tasks as well as the *Cartoon Conservation Scales* have been critically important in establishing a more accurate estimate of Johnny's potential to learn and to function in regular classes. A recent conference which included this examiner, the school psychologist, Johnny's mother, the school principal and guidance counselor, confirmed that recent test results by the school psychologist did *not* support Johnny's referral for a formal evaluation. Johnny participated in this conference at the end of our meeting and agreed that his problems might be solved with an "in-school" homework room, a "Big Brother," and increased motivation to succeed in school.

References

Bart, W. (1971). The effect of interest on horizontal decalage at the stage of formal operations. *Journal of Psychology, 78*, 141-150.

Bart, W. (1972). Construction and validation of formal reasoning instruments. *Psychological Reports, 30*, 663-670.

Borke, H. (1978). Piaget's view of social interaction and the theoretical construct of empathy. In L. Siegel & C. Brainerd (Eds.), *Alternatives to Piaget: Critical essays on the theory* (pp. 29- 41). New York: Academic Press.

Connolly, A.J., Nachtman, W., & Pritchett, E.M. (1972). *Key Math Diagnostic Arithmetic Test*. Circle Pines, MN: American Guidance Service.

Copeland, R. (1974). *Diagnostic and learning activities in mathematics for children*. New York: Macmillan.

Copeland, R. (1979). *How children learn mathematics*. New York: Macmillan.De Avila, E. (1980). *Cartoon Conservation Scales*. Corte Madera, CA: Linguametrics Press.

De Avila, E. (1981). *Finding Out*. Corte Madera, CA: Linguametrics Press.

De Avila, E., & Havassy, B.E. (1974). *Intelligence of Mexican- American children: A field study comparing neo-Piagetian and traditional capacity and achievement measures*. (Multilingual assessment project.) Stockton, CA: Stockton Unified School District.

Ducksworth, E. (1972). The having of wonderful ideas. *Harvard Educational Review, 42*, 217-231.Dunn, L. (1973). *Exceptional children in the schools*. New York: Holt, Rinehart & Winston.

Durrell, D.D. (1955). *Durrell Analysis of Reading Difficulty*. New York: Harcourt, Brace, Jovanovich.

Elkind, D. (1966). Conceptual orientation shifts in children and adolescents. *Child Development, 37*, 493-498.

Elkind, D. (1974). *Children and adolescence*. New York: Oxford University Press.

Elkind, D., Barocas, R., & Rosenthal, B. (1968). Combinatorial thinking in adolescents from graded and ungraded classrooms. *Perceptual-Motor Skills, 27*, 1015-1018.

Elkind, D., & Johnson, P. (1969). Concept production in children and adolescents. *Human Development, 12*, 10-21.

Ennis, R.H. (1976). An alternative to Piaget's conceptualization of logical competence. *Child Development, 47*, 903-919.

Ennis, R.H. (1978). Conceptualization of children's logical competence: Piaget's propositional logic and an alternative proposal. In L. Siegel & C. Brainerd (Eds.), *Alternatives to Piaget: Critical essays on the theory* (pp. 201-257). New York: Academic Press.

Feuerstein, R. (1981). *Instrumental enrichment*. Baltimore: University Park Press.

Feuerstein, R. (1981). *Dynamic assessment of retarded performers: Learning Potential Assessment Device*. Baltimore: University Park Press.

Formanek, R., & Gurian, A. (1976). *Charting intellectual development: A practical guide to Piagetian tasks*. Springfield, IL: Charles C. Thomas.

Furth, H. (1970). On language and knowing in Piaget's developmental theory. *Human Development, 13*, 241-257.

Furth, H. (1970). *Piaget for teachers*. Englewood Cliffs, NJ: Prentice Hall.

Furth, H. (1971). Linguistic deficiency and thinking: Research with deaf subjects, 1964-1969. *Psychological Bulletin, 76,* 58- 72.

Furth, H. (1974). *Thinking goes to school: Piaget's theory in practice.* New York: Oxford University Press.

Furth, H., & Youniss, J. (1969). Thinking in deaf adolescents: Language and formal operations. *Journal of Communication Disorders, 2,* 195-202.

Harris, A., & Moore, T. (1978). Language and thought in Piagetian theory. In L. Siegel & C. Brainerd (Eds.), *Alternatives to Piaget: Critical essays on te theory* (pp. 131-150). New York: Academic Press.

Inhelder, B. (1968). *The diagnosis of reasoning in the mentally retarded.* New York: John Day.

Janowitz, K. (1979). The relationships among algorithmic skills, concrete operational tasks and formal operational logic in black, urban high school students. *Dissertation Abstracts International, 39,* (II-A), 6697.

Jastak, J.F., & Jastak, S. (1965). *Wide Range Achievement Test.* Wilmington: Guidance Associates of Delaware.

Larue, G. (1974). The acquisition of concepts of conservation of matter in black adolescents. In G.I. Lubin, J.F. Magary, & M.K. Poulson (Eds.), *Proceedings of the Fourth Interdisciplinary Seminar: Piagetian Theory and Its Implications for the Helping Professions.* Los Angeles: University of Southern California.

Martorano, S.C. (1973). The development of formal operations thinking. *Dissertation Abstracts International, 35* (I-B), 515-516.

Mogdil, S., & Mogdil, C. (1976). *Piagetian research: Compilation and commentary.* Highlands, NJ: Humanities Press.

Mogdil, S., & Mogdil, C. (1982). *Jean Piaget: Consensus and controversy.* New York: Praeger.

Morf, A. (1957). Les relations entre la logique et la langage lors du passage du raisonnement concret au raisonnement formal. *Etudes D'Epistemologie Genetique, 3,* 173-203. Cited in W. Bart, *Development of a formal reasoning instrument.* Unpublished monograph, 1973.

Odom, R. (1978). A perceptual-salience account of decalage relations and developmental change. In L. Siegel & C. Brainerd (Eds.), *Alternatives to Piaget: Critical essays on the theory* (pp. 111- 129). New York: Academic Press.

Piaget, J., & Inhelder, B. (1958). *The growth of logical thinking from childhood to adolescence.* New York: Basic Books.

Pulaski, M. (1971). *Understanding Piaget.* New York: Harper & Row.Siegel, L., & Brainerd, C. (Eds.) (1978). *Alternatives to Piaget: Critical essays on the theory.* New York: Academic Press.

Schwebel, M., & Raph, J. (1973). *Piaget in the classroom.* New York: Basic Books.

Slosson, R.L. (1963). *Slosson Intelligence Test.* East Aurora, NY: Slosson Educational Publications.

Wadsworth, B. (1971). *Piaget's theory of cognitive development.* New York: McKay.

Wadsworth, B. (1978). *Piaget for the classroom teacher.* New York: Longman.

Appendix

Combinations

The combinations task was described by Elkind (1968) in a study which combined combinatorial thinking in adolescents from graded and ungraded classrooms.

Purpose

To assess the student's ability to do combinatorial thinking; to explore all possible combinations. Piaget described the adolescent's approach based upon his use of formal operations as systematic, holding one element constant while systematically combining it with others (Piaget and Inhelder, 1958). For a group of four elements, there is a constant of 16 possible combinations. As Elkind noted, since one of these possibilities is "None", 15 combinations are more likely to be identified.

Materials

Red, blue, black and white poker chips and/or any four objects with which the student is familiar. This author has used boys and girls, short and tall, and numbers.

Procedure

Establish that the child understands the word combinations and that one, two, three or more may be used to make these. Elkind provided a brief training example in his study cited earlier. The student is told to combine the objects in all the possible ways. Responses are easily recorded on scratch paper or the student may write them. Some students sketch a matrix or other scheme with which they "solve the problem". The scratch paper becomes a valuable record of the student's approach to the problem.

Evaluation

The number of combinations and the approach to identifying the possible combinations are evaluated. The student who demonstrates combinatorial thinking will use a systematic, orderly approach to naming possible combinations. He/she will also identify most if not all of the 16 possible combinations. The examiner must remember that this is an informal approach to the identification of adolescents who are thinking in age- appropriate ways based upon performance on these tasks. One may view this as a screening process which can be very helpful in the evaluation of ability in black, disadvantaged students whose verbal language is limited and whose achievement and intelligence scores on traditional measures are below average. Obviously, additional evaluation is important and required in decisions concerning retardation.

red
blue
black
white
red, blue
red, black
red, white
red, blue, black
red, blue, white
blue, black
blue, white
blue, black, white
black, white
black, white, red
black, white, red, blue
none

The second type of task involves assessment of the child's understanding of probability. This task has been described by Wadsworth (1979). In this author's adaptation of the probability task, blocks are replaced by coins.

Purpose

To assess the student's understanding of probability.

Materials

96 coins, four different types—pennies, nickels, dimes, quarters—in the following quantities:

36 pennies   36 nickels   20 dimes   4 quarters

Procedure

Divide the coins into two equal groups as follows:

18 pennies   18 nickels   10 dimes   2 quarters

Place one group of coins (total number is 48) into a paper bag or box. Place the other group of 48 coins in front of the child on the table to be used as a reference group. Tell the child that you are going to take two coins at a time from the bag without looking. Shake them up or mix them before each drawing. Ask the child to guess what the coin will be each time. Continue until all coins have been drawn. From time to time ask the child how or why he gives that answer. Each time you draw two coins, place them on the table in view, but separated from the reference set.

Evaluation

Probability is understood if the child uses the reference to make predictions. He may actually count the coins or describe the numbers. According to Piaget, the ability to make predictions based on probability appears to occur around 12 years of age.

KEY MATH TEST—Johnny

Subtest Scores:

Numeration	17/24
Fractions	5/11
Geometry and Symbols	16/20
Addition	12/15
Subtraction	2/14
Multiplication	10/11
Division	5/10

Mental Computation 9/10
Numerical Reasoning 10/12
Word Problems 10/14
Missing Elements 7/7
Money 10/15
Measurement 10/27
Time 15/19

Spelling Test

The words on the right were dictated. Johnny's responses are on the left.

Johnny's response	Dictated word
Cat	cat
See	see
red	red
too	too
big	big
work	work
book	book
chelf	shelf
lane	lame
stork	struck
aper	approve
Plack	plot

Writing Exercise

The worst day of my life
is when my bike got a
flate tire I had two new
tube for my tire my
freind tire was new tire.
I put in a new tube on my
bike, and on my bike I

Cartoon Conservation Scales—Johnny

The *Cartoon Conservation Scales*, developed by Edward De Avila and published by Linguametrics Group, Corte Madera, California, is described in the administration manual as a "measure of intellectual development derived from the theory of Jean Piaget." It consists of 32 test items which assess the student's understanding of the following: conservation of number, length, substance, distance, and volume. Horizonality of water, probability, and egocentricity/perspective. The format consists of pictures (cartoon format) and three answer choices which are presented in "bubbles".

Johnny answered all four items correctly for the following: conservation of number, length, substance horizonality, volume, egocentricity, and probability. He answered two of the items on conservation of distance. (This is a somewhat difficult item to present and the language may have been a problem.) However, the student's performance on this test is impressive and supports and confirms his performance on the informally administered probability task as well as his ability to do formal operational, age-appropriate thinking. While the developmental scales for comparison end at 150 months, and the test author notes that guessing may be involved, a simple addition of Johnny's correct responses across subscales demonstrates sufficient ability.

381

USING STUDENT PERFORMANCE DATA IN ACADEMICS: A PRAGMATIC AND DEFENSIBLE APPROACH TO NON-DISCRIMINATORY ASSESSMENT

Mark R. Shinn and Gerald A. Tindal

The realization that many current assessment practices have been discriminatory to members of minority cultures and the entry of increasingly larger numbers of non-English speaking children to the United States have brought new challenges to personnel charged with identifying students as being eligible for special education services. School districts have been faced with the difficult task of operationalizing the mandate of Public Law 94-142 which calls for a non-discriminatory evaluation. This mandate is further confounded by the task of differentiating the handicapped from students whose primary language is not English. Some unknown proportion of limited English proficient students does indeed have learning and social-behavioral difficulties which are not attributable to their language deficiencies. Similarly, some minority students manifest problems which are not attributable to cultural differences. Schools have utilized a number of assessment models (Ysseldyke & Regan, 1979) in their attempts to allocate special education services and to write Individual Educational Plans that avoid overinclusion and underinclusion of these two groups of children. Yet from an historical perspective, special education has not been noted for its responsiveness to cultural differences (Kaufman, Semmel, & Agard, 1973). In part, this lack of responsiveness stems from heavy reliance upon traditional, published norm-referenced tests. As pointed out by Bernal (1977), the "typical methods of appraisal... have been devised with children from the dominant white population in mind." (p. xii) We still witness the administration of many tests developed in this manner to students of dissimilar backgrounds.

When a norm-referenced test is to be used, assessors must address the acculturation of the student to be tested. Acculturation includes the notion that the student's background is similar to those on whom the test is normed, and that the student has had similar experiences or learning opportunities. Similar does not imply "identical." The Standards for Educational and Psychological Tests (APA, 1974) clearly address this issue. The Standards state "a test user should examine differences between characteristics of a person tested and those of the population on whom the test was developed or norms developed. His/her responsibility includes deciding whether the differences are so great that the test should not be used for that person." (p. 71) As a student's acculturation differs more obviously or extremely from those represented in the normative sample, the less valid and more biased the results become.

Current Approaches to Nondiscriminatory Assessment

In attempting to overcome the problems involved in the differing acculturation backgrounds and languages of many students, assessors have used three approaches. The first approach involves the administration of published tests that do not require verbal responses, which are often incorrectly described as "non-verbal" tasks. For example, the WISC-R Performance Scale subtests are often described in this manner and are subsequently given to students who do not speak the dominant English language. Such a scheme has a number of pitfalls. The fact that a test does not require a verbal response from the student does not mean that language skills are not necessary for appropriate performance on the task. The height of such illogic is the description of the Peabody Picture Vocabulary Test (PPVT) as a non-verbal measure and its use as a measure of global intelligence with non-English speakers. The test publishers claim that the test measures a student's receptive vocabulary and, therefore, should be viewed as language biased. The PPVT also cannot be used as a comprehensive measure of intelligence (Salvia and Ysseldyke, 1981). While the use of tests requiring no verbal responses may alleviate "surface discrimination" against members of the non-dominant culture, their use still often violates the basic assumptions of acculturation discussed earlier. A final consideration involves the technical qualities of many "non-verbal" tests. These tests are frequently plagued with problems of reliability (Leiter International Performance Scale), validity (Raven's Progressive Matrices), and normative samples (Culture Fair Tests).

The second approach to nondiscriminatory assessment involves the interpretation or translation of the test into the student's language. Again, this is an attempt to eliminate obvious bias against a student who may be of a differing background. However, when such a practice takes place and scores are calculated and interpreted using the device's norms, the assessor should understand the ramifications of doing so. The practice is clearly a violation of the practices recommended by the Standards for Educational and Psychological Tests. These Standards state that:

> A test user is expected to follow carefully the standardized procedures described in the manual for administering a test... When there is any deviation from standard practice, it should be duly noted and interpretations of scores should not be made in terms of normative data provided in the manual. (APA, 1974, p. 64)

Clearly, administering a test in another language or colloquially interpreting it to a student is a violation of the standardized procedures; scores obtained using such procedures, therefore, should not be calculated and used. Such practices are not only indefensible on professional grounds, but they often lack common sense. By changing the language, examiners are still avoiding the basic issue of acculturation. Imagine asking a student of Southeast Asian background to name, in Vietnamese, four presidents of the United States since 1900. It just doesn't work too well sometimes. Testing in another language does not mean that the test cannot be interpreted or modified to determine the student's current level of performance on such tasks (i.e., what the student can and cannot do), regardless of normative reference. Indeed, such a strategy can provide very useful information to practitioners. Rather, it is the practice of using such procedures *to determine scores* from the normative sample that is discriminatory.

The third approach to nondiscriminatory assessment involves the use of multiple models of nondiscriminatory assessment practices. Ysseldyke and Regan (1980) have identified and described five such models. The type of model and the weaknesses associated with each are listed in Table 1.

Regardless of the failures of these models, it is imperative that educators and psychologists continue their efforts to assess students' academic and social behaviors in a nondiscriminatory fashion. We agree with the sentiments of Tucker (1977), who stated that "We cannot wait for that magical test that will be non-biased or culture fair—administrable in any language, and equally valid for all children, regardless of age, sex, social class, or racial ethnic origin. Such a test measuring significant behaviors never will be produced." (pp. 91-92) Others (Oakland & Matuszek, 1977; Ysseldyke & Regan, 1980) have echoed these sentiments. Yet, the lack of "the test" does not mean that real students with real needs disappear. Students with problems continue to exist. As strongly as the standards that serve to guide our assessments seek to prescribe appropriate activities, so do they assert the need to solve

Table 1
Models of Non-Discriminatory Assessment

Model	Weaknesses
Culture Free Tests	Such attempts have failed because learning occurs in environmental contexts and therefore cannot be culture free.
Culture Fair Tests	Such attempts have not demonstrated good predictive validity and are poor predicators of success in a mono-cultural school system. They have also been rejected by the dominant culture for the most part.
Culture Specific Tests	Specific items are culturally dependent and again of low predictive validity.
Pluralistic Assessment Tests	There is an extremely heterogeneous acculturation within any one specific ethnic group. The results of at least one system have whites scoring higher than any other groups. (Reschly, 1979)

problems. Professional practice demands that "efforts to solve educational or psychological problems should not be abandoned simply because of the absence of an appropriate standardized instrument." (APA, 1974, p. 71)

We believe that pragmatic and defensible methods of solving students' problems need to be utilized. By pragmatic, we mean assessment practices that lead to special education service delivery on a time and cost efficient basis and that allow for a consistent database throughout the special education process. By defensible, we mean the use of procedures with adequate standards regarding reliability and validity. These procedures should allow the issues of acculturation to be accounted for and controlled to the greatest extent possible. Defensible procedures would also assess skills with which the schools are equipped to deal and change such as reading, spelling, mathematics, social behavior, etc. Lastly, a system that is indeed pragmatic and defensible should lead to the documentation of effective interventions. As Reschly states:

> If the assessment activities do not lead to appropriate services and are not related to effective interventions, then the assessment activities must be regarded as useless for the individual, and biased and unfair if members of minority groups are differentially exposed to inappropriate services or ineffective interventions as a result of the assessment activities. The major problem then in nonbiased assessment is ensuring usefulness and fairness of assessment and interventions for all persons. (Reschly, 1979)

Alternative Procedures to Nondiscriminatory Assessment

This section explores in depth the characteristics of an alternative procedure. The focus in evaluating whether or not an assessment is discriminatory extends well beyond the immediate assessment situation and is incorporated into the development of an appropriate educational program. As Salvia and Ysseldyke (1981) have noted, there are a series of psychoeducational decisions involving screening, determination of eligibility, instructional planning and program outcome. Nondiscriminatory assessment has focused on the eligibility decision. Although it is imperative that the information collected during the eligibility process be free of bias to the greatest extent possible, other assessment procedures that are part of providing an educationally relevant program must also be free of bias. It is these latter educational decisions which have been ignored by most previous and current attempts to develop nondiscriminatory assessment practices, primarily due to the fact that most assessments stop at the point of determining eligibility. Once students are deemed eligible for special education and classified according to disability, often no further information is formally and systematically collected and utilized. The "assessment" has been conducted and completed, with little or no concern for the determination of an appropriate useful educational program. The student has entered the door with little chance to return.

To ensure nondiscriminatory practices, an alternative measurement strategy must be based on the formal, continuous collection of data from the initial phase—prior to educational intervention—through the actual implementation of any program to termination or review. With such a strategy, a determination can be made of both the student's eligibility for special education and the appropriateness of the program for that student. The critical issue is the development of an assessment system which can provide an accurate index for use in different educational decisions. In an effort to relate one decision to the next and provide a framework for the systematic evaluation of each decision, it is imperative that a continuous, and consistent, measurement system be incorporated into all of these decisions.

A series of recent studies (Deno, Mirkin, & Chiang, 1982; Deno, Mirkin, Lowry, & Kuehnle, 1980; and Deno, Marston, & Mirkin, 1982) investigated the technical adequacy—reliability and validity—of an alternative measurement system to the more commonly used published tests of ability and achievement in the areas of reading, spelling, and written expression. The initial framework for this research specified a number of criteria for including any given measure in the research. The conceptual theme underlying these various criteria involved the use of time-series data collected through the use of frequent and continuous measurement of student performance in a curriculum. Given an emphasis on the direct measurement of student performance, the curriculum served as the domain for generating measurement items, avoiding the bias noted by Jenkins and Pany (1978) concerning the test-item by curriculum interaction. In addition, the measurement system would have to be reliable and valid with respect to acceptable measures of achievement. Characteristics of measurements necessary for frequent and continuous administration are that the measures be time efficient, easy to administer, simple to teach, inexpensive to produce, and capable of multiple alternate forms. The strategy for conducting the research included the identification of potential procedures within the content area which appeared to fulfill the characteristics noted above. These measurement procedures were then (criterion) validated with respect to several technically adequate published achievement tests.

In the area of reading, five measures were investigated, including: (a) having the student read aloud words from a list of words randomly sampled from the basal reader; (b) having the student read aloud passages taken out of the basal reader; (c) having the student orally define the meaning of words appearing in the basal reader; (d) having the student provide the word(s) which had been deleted in a passage sampled from the basal reader; and (e) having the student read words which were underlined in a passage taken out of the basal reader (Deno, Mirkin, & Chiang, 1982). For all five measurement procedures, the number of words read correctly and incorrectly served as the dependent measures. The same students were also administered the following achievement tests: Subtest Five, Part A (Reading Comprehension) of Form B from the Stanford Diagnostic Reading Test (Karlsen, Madden, & Gardner, 1975), the Reading Comprehension subtest from the Peabody Individual Achievement Test (Dunn & Markwardt, 1970), the Word Identification and Word Comprehension subtests of Form A from the Woodcock Reading Mastery Test (Woodcock, 1973), and the Phonetic Analysis and the Reading Comprehension subtests from the Stanford Achievement Test (Madden, Gardner, Rudman, Karlsen, & Merwin, 1973). After the issue of what to measure was investigated, research began on logistical considerations including what to measure (the domain of sampling), how long to measure (length of administration), and how to score (dependent measure). From this research, the investigators determined that counting the number of words read aloud in one minute from either a word list or a passage in the basal reader would serve as a reliable and valid measure of a student's reading proficiency and can be used to measure progress in his/her curriculum.

In the area of spelling, the same procedures were used to identify a system for measuring student performance (Deno, Mirkin, Lowry, Kuehnle, 1980). The parameters of this measurement system again included the domain for sampling words, the length of test administration, and various scoring procedures. In addition, units of measurement for analyzing spelling performance were investigated, comparing words spelled correctly and incorrectly with correct and incorrect letter sequences (White & Haring, 1980). The published achievement tests of spelling which were administered included the Test of Written Spelling (Larsen & Hammill, 1976), the spelling subtest from the Peabody Individual Achievement Test (Dunn & Markwardt, 1970), and the spelling section of the Stanford Achievement Test Primary III (Madden, Gardner, Rudman, Karlsen, & Merwin, 1973). Findings from this research indicated that the number of words spelled correctly or the number of correct letter sequences in response to a dictated word list would serve as appropriate measures of spelling. Further, tests of one, two and three minutes duration provided indices of spelling achievement consistent with the longer published tests of achievement.

In the area of written expression, the research focused on procedures for measuring performance, including: (a) the total number of words written; (b) the number of words spelled correctly; (c) the number of large words written (words with six or more letters); (d) the number of uncommon words (those not appearing in a list of common words compiled by Finn, 1977); and (e) the average number of words per T-unit (Hunt, 1965). The parameters of the measurement system which were investigated included the use of different stimuli for generating writing—pictures, story starters, and topic sentences—and various time limits. The criterion measures used to establish the validity of the measures included the Test of Written Language (Hammill & Larsen, 1978), the Stanford Achievement Test, Intermediate I, Word Usage Subtest (Madden, et al., 1978), and the Developmental Sentence Scoring System (Lee & Canter, 1971). The results from this research indicate that counting the total number of words written or total spelled correctly, in response to either a story a story starter or a topic sentence, provided an appropriate index of writing proficiency and correlated highly with the

Table 2
Description of Measure Used in Assessing Student Performance

Academic Area	Administration Time	What to Measure
reading	1 minute	number of words read correctly
spelling	2 minutes	number of: (a) correct letter sequences (b) words spelled correctly
written expression	3 minutes	number of words written number of words spelled correctly
math	2 minutes	number of digits correct

published achievement test (Deno, Marston, & Mirkin, 1982). A summary of the Deno, et al., research is presented in Table 2.

Findings from this line of research have established that not only are abbreviated measures of reading, spelling, and writing highly related to more accepted and commonly used measures of achievement in each of the respective areas, but that the measures are sensitive to growth and show developmental changes over grades and ages. Additionally, data from the abbreviated measures can be used to provide an index for monitoring Individual Educational Plans and to evaluate the instructional effectiveness of special education programs (Tindal, Wesson, & Germann, in press).

While the measures were initially developed for use by the classroom teacher in the evaluation of instructional programs, recent research has focused on using this same data base in initial assessment for determining eligibility. In a study by Shinn, Ysseldyke, Deno, and Tindal (in press), 49 students were administered the abbreviated measures of reading, spelling, and writing. The students were a subset of those who had been tested earlier in the year, on a wide range of commonly used psychometric tests (Ysseldyke, Algozzine, Shinn, & McGue, 1982). Although results from the published psychometric instruments revealed extreme overlap in the scores between learning disabled students and low-achieving students, results from the direct measures of students' reading, writing, and spelling skills indicated considerably less overlap, with the performance of learning disabled students reliably lower than their low-achieving counterparts.

Marston (1982) found that a student's average performance over a ten week period on measures of reading, spelling, and written expression correlated highly with achievement tests. The measures also identified students with remedial education needs. In addition, these measurement procedures were more sensitive to student improvement over the ten week period than the published standardized test which was used. Slope of improvement and standard error of estimate indices were not related to achievement or predictor variables. In a study by Deno, Marston, Shinn, and Tindal (1983), direct and repeated measures of student performance on material from the curriculum were found to differentiate students receiving LD from Title I services. Marston, Mirkin, and Deno (1982) investigated the referral of students to special education, using the Woodcock-Johnson Psychoeducational Battery (1977) and direct measures of students' writing, reading, and spelling skills. These researchers found the same students eligible using either measurement method.

The accuracy of classification into special education resource rooms using measures of reading and writing performance was investigated by Marston, Tindal, and Deno (1982). The results of this study indicated that using measures of achievement alone—either direct measures or published achievement tests—students could be reliably classified into either the special education resource room or the regular classroom. Using the direct and continuous reading measures, the accuracy of classification approached 82 percent, while the use of the direct and continuous writing measures achieved an accuracy of classification of 75 percent.

Another investigation by Marston, Tindal, and Deno (1984) revealed that students performing at a level of half the rate of average peers on these measures would be classified as eligible for special education services (representing approximately 4-6 percent of the total normative sample). This percentage concurs with the percentage typically identified in school districts using more traditional procedures. The relative performance difference, referred to as the discrepancy ratio, advocated by Deno and Mirkin (1977) and utilized in the Pine County Special Education Cooperative, identifies students as eligible for services if their (median) performance is two or more times discrepant from the median performance of their peers.

As can be seen from this research, the measurement strategy developed to evaluate educational progress and instructional programs may also serve well for initial assessments and eligibility determination. The measurement system has the advantage of providing a continuous data base throughout the various decisions in developing and implementing an appropriate educational program. By incorporating a consistent measurement program into the assessment-intervention process, a conceptual framework is provided to the entire enterprise. Each decision in the sequence has data from a common scale prior to and following the assessment, which allows a broader and integrated evaluation. Determination of (non) discriminatory practice is thus made more feasible and may be used to validate earlier decisions made during the assessment intervention process.

A frequent and continuous measurement program will result in not only an appropriate evaluation of educational usefulness but one which is concurrent with implementation, and, therefore, capable of change at appropriate times, not after it is too late. That is, effective programs will be documented and ineffective programs can be changed. The data base is tied to the students' curriculum and focuses on observed skills relevant to the classroom, avoiding the problems pointed out by Jenkins and Pany (1978). When changes are indicated in the program, the data may be used to help structure those changes and evaluate their effects. As Thurlow and Ysseldyke (1982) have determined, teachers currently have little use for most assessment information in their classroom practices. In contrast, the measurement system described above provides instructionally relevant data which are useful for collecting material, setting goals, and planning instructional procedures.

The final advantage to the use of the procedures is the ease with which local norms may be developed. In establishing normative performance using peers from the local school or district, issues of comparability of acculturation and background can be addressed. A student can be fairly compared to students of similar background and opportunity. Oakland and Matuszek (1977) argue that local norms are desirable for alleviating decision-making difficulties for districts. Additionally, performance standards are established in the local curriculum which will serve as a reference for evaluating individual programs. In summary, we believe the measurement system developed by Deno et al. meets the requirements of a pragmatic and defensible process of non-discriminatory assessment. A summary of the characteristics of such procedures is given in Table 3.

Case Studies

Three case studies will be presented to illustrate the use of direct measurement procedures for non-discriminatory assessment. The first two cases involve two elementary school age Southeast Asian students, one of whom was determined to be eligible for special education and the other who was deemed to be ineligible. As is typical of most school districts, the assessment process in these cases stopped at the point of eligibility determination. The third case involves an elementary school aged student of Native American background for whom eligibility and instructional effectiveness data were collected.

Pham and Neng

Pham and Neng were both fourth graders referred by different teachers for learning problems. Pham was a nine year old Laotian girl who came to this country in December of 1979. The next month she was enrolled in an elementary school English-as-a-Second-Language program. The following fall, Pham was placed in a regular third grade classroom where she remained for the school year. She was subsequently placed in fourth grade in the fall and was referred for special

393

Table 3
Characteristics of Nondiscriminatory Assessment Procedures

reliable	reliability should be determined using test-retest, alternative form, internal consistency, and inter-scorer agreement.
valid	validity should include content validity and criterion validity (either concurrent or predictive) with respect to other measures of instructional relevance.
appropriate norms	the reference group against which the student is being compared should have comparable background characteristics.
instructional relevance	data should be provided which may be used both to plan and to evaluate instructional programs.
sensitive	changes in student performance should be reflected in the data which are collected during implementation of the program.
continuity of data	the data collected during each phase of the student's education should validate previous decisions and provide baseline data for future decisions.
documentation of effects	all aspects of the student's educational program should include data within the student's record which can be referred to for documentation of Least Restrictive Alternatives.

education services shortly thereafter in mid-October. Pham's referral problems included poor basic math and reading skills.

In assessing students with radically different cultural backgrounds, a number of questions must be addressed prior to consideration of the students as handicapped. These questions include:

1) Does the student have any obvious physiologically based handicaps? Students with severe, physically determined handicaps are not usually difficult to detect. (Tucker, 1980)

2) How long has the student been exposed to the dominant culture or how long has the student been in the country? Identifying a student as having a mildly handicapping condition that makes him/her eligible for special education is extremely difficult given that the student has had little opportunity to learn.

3) In a related vein, are the student's difficulties in making progress attributable to those of learning a second language? Not knowing the language of instruction makes it extremely difficult for a student to learn. Yet such learning difficulties are not a "special education" handicapping condition.

The multidisciplinary team believed that Pham was not obviously physically handicapped, nor had she had problems with vision or hearing. Pham was given two years of "opportunity" to learn a curriculum, and the team believed that her "lack of progress" was not caused by difficulties in learning English.

One advantage of procedures discussed earlier was the ease of collecting data for local norms. By comparing Pham to average peers, the examiners can legitimately operationalize the discrepancy between actual achievement and expected achievement without the technical difficulties of measuring intra-individual differences on highly related instruments (Salvia & Clark, 1973; Senf, 1981). The use of local norms also makes it possible to address the probable impact of experiential differences on Pham's performance. Pham obviously had not had the same background experiences or opportunities as most of her non-minority classmates nor certainly those of a large, unclearly defined national norm group. However, Pham had had about two years of learning experiences in an academic curriculum as had many other students of Pham's background. Thus, her progress was compared to this more legitimate group to determine if indeed she was significantly different from what was expected for that group.

Pham was different in her performance compared to her regular classroom peers. Should one expect her to be otherwise? The more pertinent question was, is she different from students of similar opportunities? Such a group of students was selected based upon factors of age, years in school, and direct experience in learning English-as-a-second-language. Pham was compared to this local norm group using the Deno et al. measures. Data from the areas of reading, math (subtraction), and spelling were collected daily for three days to allow for a

---

Table 4
A Comparison of Pham's Academic Skills to Those of Her Peers

Area	Material	Pham's Rate	Peer Std.	Difference
Reading	Ginn 9			
Words Correct		124 wpm	162 wpm	1.3 x less
Errors		1	0	
Math				
Subtraction	Simple facts	24 correct digits/min.	40 correct digits/min.	1.7 x less
Spelling	Randomly selected			
No. of Correct Letter Sequences	words from a list of most common grade 2, 3, 4 words	65 correct letter sequences	68 correct letter sequences	No difference

---

stable (reliable) estimate of both Pham's skills and those of her peers. The results are presented in Table 4.

When Pham was compared to standards of similar background peers in reading, material from Ginn 360, Level 9, was selected. This constituted average level material for the comparison group. Pham read aloud from randomly selected pages over three days at a median rate of 124 words per minute with one error. Her peers read the same passages at 162 words per minute. To determine the discrepancy between what is expected and actual performance, the peer's rate was divided by Pham's rate using the discrepancy ratio discussed earlier. Differences of two or more times discrepant were considered significant (Deno &

Mirkin, 1977; Marston & Tindal, 1982). In this case, Pham's reading skills were not considered significantly different.

In mathematics, the number of correctly written digits on subtraction problems with and without regrouping were counted. While Pham was slower than her peers (24 digits versus 40 digits), such differences should not be considered significant.

Finally, in the area of spelling, both Pham and her peers spelled randomly selected words from lists of the most common grades two, three, and four words, for two minutes for three days. In this area, Pham also performed at the same rate as her peers.

In summary, in the areas of concern as expressed by her classroom teacher, Pham was not significantly discrepant in her performance compared to other students who were not viewed as being different from the teacher's expectations; their skills were essentially equivalent. Because a fair comparison was made regarding what was appropriate to expect from Pham and no significant differences were documented, no special education services were offered at that time.

Neng was an eleven year old boy of Hmong background who came to this country from Laos with his family in 1976. At that time, he was enrolled in regular kindergarten until the end of the school year. The following school year, he was placed in an English-as-a-Second-Language classroom. In 1978-79 and 1979-80, Neng attended school in regular first and second grade classrooms. Neng's family then moved outside the district for one year. When he returned, he was placed in a fourth grade classroom. Neng was referred for special education assessment shortly after that time. The multidisciplinary team again believed that he had received ample opportunity to learn a curriculum and that his problems were not attributable to those of learning English-as-a-Second-Language. Neng's classroom teacher reported that he had significant difficulty in reading; spelling; and math, especially subtraction. After hearing and vision tests ruled out physical causes of Neng's problems, a comparison group consisting of students of similar ESL background and curricular opportunities was assembled. Five students from this sample were randomly selected to determine the expectancy standards appropriate for Neng. The results of Neng's assessment are presented in Table 5.

Again, multiple samples were collected over three days to obtain a reliable estimate of skills. In Neng's school, Level 8 from Ginn 360 was considered average material for the group. Neng read this material at a rate of 68 words per minute compared to the expectancy standard of 154 words per minute. This resulted in a discrepancy ratio of 2.3 x less, a significant difference. When assessed on subtraction skills, with and without regrouping, Neng was slower than his peers but not sig-

Table 5
A Comparison of Neng's Academic Skills to Those of His Peers (N=5)

Area	Material	Neng's Rate	Peer Std.	Difference
Reading	Ginn 8			
Words Read Correctly		68 wpm	154 wpm	2.3 x less
Errors		6	2	3.0 x more
Math				
Subtraction	Simple facts without regrouping	30 correct digits	40 correct digits	1.3 x less
Spelling	Randomly selected			
No. of Correct Letter Sequences	words from a list of most common grade 2, 3, 4 words	16 correct letter sequences	66 correct letter sequences	4.1 x less

nificantly discrepant. Finally, Neng's spelling skills were significantly below those of his peers as he correctly wrote only 16 correct letter sequences
when words from grades two, three and four were dictated to him in two minutes. On the basis of these performances, the multidisciplinary team determined that Neng was eligible for special education services.

These cases illustrate how student needs and areas of strengths and weaknesses within a curriculum can be assessed using procedures that do not automatically "stack the deck" against the minority student. By using measures of a student's "vital signs," which have been empirically validated with respect to other accepted measures, a referred student can often be legitimately compared to students of similar acculturation. The last statement is qualified by the word "often." There are occasions in many school systems when adequate comparison groups cannot be constructed; in many respects, the construction of comparison groups is a big city luxury. If comparison group norms cannot be developed, examiners should ask whether the use of any "norms" is appropriate. Another caution relates to the concept of acculturation in selecting students for the development of local norms. We have advocated that referred students be compared to students of similar educational experiences and opportunities. We would not argue for the necessity to compare a referred student of educational background A and race B only to typical students of educational background A and race B. Rather, we would emphasize the need for a comparison of the former factors, i.e., similar educational experiences and opportunities.

In summary, we believe that many of the characteristics of a pragmatic and defensible assessment system have been addressed in the cases of Pham and Neng. However, we did not address the outcomes of programming. Did regular education programming continue to meet Pham's needs? Did Neng profit from special education?

Dan

The last case report in this chapter provides data to help answer the questions just raised. The case concerns Dan, a Native American boy living in a rural area in the Midwest. At the time of initial assessment, Dan was 10 years old and attending third grade in a small school (total elementary population of approximately 150 students). The referral to the multidisciplinary team was initiated by the classroom teacher, who indicated that Dan was having problems in reading, math, spelling, and writing, sufficient to interfere with normal educational progress. The teacher also indicated that Dan appeared to have a short attention span and needed to be reminded to "get to work." She ranked reading and math as the areas of highest priority and thought spelling would progress with improvement in reading.

In an interview, Dan's school achievement was a concern of both Dan and his mother. Both ranked reading and math as top priorities. Dan's mother thought the school should attend to his skills in written expression; she was least troubled with his spelling. The mother's concern was that Dan develop skills to enable his survival upon high school graduation. She thought some of the problem with his school performance was due to the family's frequent moving: Dan had been in first grade in the school from which he was currently referred, attended a school in a suburb of a large urban area in second grade, and later that year had moved back to the same rural area, attending a different

Table 6
Comparison of Performance between Dan and Peers (N=15) in the
Areas of Reading, Math, Spelling, and Written Expression

Academic Area	Dan's Median Performance	Median Peer Performance	Difference
Reading passages	18 words correct/min	90 words correct/min	5.0 x less
	10 words incorrect/min	2 words incorrect/min	5.0 x less
Math	2 digits correct/min	12 digits correct/min	6.0 x less
Spelling	15 correct letter sequences	31 digits correct/2 min	2.1 x less
Written Expression	13 words spelled correct/3 min	25 words spelled correct/3 min	1.9 x less
	19 words written/3 min	26 words written/3 min	1.4 x less

school. He returned to his original school for third grade. At the same time, he alternated living with his parents and grandparents.

Assessment data collected for determining special education eligibility indicated that Dan was discrepant in all academic areas. Table 6 summarizes Dan's median performance and the median performance of his peers for reading, math, spelling, and written expression.

Since the classroom teacher had initially noted a short attention span, the psychologist conducted a systematic observation of Dan in the classroom. Using a ten-second (whole) interval recording of on- off task behavior, both Dan and his (male) peers were observed during randomly sampled 20-minute periods when they were engaged in academic work. No difference was found in the percent of time spent on-off task between Dan and his peers, with an average of 83 percent of the time recorded on-task.

All assessment information was compiled and presented at the Student Support Team meeting where Dan was found eligible for special education in reading and math. He was assigned to the resource room for two periods every day for forty-five minutes in reading and thirty-five minutes in math. An Individual Educational Plan was developed in each of the two areas, specifying the following goals, objectives, arrangements for service and providing for the measurement of progress towards the long range goal.

This latter procedure allows for the validation of effective special education programs.

Reading

Long Range Goal:

By June 1, 1980, when presented with stories from the Houghton-Mifflin Series, *Rewards*, Dan will read aloud at the rate of forty words per minute or better with five or fewer errors.

Short Term Objective:

Each week, when presented with successive stories from *Rainbows to Rewards* in the Houghton-Mifflin Series, Dan will master (read forty words per minute or better with five or fewer errors) an average of 1.2 stories per week.

Arrangement for Service:

Dan will be seen in the resource room from 2:00 -2:45 Monday through Friday and given direct instruction in reading individually as well as within a group.

Measurement Procedures:

Three times a week, Dan read aloud for one minute from successive stories from the Houghton-Mifflin Reading Series. The number of words read correctly and incorrectly was recorded on a graph. Each time Dan read a story at a rate of fifty words correct (or more) and five errors (or less), the teacher scored the story as mastered and moved on to the next story. Measurement remained at the same story until such mastery occurred.

Math

Long Range Goal:

By June 1, 1980, when presented with problems from Book Two (Addison-Wesley), Dan will compute the answers at a rate of twelve digits correct and fewer than one digit incorrect.

Short Term Objective:

Each week, when presented with drill sheets from Book Two (Addison-Wesley), Dan will compute the answers at a rate of twelve digits correct (or more) and one error (or less).

Arrangement for Service:

Dan will be seen in the resource room from 11:45 a.m. to 12:20 p.m. Monday through Friday and given direct instruction individually and within a group.

Measurement Procedures:

A random sample of math problems appeared in Book Two of Addison- Wesley (the level specified in the long range goal) and was given to Dan once a week, with the number of digits correct and incorrect recorded on a graph.

At an implementation review held three weeks following the writing of the Individual Educational Plan, the student's program was reviewed. The teacher kept two graphs on Dan's reading performance—one recording the number of stories mastered (Figure 1) and the other recording the actual level of oral reading on the long range goal Rewards (Figure 2). One graph was kept in math—recording the number of correctly written digits on the long range goal material, Book Two (Figure 3). These data indicated satisfactory improvement in reading, with the student averaging mastery of 1.7 stories per week (or five stories in less than three weeks). At the same time, his performance on the long-range goal in reading (Figure 2) consistently remained above the mastery level of forty words per minute. On three occasions, he read

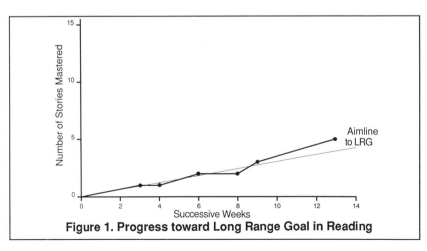

Figure 1. Progress toward Long Range Goal in Reading

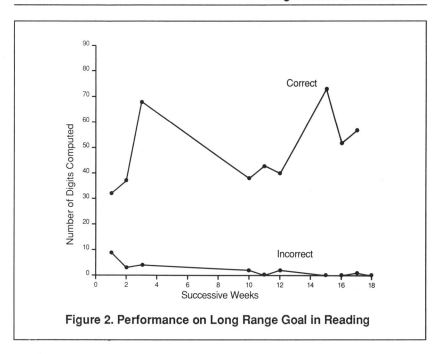

Figure 2. Performance on Long Range Goal in Reading

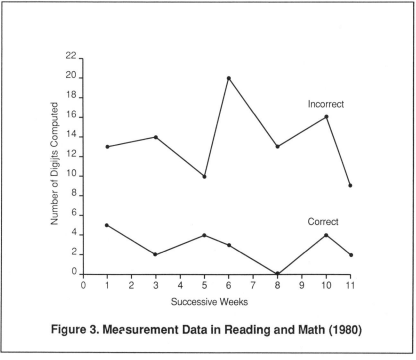

Figure 3. Measurement Data in Reading and Math (1980)

below the mastery level on the long range goal, while on six occasions he read above the mastery level. However, his performance in math was not satisfactory; progress toward his long-range goal was less than expected. Dan's performance consistently remained at a level of seven digits or less correct and nine digits or more incorrect.

Immediately following the implementation review, the family moved out of the area. Although an effective program in reading had been implemented, there had not been enough time to develop an appropriate program in math. If he had remained in the school, Dan's teacher probably would have changed her instructional program soon, in an effort to achieve the long range goal in math. Further changes would have been systematically implemented throughout the year, and would have provided documentation of both the particular characteristics of successful programs as well as their effects.

Summary

The added component of continuous assessment after eligibility for special education has been determined provides the documentation of effective programs that make a difference. When special education programs are ineffective, the procedures allow for alternative instructional strategies to be implemented and evaluated. And, importantly, students whose performance in more restrictive settings is carefully and continuously assessed should have a greater likelihood of returning to the mainstream. We have emphasized throughout this process the terms "pragmatic" and "defensible." We have maintained that methods can be developed to allocate services reliably to students with documented needs for whom regular education has not been effective. In our quest for pragmatism, we have purposely avoided the definitional dilemmas regarding issues of learning disabilities, educable mental retardation, and so on. Given the current debates regarding differential diagnosis of the mildly handicapped (cf. Hallahan & Bryan, 1981; Neisworth & Greer, 1975; Senf, 1981; Ysseldyke, Algozzine, Shinn, & McGue, 1982), we believed it to be unpragmatic to try to do so. As Tucker (1977) states, "These categories... are problems because they are based upon social norms or ill-defined symptoms which appear as easily because of normal cultural diversity as because of some handicapping condition. It is sometimes impossible to tell the difference." (p. 94)

We believe it to be pragmatic to apply operationally defined terms to differentiate students according to individual needs. Finally, we believe that ultimately educational needs must pass the test of documented program effectiveness. As we have characterized the 70s as the era of identification and definition, we characterize the 80s as an era of accountability and instruction.

References

American Psychological Association (1974). *Standards for educational and psychological tests and manuals*. Washington, D.C.: A.P.A.

Bernal, E. (1977). Introduction: Perspectives on nondiscriminatory assessment. In T. Oakland (Ed.), *Psychological and educational assessment of minority children* (pp. xi-xiv). New York: Brunner/Mazel.

Deno, S.L., Marston, D., & Mirkin, P. (1982). Valid measurement procedures for continuous evaluation of written expression. *Exceptional Children, 48,* 368-371.

Deno, S.L., Marston, D., Shinn, M., & Tindal, G. (1983). Oral reading fluency: A simple datum for scaling reading disability. *Topics in Learning and Learning Disabilities, 2,* 53-59.

Deno, S.L., & Mirkin, P. (1977). *Data-based program modification: A manual*. Minneapolis: University of Minnesota Leadership Training Institute/Special Education.

Deno, S.L., Mirkin, P., & Chiang, B. (1982). Identifying valid measures of reading for use in continuous evaluation of educational programs. *Exceptional Children, 49,* 36-45.

Deno, S.L., Mirkin, P., Lowry, L., & Kuehnle, K. (1980, Jan.). *Relationships among simple measures of spelling and performance on standardized achievement tests*. Research Report No. 21. Minneapolis: University of Minnesota Institute for Research on Learning Disabilities.

Deno, S.L., Marston, D., & Mirkin, P. (1982). Valid measurement procedures for continuous evaluation of written expression. *Exceptional Children, 48,* 368-371.

Dunn, L.M., & Markwardt, F.C. (1970). *Peabody Individual Achievement Test*. Circle Pines, MN: American Guidance Service.

Finn, P. (1977). Computer-aided description of mature word choices in writing. In C.R. Cooper & L. Odell (Eds.), *Evaluating writing: Describing, measuring, judging*. Urbana, Ill: National Council of Teachers of English.

Hallahan, D., & Bryan, T. (1981). Learning disabilities. In J. Kauffman, D. Hallahan (Eds.), *Handbook of special education* (pp. 141-164). Englewood Cliffs, NJ: Prentice Hall.

Hammill, D.D., & Larsen, S.C. (1978). *The test of written language*. Austin, TX: Pro-Ed.

Hunt, K.W. (1965). *Grammatical structures written at three grade levels*. Research Report No. 3. Champaign, Ill: National Council of Teachers of English.

Jenkins, J., & Pany, D. (1978). Standardized achievement tests: How useful for special education? *Exceptional Children, 44*(6), 448-453.

Karlsen, B., Madden, R., & Gardner, E.F. (1975). *Stanford diagnostic reading test* (reen Level Form B). New York: Harcourt Brace Jovanovich.

Kaufman, M., Semmel, M., & Agard, J. (1973). *Project PRIME: An overview.* Austin, TX: Texas Education Agency.

Larsen, S.C., & Hammill, D.D. (1976). *Test of written spelling.* Austin, TX: Empiric Press.

Lee, L., & Canter, S.M. (1971). Developmental sentence scoring. *Journal of Speech and Hearing Disorders, 36,* 335-340.

Madden, R., Gardner, E., Rudman, H., Karlsen, B., & Merwin, J. (1973). *Stanford achievement test,* Primary Level III. New York: Harcourt Brace Jovanovich.

Madden, R., Gardner, E.F., Rudman, H.C., Karlsen, B., & Merwin, J.C. (1978). *Stanford achievement test.* New York: Harcourt Brace Jovanovich.

Marston, D. (1982). *The technical adequacy of direct and repeated measurement of academic skills in low achieving elementary students.* Doctoral dissertation, University of Minnesota.

Marston, D., Mirkin, P., & Deno, S.L. (1984). Direct and repeated measurement of academic skills: An alternative to traditional screening, referral, and identification of learning disabled students. *Journal of Special Education,18,* 109-117.

Marston, D., Tindal, G., & Deno, S. (1982). *A comparison of direct measures of student performance and standardized achievement tests in the accuracy of classification* (pp. 742-775). Research Report. Minneapolis: University of Minnesota Institute for Research on Learning Disabilities.

Marston, D., Tindal, G., & Deno, S. (1984). Eligibility for learning disability services: A direct and repeated measurement approach. *Exceptional Children, 50,* 554-555.

Neisworth, J.T., & Greer, S.G. (1975). Functional similarities of LD and mild retardation. *Exceptional Children, 42*(11), 17-26.

Oakland, T., & Matuszek, P. (1977). Using tests in a nondiscriminatory fashion. In T. Oakland (Ed.), *Psychological and educational assessment of minority children* (pp. 52-69). New York: Brunner/Mazel.

Reschly, D. (1979). Nonbiased assessment. In G. Phye and D. Reschly (Eds.), *School psychology: Perspectives and issues* (pp. 215-256). New York: Academic Press.

Salvia, J., & Clark, J. (1973). Use of deficits to identify the learning disabled. *Exceptional Children, 39,* 305-308.

Salvia, J., & Ysseldyke, J. (1981). *Assessment in special and remedial education.* Boston: Houghton-Mifflin.

Senf, G. (1981). Issues surrounding the diagnosis of learning disabilities: Child handicap vs. failure of the child-school interaction. In T. Kratochwill (Ed.), *Advances in school psychology* (pp. 83-131). Hillsdale, NJ: Lawrence Erlbaum.

Shinn, M., Ysseldyke, J., Deno, S., & Tindal, G. (in press). *A comparison of differences between students labeled learning disabled and low achieving on measures of classroom performance. Journal of Learning Disabilities.*

Thurlow, M.L., & Ysseldyke, J. (1982). Instructional planning: Information collected by school psychologists vs. information considered useful by teachers. *Journal of School Psychology, 20,* 3-10.

Tindal, G., Wesson, C., & Germann, G. (in press). The Pine County model for special education delivery: A data-based system. In T. Kratochwill (Ed.), *Advances in school psychology.* Hillsdale, NJ: Lawrence Erlbaum.

Tucker, J. (1977). Operationalizing the diagnostic-intervention process. In T. Oakland (Ed.), *Psychological and educational assessment of minority children* (pp. 91-110). New York: Brunner/Mazel.

Tucker, J. (1980). Ethnic proportions in classes for the learning disabled: Issues in nonbiased assessment. *Journal of Special Education, 14*(1), 93-105.

White, O., & Haring, N. (1980). *Exceptional teaching* (2nd ed.). Columbus: Charles E. Merrill.

Woodcock, R.M. (1973). *Woodcock reading mastery tests* (Form A). Circle Pines, MN: American Guidance Service.

Woodcock, R.M., & Johnson, M.B. (1977). *Woodcock-Johnson psychoeducational battery*. Boston: Teaching Resources.

Ysseldyke, J., Algozzine, B., Shinn, M., & McGue, M. (1982). Similarities and differences between low achievers and students labeled learning disabled: Identical twins with different mothers. *Journal of Special Education, 16*, 73-85.

Ysseldyke, J., & Regan, R. (1980). Non-discriminatory assessment: A formative model. *Exceptional Children, 46*, 465-468.

Biographical Sketches
and Indexes

Biographical Sketches

WILLIAM H. ANDERSON, JR. is Associate Professor in the Counseling Center and in the Institute of Clinical Psychology at the University of Virginia where he trains graduate psychology students in the use of Cognitive Behavioral approaches in assessment and therapy. He received his doctorate in Clinical Psychology from the State University of New York at Stony Brook and has pursued postdoctoral studies in Pediatric Psychology at the University of North Carolina's Division for Disorders of Development and Learning. An active member of the American Psychological Association, the Association for the Advancement of Behavior Therapy, and the Association of Black Psychologists, Dr. Anderson has done research and writing emphasizing the interface of empirically based clinical procedures and the application of these procedures to the needs of minority group members.

DAVID W. BARNETT is an Associate Professor of School Psychology at the University of Cincinnati. He earned his Ph.D. in School Psychology at Indiana State University. Prior to his present position, he was a Supervisor of Psychological Services and Coordinator of Learning Disabled and Emotionally Disturbed Children in the public schools. For the past seven years he has served as a consultant to preschool programs and other public agencies in a number of states. Recent publications include a book, *Nondiscriminatory Multifactored Assessment: A Sourcebook*, and chapters and articles on the topics of preschool psychological services and the assessment of children's personal and social functioning.

HERBERT G. W. BISCHOFF, Ph.D. is a psychologist in private practice with Psychology Resources in Anchorage, Alaska. He is a school psychologist with a primary interest in working with adolescents. Dr. Bischoff recently completed a three-year term as Chairman of the State Mental Health Advisory Council, serves on the Medical Executive Committee of a local psychiatric hospital and is the current President of the International School Psychology Association. Dr. Bischoff has traveled extensively, particularly throughout Alaska, and is interested in cross-cultural issues in mental health and education.

HERMES T. CERVANTES is a School Psychologist with the Denver, Colorado, public schools where he is assigned to schools in predominantly bilingual-multicultural communities. Dr. Cervantes has been on the Graduate Faculty at the University of Colorado and Metropolitan State College where he has taught classes on the Education of Exceptional Children and Diagnostic Assessment in Bilingual and Special Education. The psychological and educational assessment of linguistic minorities is a particular research interest for Dr. Cervantes, and he has published numerous articles in that area. He has also coauthored with Dr. Leonard M. Baca a text in the new field of Bilingual Special Education, *The Bilingual Special Education Interface*, (1984), C.V. Mosby. Dr. Cervantes received his B.A. and M.Ed. from the University of Texas at El Paso and his Ph.D. from the University of Colorado.

MARGARET G. DABNEY is Dean of the School of Education, Virginia State University at Petersburg. She coordinates the Secondary School Experiential Learning Community (SSELC) Project, a joint effort of Richmond Public Schools, a group of private citizens, and Virginia State University. SSELC's purpose is to identify and educate gifted disadvantaged children. Dr. Dabney currently serves as member of the Board of Directors of the Virginia Advisory Committee on Gifted Education and has been a member of the Board of Directors of the Virginia Association for Education of the Gifted and a member of the Task Force that drafted the Virginia Plan for Gifted Education. She served as Coordinator for the Project to Evaluate Teacher Training in Developing Institutions' Program of EPDA (1973-75) and Director of the Virginia Teacher Corps Consortium, Virginia State University and Virginia Commonwealth University, 1970-76.

She has published *Lessons Learned: Teacher Training in Developing Institutions' Program of the Education Professions Development Act* (1975, July), Washington, D.C., Division of Educational Systems Development, U.S. Office of Education; and "Curriculum Building and Implementation in Mainstream Settings: Some Concepts and Propositions," in R.L. Jones (Ed.) (1976), *Mainstreaming and the Minority Child*, Reston, VA: Council for Exceptional Children. Dr. Dabney received her A.B. in Sociology from Boston University, her M.A. from the Center for Human Relations Studies at New York University, and her Ph.D. from George Peabody College for Teachers.

HAROLD E. DENT is Vice President of Psychological and Human Resources Consultants of Oakland, California. Dr. Dent served for ten years as Director of Consultation and Education at the Westside Community Mental Health Center in San Francisco. He also served as

Coordinator of Pupil Personnel Services for the Berkeley Unified School District, Berkeley, California, and as Regional Mental Retardation Consultant for the Department of Health, Education and Welfare (now the Department of Health and Human Services) in San Francisco. Dr. Dent has taught at San Francisco State University, California State University at Hayward, California State University at Sonoma, and at the Wright Institute, Berkeley.

He has served as a member of the Advisory Committee to the Joint Legislative Committee on Educational Goals for the California State Legislature, Sacramento, California, and the National Advisory Council for the Developmental Disabilities Technical Assistance System (DD/TAX), University of North Carolina, Chapel Hill. He has acted as Consultant to the State Department of Education, State of Connecticut, the Superintendent of Public Instruction, Department of Special Services, Olympia, Washington, the Chicago Public Schools' Desegregation Plan Project, San Francisco Unified School District and the San Francisco Department of Social Services. He has also served as Consultant for the *Journal of Educational Measurement* and the *Journal of Applied Psychology*. Dr. Dent received his B.A. in Psychology from New York University, his M.A. in Clinical Psychology from Denver University, and his Ph.D. in Clinical/Counseling Psychology from the University of Hawaii.

ALAN T. FISHER is a psychologist in private practice in Corpus Christi, Texas. He currently consults with several independent school systems and the local mental health agency. Dr. Fisher was previously the Chief School Psychologist for the Corpus Christi Independent School District. During this time, he maintained a part-time private practice and was on the adjunct faculty of Corpus Christi State University. Dr. Fisher is coauthor of the article "Adaptive Behavior Inventory for Children: The Need for Local Norms," (1982) in the *Journal of School Psychology, 20,* 39-44, and is coauthor of the unpublished test, the *Texas Environmental Adaptation Measure*. He has conducted seminars on adaptive behavior and various childhood handicaps. Dr. Fisher is a past Director of the Division of School Psychology, Texas Psychological Association. He is a certified school psychologist (Texas Education Agency) and a member of the National Register of Health Services Providers. He received his B.S. in Psychology and his Ph.D. in Psychology from the University of Houston.

RALPH M. HAUSMAN is presently a generic/resource special education teacher as well as math and computer literacy teacher at the Ector County Alternative Education Center, Odessa, Texas. On occasion, he is also an Adjunct Associate Professor, University of Texas—Permian Basin. Dr. Hausman has been a special education Principal and teacher of a self-contained class for emotionally disturbed children and has served in the role of school psychologist for several school systems, working in a diagnostic and/or therapeutic capacity with mildly to profoundly handicapped inviduals. He has also spent ten years as an assistant or associate professor in Special Education teacher training programs and has consulted with many school systems in the development of assessment and special education programs. In addition, he continues to maintain an inservice training service.

Dr. Hausman has published (with R. Buro, K. Hargrove, & C. Adams) "The Effects of Several Confounding Variables on Color Vision Assessment in Young, Handicapped Children" (1980), in *Diagnostic, 5,* 26-31, and (with J.B. Merbler & B. Seymour) (1978) "IEP Inclusion in a Preservice and Inservice Training Program" in B.B. Weiner (Ed.), *Periscope: Views of the Individualized Education Program*, Reston, VA: Council for Exceptional Children. Other publications include (with R. Buro, N. Garret, & V. Wright) (1976) "Color Vision Anomalies in Young, Handicapped Children: An Interim Report," *Baylor Educator, 1,* 15-21; "Assessment of the Learning Potential of Exceptional Children" (1969), *IMRID Papers and Reports, 6,* No. 3; and "Individual Intelligence Testing of Visually Handicapped Children" (1968), *Peabody Papers in Human Development, 6,* No. 4. In conjunction with his university students, Dr. Hausman has presented extensively at local, state, and international conferences. Dr. Hausman received his B.A. and M.A. in Psychology/Educational Psychology at the University of Texas, Austin, an M.Ed. in Educational Psychology/Psychology from the University of Hawaii, and his Ph.D. in Special Education/School Psychology from George Peabody College for Teachers.

H. CARL HAYWOOD of Vanderbilt University is Professor of Psychology, George Peabody College, Professor of Neurology, School of Medicine, Senior Fellow in the Vanderbilt Institute for Public Policy Studies, and former Director, John F. Kennedy Center for Research on Education and Human Development. He is a past President of the American Association on Mental Deficiency and a member of numerous advisory boards of national organizations and committees. Dr. Haywood was Editor of the *American Journal of Mental Deficiency*, 1969-79. He has edited four books, *Brain Damage in School-Age Children, Social-Cultural Aspects of Mental Retardation, Prevention of Retarded Development in Psychosocially Disadvantaged Children* (with M.J. Begab & H. Garber), and *Living Environments for Developmentally Retarded Persons* (with J.R. Newbrough); and he has coauthored (with R. Feuerstein, Y.

Rand, M.B. Hoffman, & M. Jensen) *Examiner Manuals for the Learning Potential Assessment Device.* He has published over one hundred chapters and articles in professional books and journals, some of which include "Alternatives to Normative Assessment," "Assessing Cognitive Change," and "Dynamic Assessment: The Learning Potential Assessment Device (LPAD)."

Dr. Haywood's current research program includes studies of the development of personality and motivational influences on individual differences in the efficiency of learning and performance, the development of thought processes and methods to assess and modify cognitive functions of slow-learning children and adolescents by strategies ranging from the laboratory to the classroom, as well as public policy that affects children and families. Presently, he is coprincipal investigator, with John Bransford, of a federally funded project on the dynamic assessment of intellectually handicapped children and directs a current project on development, evaluation, and dissemination of a cognitive curriculum for preschool children. Dr. Haywood received his A.B. in Psychology and Speech Arts from San Diego State College, an M.A. in Psychology from San Diego State College, and his Ph.D. in Psychology from the University of Illinois.

REGINALD L. JONES is Professor of Afro-American Studies and Professor of Education at the University of California, Berkeley. His appointments have included psychologist, military and state hospitals; Professor of Psychology and Education, and Vice Chairman, Department of Psychology, The Ohio State University; Professor and Chair, Department of Education, University of California, Riverside; and Professor and Director, University Testing Center, Haile Sellassie I University, Addis Ababa, Ethiopia. He has also taught at U.C.L.A. and at Miami, Fisk, and Indiana Universities.

He has authored a number of papers on special education assessment and has edited or coauthored several books, including *New Directions in Special Education* (1970, Allyn & Bacon), *Problems and Issues in the Education of Exceptional Children* (1971, Houghton Mifflin, *Special Education in Transition* (with D. MacMillan) (1974, Allyn & Bacon), *Mainstreaming and the Minority Child* (1976, Council for Exceptional Children), and *Black Psychology* (1972, 1980, Harper & Row). *The Handbook of Tests and Measurements for Black Populations* (Cobb & Henry) is in press.

Dr. Jones has been a consulting editor to the *Journal of School Psychology, Professional Psychology, Psychological Aspects of Disability, The Journal of Social Issues,* and *The American Education Research Journal.* He has been Associate Editor of the *American Journal of Mental Deficiency* and Editor of *Mental Retardation* (official journals of the American Association on Mental Deficiency). He is the recipient of the J.E. Wallace Wallin Award of the Council for Exceptional Children and the Scholarship Award of the Association of Black Psychologists. Dr. Jones received his A.B. in Psychology from Morehouse College in 1952, his M.A. in Clinical Psychology from Wayne State University in 1954 and his Ph.D. in Psychology (with a minor in Special Education) in 1959 from The Ohio State University.

HENRIETTE W. LANGDON is a bilingual Speech and Language Consultant. She has worked as Program Specialist and Speech and Language Specialist in the Bay Area for a number of years. Her area of interest and expertise is the assessment and school programming for the Limited-English Proficient student with language/learning disabilities. She has given numerous presentations at local, state, and national conferences. Her publication in *Exceptional Children* (1983, September) is on identifying a language disorder in bilingual children. Most recently, she contributed to the development of a test to certify bilingual Speech and Language Specialists and psychologists working with Hispanic handicapped students, a project funded by the California State Department of Education (1985-86). Dr. Langdon received a B.S. from the Universidad Nacional de Mexico, Mexico City, an Ed.M. from Tufts University, and her Ed.D. from Boston University. Dr. Langdon is fluent in French, Spanish, Polish, and English.

MARCIA L. McEVOY is a practicing School Psychologist in Cincinnati, Ohio. She earned her Ph.D. in School Psychology at the University of Cincinnati in 1985. Dr. McEvoy has been on the School Psychology Faculty at Miami University in Oxford, Ohio, where she has taught classes on psychoeducational assessment of children and youth. Over the past years she has presented a number of papers at national conventions on the topics of psychoeducational assessment and preschool psychological services.

DEBRA L. McINTOSH is currently employed as a Child Development Specialist by the Umatilla Education Service District in Pendleton, Oregon. She provides a comprehensive array of school psychology services to several rural districts in Eastern Oregon. Ms. McIntosh, a 19-year resident of Alaska, previously consulted to several school districts throughout that state in the capacity of School Psychologist and doctoral intern from Northern Arizona University. She holds an Ed.D. degree in Educational Psychology and maintains an active interest in rural psychology and cross-cultural issues.

JAMES A. MORRISON is a District Psychologist for the ABC Unified School District in Cerritos, California. During the past 14 years, he has worked in the field of education as a classroom teacher, bilingual resource teacher, special education teacher, counselor and psychologist. Dr. Morrison has also been a consultant to numerous school districts in Southern California, has presented papers at several state, national, and international conferences, and has served as a member of the California State Department of Education Task Force on Bilingual Special Education.

He has published (with William B. Michael) "The Development and Validation of an Auditory Perception Test in Spanish for Hispanic Children Receiving Reading Instruction in Spanish" in *Educational and Psychological Measurement* (1982), 42, 657-699, and "Validity of Measures Reflecting Visual Discrimination and Linguistic Constructs for a Sample of Second Grade Hispanic Children Receiving Reading Instruction in Spanish" in *Educational and Psychological Measurement* (1984), and is the author (1982) of *The Assessment of Spanish Reading Problems: A Workshop Manual* (Second Experimental Edition), West Covina, CA: Author. Dr. Morrison received his B.A. in English from the University of California, Los Angeles, an M.S. in Education from the University of Southern California, a Fulbright- Hayes Foreign Study Grant to the National University of Mexico, an Adv. M.Ed. in Educational Psychology and his Ph.D. in Educational Psychology, both from the University of Southern California.

DANIEL J. RESCHLY is Professor of Psychology and Professional Studies in Education, Iowa State University, where he directs the School Psychology Graduate Program. He previously was on the faculty of the University of Arizona and served as a School Psychologist in the public schools of Iowa, Oregon, and Arizona. Dr. Reschly has coedited *School Psychology: Perspectives and Issues*, edited the *School Psychology Review*, and is on the editorial boards of six journals. He currently is President of the National Association of School Psychologists. Reschly has authored numerous articles on school psychology professional practices and has conducted extensive research on nondiscriminatory assessment and mild mental retardation. He is completing research on multitrait-multimethod assessment of adaptive behavior and social skills. Dr. Reschly received his B.S. from Iowa State University, his M.A. from the University of Iowa, and his Ph.D. from the University of Oregon.

JOSE RODRIGUEZ is currently a Guidance Specialist for the San Jose Unified School District in San Jose, California. For 15 years, he has worked as a School Psychologist in schools with predominantly bilingual students. He has also served as consultant and guest lecturer to Universities, school districts, and county offices of education. Dr. Rodriguez has conducted research investigating factors affecting college enrollment decisions of Hispanic students, the effects on learning of teaching styles and student variables, and the correlation of cognitive functioning styles and visual-motor functioning. He received his B.S. from the State University of New York, an M.S. and an advanced credential in School Psychology from California State University, and an M.A. and Ph.D. from Stanford University.

LEIGH S. SCOTT is Consultant for Appraisal Services of the Corpus Christi (Texas) Independent School District, assisting in the district-wide administration of psychological consultation and evaluation services (1980-). Scott formerly functioned as Associate School Psychologist on the district's Pluralistic Diagnostic Team, a research and development project in the field of adaptive behavior assessment. She coauthored the article "Adaptive Behavior Inventory for Children: The Need for Local Norms" in *Journal of School Psychology* (1982), *20*, 39-44 and is coauthor of the unpublished test, *The Texas Environmental Adaptation Measure*. Scott has conducted workshops throughout Texas on adaptive behavior assessment and has presented numerous papers at state and national conventions.

She is a past director of the Division of Psychological Associates of the Texas Psychological Association, a past president of the Nueces County Psychological Association, a member of the National Association of School Psychologists, and associate member of the American Psychological Association. She served as Associate Editor for the *Texas Psychologist* from 1984 to 1986 and appears in the 20th edition of *Who's Who in the South and Southwest*. Scott is certified as a psychological associate by the Texas State Board of Examiners of Psychologists and as an Associate School Psychologist by the Texas Education Agency. She has a B.S. (1974) and an M.S. (1975) in Psychology from East Texas State University.

MARK R. SHINN is currently Director of the School Psychology Program at the University of Oregon where his primary responsibilities are teaching master's and doctoral level students and conducting research into curriculum-based assessment. Prior to joining the University of Oregon, Dr. Shinn served as a psychologist on special assignment for the Minneapolis Public Schools where he trained special education teachers in curriculum-based assessment procedures and assisted in dramatically reorganizing assessment practices. Dr. Shinn worked previously for St. Paul Public Schools as a School Psychologist for the

Limited English Proficiency Program, where he assisted in the development of assessment procedures for more than 3,000 students from countries in Southeast Asia. He has coauthored a chapter with James E. Ysseldyke, "Psychoeducational Assessment" in the *Handbook of Special Education* (Hallahan & Kaufmann, Eds.) and has published in consortium with Stanley Deno, Gerald Tindal, Doug Marston, and Ysseldyke in journals such as the *Journal of Special Education, Learning Disability Quarterly, Journal of Learning Disabilities, Journal of School Psychology, Remedial and Special Education,* and *School Psychology Review.* Dr. Shinn received his B.A. in Psychology from Gustavus Adolphus and his Ph.D. in Educational Psychology from the University of Minnesota.

JOHN M. TAYLOR is presently the Executive Director of the Developmental Disabilities Center in Boulder, Colorado. Previously he was Director of Psychological and Social Work Services for the Louisiana State Department of Education, Office of Special Education Services, and prior to that, Supervisor for School Psychology. Dr. Taylor has worked as a School Psychologist, Coordinator of Psychological and Social Work Services, and acting Director of Student Services for the Leon County, Florida public school system. He has been President of the Florida Association of School Psychologists, President of the National Association of State Consultants for School Psychological Services and advisor to the Louisiana School Psychological Association. Dr. Taylor has served as West-Central Regional Director and Cochairperson of the Planning and Development Committee and Research Committee for the National Association of School Psychologists (NASP).

He has currently resumed the position of Cochairperson for the Planning and Development Committee of NASP. He is a member of the Advisory Task Force for the National School Psychology In-Service Training Network at the University of Minnesota, and is an associate or consulting editor to several professional journals such as *Exceptional Children* and the *School Psychology Review.* Dr. Taylor received his B.S. in Psychology from Pennsylvania State University and his M.S. and Ph.D. in Psychology from Florida State University.

LORRAINE S. TAYLOR is a Professor in the Special Education Program at the State University of New York, New Paltz. Previously she was an instructor at the University of Minnesota where she received her B.A. and Ph.D. She also completed a postdoctoral training program in Neuropsychology at the Tufts-New England Medical Center in Boston where she pursued her interests in learning disabilities. Her public school teaching experience has been primarily with disadvantaged black students in the Chicago Public Schools where she taught grades

K-8 and remedial reading and math. In addition, she served as Director of an alternative high school program which primarily served disadvantaged minority students in Minnesota.

GERALD A. TINDAL received his Ph.D. in Educational Psychology from the University of Minnesota where he was involved in a large-scale research project investigating assessment and skill remediation with mildly handicapped students. The particular focus of his research was on the development and validation of an alternative measurement-evaluation system that could be used across all types of educational decisions-identification, program planning, and program evaluation, at both the individual and system level. In the final phases of this research, the focus was on logistical implementation in the schools, and he began working in a six district cooperative that had adopted the entirety of the measurement-evaluation system for use in all educational decisions. He worked in this setting for the next four years, serving as a teacher consultant and continuing to investigate various aspects of the delivery of services to mildly handicapped students.

In 1984, he accepted a position as Assistant Professor in Special Education at the University of Oregon and began to coordinate the Resource Consultant Program. In this position, he has continued his research and developed a teacher training program on the delivery of alternative services for mildly handicapped students. He is currently the Project Director of three federally funded grants aimed at extending this training to teachers in regular education. In addition to this research and training, he continues to serve as a consultant with school districts in Minnesota, Washington, and Oregon.

JOSEPHINE L. YOUNG is currently a School Psychologist with the District of Columbia Public School System (DCPS). Additionally, she has served as a supervising Director of Pupil Personnel Service and as Psychology Coordinator in DCPS. She has been with the school system since 1971. Dr. Young has been an instructor of Psychology and an Associate Community Educator with the University of the District of Columbia (formerly Federal City College) and was Coordinator for a special project with the Young Men's Christian Association. She has also served as a consultant to the Peace Corps and has participated as a presenter in workshops sponsored by the District of Columbia School System, Alexandria City Public Schools, and the Council for Exceptional Children. Dr. Young received her B.S. and M.S. degrees in Psychology from Howard University and her Ph.D. in Educational Psychology from Catholic University.

Author Index

Subject Index